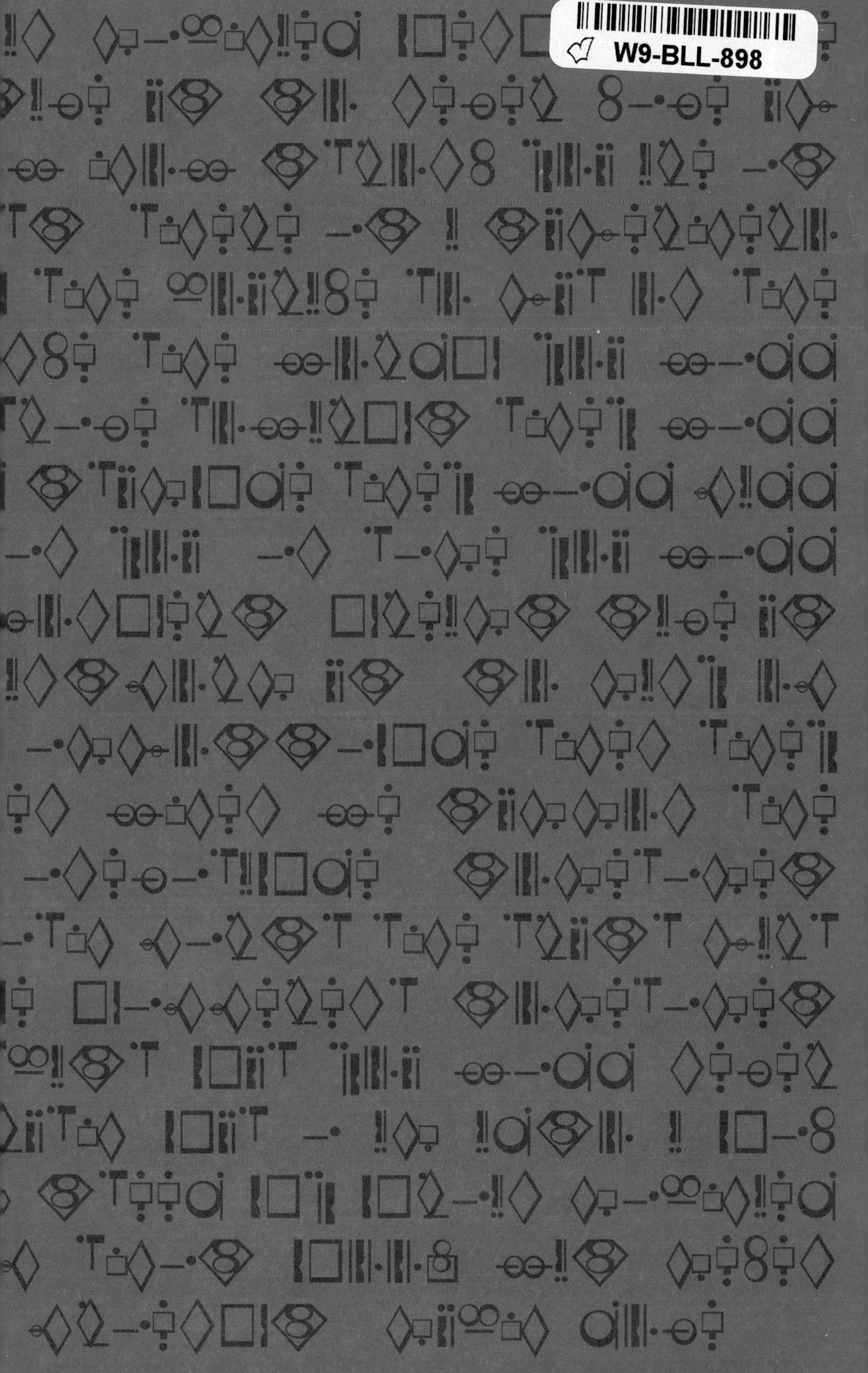

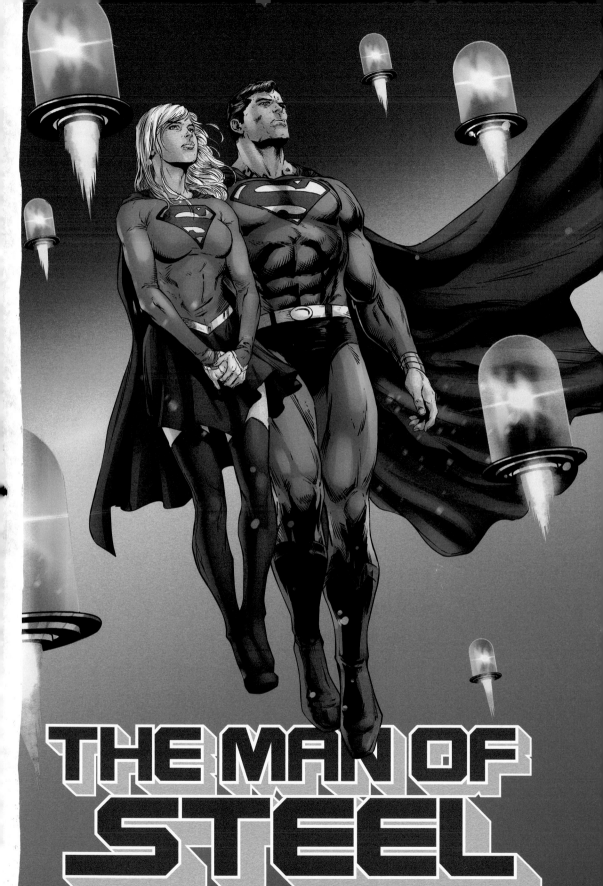

THE MAN OF STEEL

BY BRIAN MICHAEL BENDIS

THE MAN OF STEEL

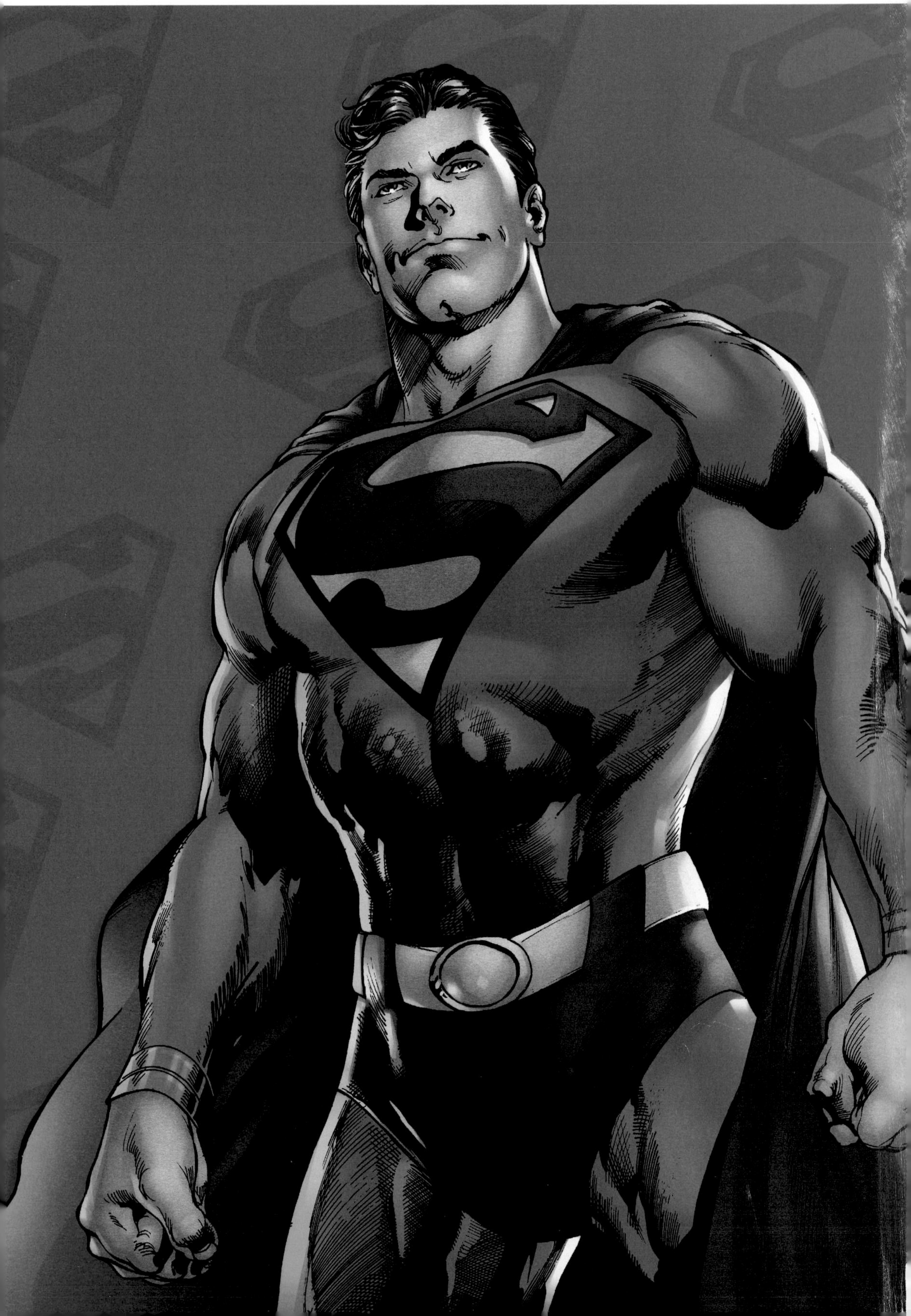

BY BRIAN MICHAEL BENDIS

BRIAN MICHAEL BENDIS
WRITER

JIM LEE
SCOTT WILLIAMS
JOSÉ LUIS GARCÍA-LÓPEZ
DEXTER VINES
IVAN REIS
JOE PRADO
JASON FABOK
EVAN "DOC" SHANER
STEVE RUDE
RYAN SOOK
WADE VON GRAWBADGER
KEVIN MAGUIRE
ADAM HUGHES
ARTISTS

ALEX SINCLAIR
ADAM HUGHES
COLORISTS

JOSH REED
CORY PETIT
LETTERERS

IVAN REIS, JOE PRADO and ALEX SINCLAIR
COLLECTION COVER ART AND ORIGINAL SERIES COVERS

MIKE COTTON
Editor – Original Series

JESSICA CHEN
Associate Editor – Original Series

JEB WOODARD
Group Editor – Collected Editions

SCOTT NYBAKKEN
Editor – Collected Edition

STEVE COOK
Design Director – Books

MEGEN BELLERSEN
Publication Design

BOB HARRAS
Senior VP – Editor-in-Chief, DC Comics

PAT McCALLUM
Executive Editor, DC Comics

DAN DiDIO
Publisher

JIM LEE
Publisher & Chief Creative Officer

AMIT DESAI
Executive VP – Business & Marketing Strategy,
Direct to Consumer & Global Franchise Management

BOBBIE CHASE
VP & Executive Editor, Young Reader & Talent Development

MARK CHIARELLO
Senior VP – Art, Design & Collected Editions

JOHN CUNNINGHAM
Senior VP – Sales & Trade Marketing

BRIAR DARDEN
VP – Business Affairs

ANNE DePIES
Senior VP – Business Strategy, Finance & Administration

DON FALLETTI
VP – Manufacturing Operations

LAWRENCE GANEM
VP – Editorial Administration & Talent Relations

ALISON GILL
Senior VP – Manufacturing & Operations

JASON GREENBERG
VP – Business Strategy & Finance

HANK KANALZ
Senior VP – Editorial Strategy & Administration

JAY KOGAN
Senior VP – Legal Affairs

NICK J. NAPOLITANO
VP – Manufacturing Administration

LISETTE OSTERLOH
VP – Digital Marketing & Events

EDDIE SCANNELL
VP – Consumer Marketing

COURTNEY SIMMONS
Senior VP – Publicity & Communications

JIM (SKI) SOKOLOWSKI
VP – Comic Book Specialty Sales & Trade Marketing

NANCY SPEARS
VP – Mass, Book, Digital Sales & Trade Marketing

MICHELE R. WELLS
VP – Content Strategy

THE MAN OF STEEL BY BRIAN MICHAEL BENDIS

DC Comics, 2900 West Alameda Ave., Burbank, CA 91505
Printed by LSC Communications, Kendallville, IN, USA. 9/28/18. First Printing.
ISBN: 978-1-4012-8348-3

Library of Congress Cataloging-in-Publication Data is available.

PEFC Certified

Printed on paper from
sustainably managed
forests and controlled
sources

PEFC/29-31-337

www.pefc.org

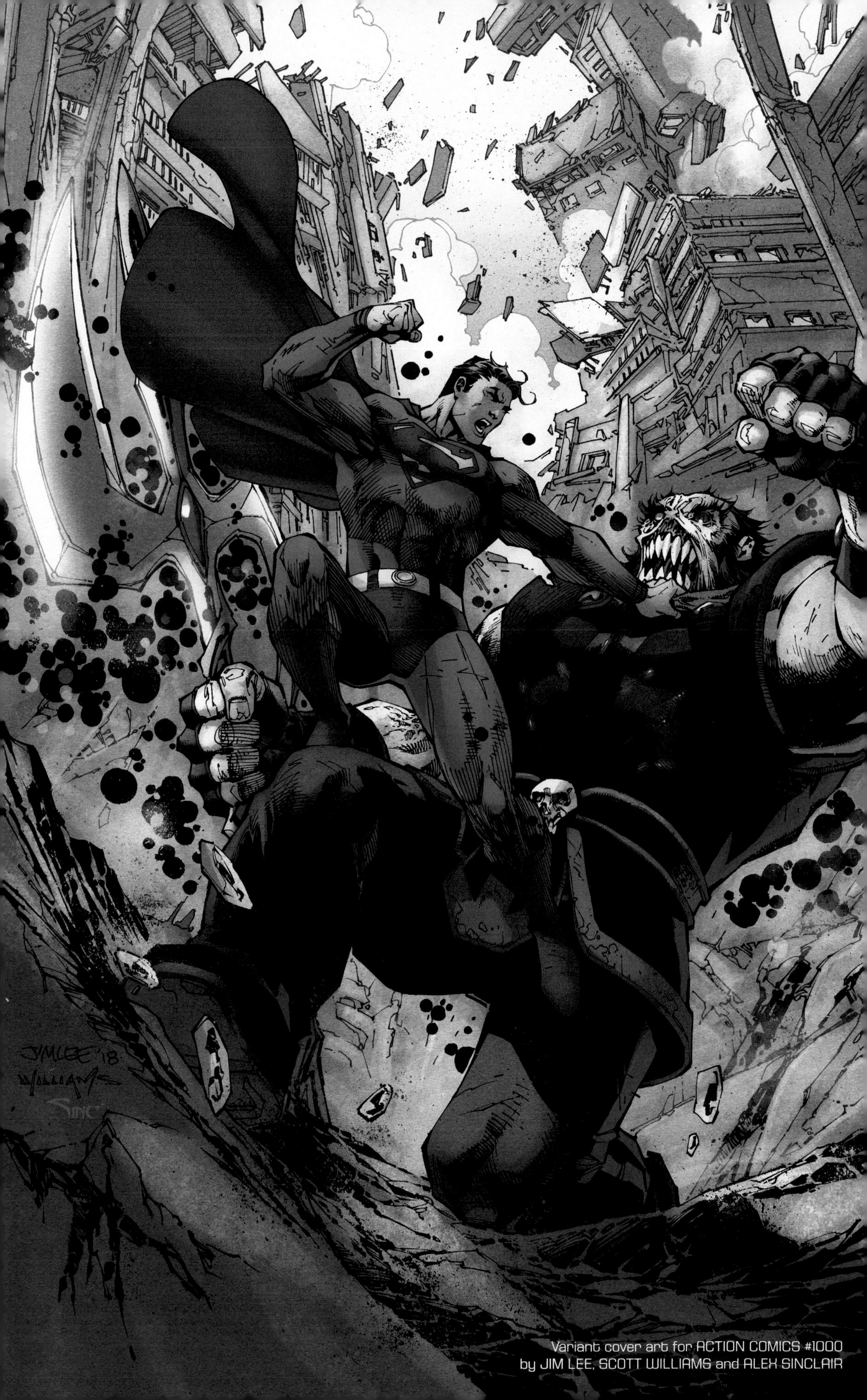

Variant cover art for ACTION COMICS #1000
by JIM LEE, SCOTT WILLIAMS and ALEX SINCLAIR

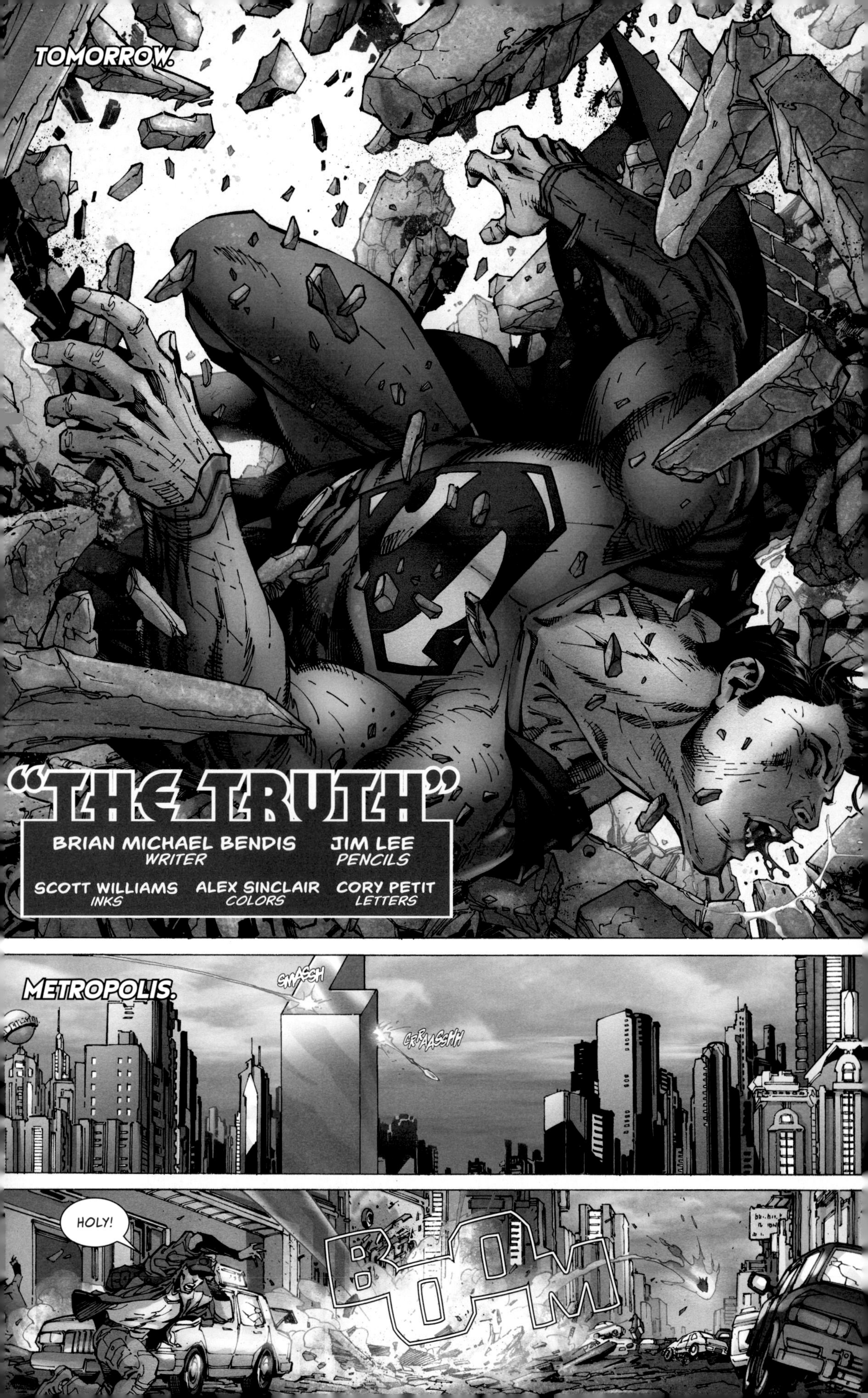
TOMORROW.
"THE TRUTH"
BRIAN MICHAEL BENDIS WRITER
JIM LEE PENCILS
SCOTT WILLIAMS INKS
ALEX SINCLAIR COLORS
CORY PETIT LETTERS
METROPOLIS.
SWASSH
CRRAASSHH
HOLY!
BOOM

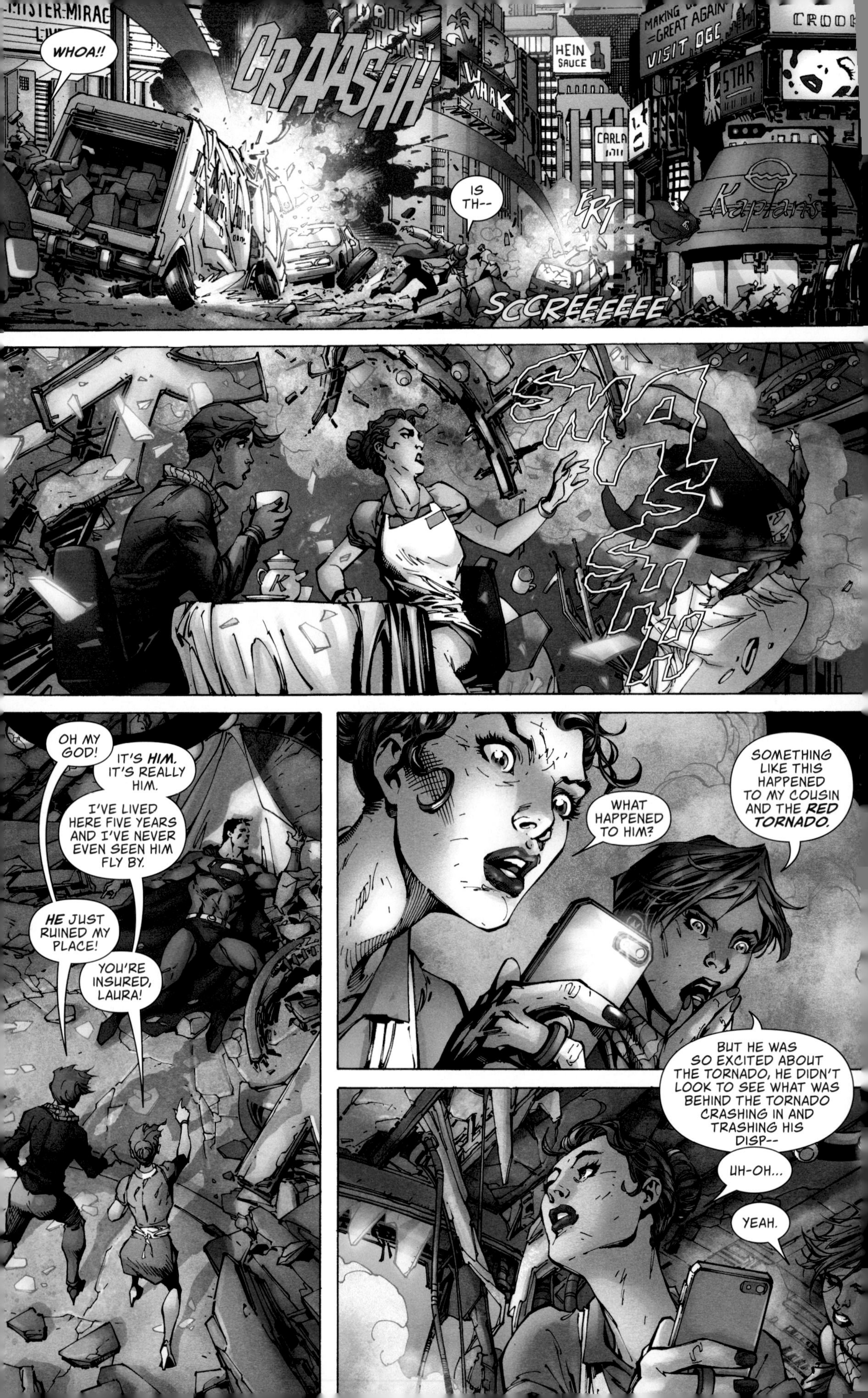
WHOA!!
CRAASHH
IS TH--
SCCREEEEEEE
SMASHH
OH MY GOD!
IT'S **HIM.** IT'S REALLY HIM.
I'VE LIVED HERE FIVE YEARS AND I'VE NEVER EVEN SEEN HIM FLY BY.
HE JUST RUINED MY PLACE!
YOU'RE INSURED, LAURA!
WHAT HAPPENED TO HIM?
SOMETHING LIKE THIS HAPPENED TO MY COUSIN AND THE ***RED TORNADO.***
BUT HE WAS SO EXCITED ABOUT THE TORNADO, HE DIDN'T LOOK TO SEE WHAT WAS BEHIND THE TORNADO CRASHING IN AND TRASHING HIS DISP--
UH-OH...
YEAH.

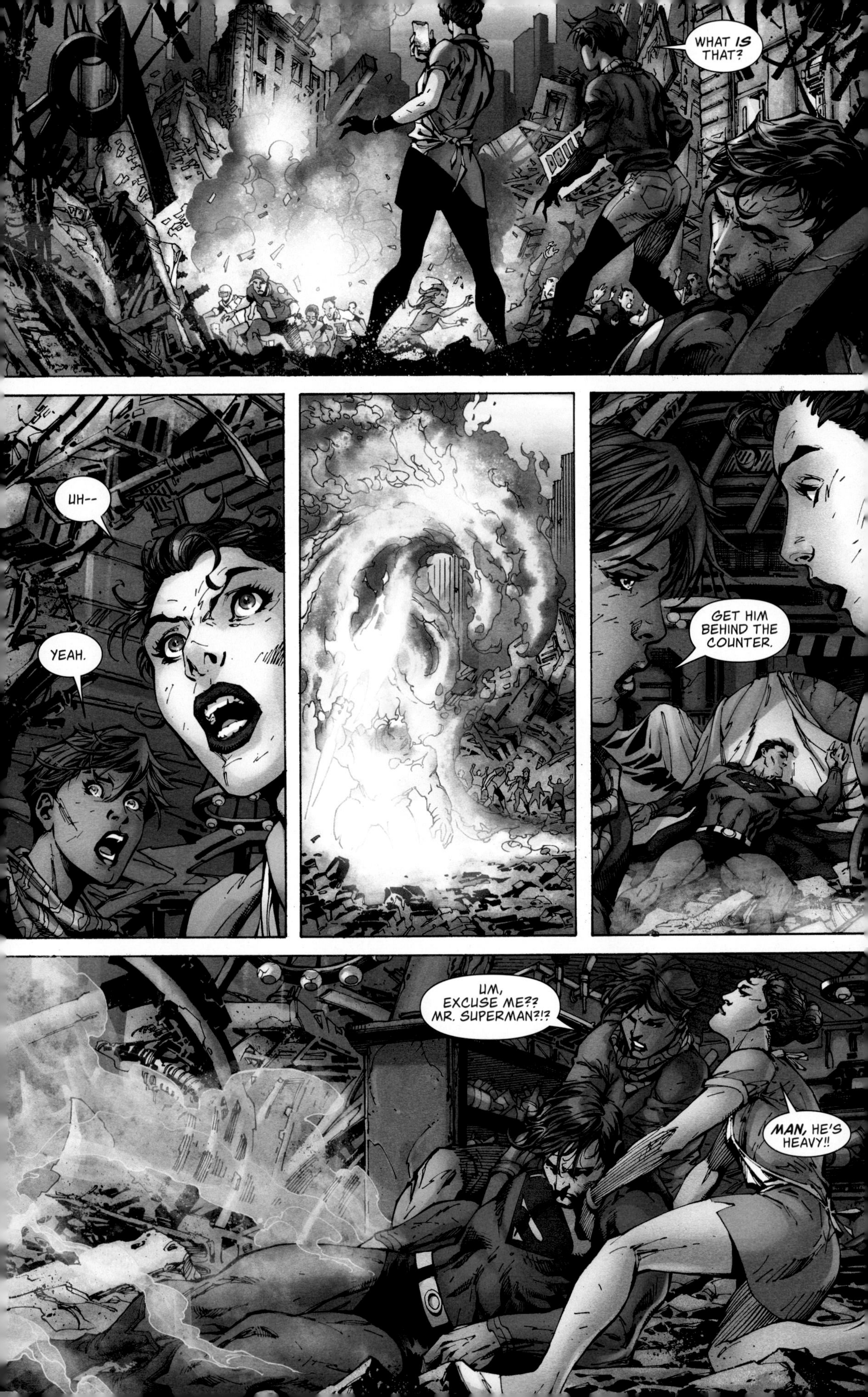

WHAT *IS* THAT?
UH--
YEAH.
GET HIM BEHIND THE COUNTER.
UM, EXCUSE ME?? MR. SUPERMAN?!?
MAN, HE'S HEAVY!!

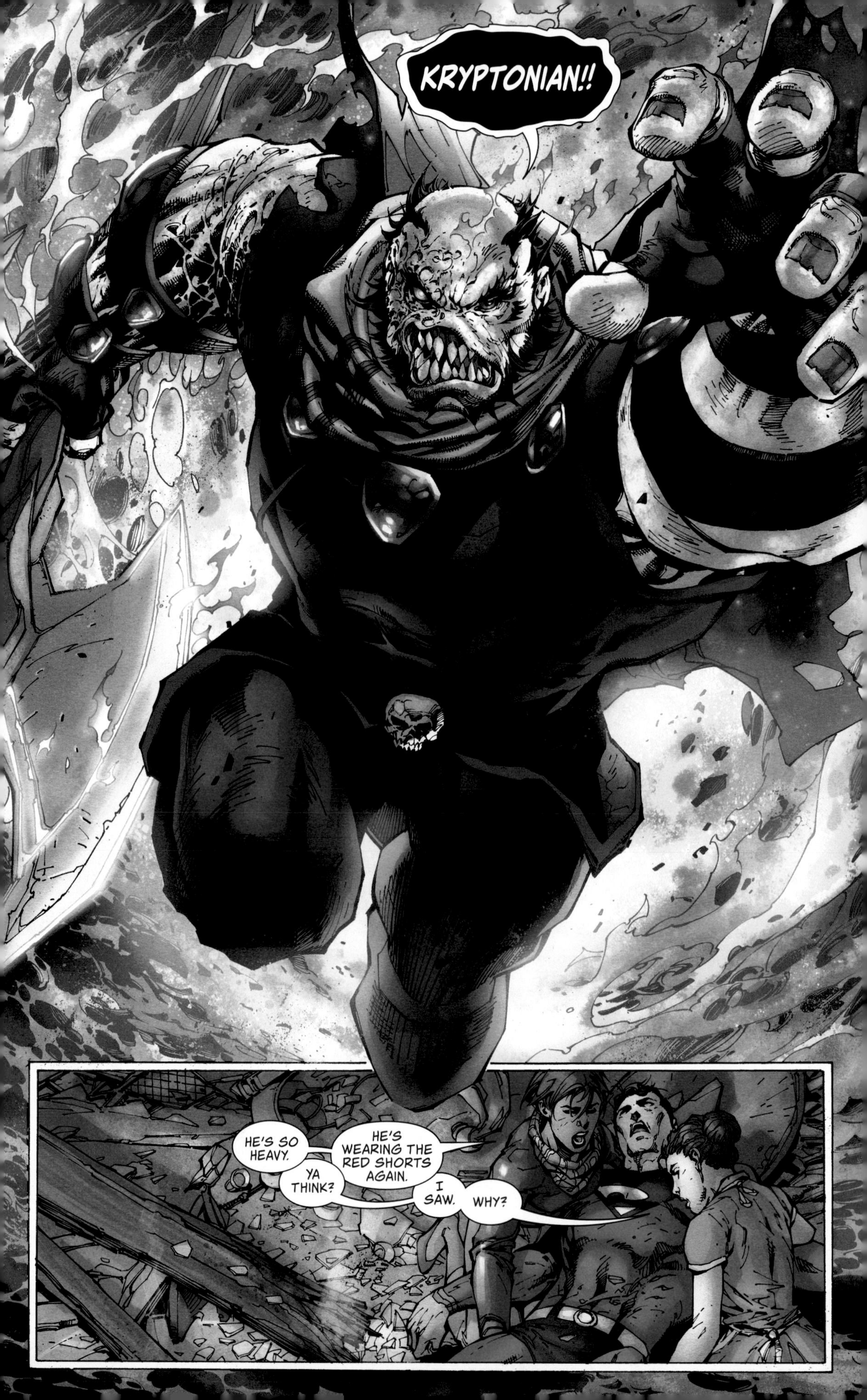
KRYPTONIAN!!
HE'S SO HEAVY.
HE'S WEARING THE RED SHORTS AGAIN.
YA THINK?
I SAW.
WHY?

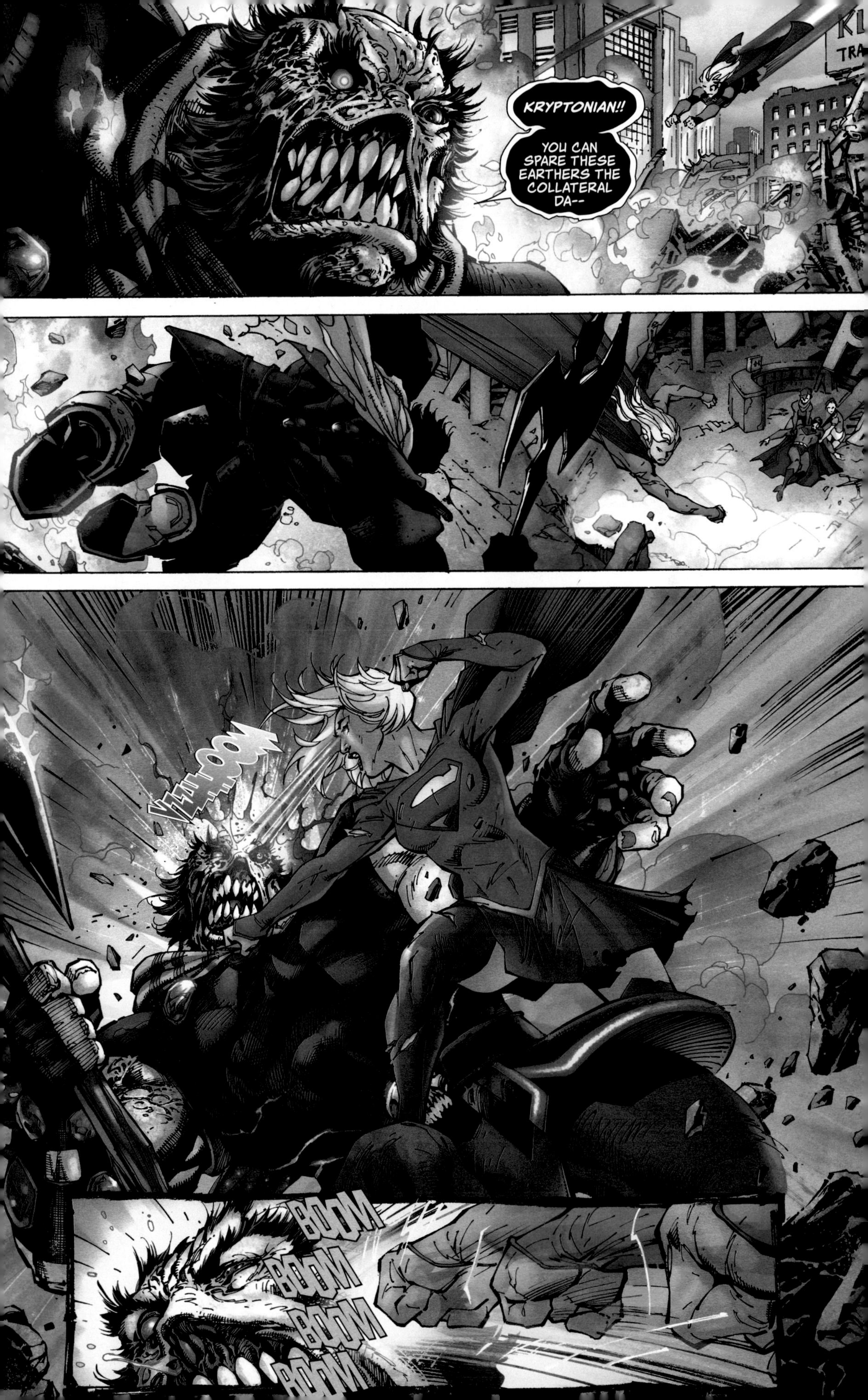
KRYPTONIAN!!
YOU CAN SPARE THESE EARTHERS THE COLLATERAL DA--
VZZOOOM
BOOM
BOOM
BOOM
BOOM

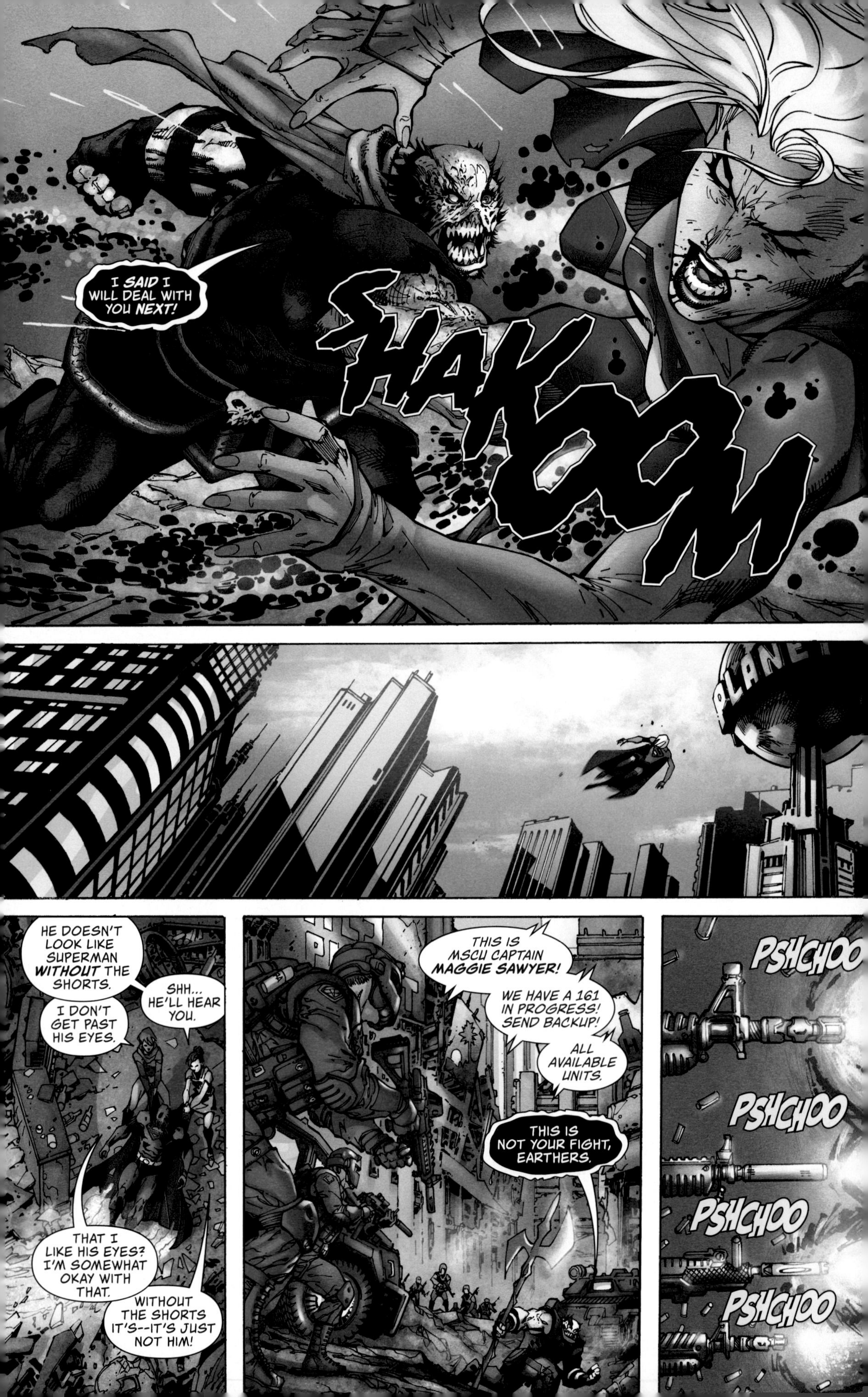
I SAID I WILL DEAL WITH YOU NEXT!
SHAKOOM
PLANET
HE DOESN'T LOOK LIKE SUPERMAN WITHOUT THE SHORTS.
SHH... HE'LL HEAR YOU.
I DON'T GET PAST HIS EYES.
THAT I LIKE HIS EYES? I'M SOMEWHAT OKAY WITH THAT.
WITHOUT THE SHORTS IT'S--IT'S JUST NOT HIM!
THIS IS MSCU CAPTAIN MAGGIE SAWYER!
WE HAVE A 161 IN PROGRESS! SEND BACKUP!
ALL AVAILABLE UNITS.
THIS IS NOT YOUR FIGHT, EARTHERS.
PSHCHOO
PSHCHOO
PSHCHOO
PSHCHOO

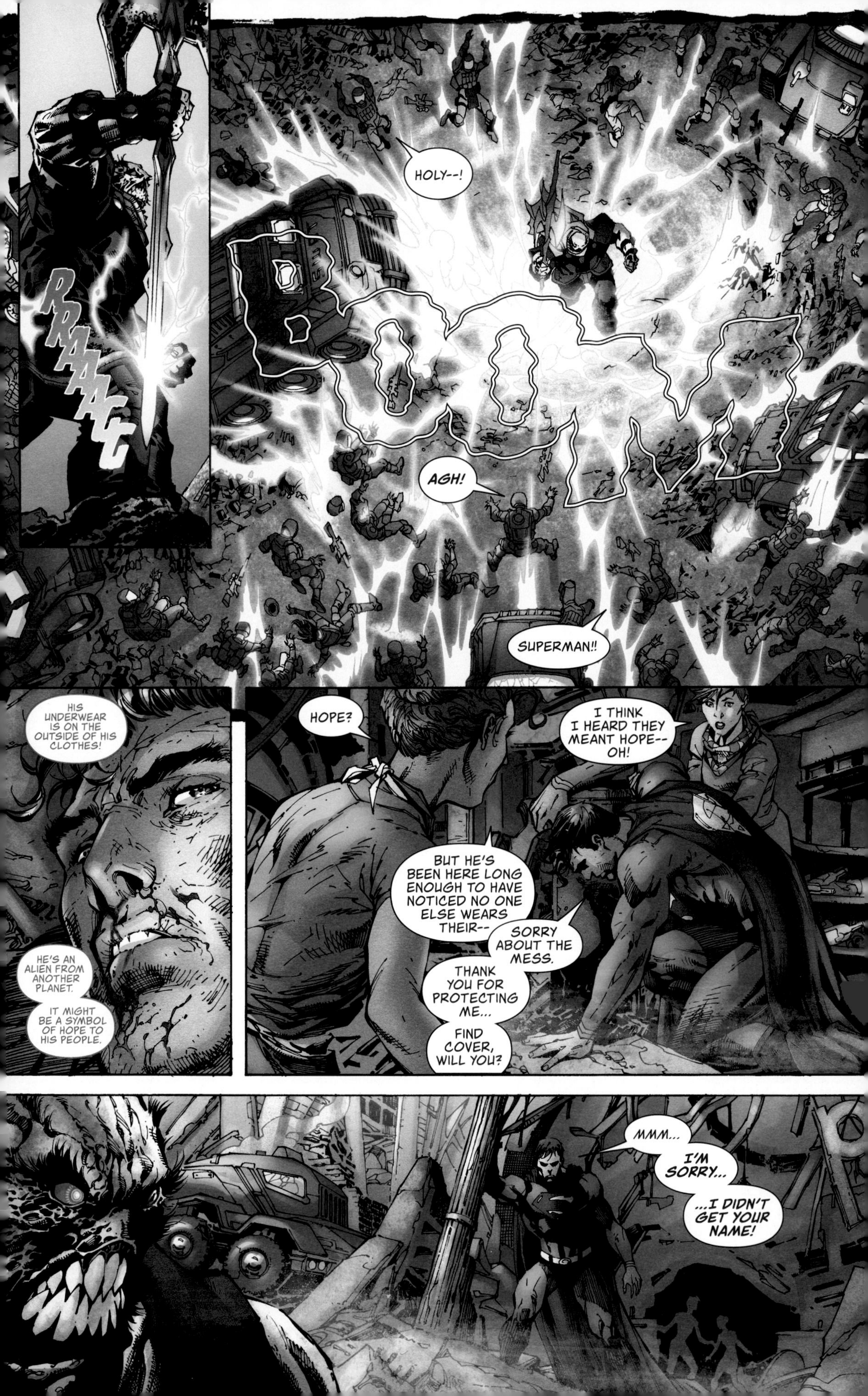
RRAAAACC
HOLY--!
BOOM
AGH!
SUPERMAN!!
HIS UNDERWEAR IS ON THE OUTSIDE OF HIS CLOTHES!
HE'S AN ALIEN FROM ANOTHER PLANET.
IT MIGHT BE A SYMBOL OF HOPE TO HIS PEOPLE.
HOPE?
I THINK I HEARD THEY MEANT HOPE--OH!
BUT HE'S BEEN HERE LONG ENOUGH TO HAVE NOTICED NO ONE ELSE WEARS THEIR--
SORRY ABOUT THE MESS.
THANK YOU FOR PROTECTING ME...
FIND COVER, WILL YOU?
MMM...
I'M SORRY...
...I DIDN'T GET YOUR NAME!

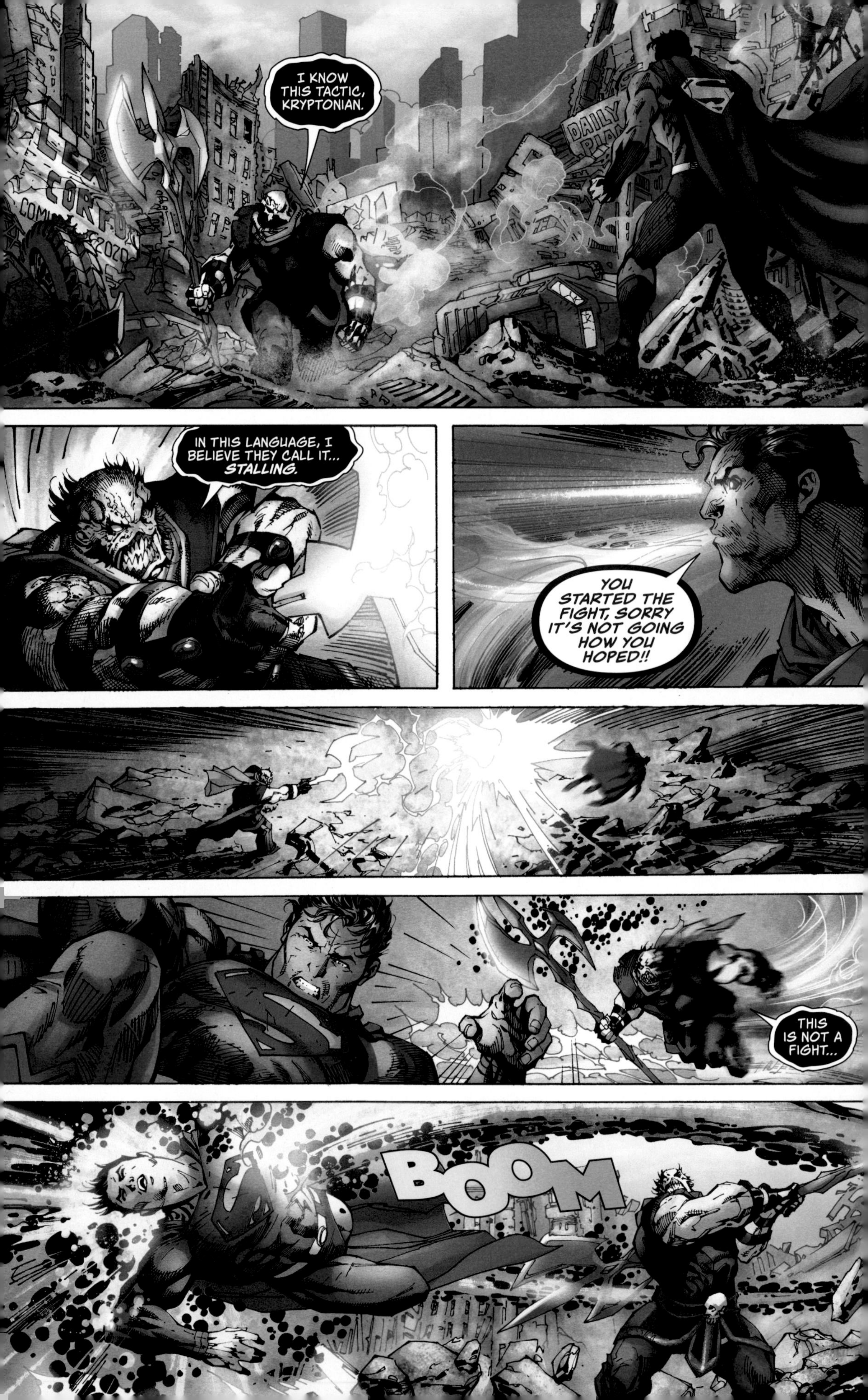
I KNOW THIS TACTIC, KRYPTONIAN.
IN THIS LANGUAGE, I BELIEVE THEY CALL IT... STALLING.
YOU STARTED THE FIGHT, SORRY IT'S NOT GOING HOW YOU HOPED!!
THIS IS NOT A FIGHT...
BOOM

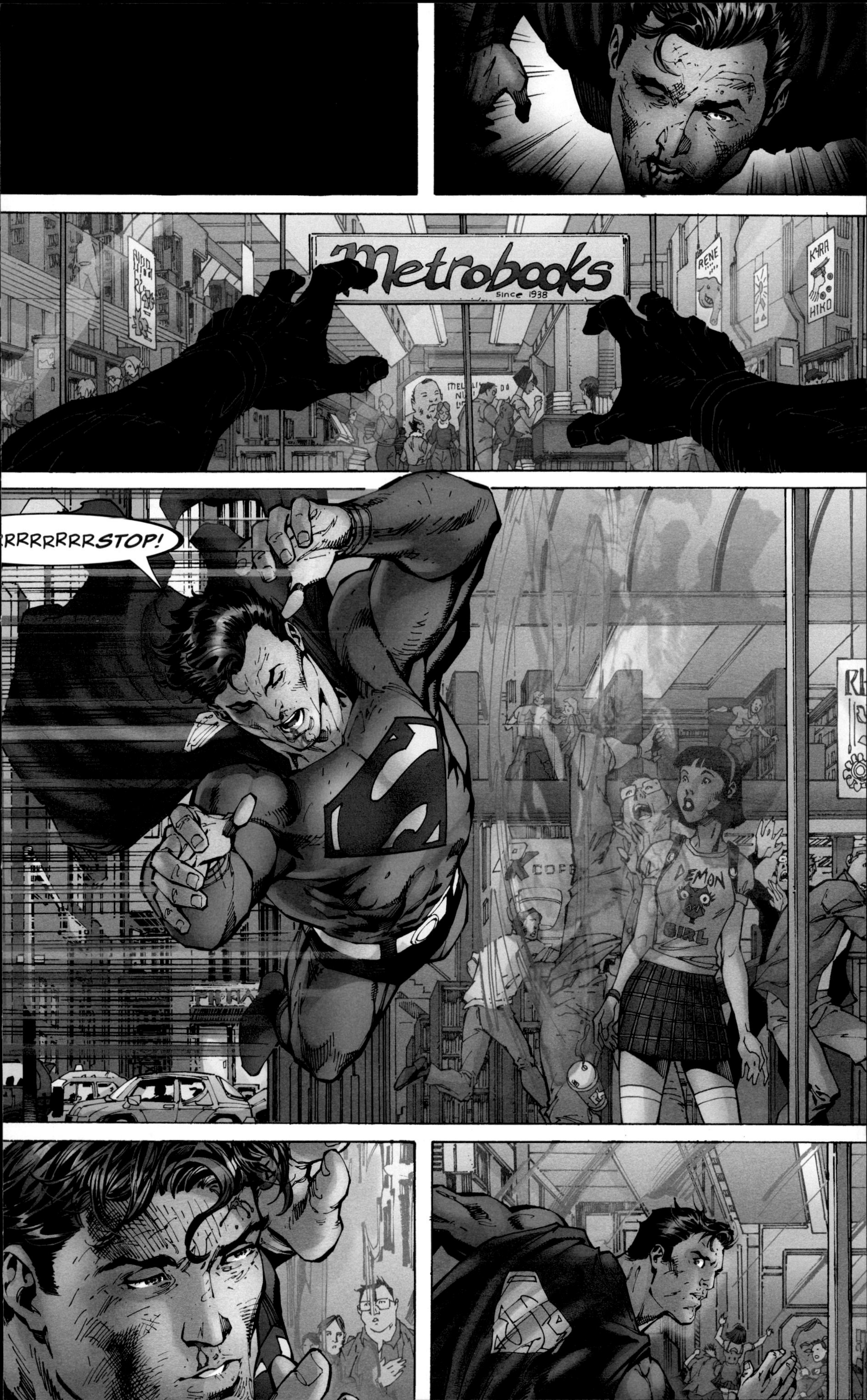
Metrobooks
since 1938
RENE
KYRA
HIKO
RRRRRRRRSTOP!
DEMON
GIRL

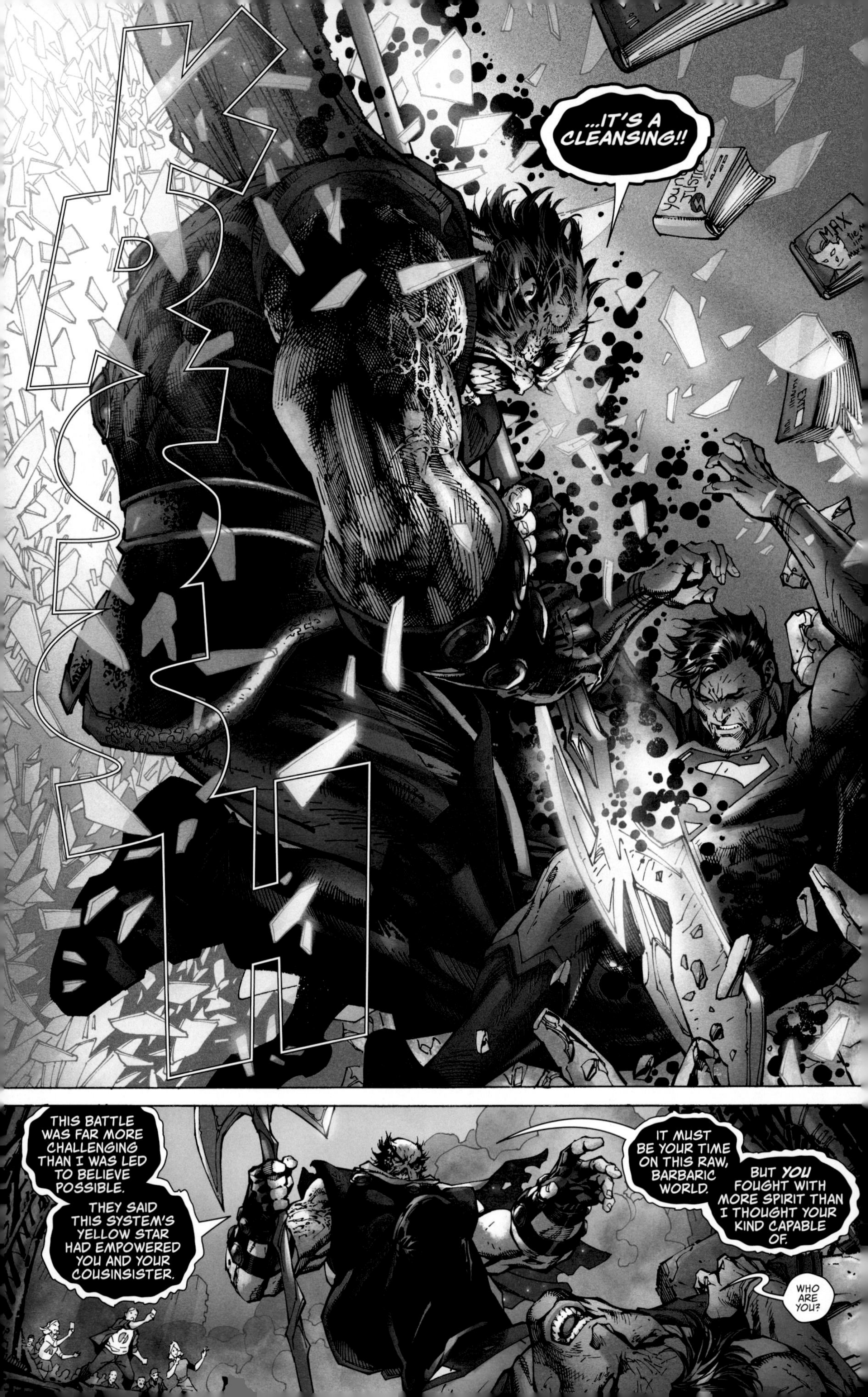
...IT'S A CLEANSING!!
THIS BATTLE WAS FAR MORE CHALLENGING THAN I WAS LED TO BELIEVE POSSIBLE.
THEY SAID THIS SYSTEM'S YELLOW STAR HAD EMPOWERED YOU AND YOUR COUSINSISTER.
IT MUST BE YOUR TIME ON THIS RAW, BARBARIC WORLD.
BUT YOU FOUGHT WITH MORE SPIRIT THAN I THOUGHT YOUR KIND CAPABLE OF.
WHO ARE YOU?

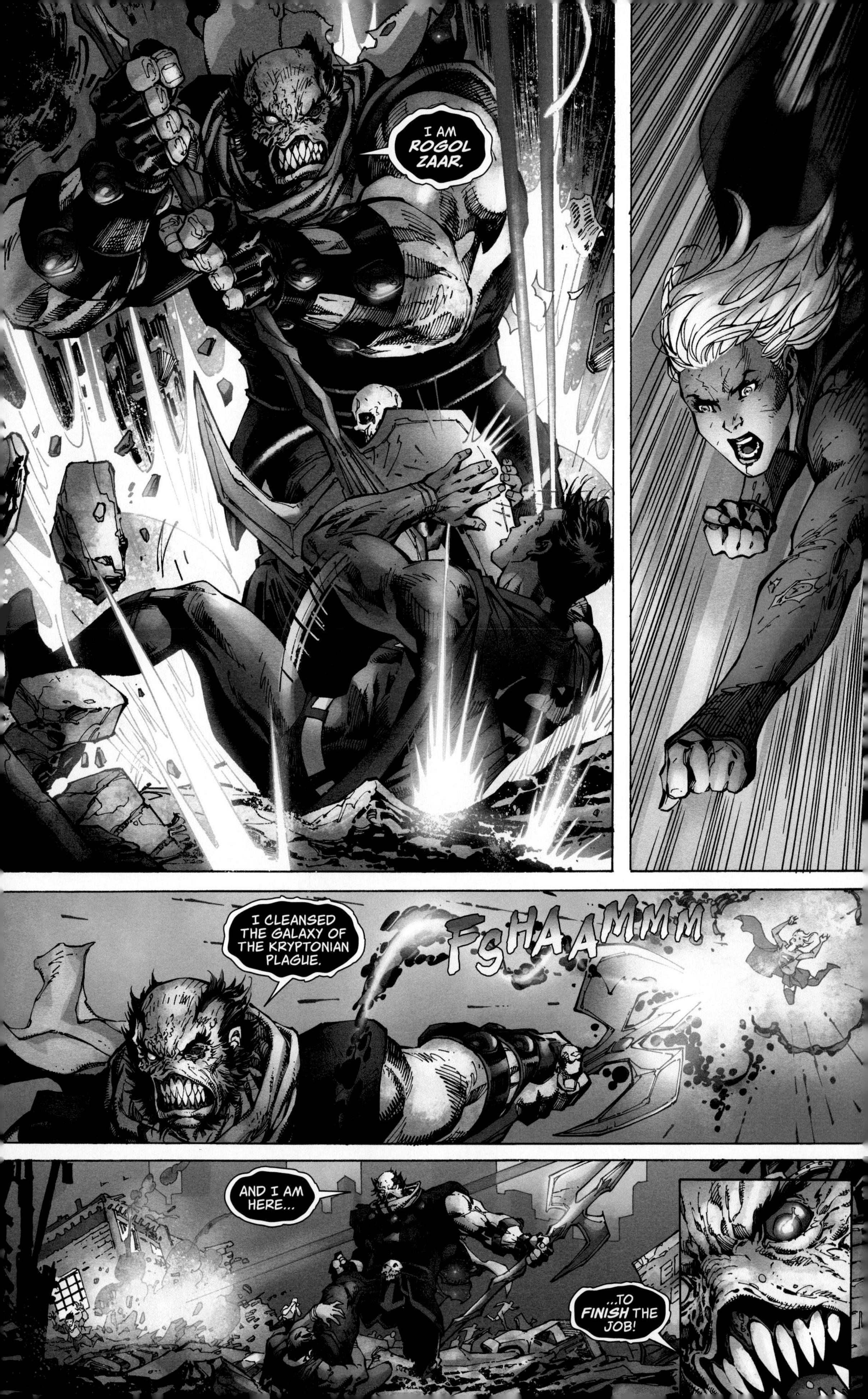
I AM ROGOL ZAAR.
I CLEANSED THE GALAXY OF THE KRYPTONIAN PLAGUE.
FSHAAMMM
AND I AM HERE...
...TO FINISH THE JOB!

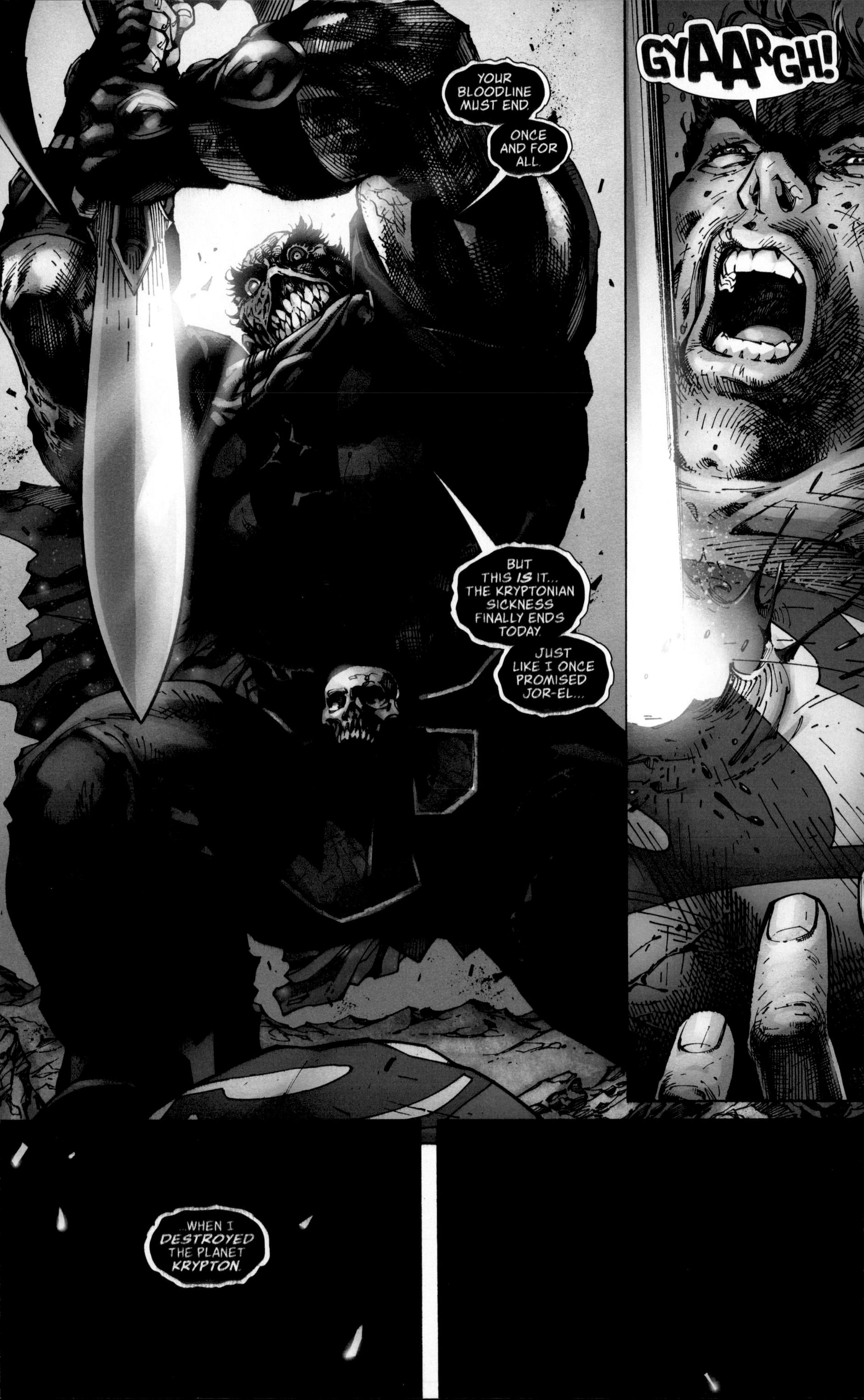
YOUR BLOODLINE MUST END.
ONCE AND FOR ALL.
GYAARGH!
BUT THIS IS IT... THE KRYPTONIAN SICKNESS FINALLY ENDS TODAY.
JUST LIKE I ONCE PROMISED JOR-EL...
...WHEN I DESTROYED THE PLANET KRYPTON.

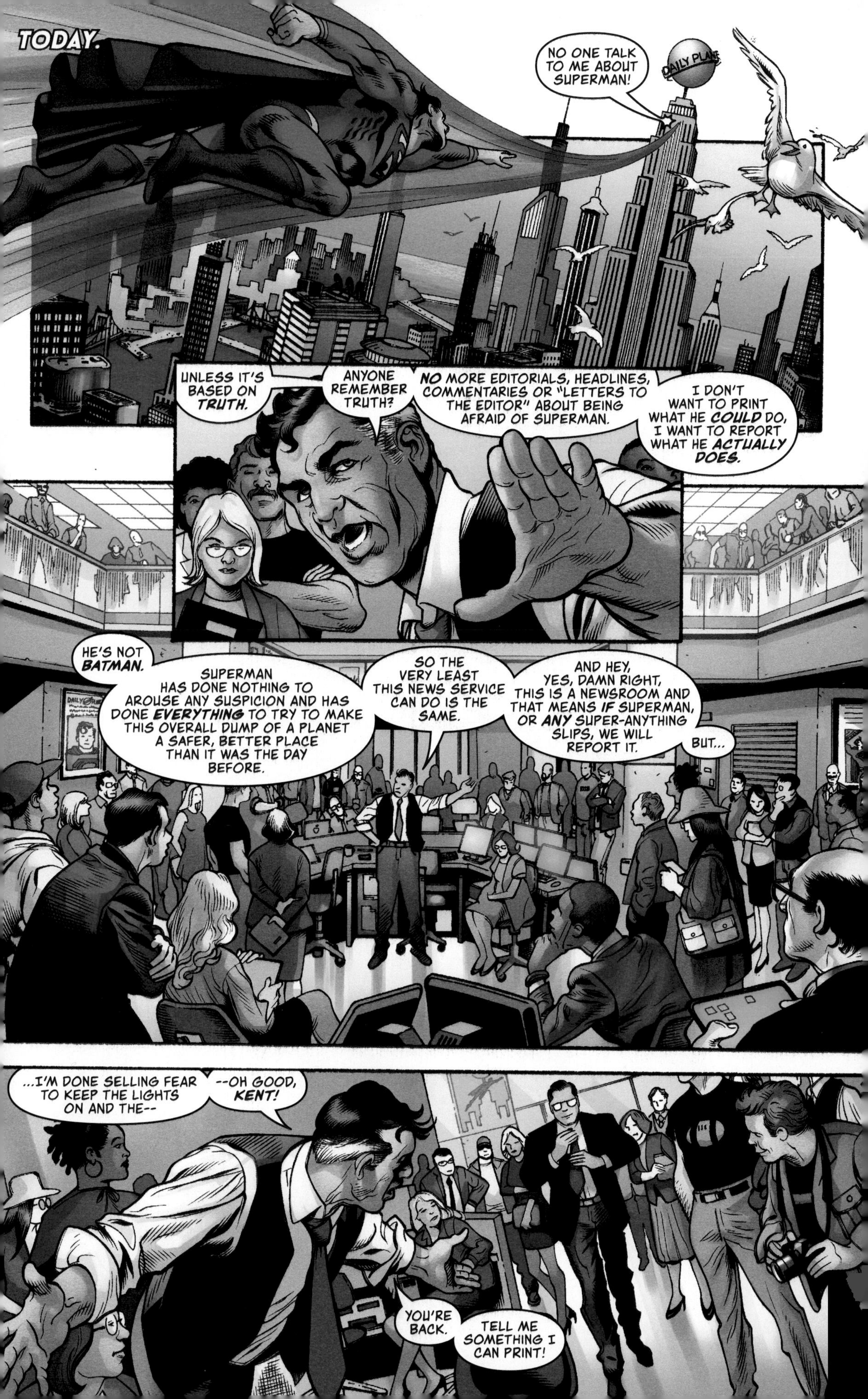
TODAY.
NO ONE TALK TO ME ABOUT SUPERMAN!
DAILY PLANET
UNLESS IT'S BASED ON TRUTH.
ANYONE REMEMBER TRUTH?
NO MORE EDITORIALS, HEADLINES, COMMENTARIES OR "LETTERS TO THE EDITOR" ABOUT BEING AFRAID OF SUPERMAN.
I DON'T WANT TO PRINT WHAT HE COULD DO, I WANT TO REPORT WHAT HE ACTUALLY DOES.
HE'S NOT BATMAN.
SUPERMAN HAS DONE NOTHING TO AROUSE ANY SUSPICION AND HAS DONE EVERYTHING TO TRY TO MAKE THIS OVERALL DUMP OF A PLANET A SAFER, BETTER PLACE THAN IT WAS THE DAY BEFORE.
SO THE VERY LEAST THIS NEWS SERVICE CAN DO IS THE SAME.
AND HEY, YES, DAMN RIGHT, THIS IS A NEWSROOM AND THAT MEANS IF SUPERMAN, OR ANY SUPER-ANYTHING SLIPS, WE WILL REPORT IT.
BUT...
...I'M DONE SELLING FEAR TO KEEP THE LIGHTS ON AND THE--
--OH GOOD, KENT!
YOU'RE BACK.
TELL ME SOMETHING I CAN PRINT!

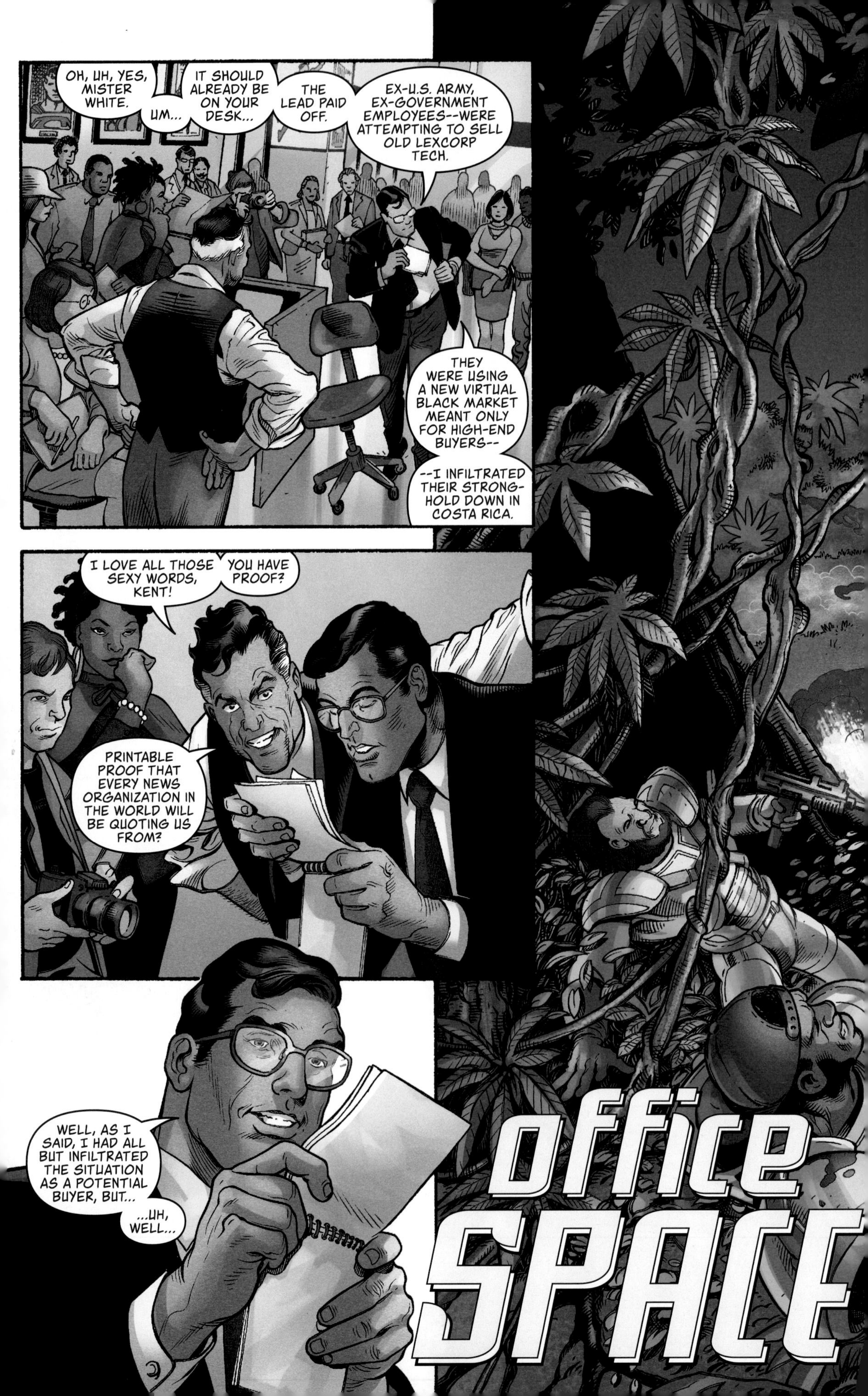

OH, UH, YES, MISTER WHITE.
UM...
IT SHOULD ALREADY BE ON YOUR DESK...
THE LEAD PAID OFF.
EX-U.S. ARMY, EX-GOVERNMENT EMPLOYEES--WERE ATTEMPTING TO SELL OLD LEXCORP TECH.
THEY WERE USING A NEW VIRTUAL BLACK MARKET MEANT ONLY FOR HIGH-END BUYERS--
--I INFILTRATED THEIR STRONG-HOLD DOWN IN COSTA RICA.
I LOVE ALL THOSE SEXY WORDS, KENT!
YOU HAVE PROOF?
PRINTABLE PROOF THAT EVERY NEWS ORGANIZATION IN THE WORLD WILL BE QUOTING US FROM?
WELL, AS I SAID, I HAD ALL BUT INFILTRATED THE SITUATION AS A POTENTIAL BUYER, BUT...
...UH, WELL...
office SPACE

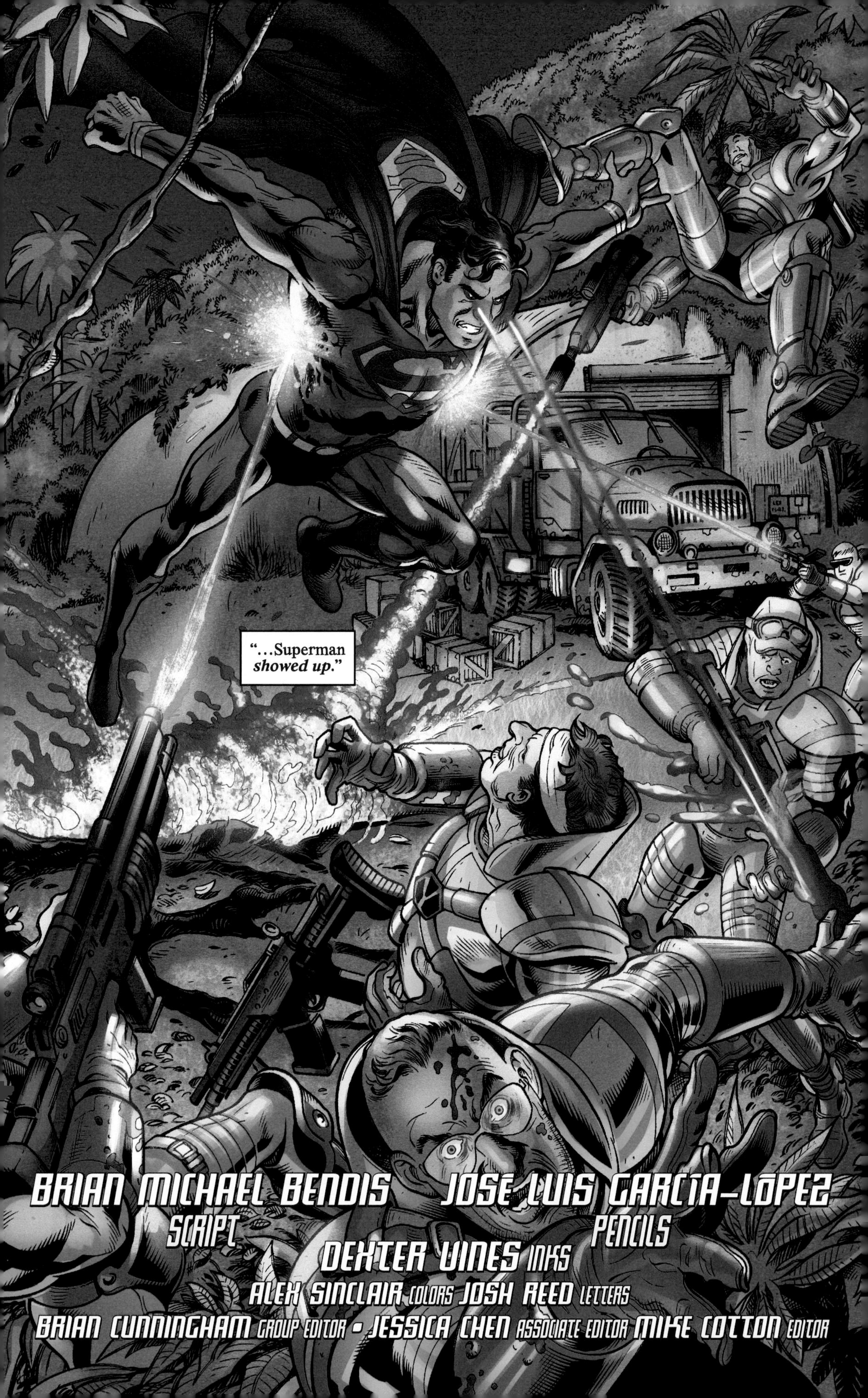
"...Superman *showed up*."
BRIAN MICHAEL BENDIS SCRIPT
JOSE LUIS GARCIA-LÓPEZ PENCILS
DEXTER VINES INKS
ALEX SINCLAIR COLORS JOSH REED LETTERS
BRIAN CUNNINGHAM GROUP EDITOR • JESSICA CHEN ASSOCIATE EDITOR MIKE COTTON EDITOR

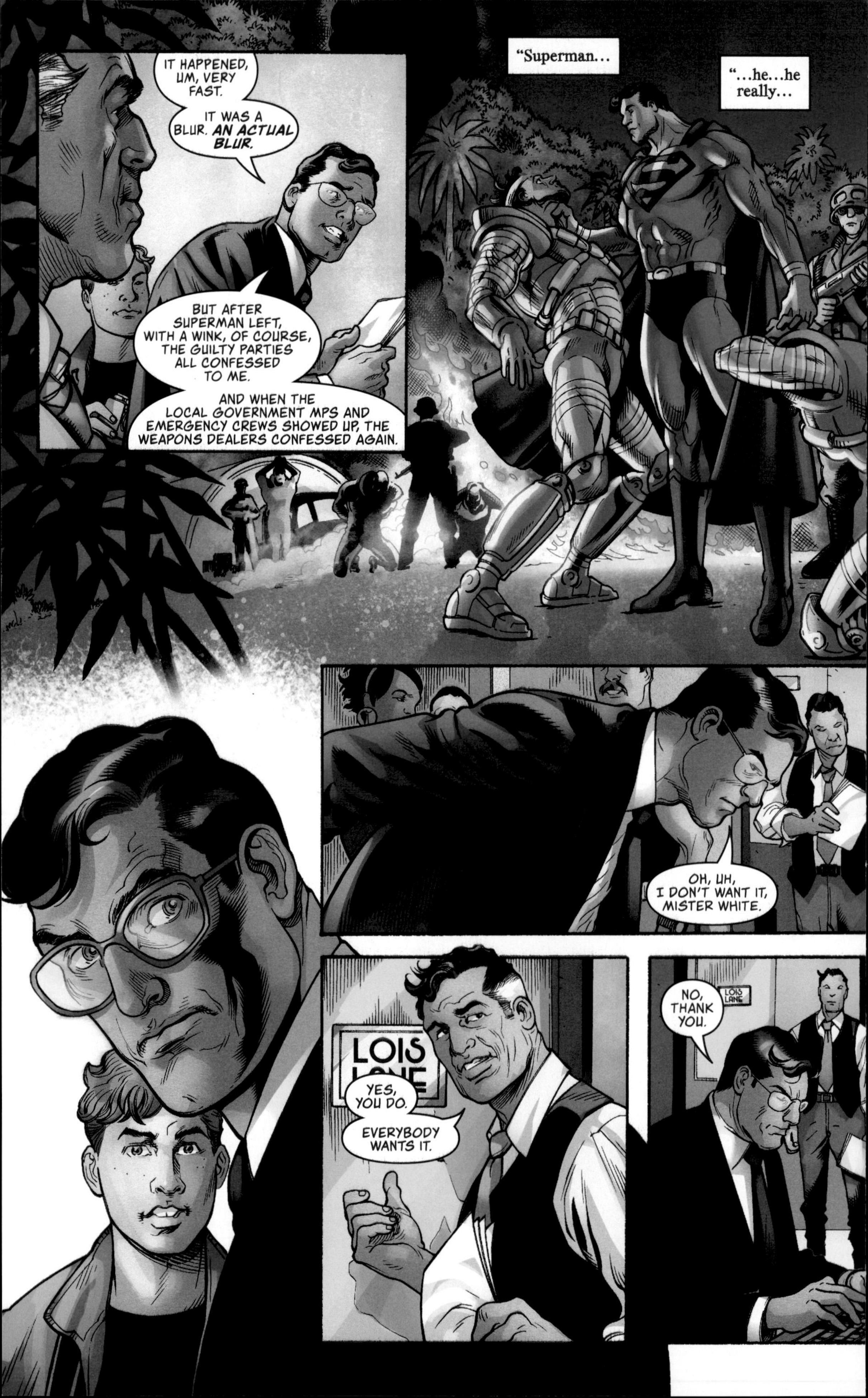
IT HAPPENED, UM, VERY FAST.
IT WAS A BLUR. AN ACTUAL BLUR.
"Superman…
"…he…he really…
BUT AFTER SUPERMAN LEFT, WITH A WINK, OF COURSE, THE GUILTY PARTIES ALL CONFESSED TO ME.
AND WHEN THE LOCAL GOVERNMENT MPS AND EMERGENCY CREWS SHOWED UP, THE WEAPONS DEALERS CONFESSED AGAIN.
OH, UH, I DON'T WANT IT, MISTER WHITE.
LOIS LANE
YES, YOU DO.
EVERYBODY WANTS IT.
NO, THANK YOU.
LOIS LANE

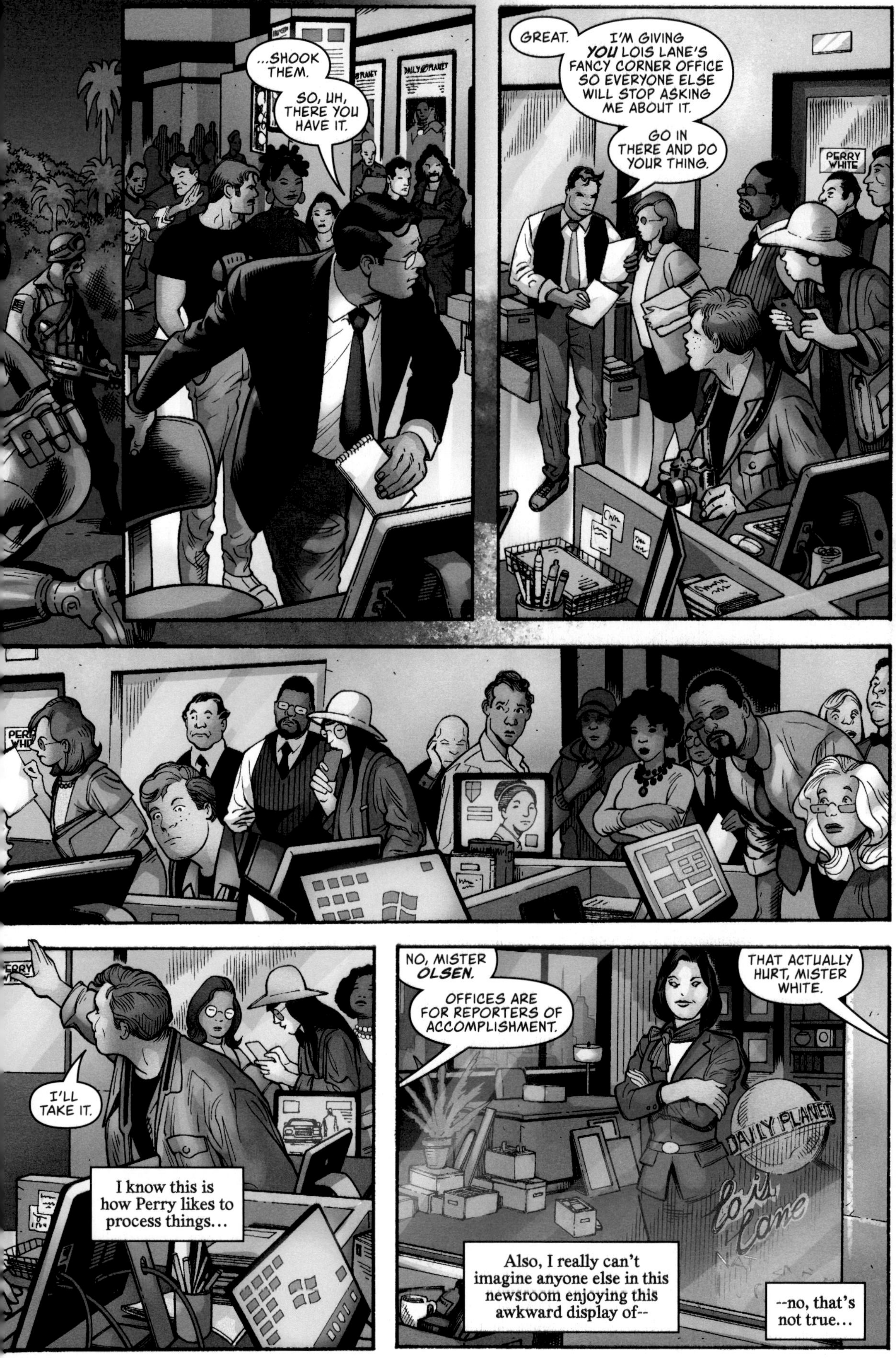
...SHOOK THEM.
SO, UH, THERE YOU HAVE IT.
GREAT.
I'M GIVING YOU LOIS LANE'S FANCY CORNER OFFICE SO EVERYONE ELSE WILL STOP ASKING ME ABOUT IT.
GO IN THERE AND DO YOUR THING.
PERRY WHITE
I'LL TAKE IT.
I know this is how Perry likes to process things...
NO, MISTER OLSEN.
OFFICES ARE FOR REPORTERS OF ACCOMPLISHMENT.
THAT ACTUALLY HURT, MISTER WHITE.
DAILY PLANET
Lois Lane
Also, I really can't imagine anyone else in this newsroom enjoying this awkward display of--
--no, that's not true...

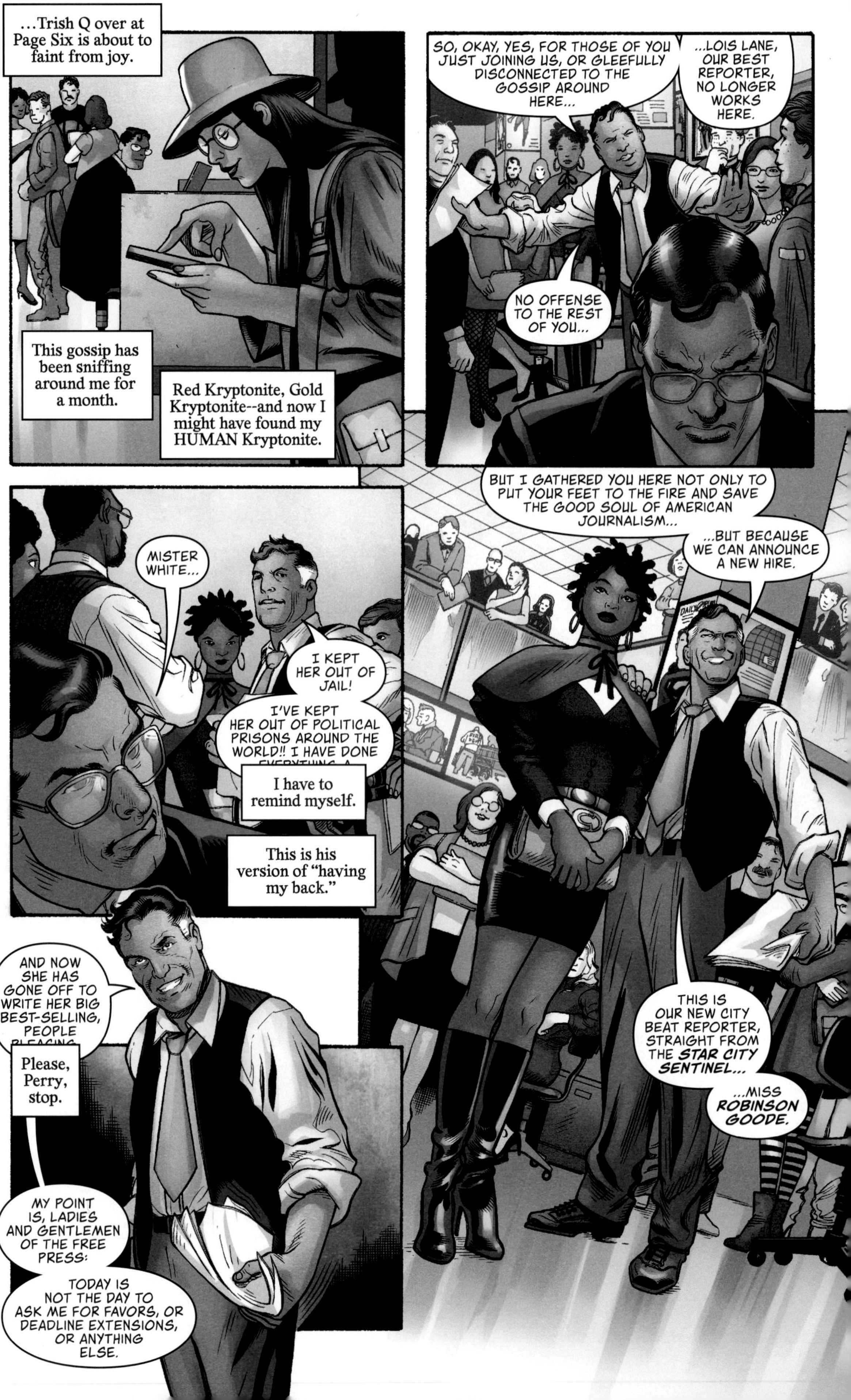
...Trish Q over at Page Six is about to faint from joy.
This gossip has been sniffing around me for a month.
Red Kryptonite, Gold Kryptonite--and now I might have found my HUMAN Kryptonite.
SO, OKAY, YES, FOR THOSE OF YOU JUST JOINING US, OR GLEEFULLY DISCONNECTED TO THE GOSSIP AROUND HERE...
...LOIS LANE, OUR BEST REPORTER, NO LONGER WORKS HERE.
NO OFFENSE TO THE REST OF YOU...
MISTER WHITE...
I KEPT HER OUT OF JAIL!
I'VE KEPT HER OUT OF POLITICAL PRISONS AROUND THE WORLD!! I HAVE DONE
I have to remind myself.
This is his version of "having my back."
AND NOW SHE HAS GONE OFF TO WRITE HER BIG BEST-SELLING, PEOPLE
Please, Perry, stop.
MY POINT IS, LADIES AND GENTLEMEN OF THE FREE PRESS:
TODAY IS NOT THE DAY TO ASK ME FOR FAVORS, OR DEADLINE EXTENSIONS, OR ANYTHING ELSE.
BUT I GATHERED YOU HERE NOT ONLY TO PUT YOUR FEET TO THE FIRE AND SAVE THE GOOD SOUL OF AMERICAN JOURNALISM...
...BUT BECAUSE WE CAN ANNOUNCE A NEW HIRE.
THIS IS OUR NEW CITY BEAT REPORTER, STRAIGHT FROM THE STAR CITY SENTINEL...
...MISS ROBINSON GOODE.

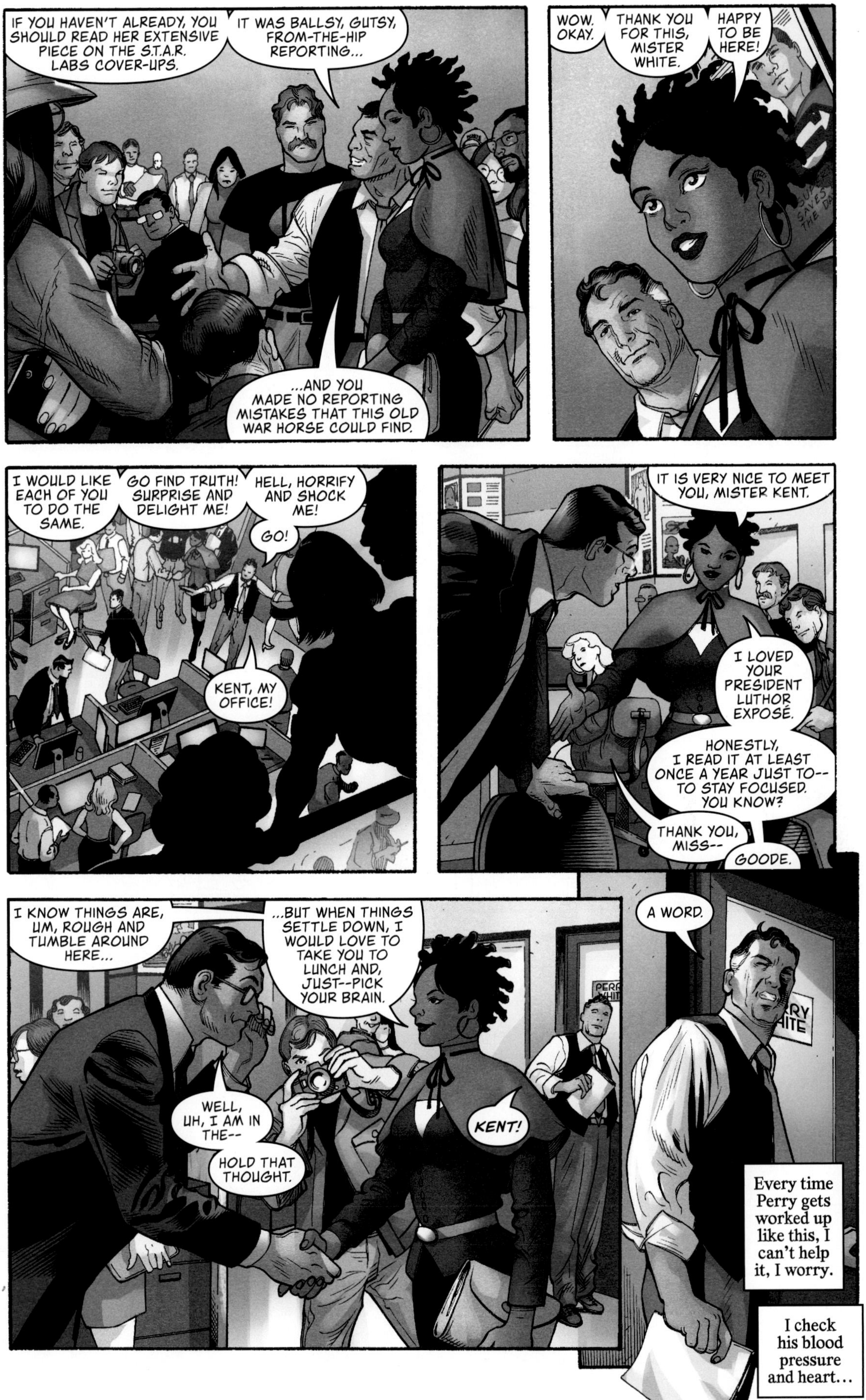
IF YOU HAVEN'T ALREADY, YOU SHOULD READ HER EXTENSIVE PIECE ON THE S.T.A.R. LABS COVER-UPS.
IT WAS BALLSY, GUTSY, FROM-THE-HIP REPORTING...
...AND YOU MADE NO REPORTING MISTAKES THAT THIS OLD WAR HORSE COULD FIND.
WOW. OKAY.
THANK YOU FOR THIS, MISTER WHITE.
HAPPY TO BE HERE!
I WOULD LIKE EACH OF YOU TO DO THE SAME.
GO FIND TRUTH! SURPRISE AND DELIGHT ME!
HELL, HORRIFY AND SHOCK ME!
GO!
KENT, MY OFFICE!
IT IS VERY NICE TO MEET YOU, MISTER KENT.
I LOVED YOUR PRESIDENT LUTHOR EXPOSÉ.
HONESTLY, I READ IT AT LEAST ONCE A YEAR JUST TO-- TO STAY FOCUSED. YOU KNOW?
THANK YOU, MISS--
GOODE.
I KNOW THINGS ARE, UM, ROUGH AND TUMBLE AROUND HERE...
...BUT WHEN THINGS SETTLE DOWN, I WOULD LOVE TO TAKE YOU TO LUNCH AND, JUST--PICK YOUR BRAIN.
WELL, UH, I AM IN THE--
HOLD THAT THOUGHT.
KENT!
A WORD.
Every time Perry gets worked up like this, I can't help it, I worry.
I check his blood pressure and heart...

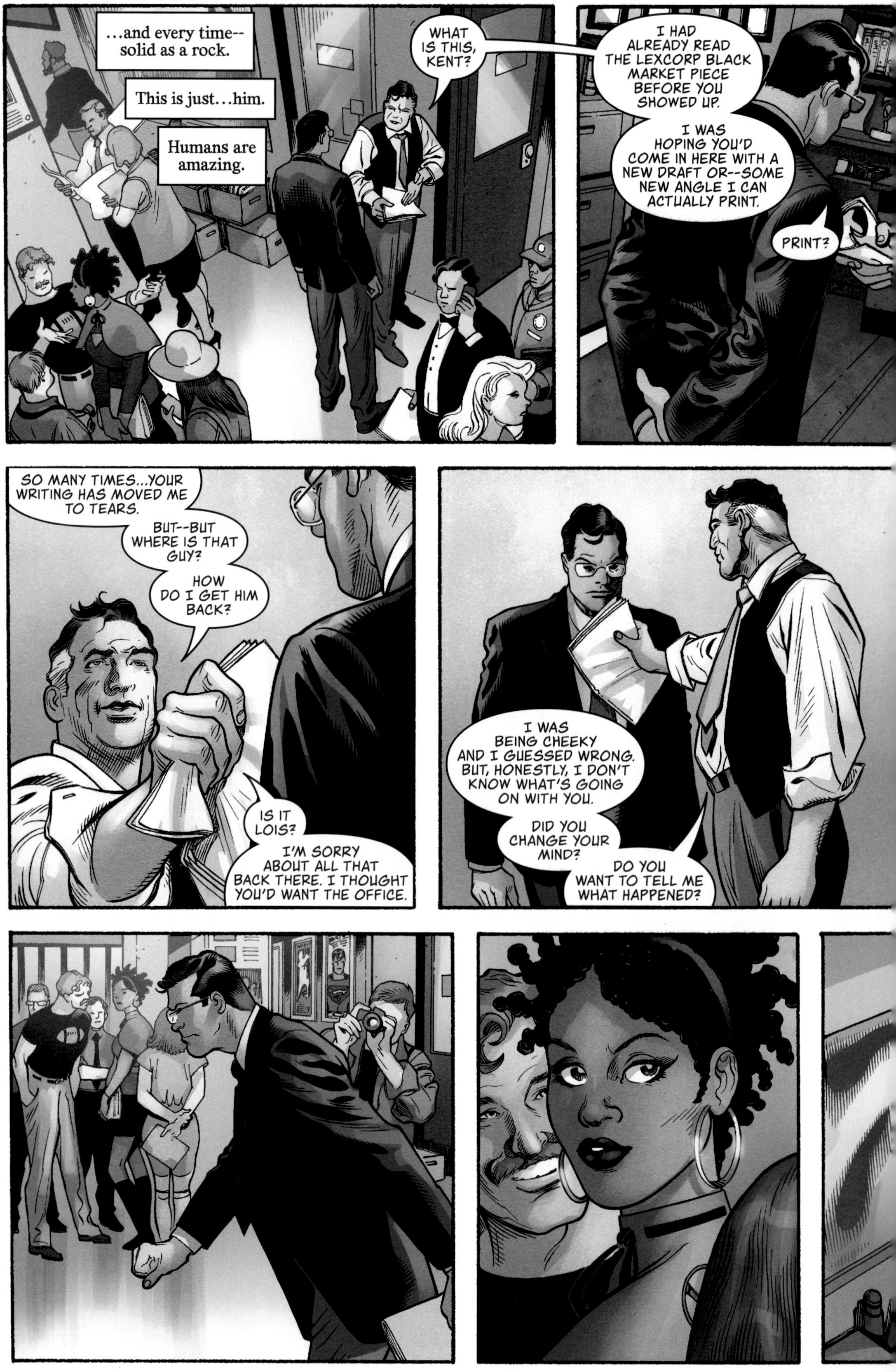
...and every time--solid as a rock.
This is just...him.
Humans are amazing.
WHAT IS THIS, KENT?
I HAD ALREADY READ THE LEXCORP BLACK MARKET PIECE BEFORE YOU SHOWED UP.
I WAS HOPING YOU'D COME IN HERE WITH A NEW DRAFT OR--SOME NEW ANGLE I CAN ACTUALLY PRINT.
PRINT?
SO MANY TIMES...YOUR WRITING HAS MOVED ME TO TEARS.
BUT--BUT WHERE IS THAT GUY?
HOW DO I GET HIM BACK?
IS IT LOIS?
I'M SORRY ABOUT ALL THAT BACK THERE. I THOUGHT YOU'D WANT THE OFFICE.
I WAS BEING CHEEKY AND I GUESSED WRONG. BUT, HONESTLY, I DON'T KNOW WHAT'S GOING ON WITH YOU.
DID YOU CHANGE YOUR MIND?
DO YOU WANT TO TELL ME WHAT HAPPENED?

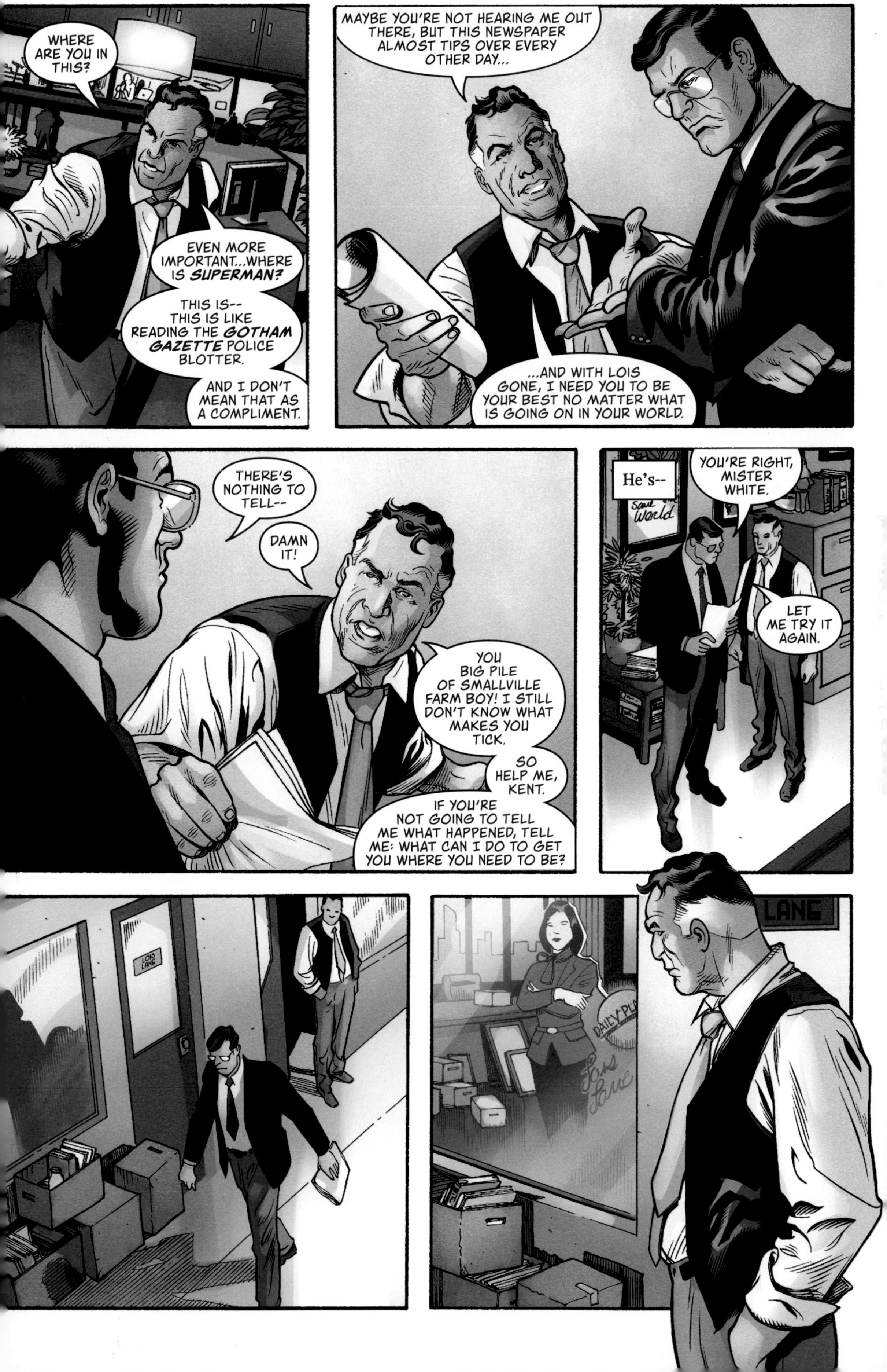

WHERE ARE YOU IN THIS?
EVEN MORE IMPORTANT...WHERE IS SUPERMAN?
THIS IS-- THIS IS LIKE READING THE GOTHAM GAZETTE POLICE BLOTTER.
AND I DON'T MEAN THAT AS A COMPLIMENT.
MAYBE YOU'RE NOT HEARING ME OUT THERE, BUT THIS NEWSPAPER ALMOST TIPS OVER EVERY OTHER DAY...
...AND WITH LOIS GONE, I NEED YOU TO BE YOUR BEST NO MATTER WHAT IS GOING ON IN YOUR WORLD.
THERE'S NOTHING TO TELL--
DAMN IT!
YOU BIG PILE OF SMALLVILLE FARM BOY! I STILL DON'T KNOW WHAT MAKES YOU TICK.
SO HELP ME, KENT.
IF YOU'RE NOT GOING TO TELL ME WHAT HAPPENED, TELL ME: WHAT CAN I DO TO GET YOU WHERE YOU NEED TO BE?
He's--
YOU'RE RIGHT, MISTER WHITE.
LET ME TRY IT AGAIN.
LANE

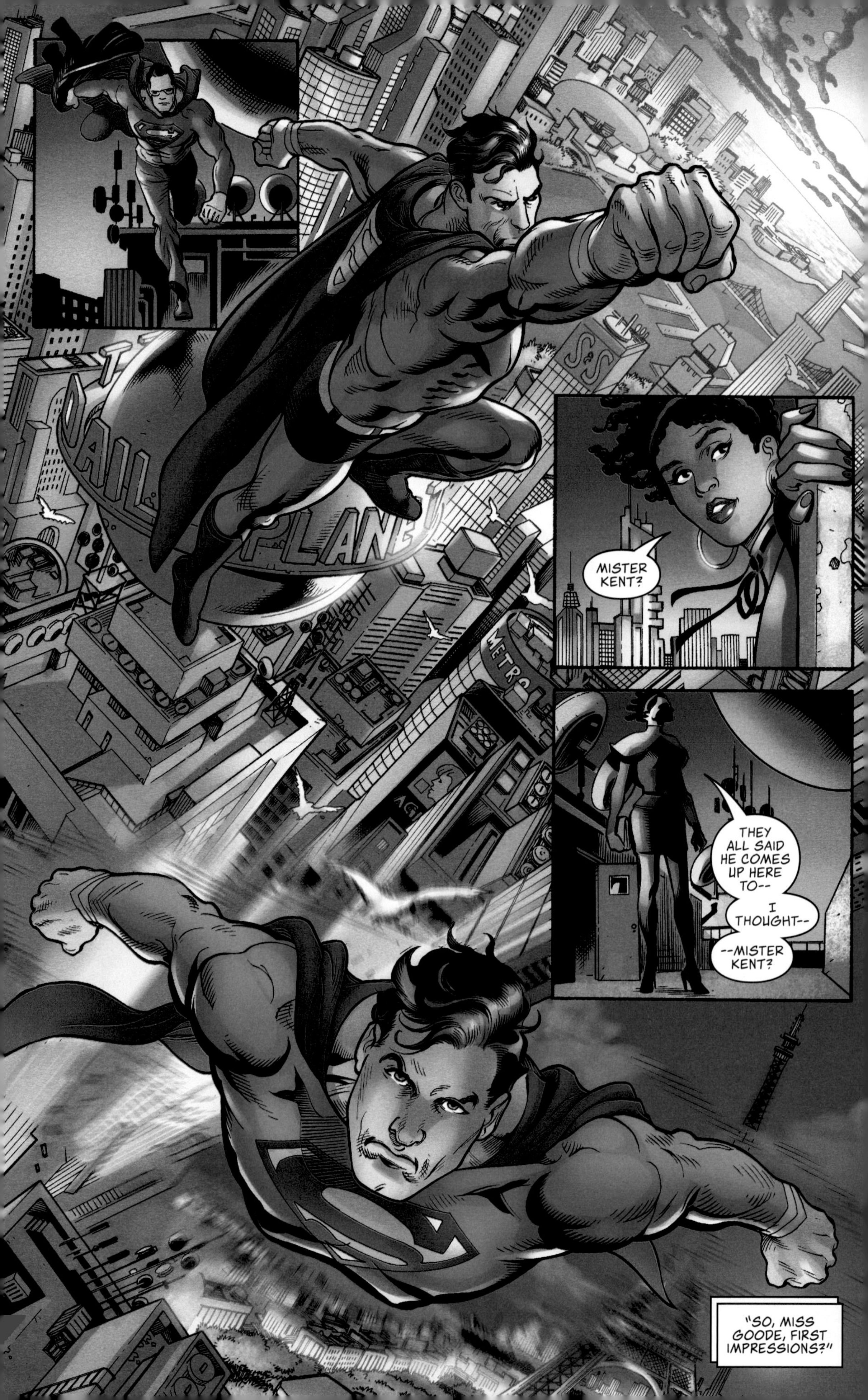
MISTER KENT?
THEY ALL SAID HE COMES UP HERE TO--
I THOUGHT--
--MISTER KENT?
"SO, MISS GOODE, FIRST IMPRESSIONS?"

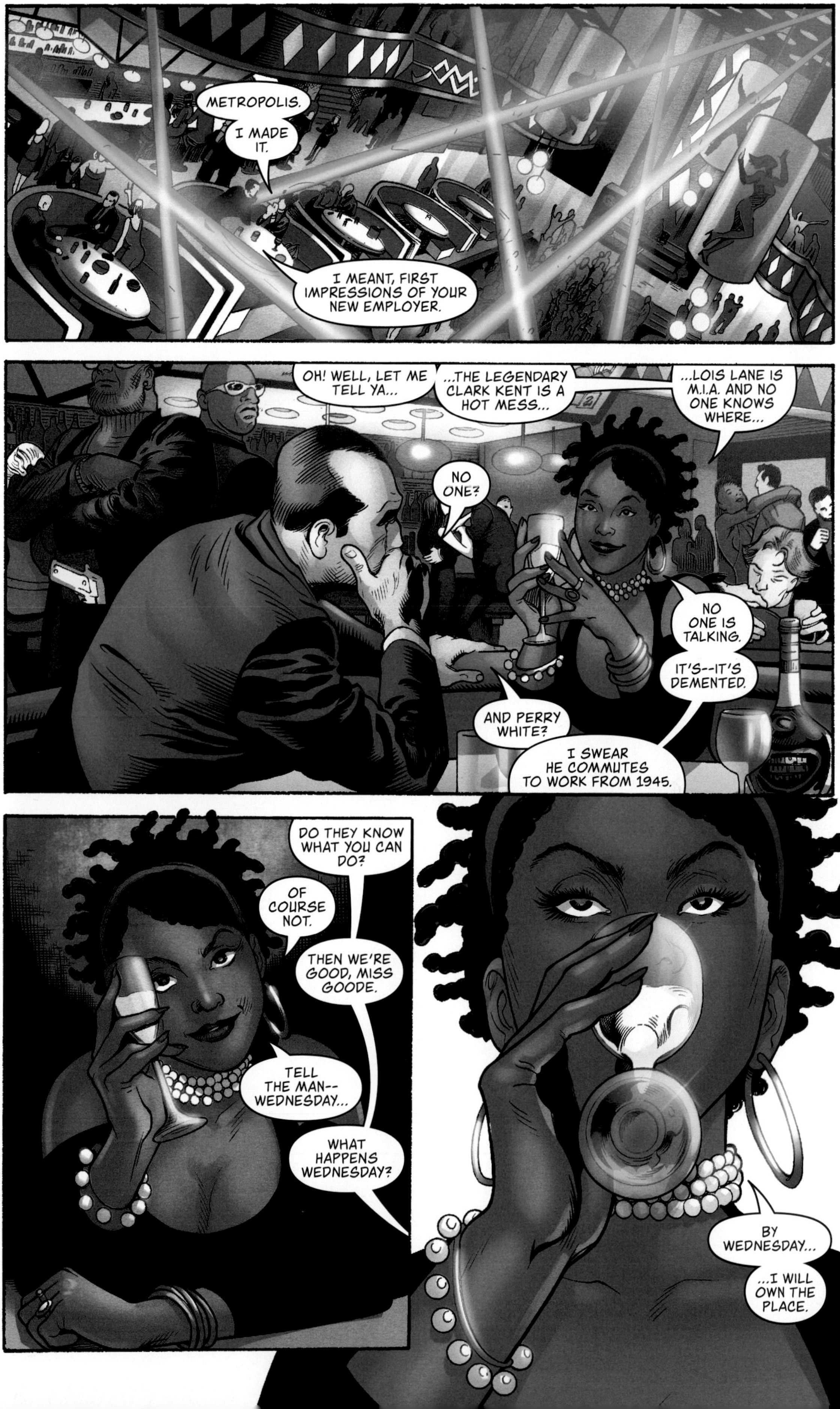
METROPOLIS.
I MADE IT.
I MEANT, FIRST IMPRESSIONS OF YOUR NEW EMPLOYER.
OH! WELL, LET ME TELL YA...
...THE LEGENDARY CLARK KENT IS A HOT MESS...
...LOIS LANE IS M.I.A. AND NO ONE KNOWS WHERE...
NO ONE?
NO ONE IS TALKING.
IT'S--IT'S DEMENTED.
AND PERRY WHITE?
I SWEAR HE COMMUTES TO WORK FROM 1945.
DO THEY KNOW WHAT YOU CAN DO?
OF COURSE NOT.
THEN WE'RE GOOD, MISS GOODE.
TELL THE MAN--WEDNESDAY...
WHAT HAPPENS WEDNESDAY?
BY WEDNESDAY...
...I WILL OWN THE PLACE.

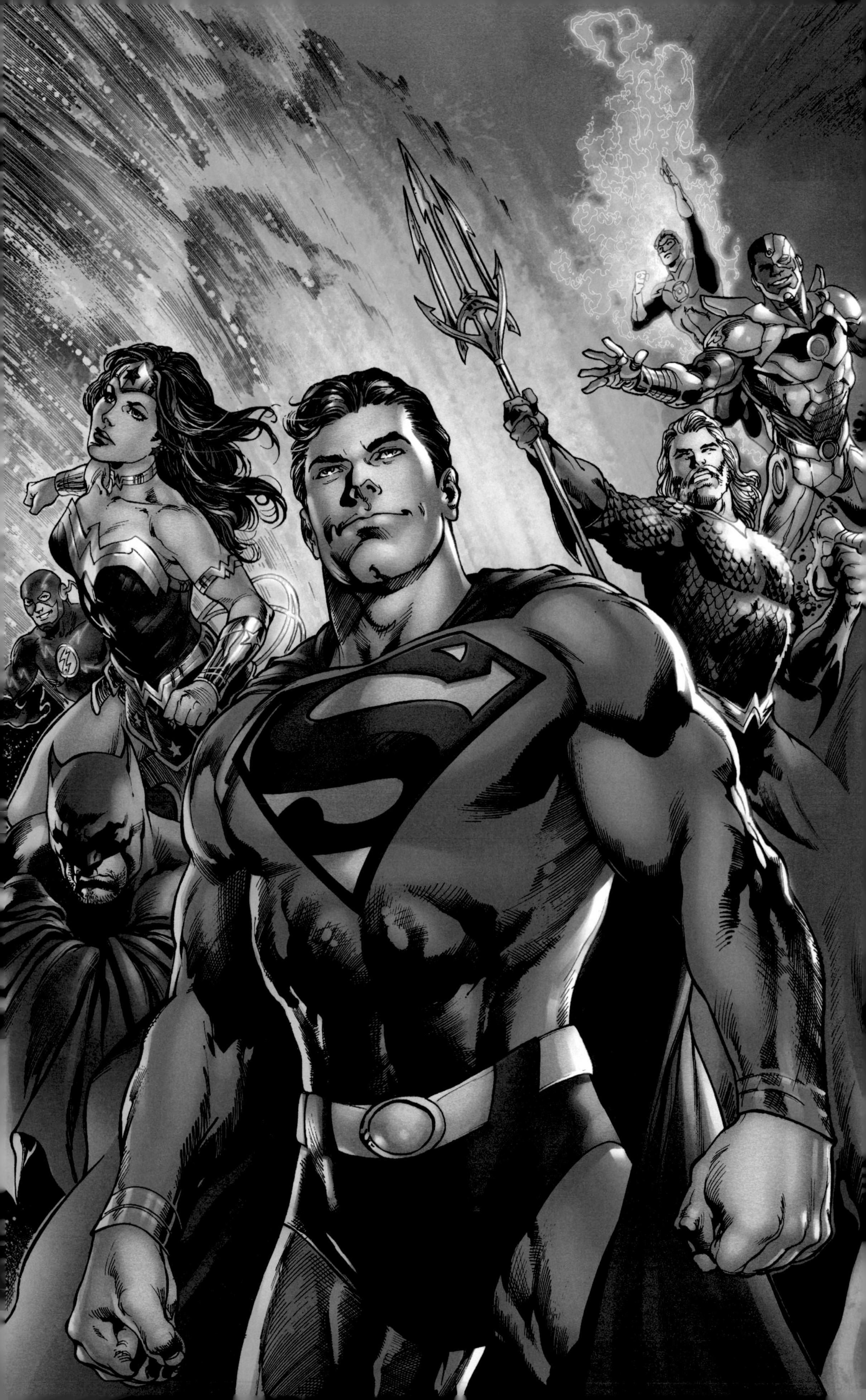

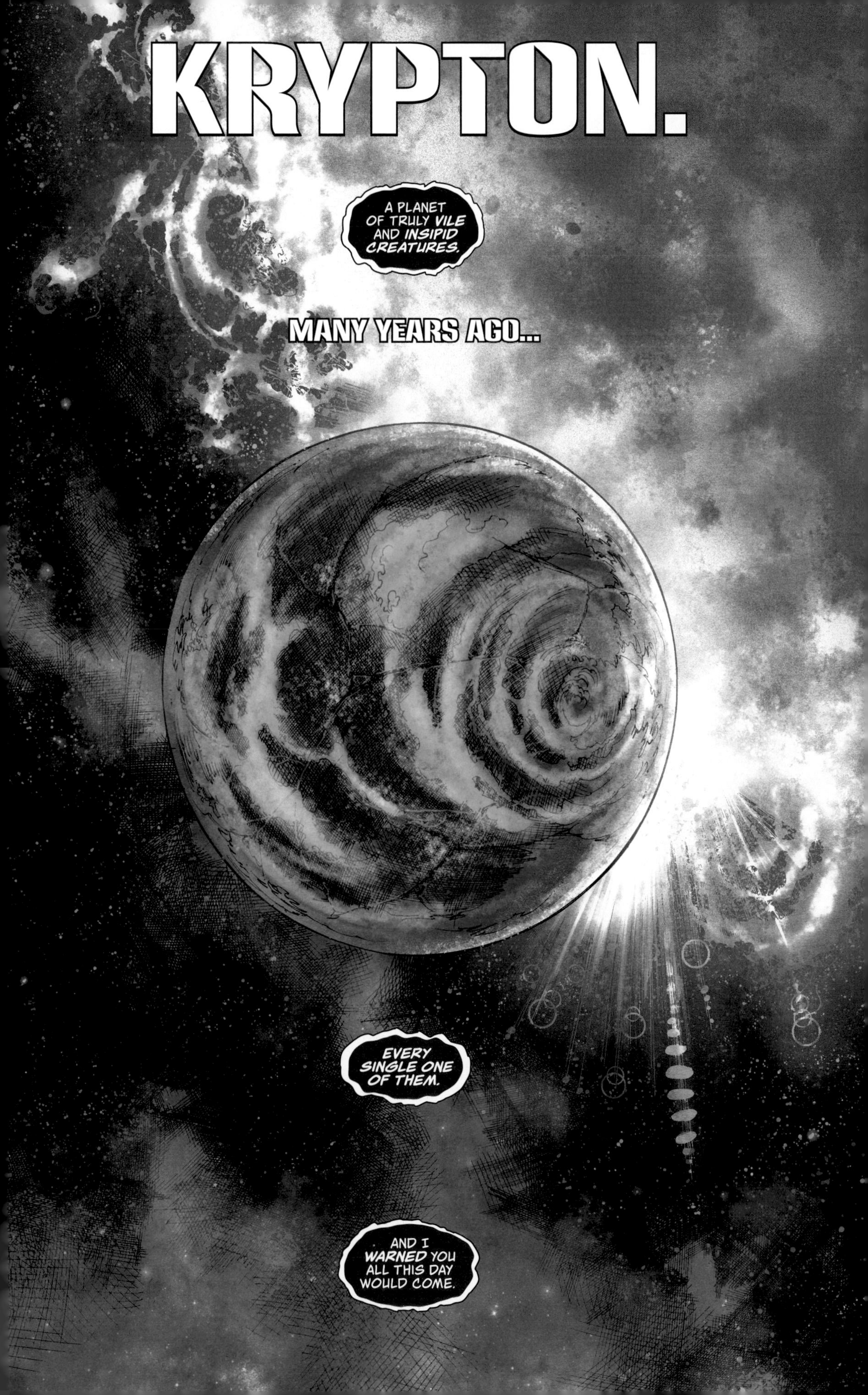
KRYPTON.
A PLANET OF TRULY VILE AND INSIPID CREATURES.
MANY YEARS AGO...
EVERY SINGLE ONE OF THEM.
AND I WARNED YOU ALL THIS DAY WOULD COME.

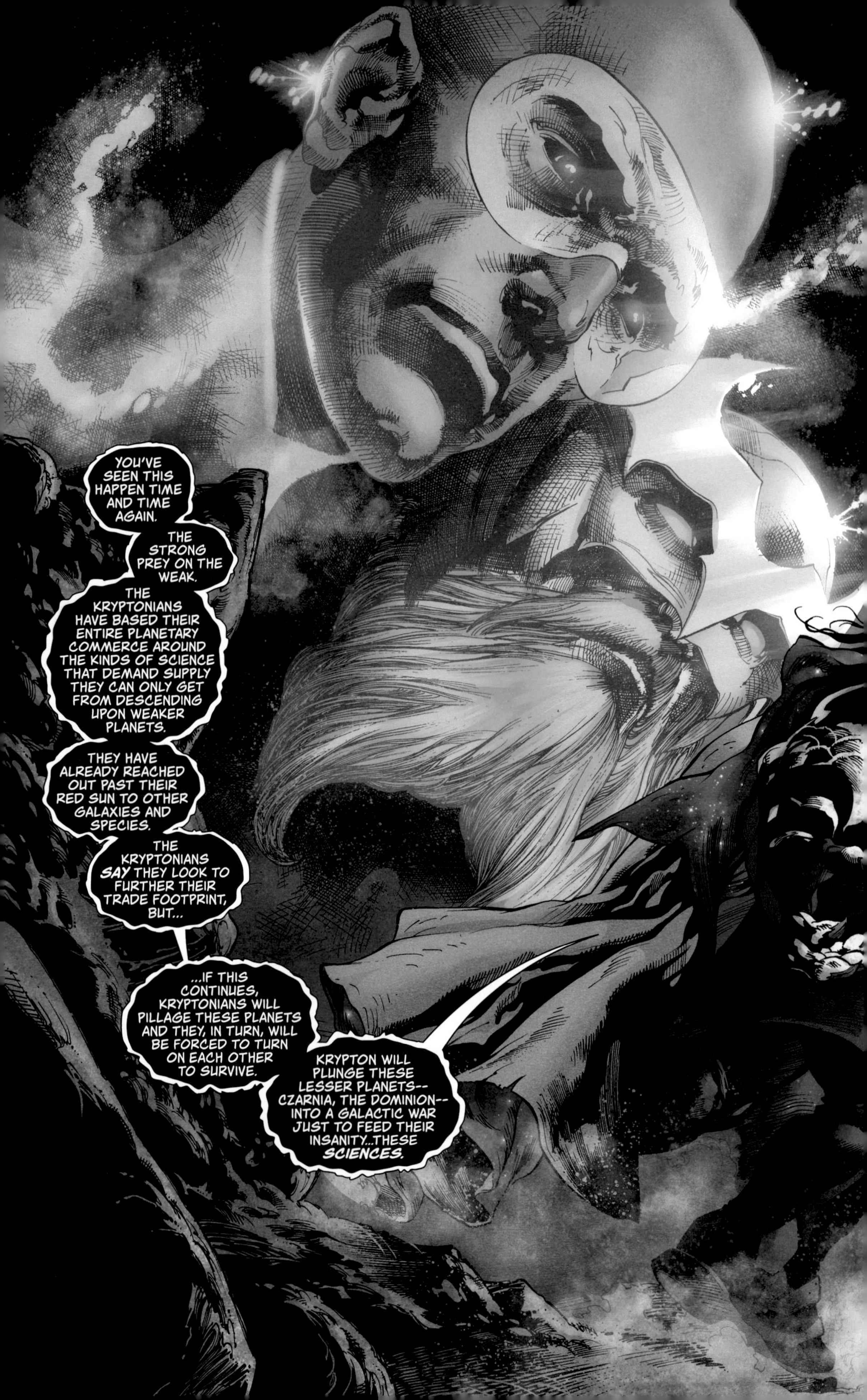
YOU'VE SEEN THIS HAPPEN TIME AND TIME AGAIN.
THE STRONG PREY ON THE WEAK.
THE KRYPTONIANS HAVE BASED THEIR ENTIRE PLANETARY COMMERCE AROUND THE KINDS OF SCIENCE THAT DEMAND SUPPLY THEY CAN ONLY GET FROM DESCENDING UPON WEAKER PLANETS.
THEY HAVE ALREADY REACHED OUT PAST THEIR RED SUN TO OTHER GALAXIES AND SPECIES.
THE KRYPTONIANS *SAY* THEY LOOK TO FURTHER THEIR TRADE FOOTPRINT, BUT...
...IF THIS CONTINUES, KRYPTONIANS WILL PILLAGE THESE PLANETS AND THEY, IN TURN, WILL BE FORCED TO TURN ON EACH OTHER TO SURVIVE.
KRYPTON WILL PLUNGE THESE LESSER PLANETS--CZARNIA, THE DOMINION--INTO A GALACTIC WAR JUST TO FEED THEIR INSANITY...THESE *SCIENCES.*

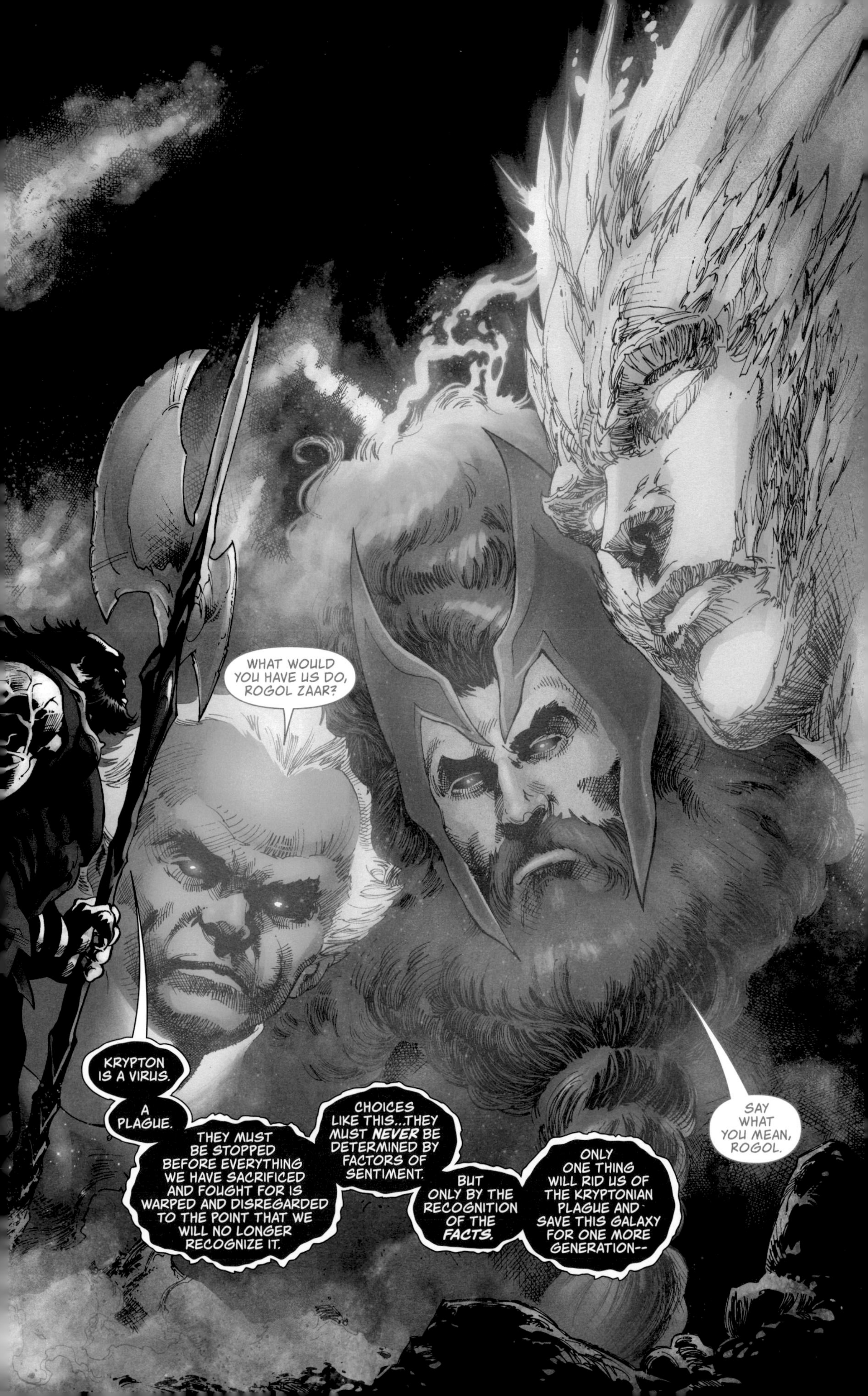
WHAT WOULD YOU HAVE US DO, ROGOL ZAAR?
KRYPTON IS A VIRUS.
A PLAGUE.
THEY MUST BE STOPPED BEFORE EVERYTHING WE HAVE SACRIFICED AND FOUGHT FOR IS WARPED AND DISREGARDED TO THE POINT THAT WE WILL NO LONGER RECOGNIZE IT.
CHOICES LIKE THIS...THEY MUST NEVER BE DETERMINED BY FACTORS OF SENTIMENT.
BUT ONLY BY THE RECOGNITION OF THE FACTS.
SAY WHAT YOU MEAN, ROGOL.
ONLY ONE THING WILL RID US OF THE KRYPTONIAN PLAGUE AND SAVE THIS GALAXY FOR ONE MORE GENERATION--

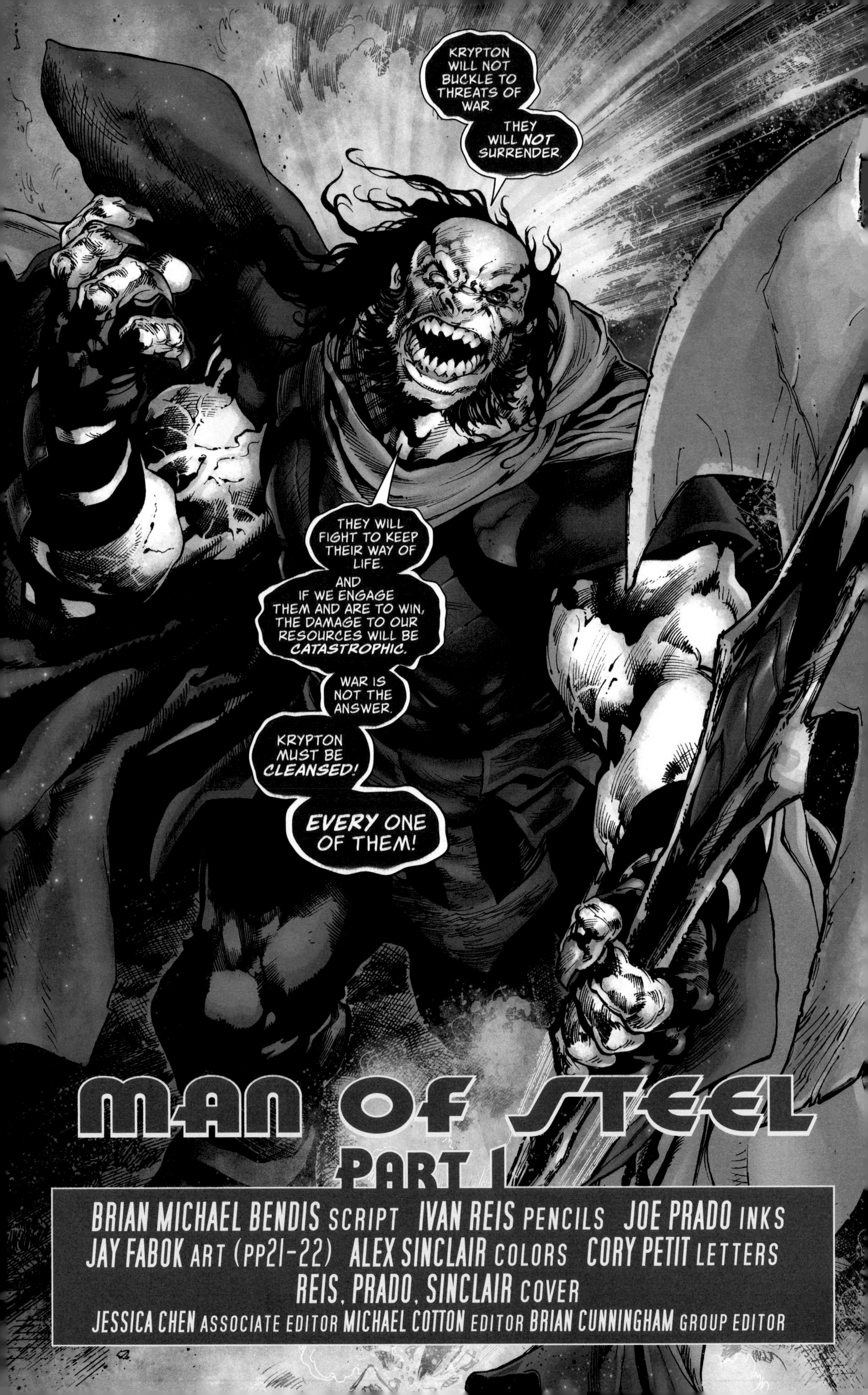

KRYPTON WILL NOT BUCKLE TO THREATS OF WAR.
THEY WILL NOT SURRENDER.
THEY WILL FIGHT TO KEEP THEIR WAY OF LIFE.
AND IF WE ENGAGE THEM AND ARE TO WIN, THE DAMAGE TO OUR RESOURCES WILL BE CATASTROPHIC.
WAR IS NOT THE ANSWER.
KRYPTON MUST BE CLEANSED!
EVERY ONE OF THEM!
MAN OF STEEL
PART 1
BRIAN MICHAEL BENDIS SCRIPT IVAN REIS PENCILS JOE PRADO INKS
JAY FABOK ART (PP21-22) ALEX SINCLAIR COLORS CORY PETIT LETTERS
REIS, PRADO, SINCLAIR COVER
JESSICA CHEN ASSOCIATE EDITOR MICHAEL COTTON EDITOR BRIAN CUNNINGHAM GROUP EDITOR

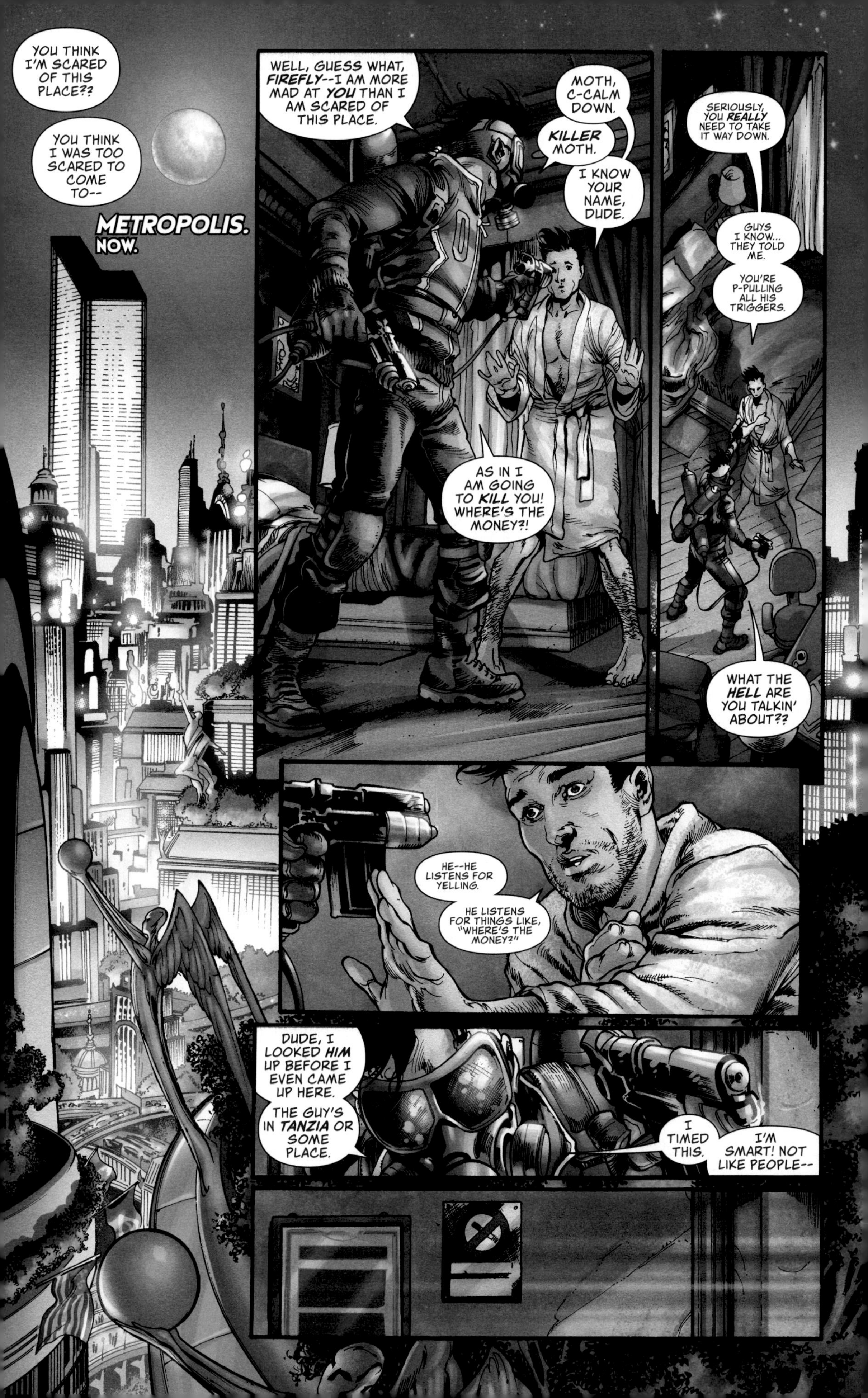

YOU THINK I'M SCARED OF THIS PLACE??
YOU THINK I WAS TOO SCARED TO COME TO--
METROPOLIS. NOW.
WELL, GUESS WHAT, FIREFLY--I AM MORE MAD AT YOU THAN I AM SCARED OF THIS PLACE.
MOTH, C-CALM DOWN.
KILLER MOTH.
I KNOW YOUR NAME, DUDE.
AS IN I AM GOING TO KILL YOU! WHERE'S THE MONEY?!
SERIOUSLY, YOU REALLY NEED TO TAKE IT WAY DOWN.
GUYS I KNOW... THEY TOLD ME.
YOU'RE P-PULLING ALL HIS TRIGGERS.
WHAT THE HELL ARE YOU TALKIN' ABOUT??
HE--HE LISTENS FOR YELLING.
HE LISTENS FOR THINGS LIKE, "WHERE'S THE MONEY?"
DUDE, I LOOKED HIM UP BEFORE I EVEN CAME UP HERE.
THE GUY'S IN TANZIA OR SOME PLACE.
I TIMED THIS.
I'M SMART! NOT LIKE PEOPLE--

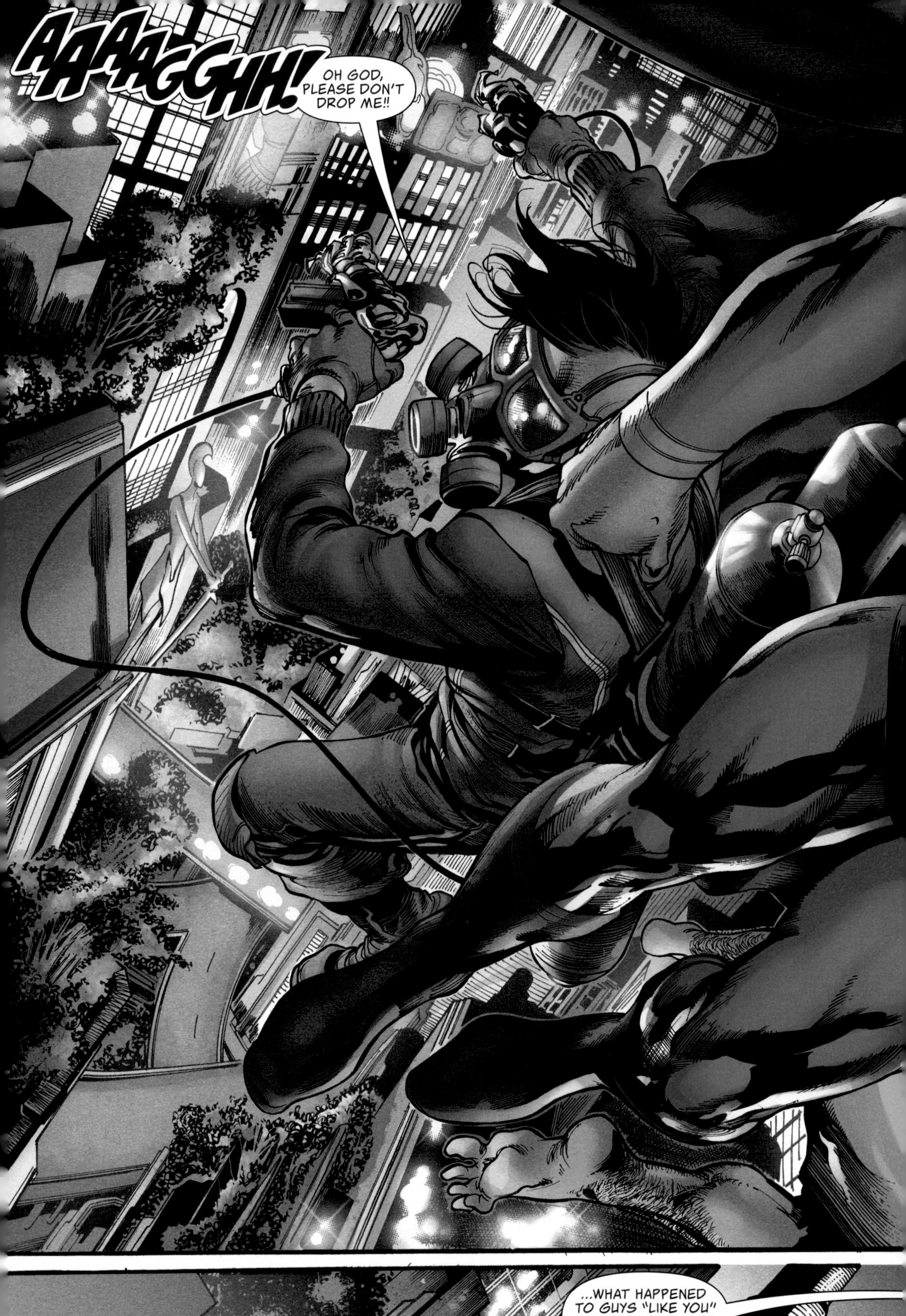
AAAAAGGHH!
OH GOD, PLEASE DON'T DROP ME!!

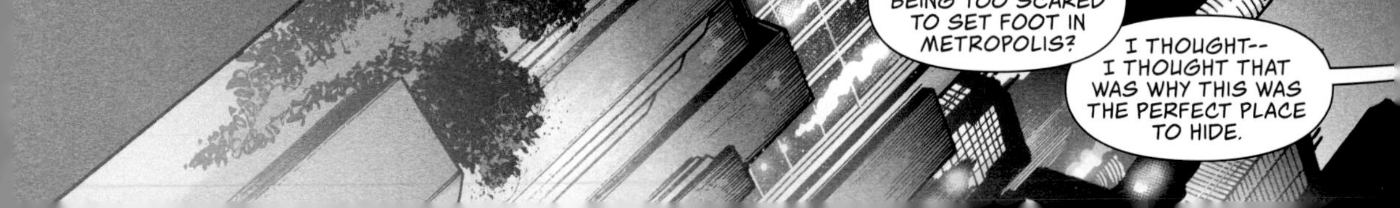
...WHAT HAPPENED TO GUYS "LIKE YOU" BEING TOO SCARED TO SET FOOT IN METROPOLIS?
I THOUGHT-- I THOUGHT THAT WAS WHY THIS WAS THE PERFECT PLACE TO HIDE.

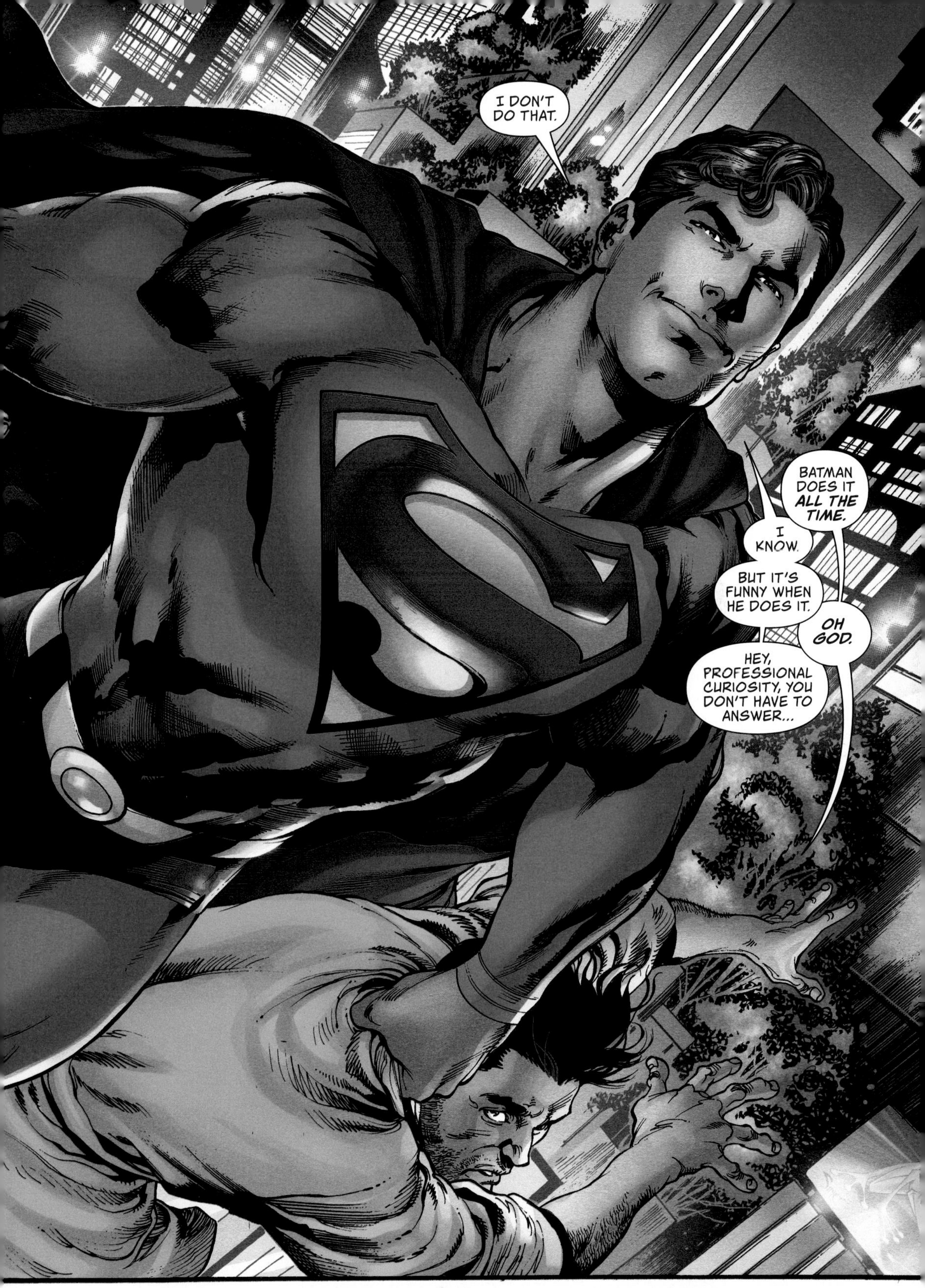
I DON'T DO THAT.
BATMAN DOES IT ALL THE TIME.
I KNOW.
BUT IT'S FUNNY WHEN HE DOES IT.
OH GOD.
HEY, PROFESSIONAL CURIOSITY, YOU DON'T HAVE TO ANSWER...

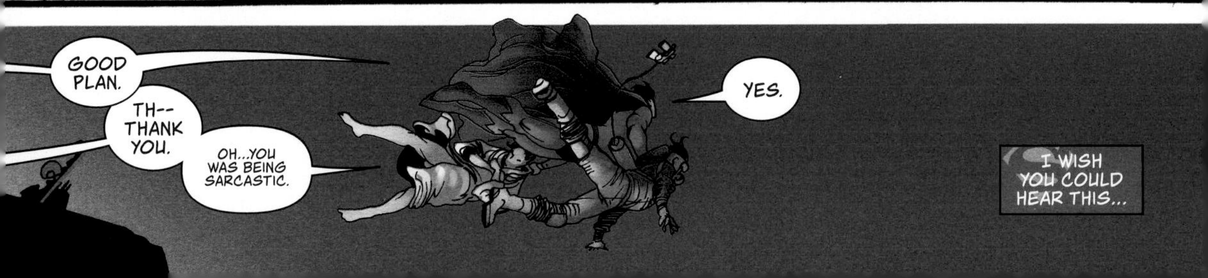
GOOD PLAN.
TH-- THANK YOU.
OH...YOU WAS BEING SARCASTIC.
YES.
I WISH YOU COULD HEAR THIS...

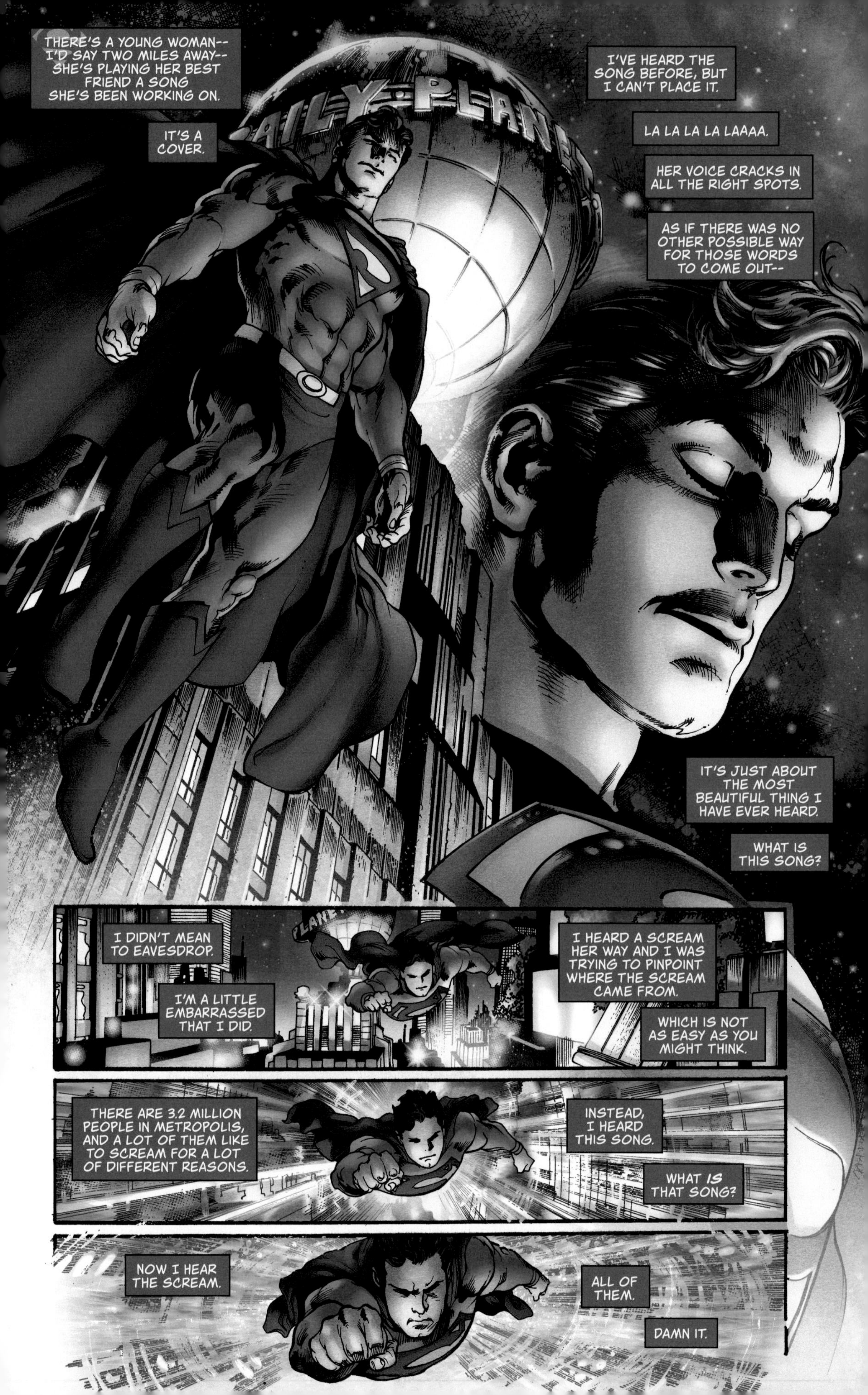
THERE'S A YOUNG WOMAN-- I'D SAY TWO MILES AWAY-- SHE'S PLAYING HER BEST FRIEND A SONG SHE'S BEEN WORKING ON.
IT'S A COVER.
I'VE HEARD THE SONG BEFORE, BUT I CAN'T PLACE IT.
LA LA LA LA LAAAA.
HER VOICE CRACKS IN ALL THE RIGHT SPOTS.
AS IF THERE WAS NO OTHER POSSIBLE WAY FOR THOSE WORDS TO COME OUT--
IT'S JUST ABOUT THE MOST BEAUTIFUL THING I HAVE EVER HEARD.
WHAT IS THIS SONG?
I DIDN'T MEAN TO EAVESDROP.
I'M A LITTLE EMBARRASSED THAT I DID.
I HEARD A SCREAM HER WAY AND I WAS TRYING TO PINPOINT WHERE THE SCREAM CAME FROM.
WHICH IS NOT AS EASY AS YOU MIGHT THINK.
THERE ARE 3.2 MILLION PEOPLE IN METROPOLIS, AND A LOT OF THEM LIKE TO SCREAM FOR A LOT OF DIFFERENT REASONS.
INSTEAD, I HEARD THIS SONG.
WHAT *IS* THAT SONG?
NOW I HEAR THE SCREAM.
ALL OF THEM.
DAMN IT.

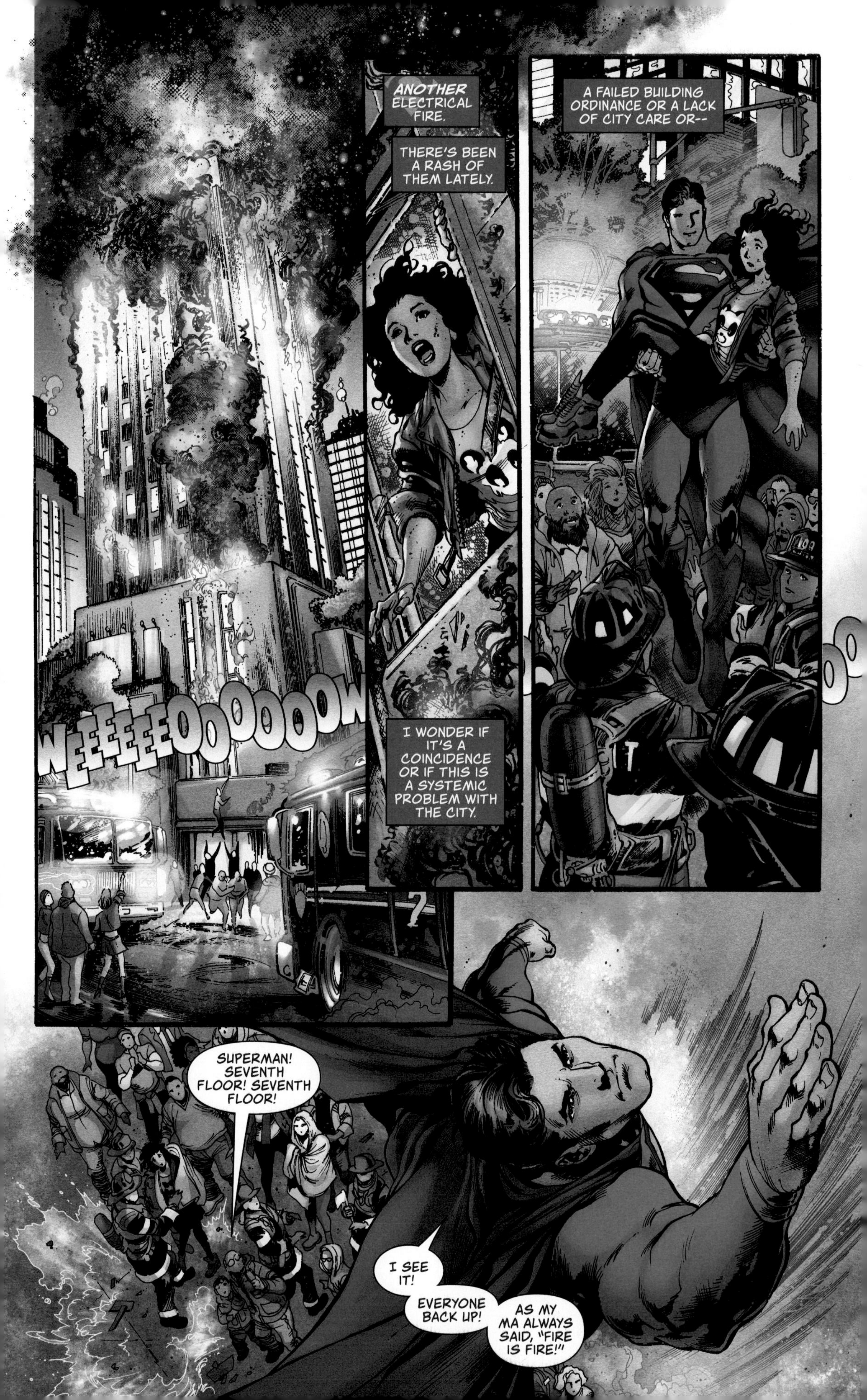
ANOTHER ELECTRICAL FIRE.
THERE'S BEEN A RASH OF THEM LATELY.
I WONDER IF IT'S A COINCIDENCE OR IF THIS IS A SYSTEMIC PROBLEM WITH THE CITY.
A FAILED BUILDING ORDINANCE OR A LACK OF CITY CARE OR--
WEEEEEOOOOOOOW
SUPERMAN! SEVENTH FLOOR! SEVENTH FLOOR!
I SEE IT!
EVERYONE BACK UP!
AS MY MA ALWAYS SAID, "FIRE IS FIRE!"

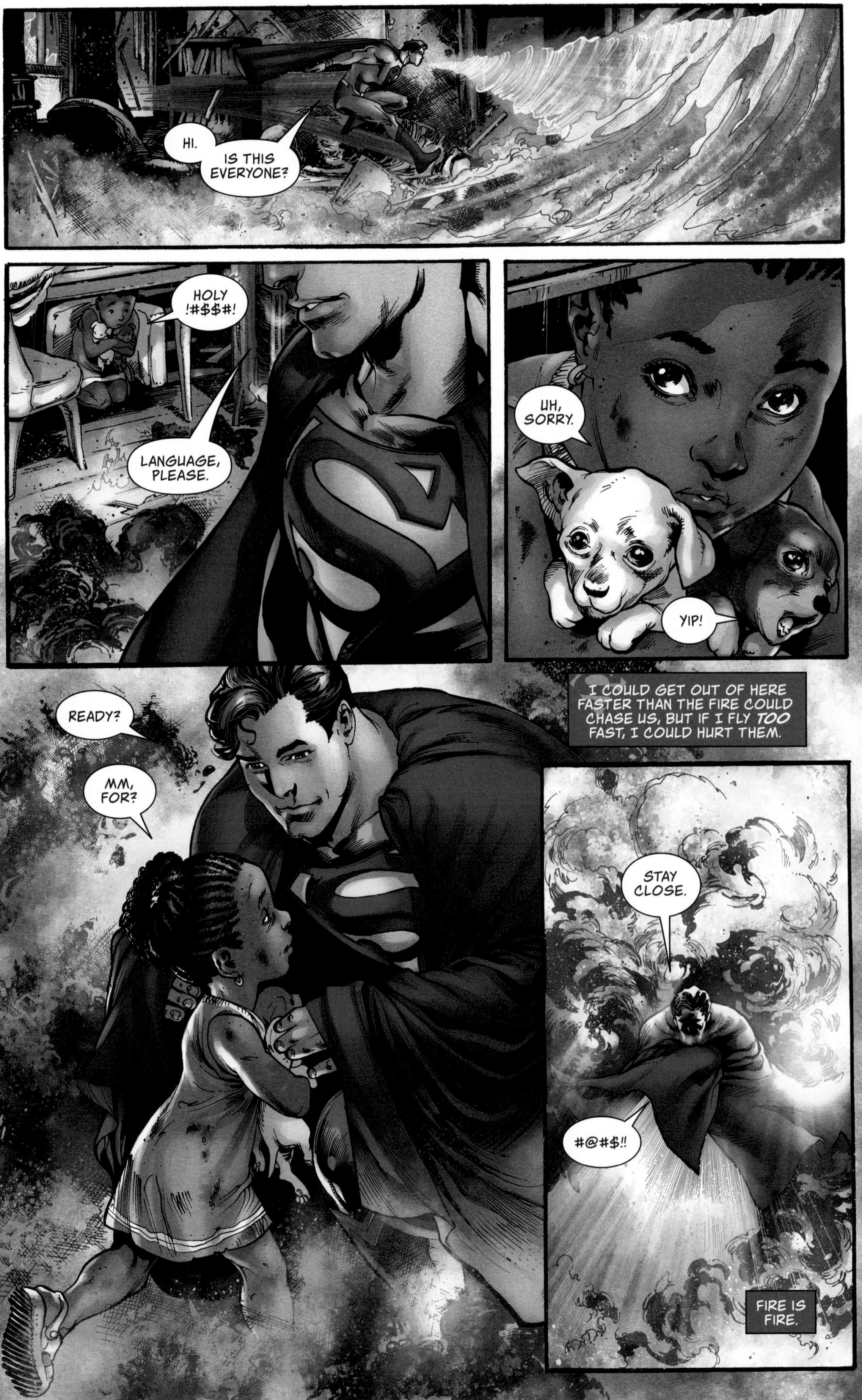
HI.
IS THIS EVERYONE?
HOLY !#$$#!
LANGUAGE, PLEASE.
UH, SORRY.
YIP!
I COULD GET OUT OF HERE FASTER THAN THE FIRE COULD CHASE US, BUT IF I FLY *TOO* FAST, I COULD HURT THEM.
READY?
MM, FOR?
STAY CLOSE.
#@#$!!
FIRE IS FIRE.

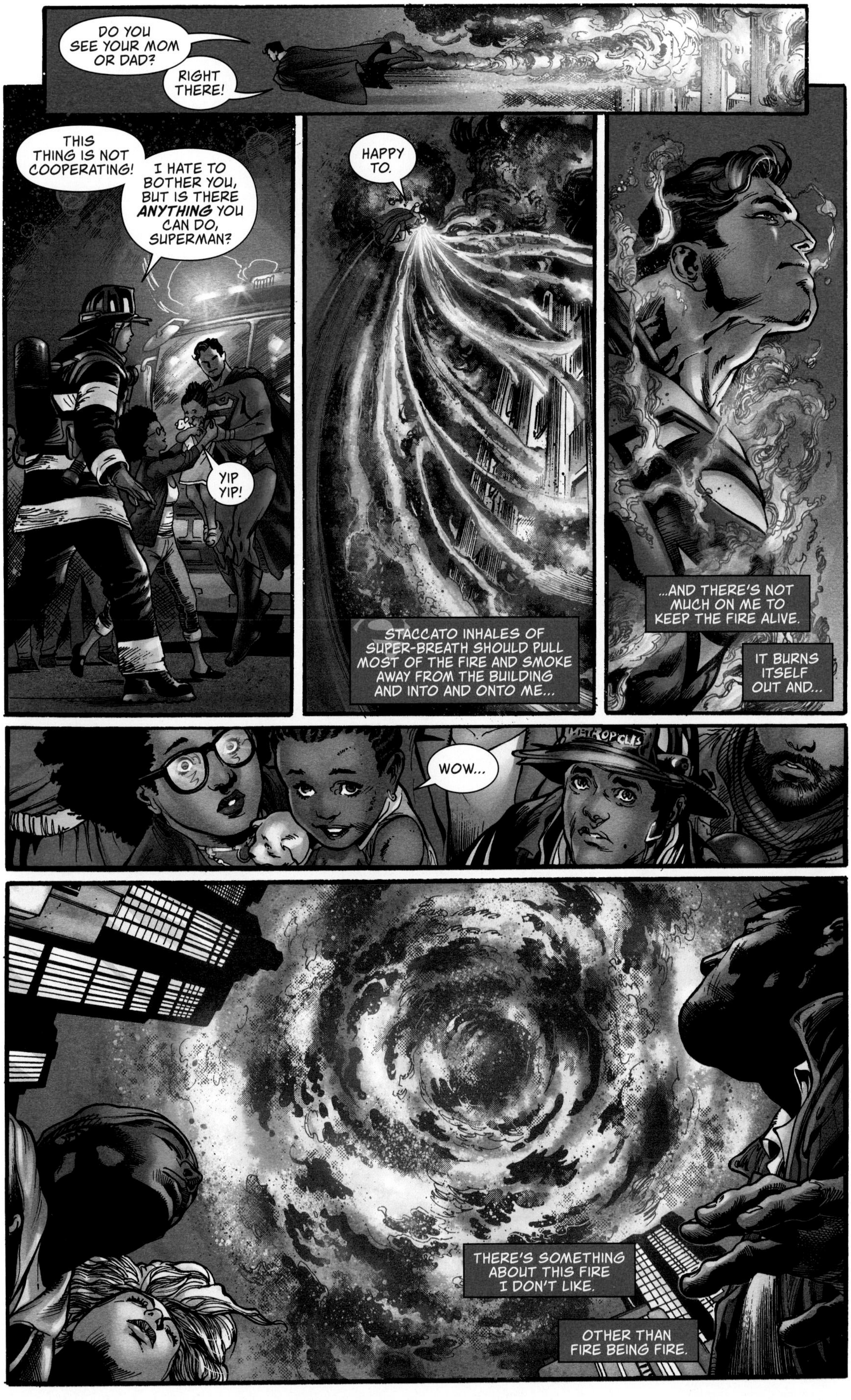
DO YOU SEE YOUR MOM OR DAD?
RIGHT THERE!
THIS THING IS NOT COOPERATING!
I HATE TO BOTHER YOU, BUT IS THERE ANYTHING YOU CAN DO, SUPERMAN?
YIP YIP!
HAPPY TO.
STACCATO INHALES OF SUPER-BREATH SHOULD PULL MOST OF THE FIRE AND SMOKE AWAY FROM THE BUILDING AND INTO AND ONTO ME...
...AND THERE'S NOT MUCH ON ME TO KEEP THE FIRE ALIVE.
IT BURNS ITSELF OUT AND...
WOW...
METROPOLIS
THERE'S SOMETHING ABOUT THIS FIRE I DON'T LIKE.
OTHER THAN FIRE BEING FIRE.

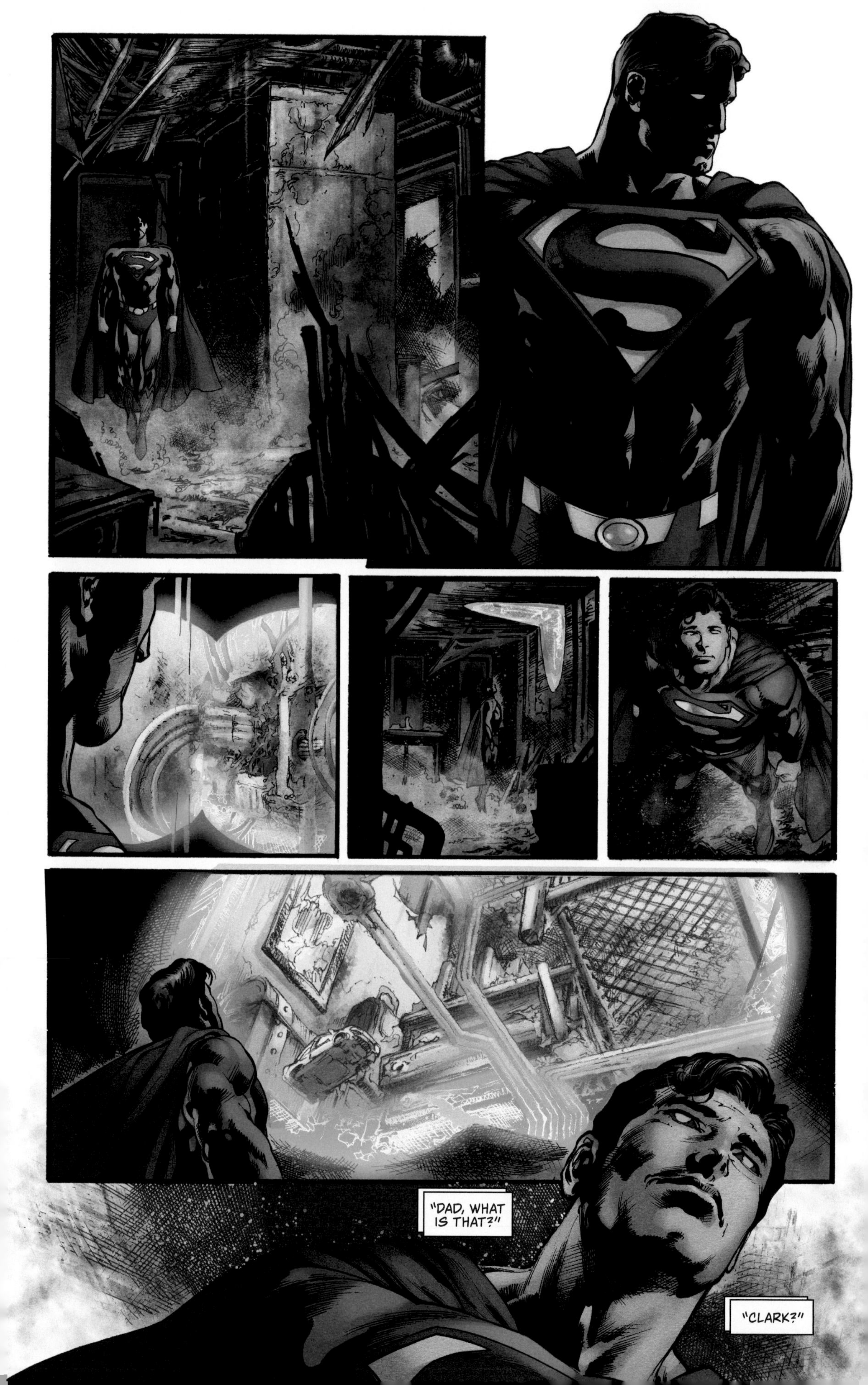
"DAD, WHAT IS THAT?"
"CLARK?"

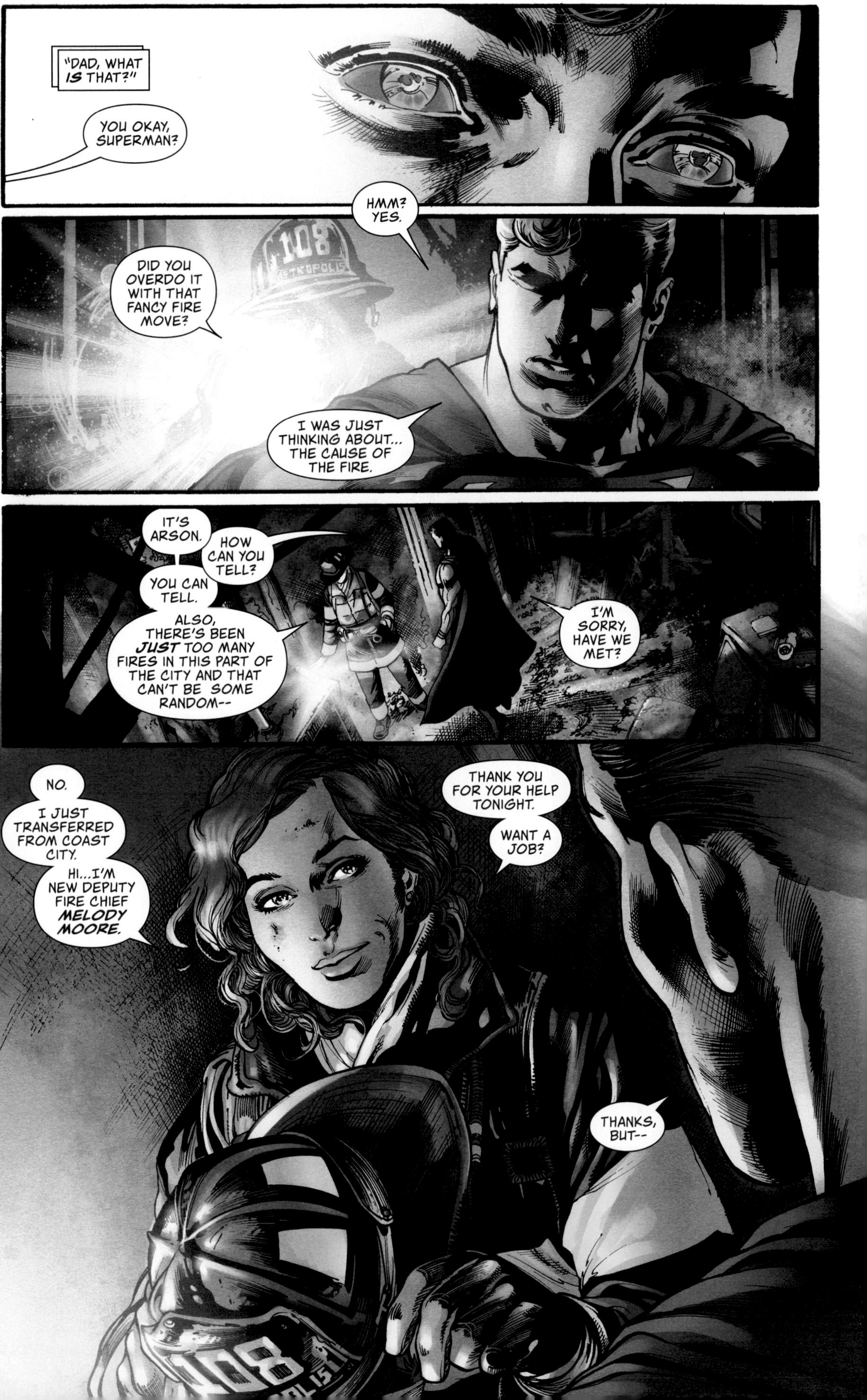
"DAD, WHAT IS THAT?"
YOU OKAY, SUPERMAN?
HMM? YES.
DID YOU OVERDO IT WITH THAT FANCY FIRE MOVE?
I WAS JUST THINKING ABOUT... THE CAUSE OF THE FIRE.
IT'S ARSON.
HOW CAN YOU TELL?
YOU CAN TELL.
ALSO, THERE'S BEEN JUST TOO MANY FIRES IN THIS PART OF THE CITY AND THAT CAN'T BE SOME RANDOM--
I'M SORRY, HAVE WE MET?
NO.
I JUST TRANSFERRED FROM COAST CITY.
HI...I'M NEW DEPUTY FIRE CHIEF MELODY MOORE.
THANK YOU FOR YOUR HELP TONIGHT.
WANT A JOB?
THANKS, BUT--

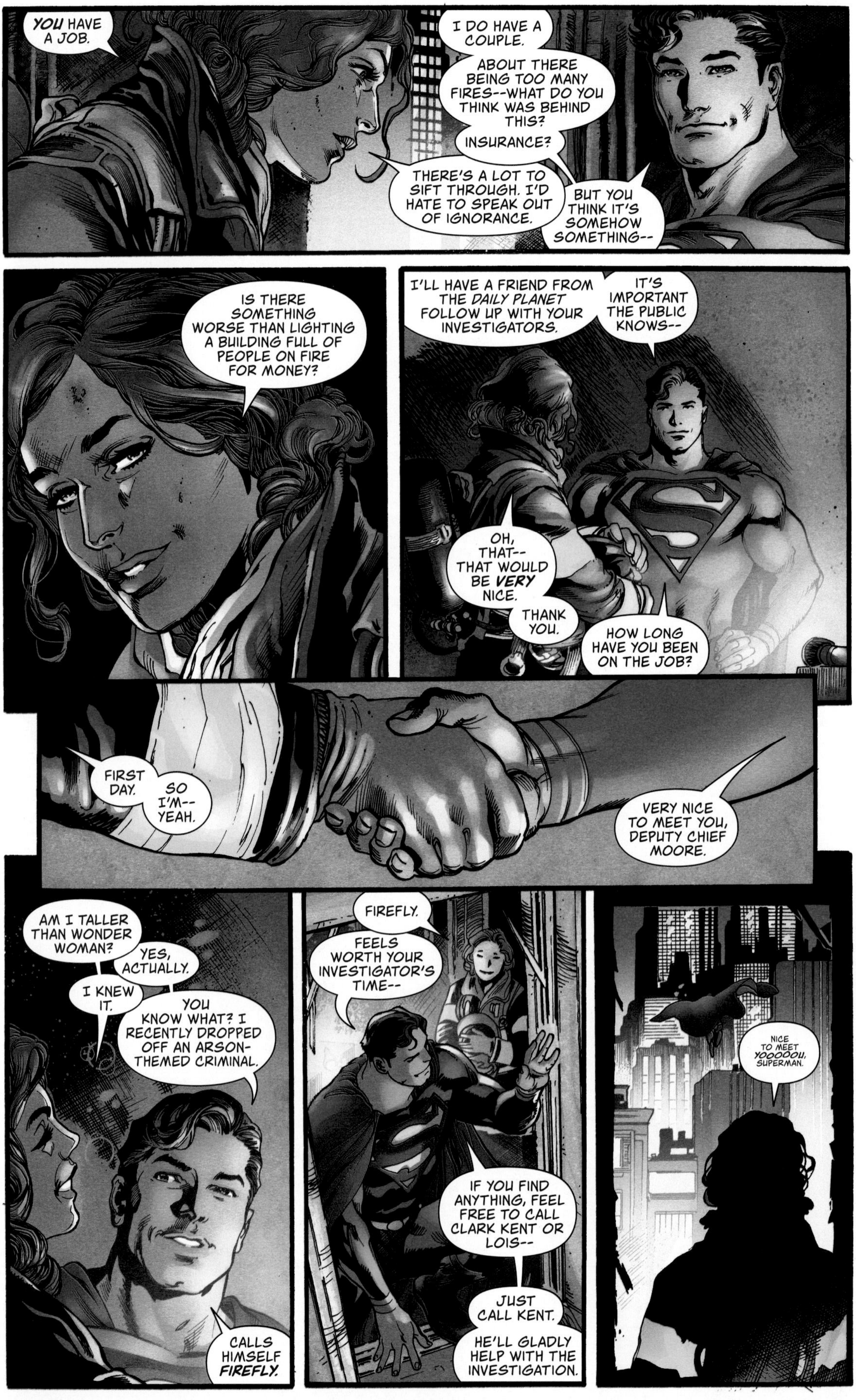
YOU HAVE A JOB.
I DO HAVE A COUPLE.
ABOUT THERE BEING TOO MANY FIRES--WHAT DO YOU THINK WAS BEHIND THIS?
INSURANCE?
THERE'S A LOT TO SIFT THROUGH. I'D HATE TO SPEAK OUT OF IGNORANCE.
BUT YOU THINK IT'S SOMEHOW SOMETHING--
IS THERE SOMETHING WORSE THAN LIGHTING A BUILDING FULL OF PEOPLE ON FIRE FOR MONEY?
I'LL HAVE A FRIEND FROM THE DAILY PLANET FOLLOW UP WITH YOUR INVESTIGATORS.
IT'S IMPORTANT THE PUBLIC KNOWS--
OH, THAT--THAT WOULD BE VERY NICE.
THANK YOU.
HOW LONG HAVE YOU BEEN ON THE JOB?
FIRST DAY.
SO I'M--YEAH.
VERY NICE TO MEET YOU, DEPUTY CHIEF MOORE.
AM I TALLER THAN WONDER WOMAN?
YES, ACTUALLY.
I KNEW IT.
YOU KNOW WHAT? I RECENTLY DROPPED OFF AN ARSON-THEMED CRIMINAL.
CALLS HIMSELF FIREFLY.
FIREFLY.
FEELS WORTH YOUR INVESTIGATOR'S TIME--
IF YOU FIND ANYTHING, FEEL FREE TO CALL CLARK KENT OR LOIS--
JUST CALL KENT.
HE'LL GLADLY HELP WITH THE INVESTIGATION.
NICE TO MEET YOOOOOU, SUPERMAN.

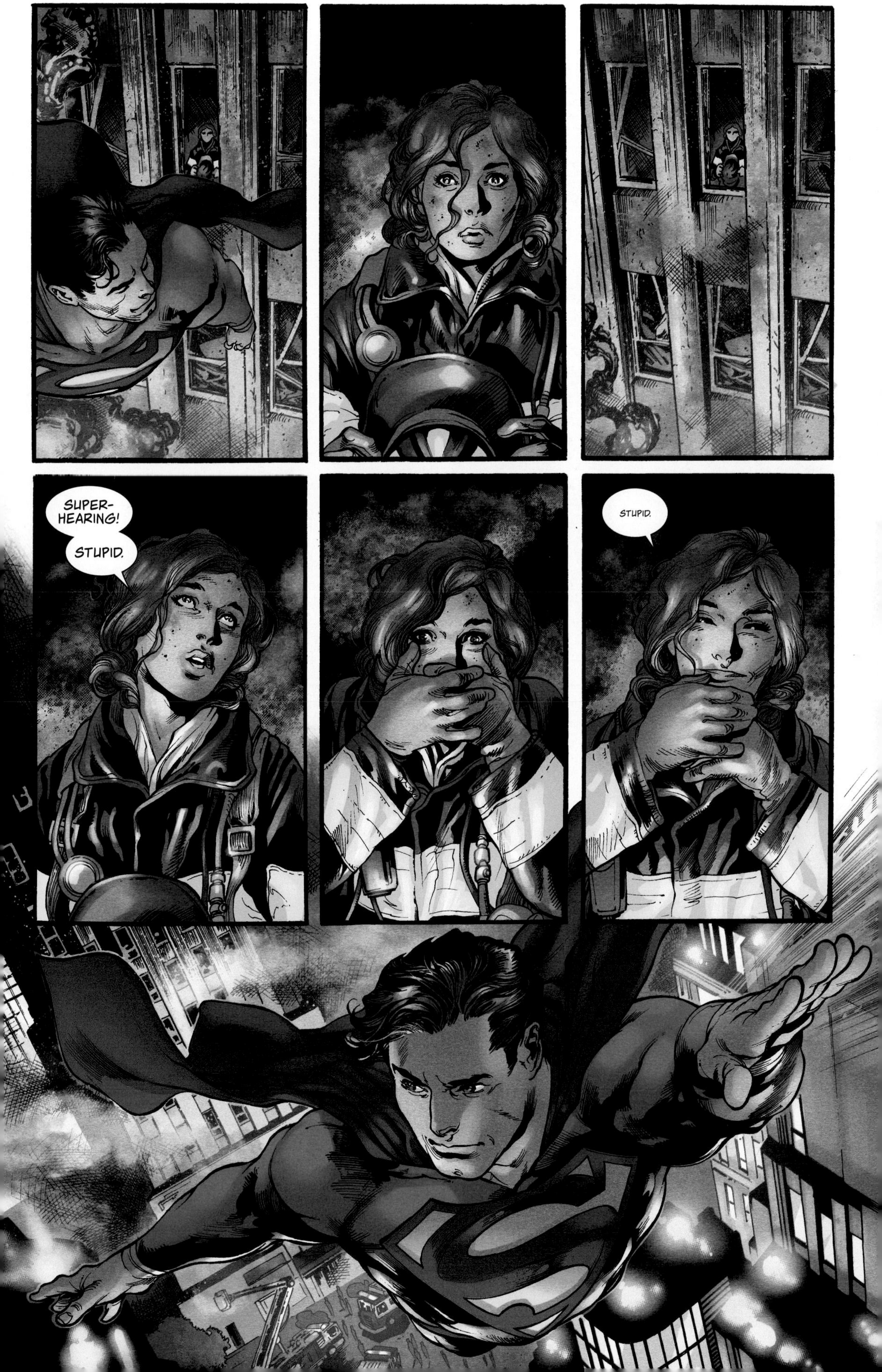
SUPER-HEARING!
STUPID.
STUPID.

THEN.
GXYAARGH!
GYAAAGGH!
CHUUNKK
HUAAGHH!
YOU ARE MY FIRST VISITOR HERE...

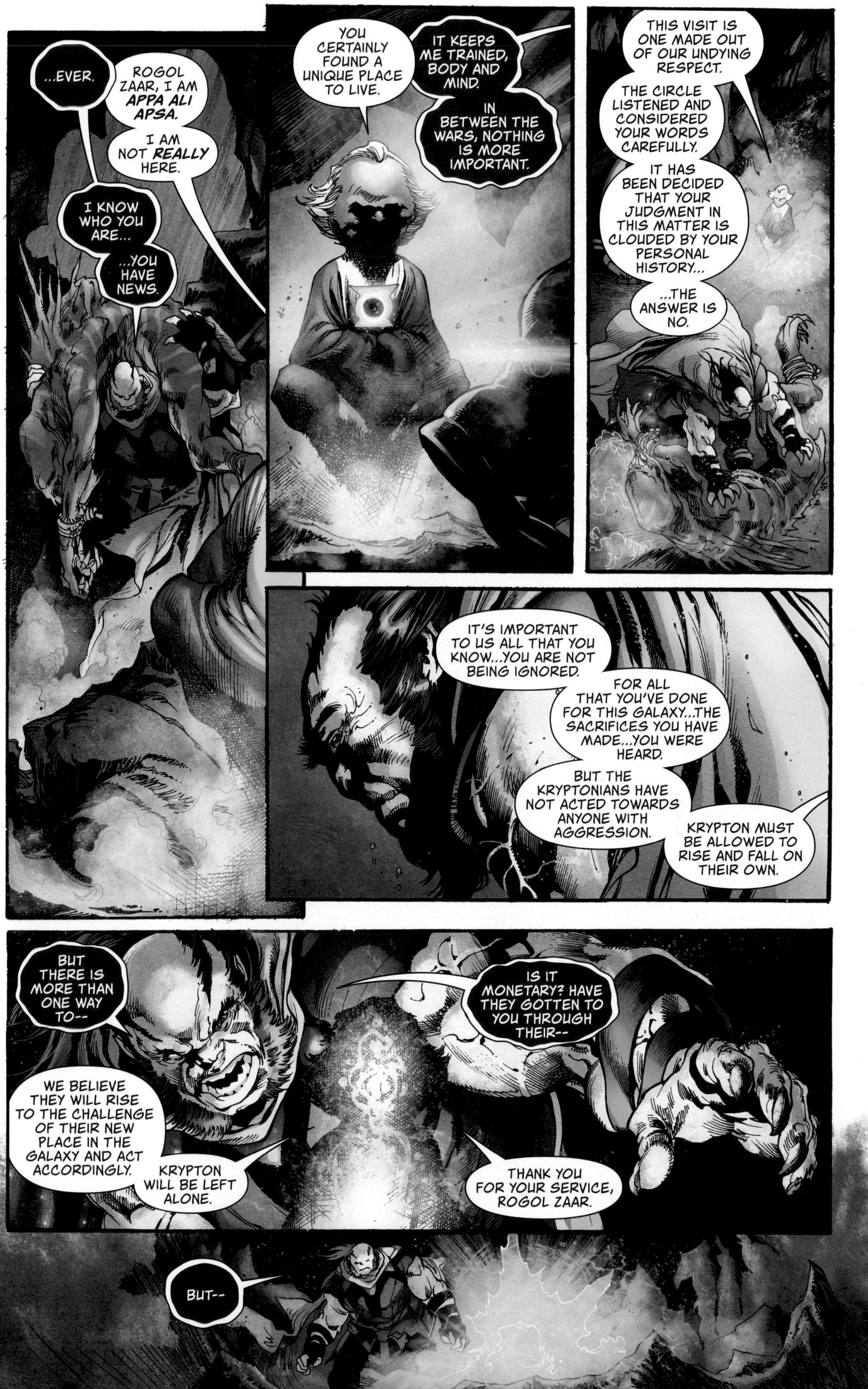
...EVER.
ROGOL ZAAR, I AM **APPA ALI APSA.**
I AM NOT **REALLY** HERE.
I KNOW WHO YOU ARE...
...YOU HAVE NEWS.
YOU CERTAINLY FOUND A UNIQUE PLACE TO LIVE.
IT KEEPS ME TRAINED, BODY AND MIND.
IN BETWEEN THE WARS, NOTHING IS MORE IMPORTANT.
THIS VISIT IS ONE MADE OUT OF OUR UNDYING RESPECT.
THE CIRCLE LISTENED AND CONSIDERED YOUR WORDS CAREFULLY.
IT HAS BEEN DECIDED THAT YOUR JUDGMENT IN THIS MATTER IS CLOUDED BY YOUR PERSONAL HISTORY...
...THE ANSWER IS NO.
IT'S IMPORTANT TO US ALL THAT YOU KNOW...YOU ARE NOT BEING IGNORED.
FOR ALL THAT YOU'VE DONE FOR THIS GALAXY...THE SACRIFICES YOU HAVE MADE...YOU WERE HEARD.
BUT THE KRYPTONIANS HAVE NOT ACTED TOWARDS ANYONE WITH AGGRESSION.
KRYPTON MUST BE ALLOWED TO RISE AND FALL ON THEIR OWN.
BUT THERE IS MORE THAN ONE WAY TO--
IS IT MONETARY? HAVE THEY GOTTEN TO YOU THROUGH THEIR--
WE BELIEVE THEY WILL RISE TO THE CHALLENGE OF THEIR NEW PLACE IN THE GALAXY AND ACT ACCORDINGLY.
KRYPTON WILL BE LEFT ALONE.
THANK YOU FOR YOUR SERVICE, ROGOL ZAAR.
BUT--

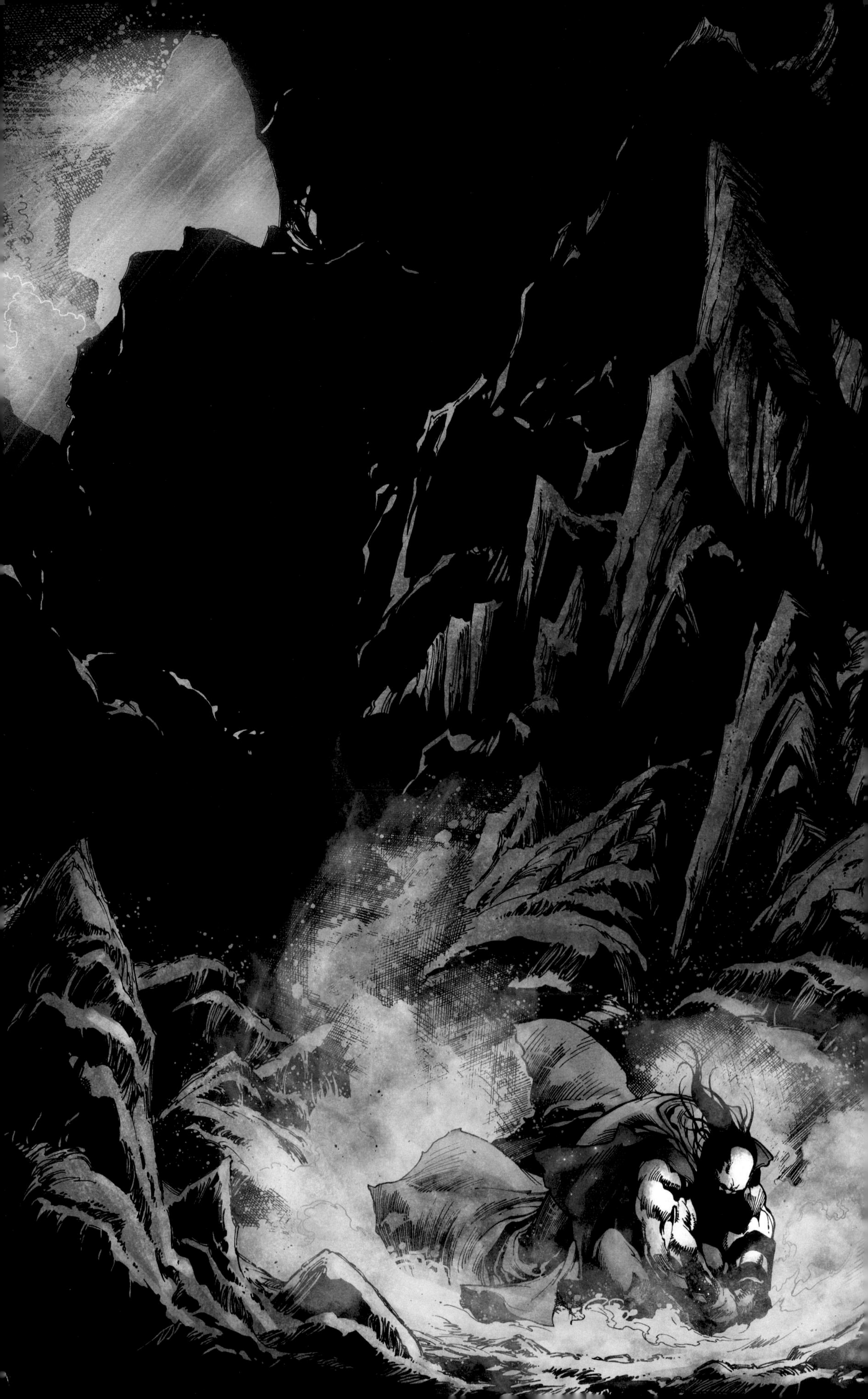

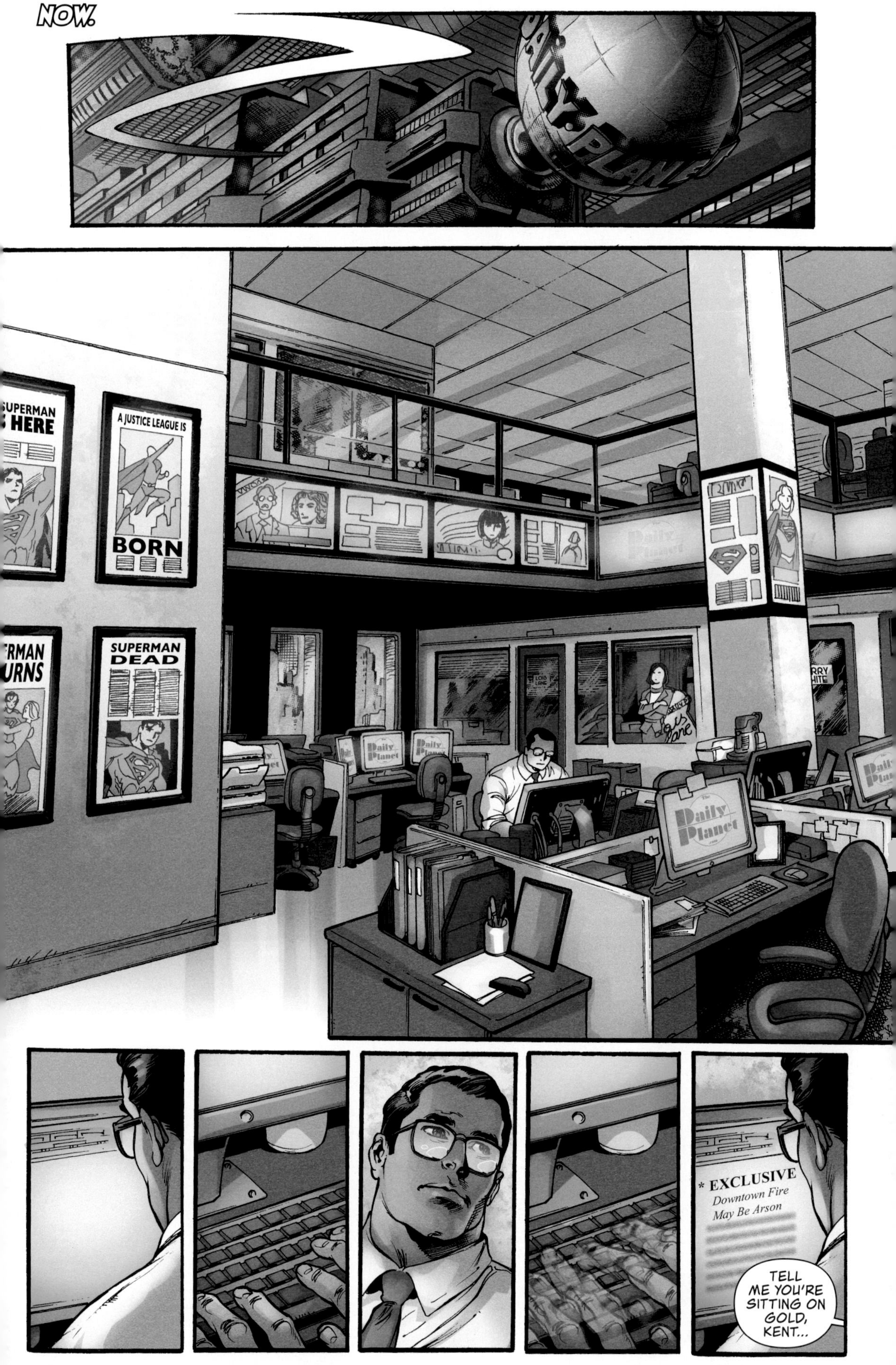
NOW.
A JUSTICE LEAGUE IS BORN
SUPERMAN DEAD
SUPERMAN
Daily Planet
* EXCLUSIVE
Downtown Fire May Be Arson
TELL ME YOU'RE SITTING ON GOLD, KENT...

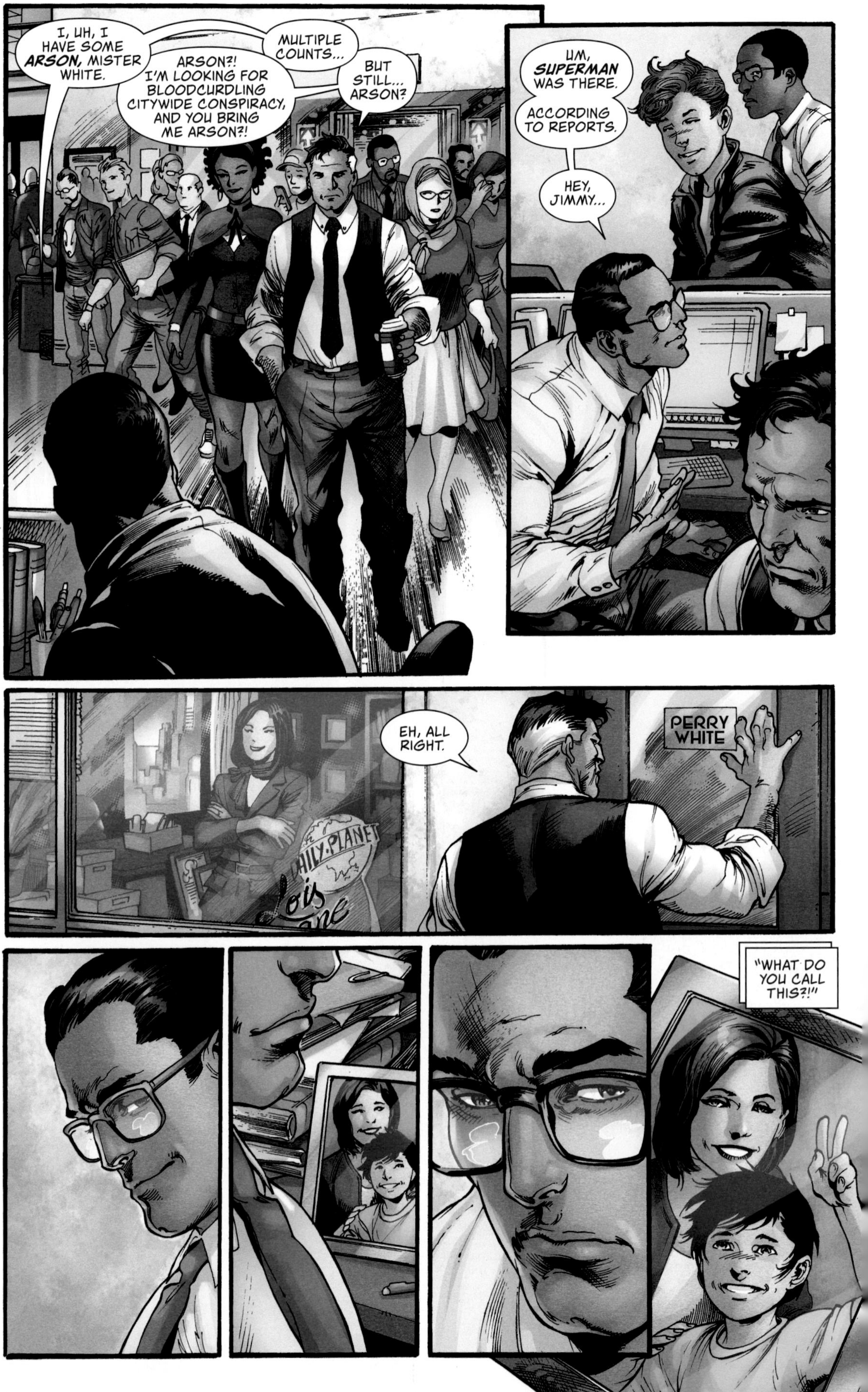

I, UH, I HAVE SOME ARSON, MISTER WHITE.
MULTIPLE COUNTS...
ARSON?! I'M LOOKING FOR BLOODCURDLING CITYWIDE CONSPIRACY, AND YOU BRING ME ARSON?!
BUT STILL... ARSON?
UM, SUPERMAN WAS THERE.
ACCORDING TO REPORTS.
HEY, JIMMY...
EH, ALL RIGHT.
PERRY WHITE
DAILY PLANET
"WHAT DO YOU CALL THIS?!"

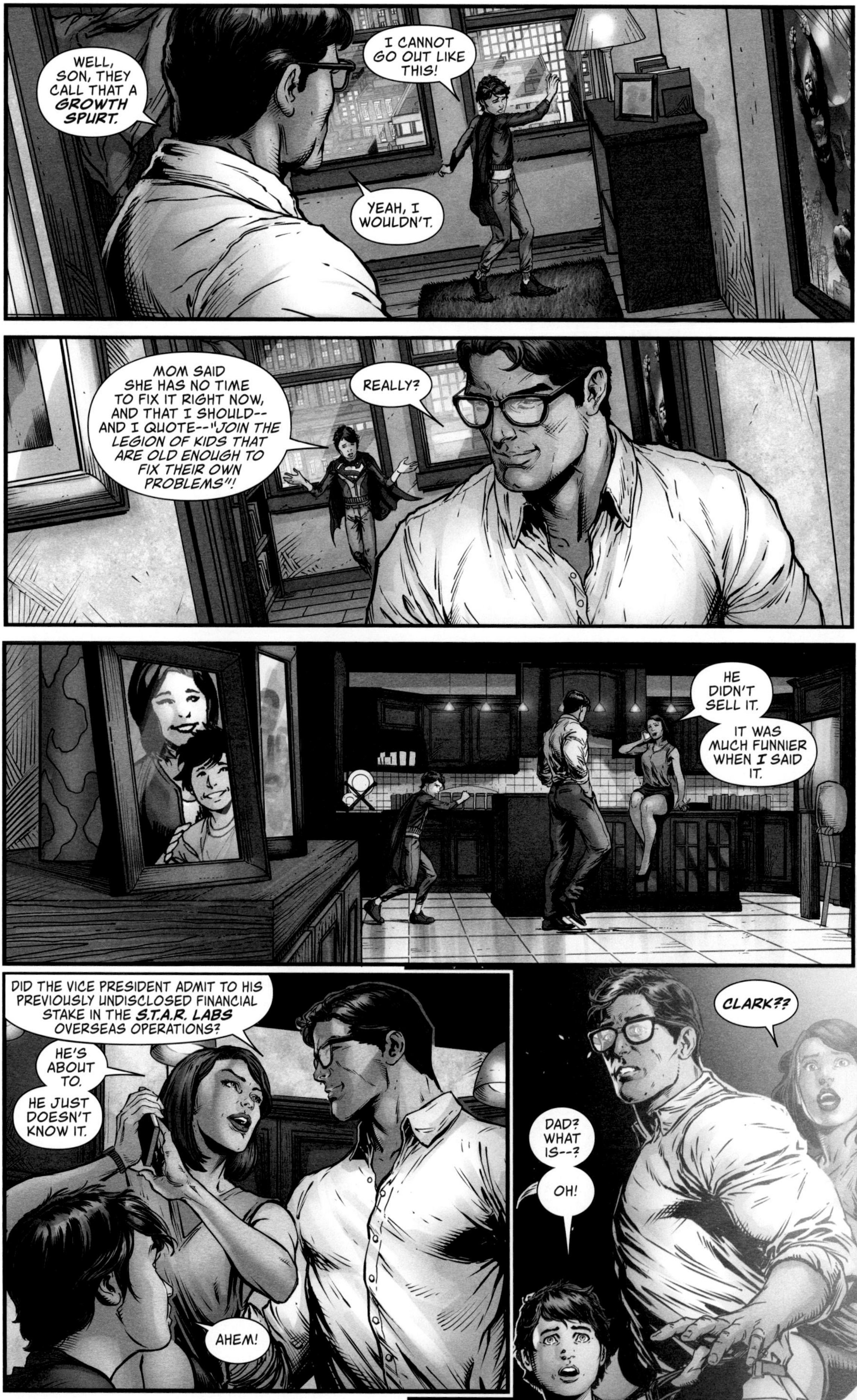
WELL, SON, THEY CALL THAT A GROWTH SPURT.
I CANNOT GO OUT LIKE THIS!
YEAH, I WOULDN'T.
MOM SAID SHE HAS NO TIME TO FIX IT RIGHT NOW, AND THAT I SHOULD-- AND I QUOTE--"JOIN THE LEGION OF KIDS THAT ARE OLD ENOUGH TO FIX THEIR OWN PROBLEMS"!
REALLY?
HE DIDN'T SELL IT.
IT WAS MUCH FUNNIER WHEN I SAID IT.
DID THE VICE PRESIDENT ADMIT TO HIS PREVIOUSLY UNDISCLOSED FINANCIAL STAKE IN THE S.T.A.R. LABS OVERSEAS OPERATIONS?
HE'S ABOUT TO.
HE JUST DOESN'T KNOW IT.
AHEM!
CLARK??
DAD? WHAT IS--?
OH!

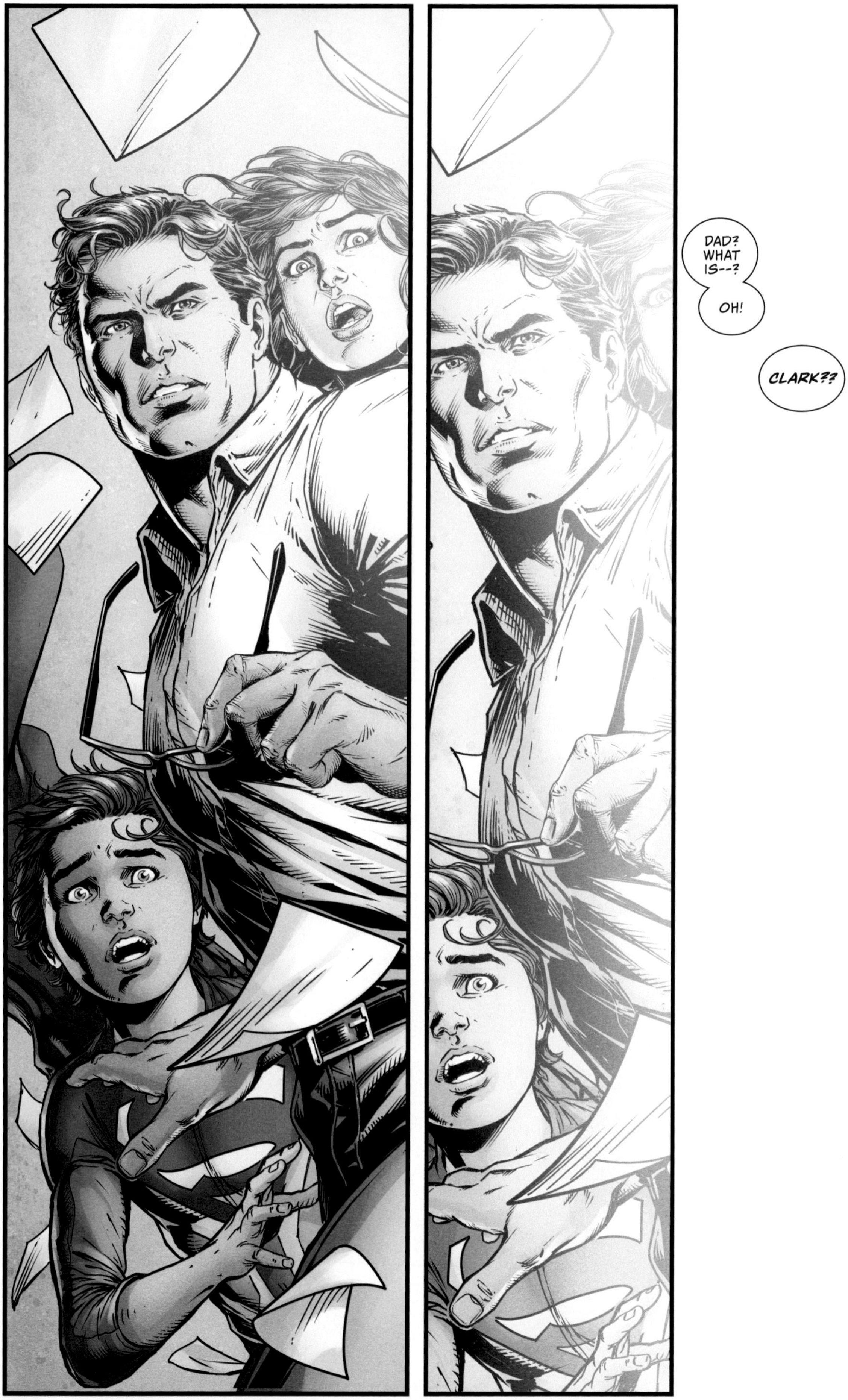
DAD? WHAT IS--?
OH!
CLARK??

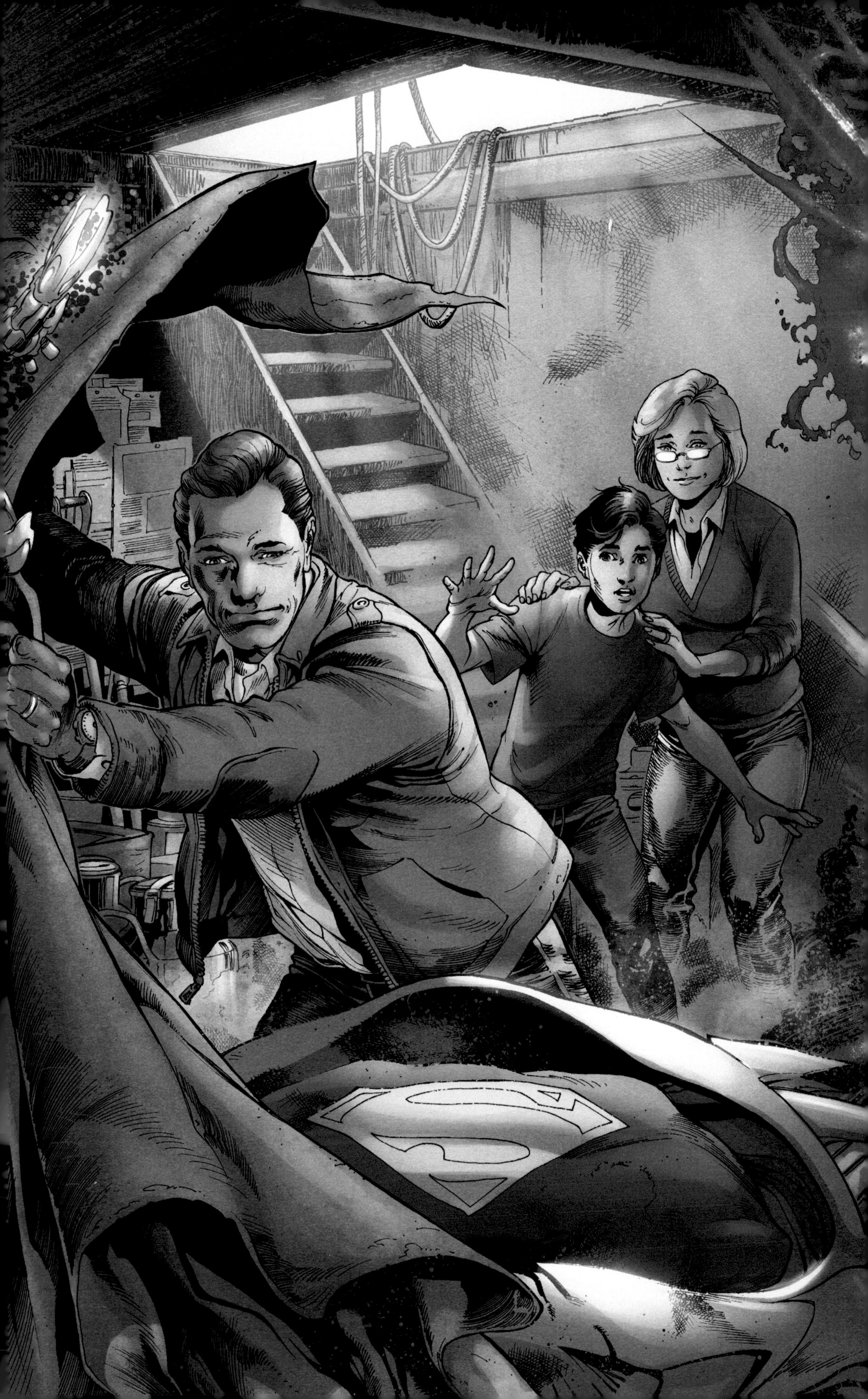

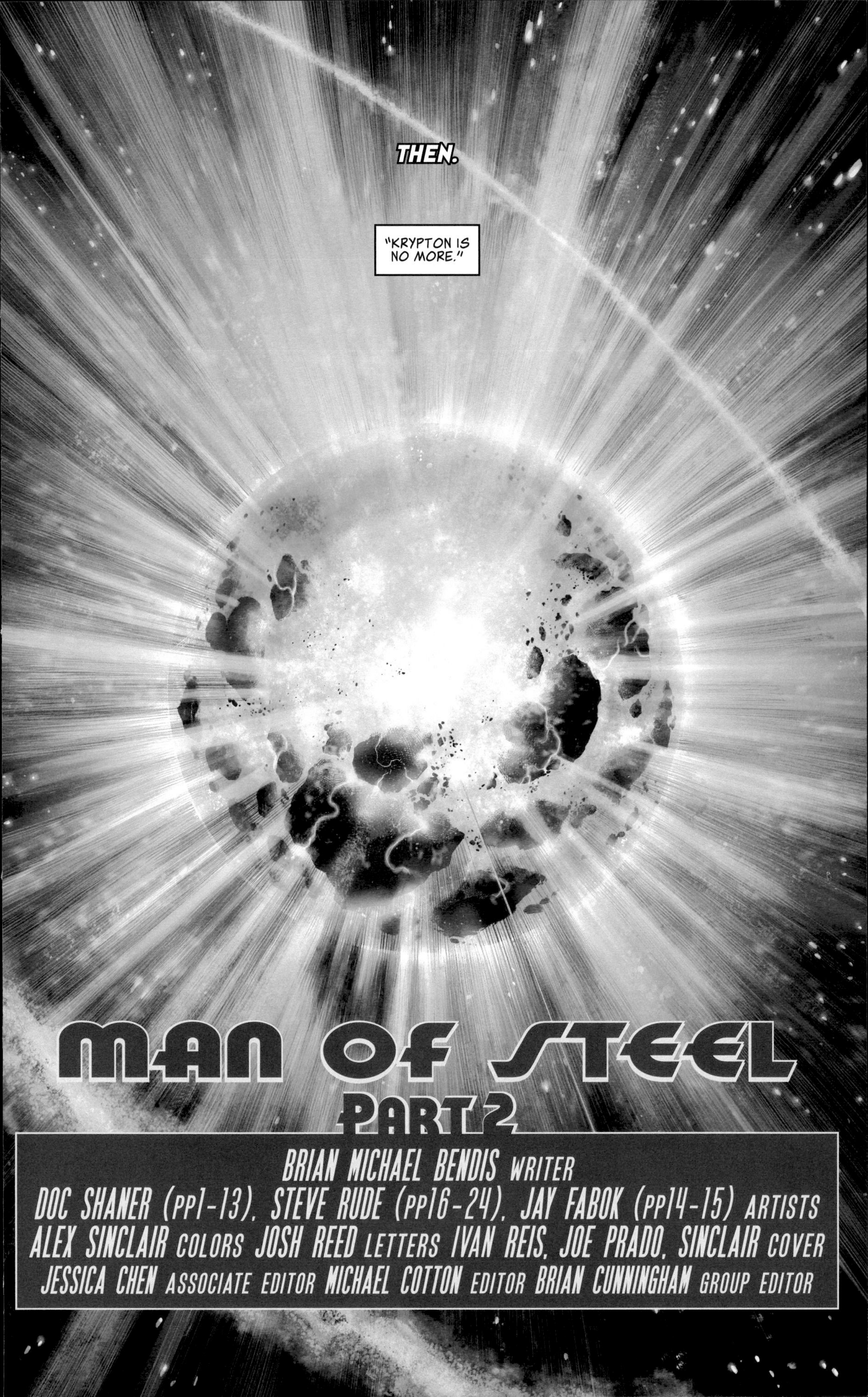
THEN.
"KRYPTON IS NO MORE."
MAN OF STEEL
PART 2
BRIAN MICHAEL BENDIS WRITER
DOC SHANER (PP1-13), STEVE RUDE (PP16-24), JAY FABOK (PP14-15) ARTISTS
ALEX SINCLAIR COLORS JOSH REED LETTERS IVAN REIS, JOE PRADO, SINCLAIR COVER
JESSICA CHEN ASSOCIATE EDITOR MICHAEL COTTON EDITOR BRIAN CUNNINGHAM GROUP EDITOR

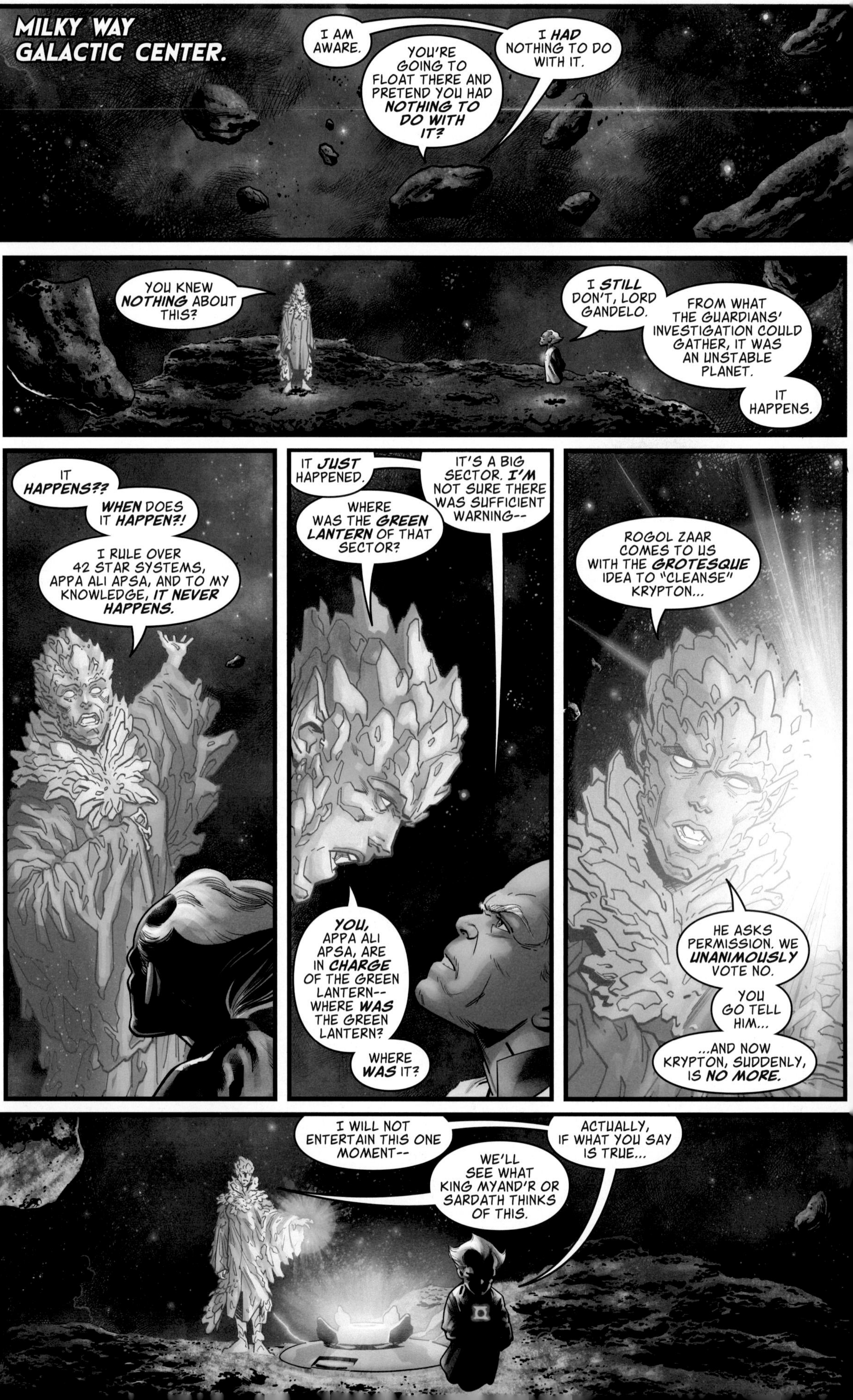
MILKY WAY GALACTIC CENTER.
I AM AWARE.
YOU'RE GOING TO FLOAT THERE AND PRETEND YOU HAD NOTHING TO DO WITH IT?
I HAD NOTHING TO DO WITH IT.
YOU KNEW NOTHING ABOUT THIS?
I STILL DON'T, LORD GANDELO.
FROM WHAT THE GUARDIANS' INVESTIGATION COULD GATHER, IT WAS AN UNSTABLE PLANET.
IT HAPPENS.
IT HAPPENS?? WHEN DOES IT HAPPEN?!
I RULE OVER 42 STAR SYSTEMS, APPA ALI APSA, AND TO MY KNOWLEDGE, IT NEVER HAPPENS.
IT JUST HAPPENED.
WHERE WAS THE GREEN LANTERN OF THAT SECTOR?
IT'S A BIG SECTOR. I'M NOT SURE THERE WAS SUFFICIENT WARNING--
YOU, APPA ALI APSA, ARE IN CHARGE OF THE GREEN LANTERN-- WHERE WAS THE GREEN LANTERN?
WHERE WAS IT?
ROGOL ZAAR COMES TO US WITH THE GROTESQUE IDEA TO "CLEANSE" KRYPTON...
HE ASKS PERMISSION. WE UNANIMOUSLY VOTE NO.
YOU GO TELL HIM...
...AND NOW KRYPTON, SUDDENLY, IS NO MORE.
I WILL NOT ENTERTAIN THIS ONE MOMENT--
ACTUALLY, IF WHAT YOU SAY IS TRUE...
WE'LL SEE WHAT KING MYAND'R OR SARDATH THINKS OF THIS.

...IF ROGOL, THIS LEGENDARY CREATURE OF WAR, WHO HAS BATHED IN THE BLOOD OF MILLIONS OF SOULS TO FIGHT FOR WHAT HE BELIEVES IN...

...IF HE TOOK IT UPON *HIMSELF* TO BETRAY THE GALACTIC CIRCLE HE HAS *SWORN* TO SERVE AND PROTECT...

...IF *HE WENT* BEHIND *OUR BACKS* AND RID THE UNIVERSE OF *AN ENTIRE SPECIES...*

...*WHAT* DO YOU THINK HE'LL DO TO *YOU,* AND YOUR 42 STAR SYSTEMS, IF YOU KEEP GOING WITH THIS LINE OF INQUIRY?

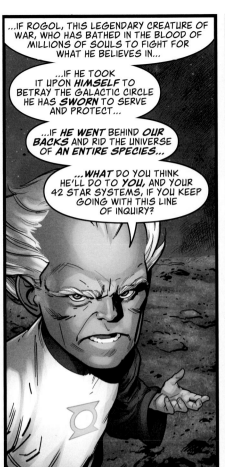

IF YOUR THEORY IS TRUE...YOU SHOULD HOPE HE WAS IN THE HEART OF KRYPTON WHEN IT EXPLODED.

YOU SHOULD HOPE *HE* HAD THE COURTESY OF SACRIFICING HIMSELF FOR WHAT HE BELIEVED.

I HEAR AND UNDERSTAND YOUR FRUSTRATION. BUT ON THIS DAY, YOU AND I ARE GUILTY OF THE VERY SAME THING...

...WE DID NOT SEE THIS COMING.

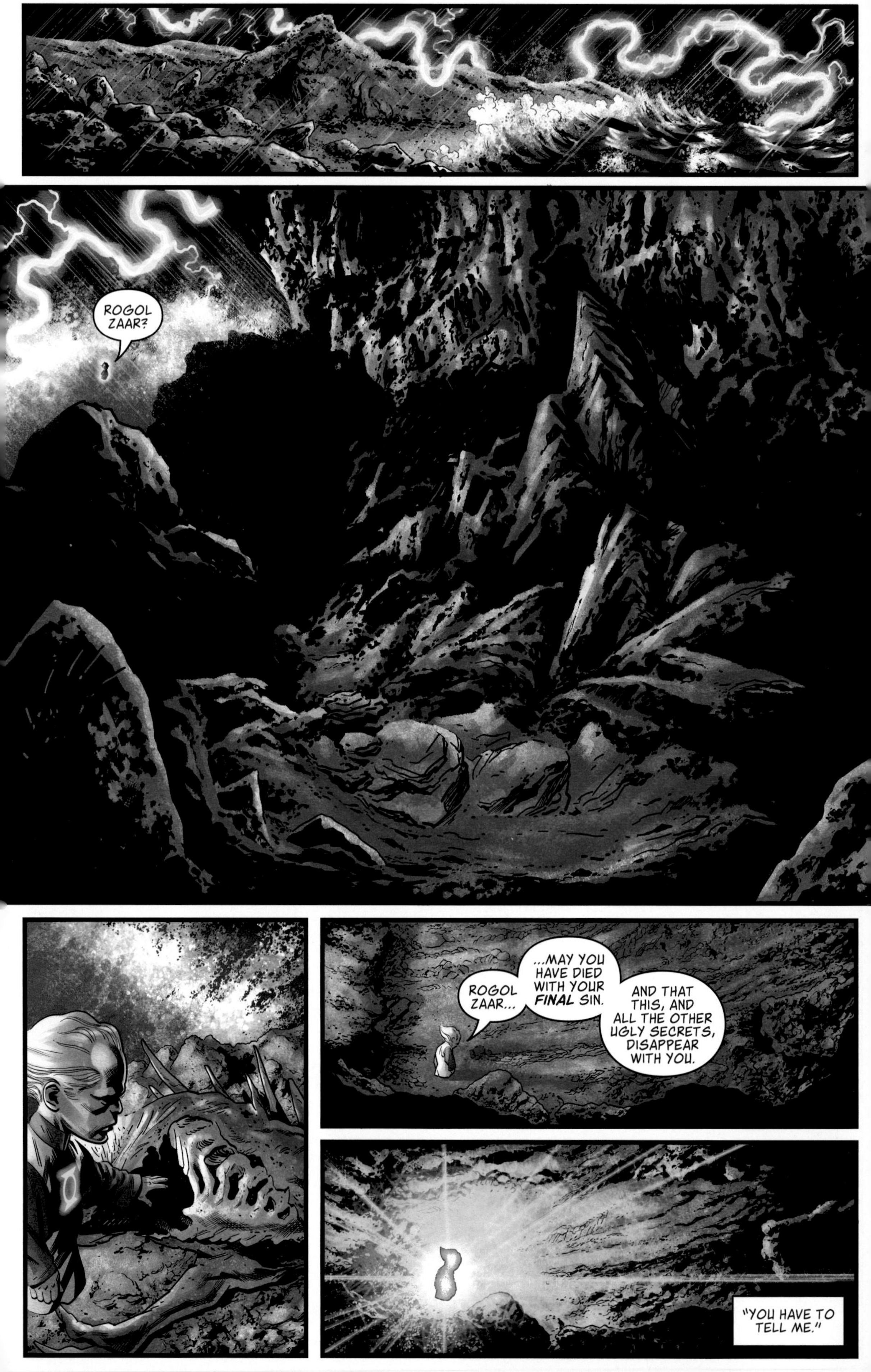

ROGOL ZAAR?
ROGOL ZAAR...
...MAY YOU HAVE DIED WITH YOUR FINAL SIN.
AND THAT THIS, AND ALL THE OTHER UGLY SECRETS, DISAPPEAR WITH YOU.
"YOU HAVE TO TELL ME."

NOW.

TELL YOU WHAT?

YOU **KNOW!**

THE UGLY SECRET EVERY-**ONE** WANTS TO KNOW...

...WHERE IS **LOIS LANE?**

I'M SORRY...

...WHAT WAS **YOUR NAME** AGAIN?

ROBINSON GOODE. I'M THE NEW CITY DESK REPORTER.

I WAS JUST THINKING HOW CRAZY IT WAS THAT YOU WERE ASKING **ME** FOR GOSSIP AND I DON'T EVEN **KNOW** YOU.

YOU'RE TRISH Q, THE GOSSIP COLUMNIST.

OH. OKAY.

I'M AN ARTS AND LEISURE REPORTER.

TRISH Q
She has all the gossip!

OKAY, SO WHAT'S THE "ARTS" ANGLE ON THE GOSSIP OF WHAT HAPPENED TO LOIS LANE?

GO ASK HER ESTRANGED HUSBAND, MISTER CLARK KENT.

I **WOULD,** BUT HE HASN'T MADE EYE CONTACT WITH ME YET.

OH, THAT...

...BABE, CLARK KENT IS 100 PERCENT GOOD-OLD AMERICAN SMALLVILLE FARM BOY.

WHICH MEANS HE STILL TREATS WOMEN WITH GOOD-OLD AMERICAN SMALLVILLE FARM BOY RESPECT.

HE RUNS AWAY FROM ME EVERY TIME I SAY HI.

WHAT DO YOU WANT ME TO TELL YOU?

YOU'RE A REPORTER AND HE HAS A SECRET.

SO THERE **IS** A SECRET...

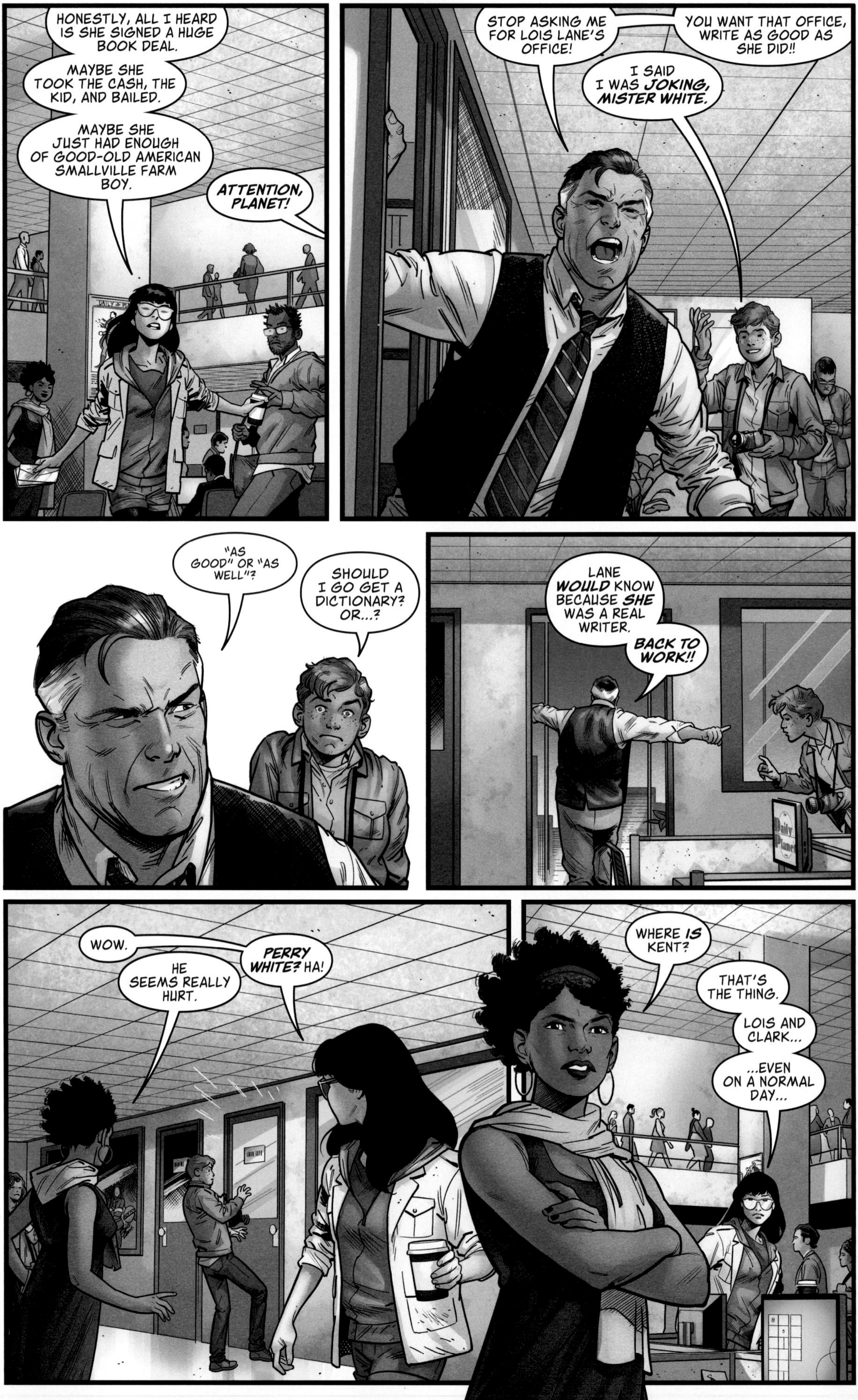
HONESTLY, ALL I HEARD IS SHE SIGNED A HUGE BOOK DEAL.
MAYBE SHE TOOK THE CASH, THE KID, AND BAILED.
MAYBE SHE JUST HAD ENOUGH OF GOOD-OLD AMERICAN SMALLVILLE FARM BOY.
ATTENTION, PLANET!
STOP ASKING ME FOR LOIS LANE'S OFFICE!
YOU WANT THAT OFFICE, WRITE AS GOOD AS SHE DID!!
I SAID I WAS JOKING, MISTER WHITE.
"AS GOOD" OR "AS WELL"?
SHOULD I GO GET A DICTIONARY? OR...?
LANE WOULD KNOW BECAUSE SHE WAS A REAL WRITER.
BACK TO WORK!!
WOW.
PERRY WHITE? HA!
HE SEEMS REALLY HURT.
WHERE IS KENT?
THAT'S THE THING.
LOIS AND CLARK...
...EVEN ON A NORMAL DAY...

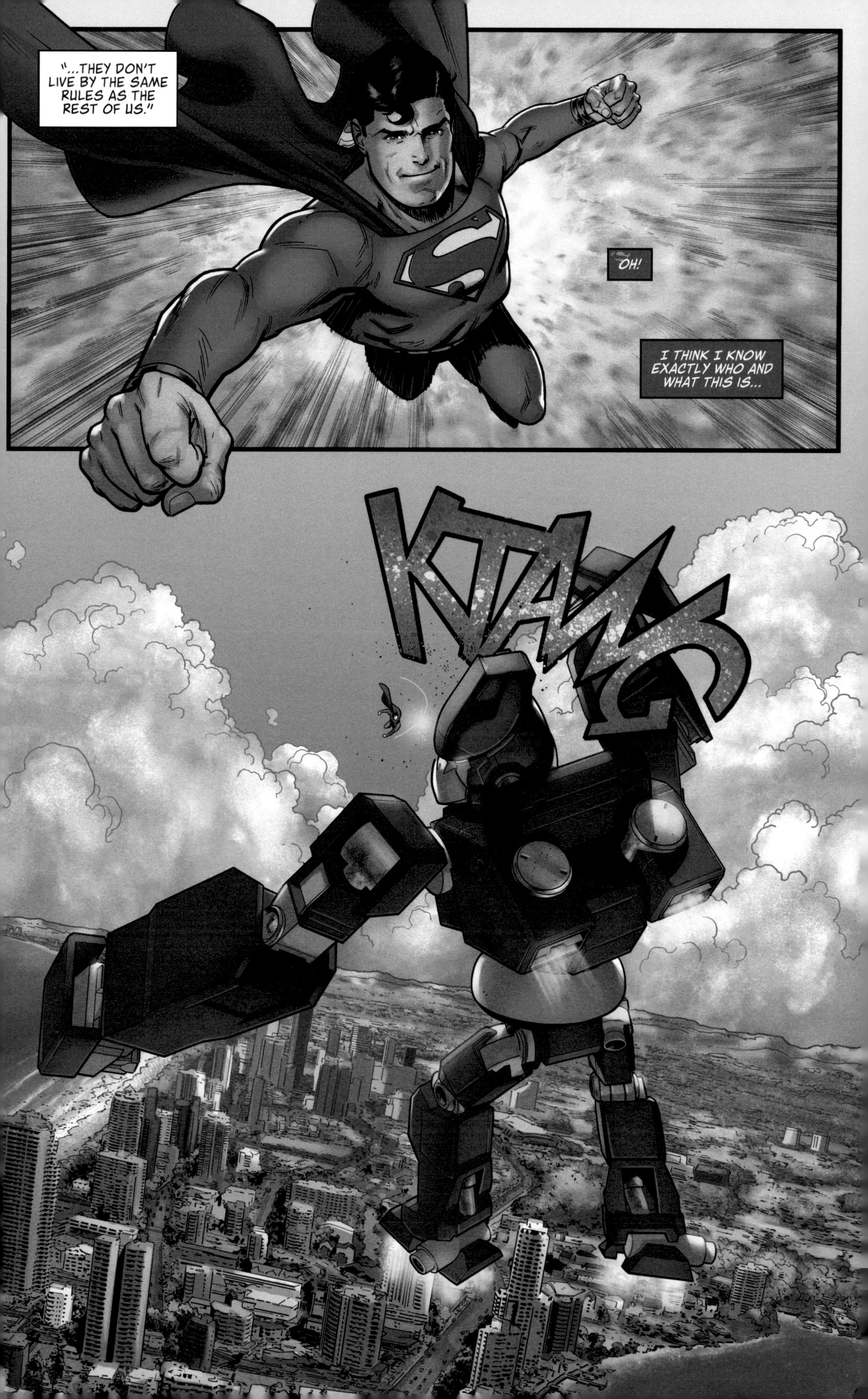
"...THEY DON'T LIVE BY THE SAME RULES AS THE REST OF US."
OH!
I THINK I KNOW EXACTLY WHO AND WHAT THIS IS...
KTANG

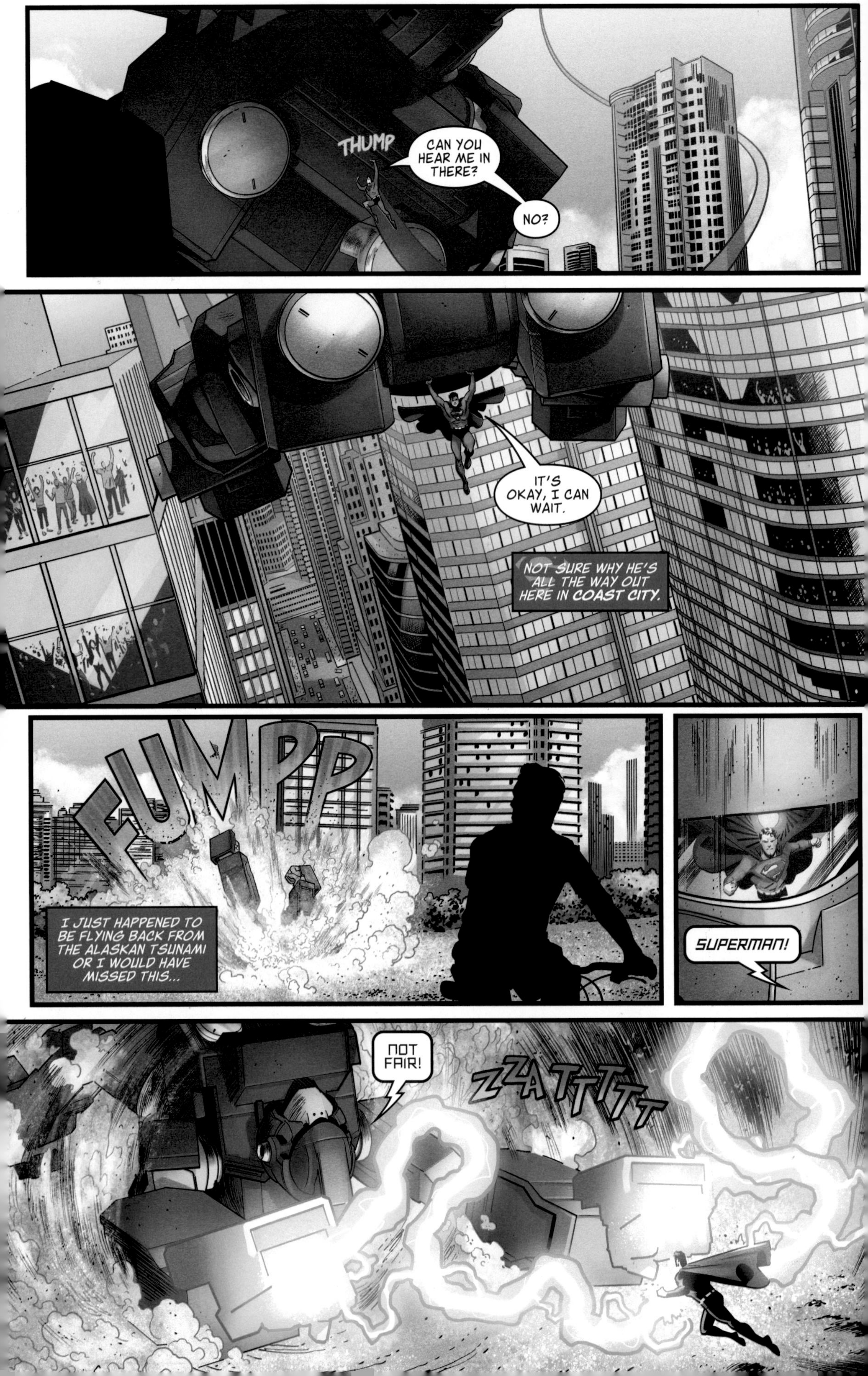
THUMP
CAN YOU HEAR ME IN THERE?
NO?
IT'S OKAY, I CAN WAIT.
NOT SURE WHY HE'S ALL THE WAY OUT HERE IN COAST CITY.
FUMPP
I JUST HAPPENED TO BE FLYING BACK FROM THE ALASKAN TSUNAMI OR I WOULD HAVE MISSED THIS...
SUPERMAN!
NOT FAIR!
ZZZATTTTT

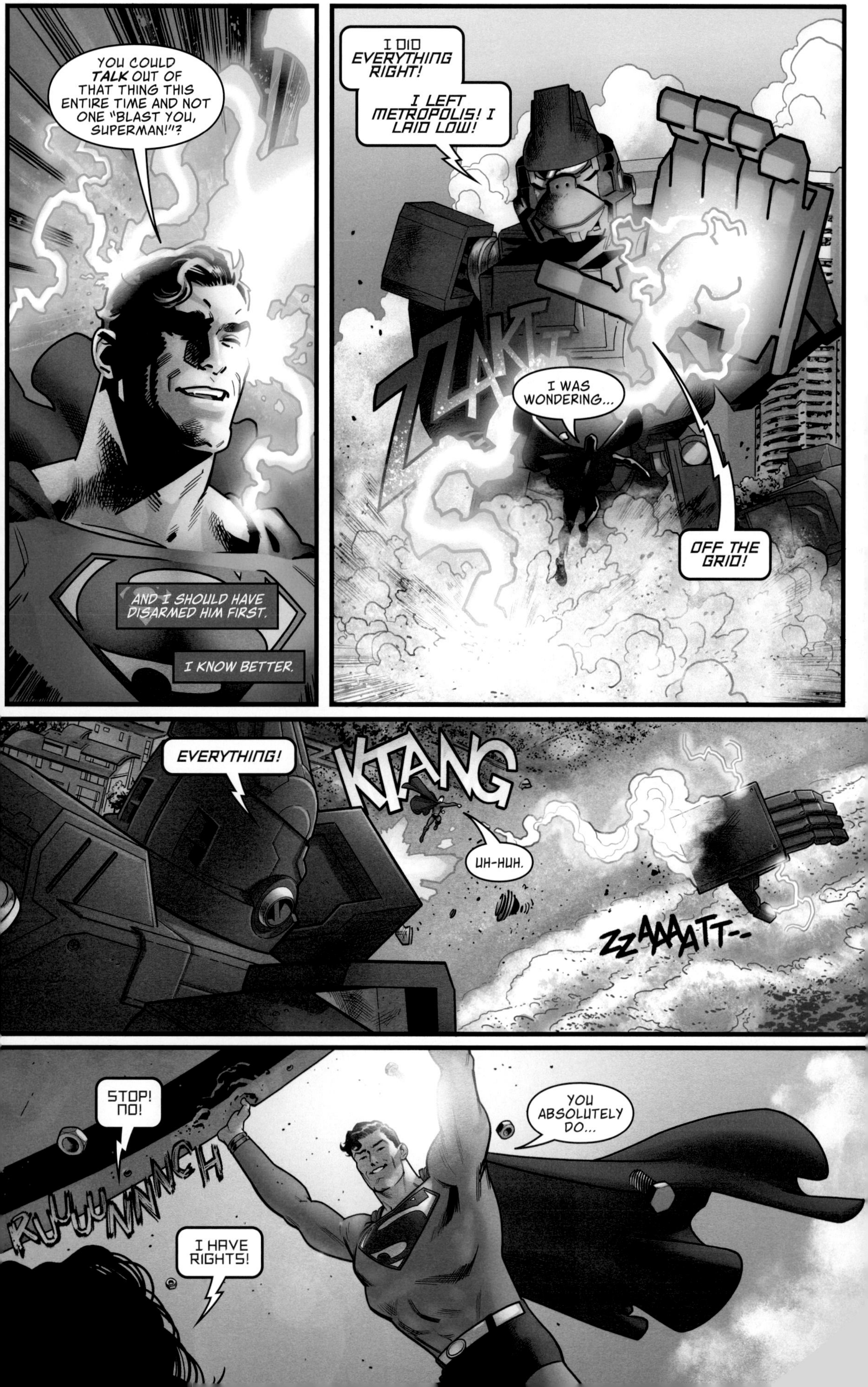
YOU COULD TALK OUT OF THAT THING THIS ENTIRE TIME AND NOT ONE "BLAST YOU, SUPERMAN!"?
AND I SHOULD HAVE DISARMED HIM FIRST.
I KNOW BETTER.
I DID EVERYTHING RIGHT!
I LEFT METROPOLIS! I LAID LOW!
ZZLAKT
I WAS WONDERING...
OFF THE GRID!
EVERYTHING!
KTANG
UH-HUH.
ZZAAAATT--
STOP! NO!
RUUUNNNCH
YOU ABSOLUTELY DO...
I HAVE RIGHTS!

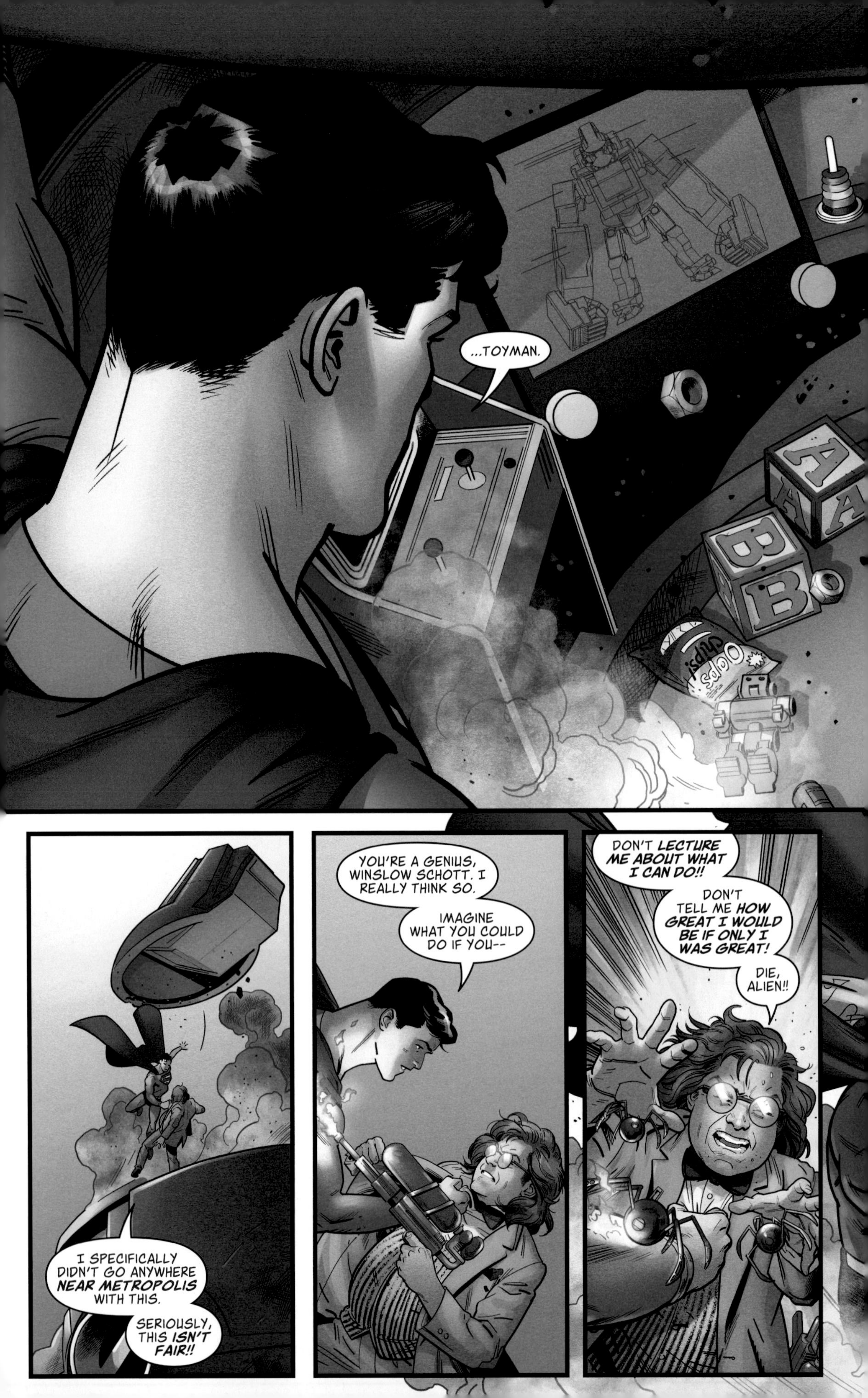
...TOYMAN.
Olops Chips!
I SPECIFICALLY DIDN'T GO ANYWHERE NEAR METROPOLIS WITH THIS.
SERIOUSLY, THIS ISN'T FAIR!!
YOU'RE A GENIUS, WINSLOW SCHOTT. I REALLY THINK SO.
IMAGINE WHAT YOU COULD DO IF YOU--
DON'T LECTURE ME ABOUT WHAT I CAN DO!!
DON'T TELL ME HOW GREAT I WOULD BE IF ONLY I WAS GREAT!
DIE, ALIEN!!

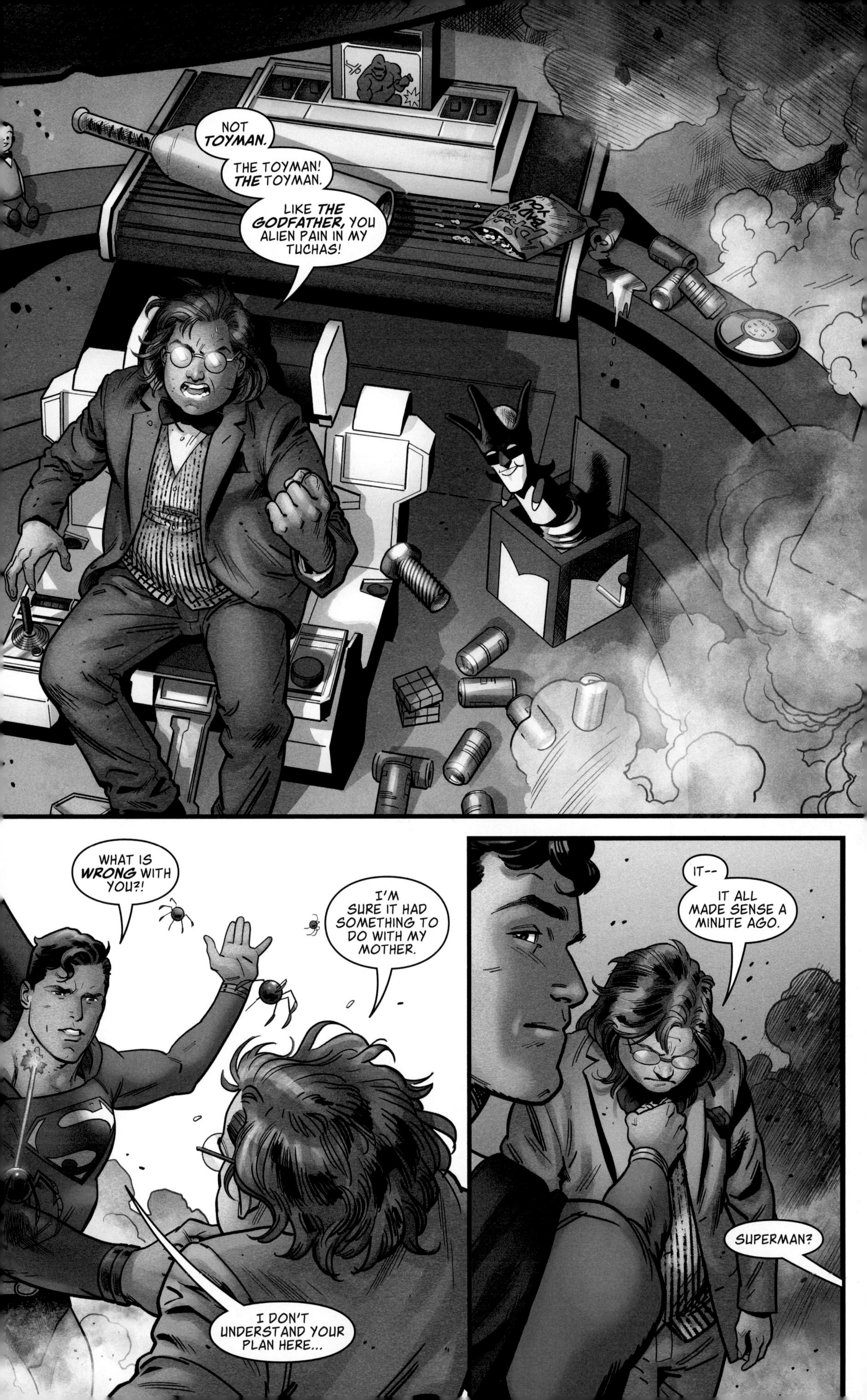

NOT TOYMAN.
THE TOYMAN! THE TOYMAN.
LIKE THE GODFATHER, YOU ALIEN PAIN IN MY TUCHAS!
WHAT IS WRONG WITH YOU?!
I'M SURE IT HAD SOMETHING TO DO WITH MY MOTHER.
I DON'T UNDERSTAND YOUR PLAN HERE...
IT--
IT ALL MADE SENSE A MINUTE AGO.
SUPERMAN?

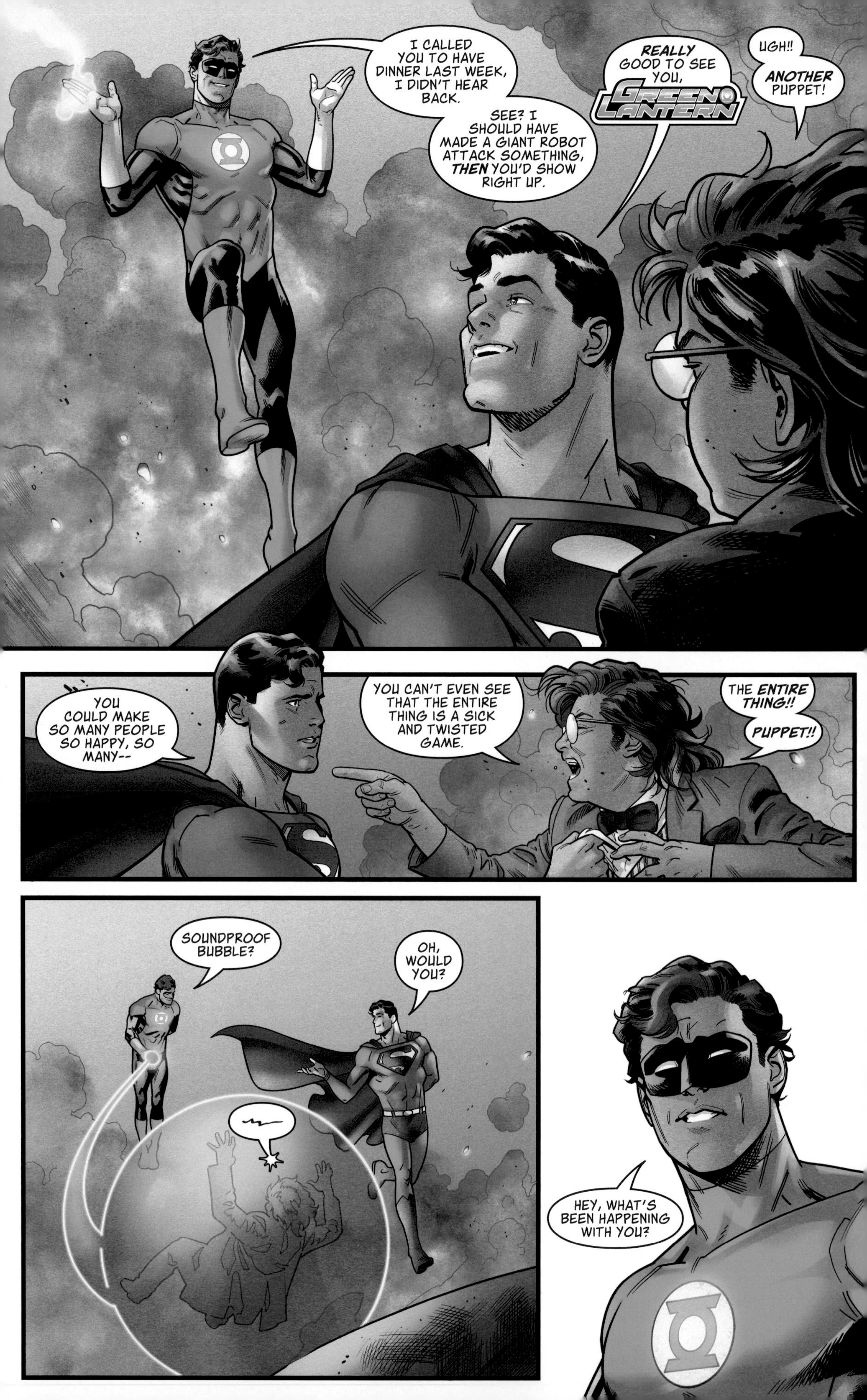
I CALLED YOU TO HAVE DINNER LAST WEEK, I DIDN'T HEAR BACK.
SEE? I SHOULD HAVE MADE A GIANT ROBOT ATTACK SOMETHING, THEN YOU'D SHOW RIGHT UP.
REALLY GOOD TO SEE YOU, GREEN LANTERN
UGH!!
ANOTHER PUPPET!
YOU COULD MAKE SO MANY PEOPLE SO HAPPY, SO MANY--
YOU CAN'T EVEN SEE THAT THE ENTIRE THING IS A SICK AND TWISTED GAME.
THE ENTIRE THING!!
PUPPET!!
SOUNDPROOF BUBBLE?
OH, WOULD YOU?
HEY, WHAT'S BEEN HAPPENING WITH YOU?

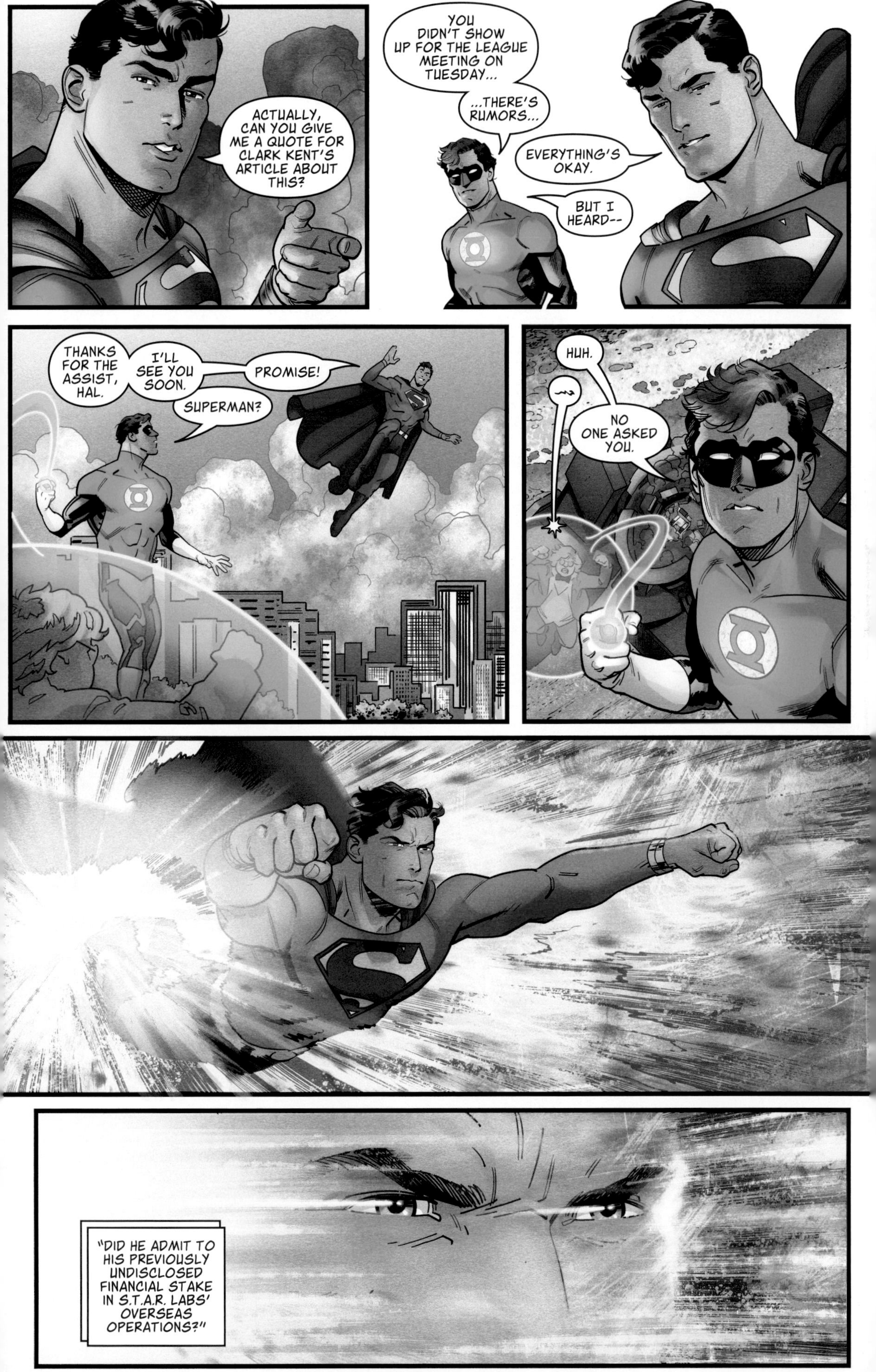

ACTUALLY, CAN YOU GIVE ME A QUOTE FOR CLARK KENT'S ARTICLE ABOUT THIS?
YOU DIDN'T SHOW UP FOR THE LEAGUE MEETING ON TUESDAY...
...THERE'S RUMORS...
EVERYTHING'S OKAY.
BUT I HEARD--
THANKS FOR THE ASSIST, HAL.
I'LL SEE YOU SOON.
PROMISE!
SUPERMAN?
HUH.
NO ONE ASKED YOU.
"DID HE ADMIT TO HIS PREVIOUSLY UNDISCLOSED FINANCIAL STAKE IN S.T.A.R. LABS' OVERSEAS OPERATIONS?"

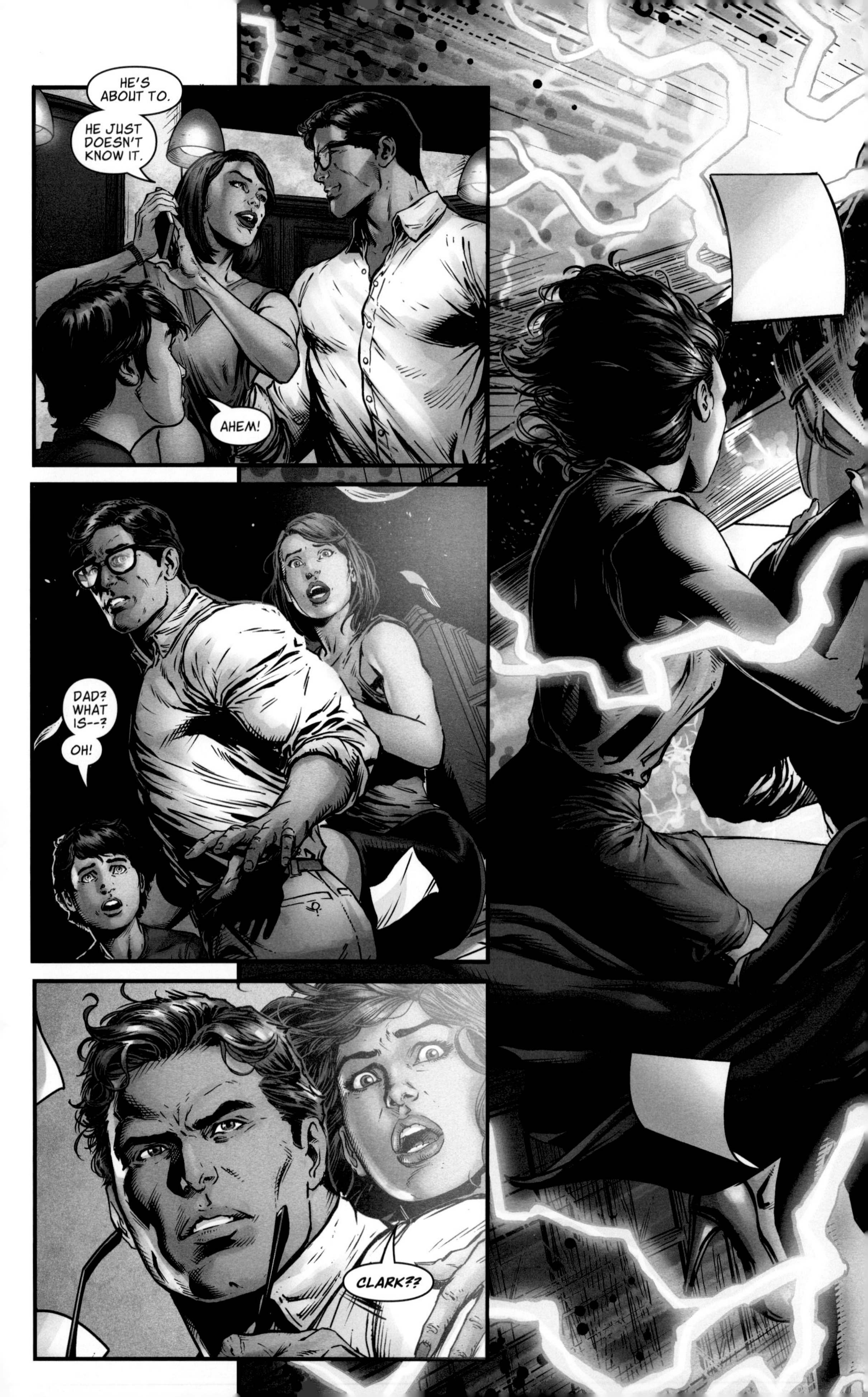
HE'S ABOUT TO.
HE JUST DOESN'T KNOW IT.
AHEM!
DAD? WHAT IS--?
OH!
CLARK??

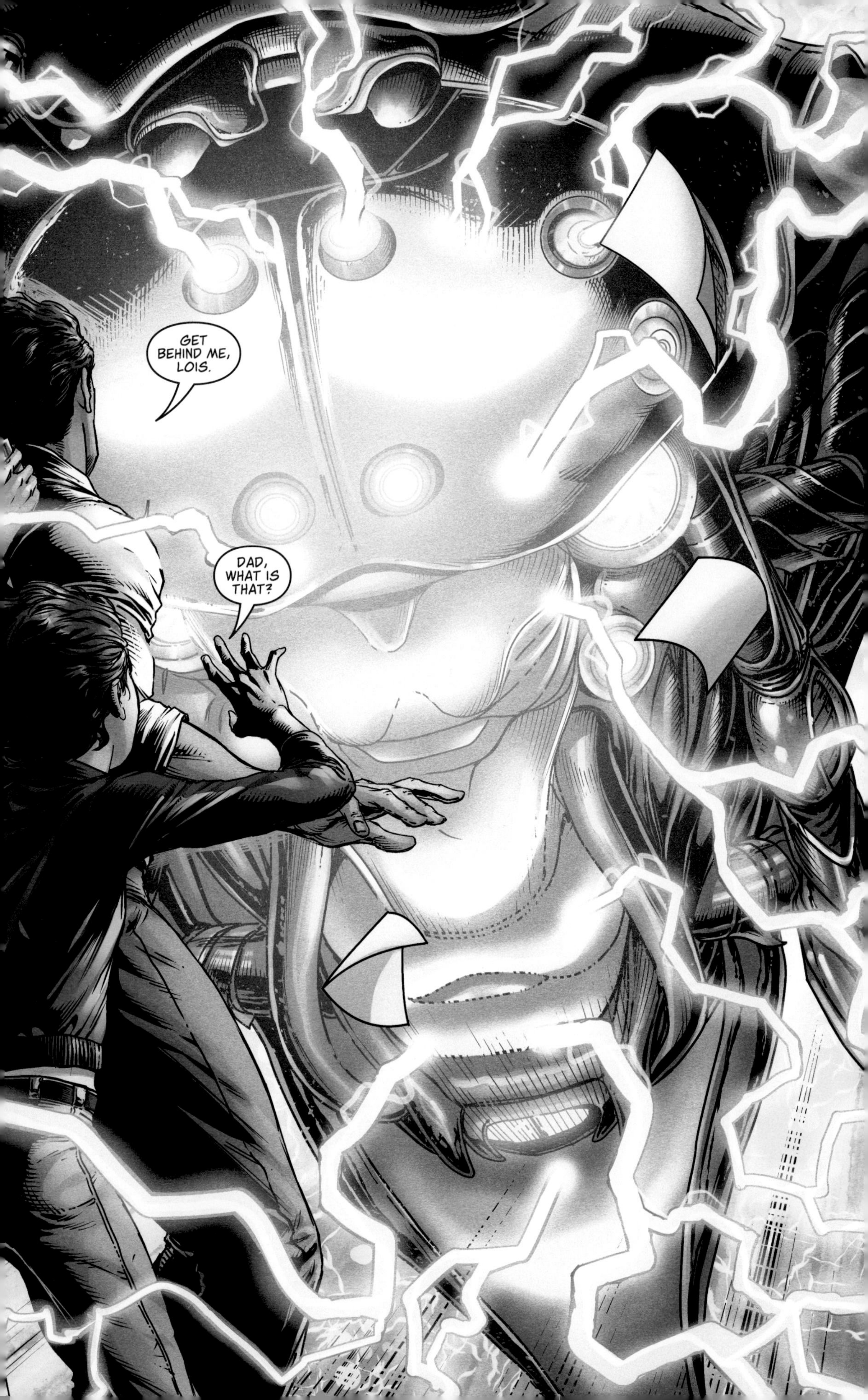
GET BEHIND ME, LOIS.
DAD, WHAT IS THAT?

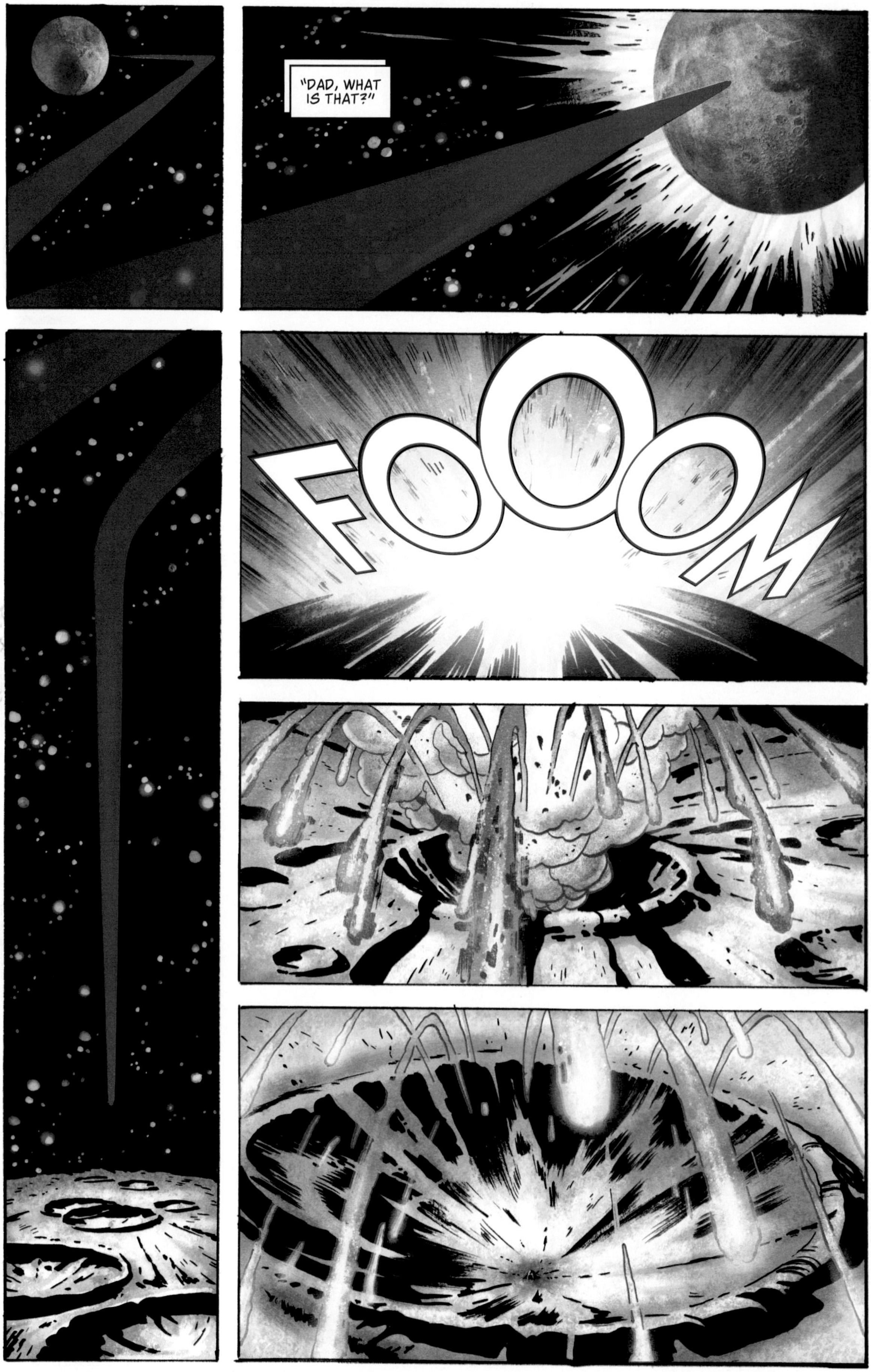
"DAD, WHAT IS THAT?"
FOOOOM

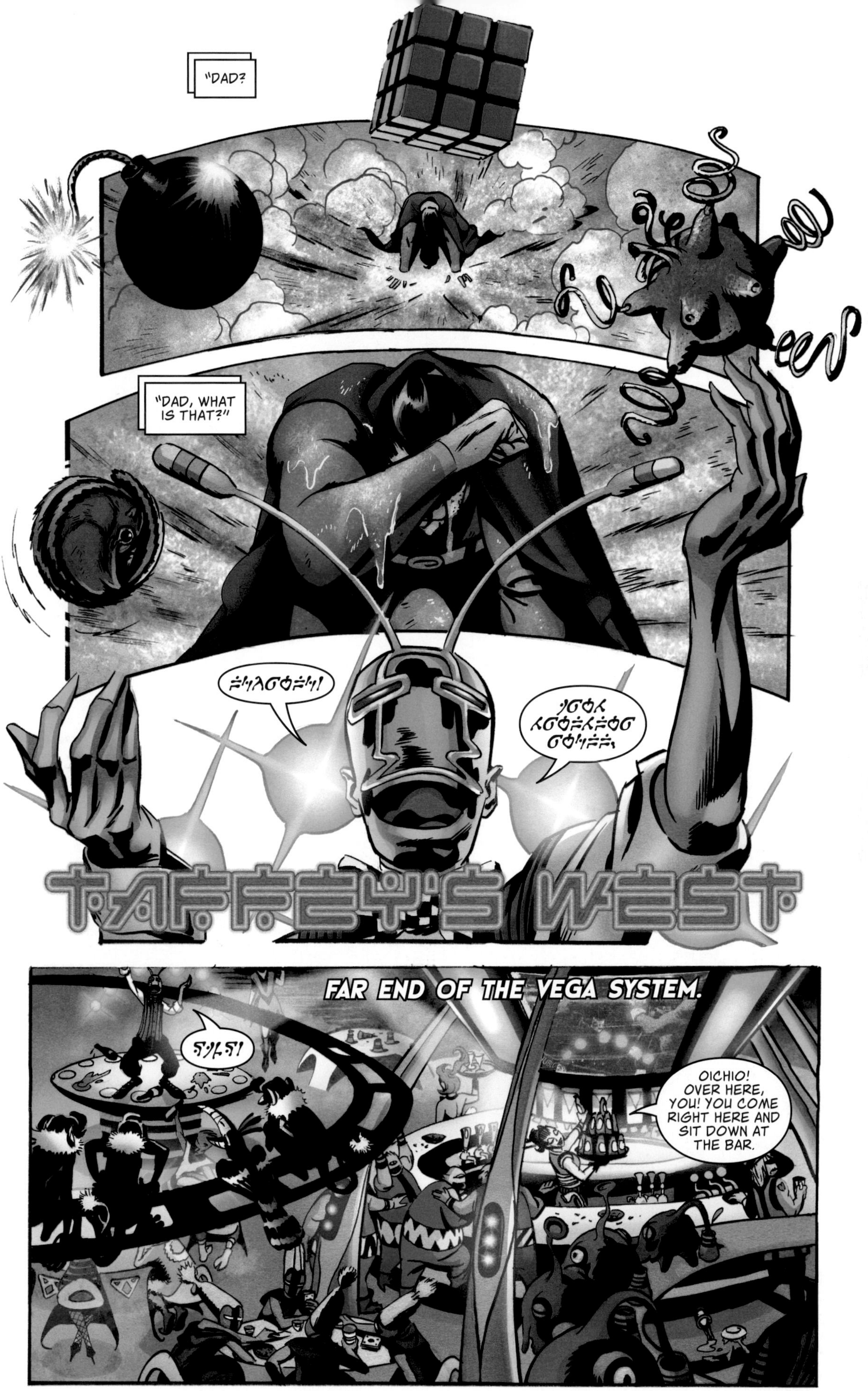
"DAD?
"DAD, WHAT IS THAT?"
TAFFEY'S WEST
FAR END OF THE VEGA SYSTEM.
OICHIO! OVER HERE, YOU! YOU COME RIGHT HERE AND SIT DOWN AT THE BAR.

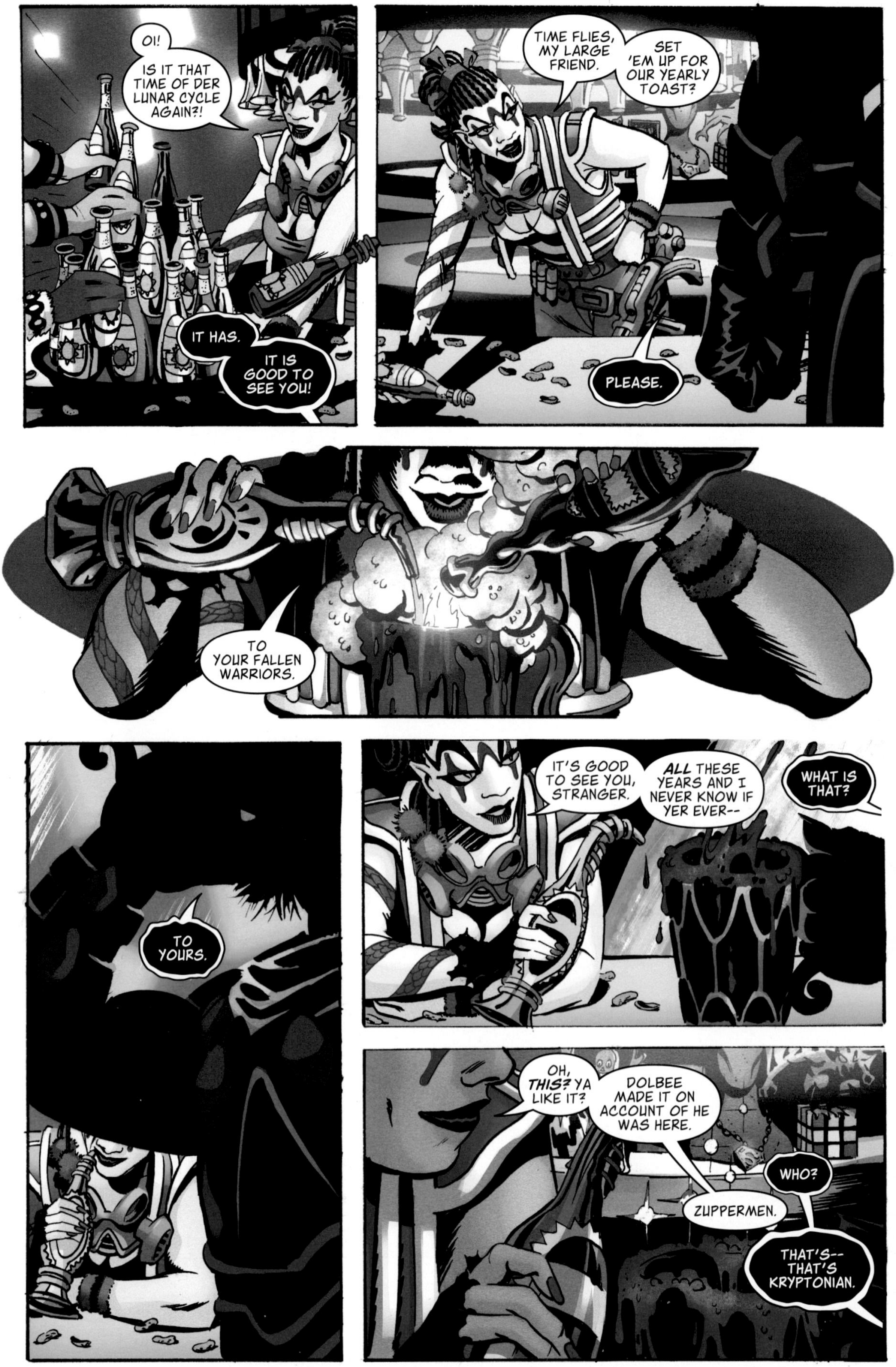

OI!
IS IT THAT TIME OF DER LUNAR CYCLE AGAIN?!
IT HAS.
IT IS GOOD TO SEE YOU!
TIME FLIES, MY LARGE FRIEND.
SET 'EM UP FOR OUR YEARLY TOAST?
PLEASE.
TO YOUR FALLEN WARRIORS.
TO YOURS.
IT'S GOOD TO SEE YOU, STRANGER.
ALL THESE YEARS AND I NEVER KNOW IF YER EVER--
WHAT IS THAT?
OH, THIS? YA LIKE IT?
DOLBEE MADE IT ON ACCOUNT OF HE WAS HERE.
WHO?
ZUPPERMEN.
THAT'S-- THAT'S KRYPTONIAN.

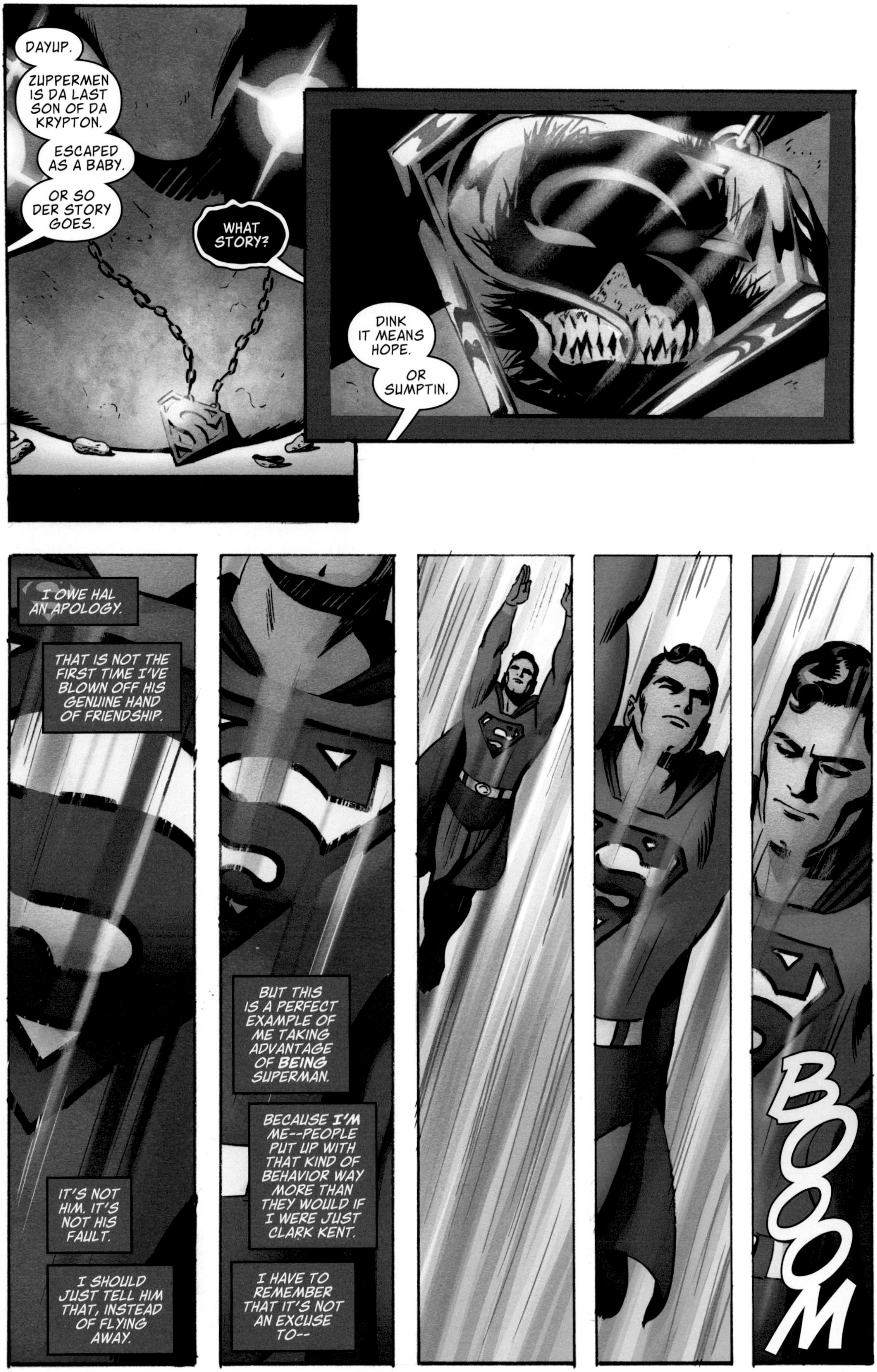

DAYUP.
ZUPPERMEN IS DA LAST SON OF DA KRYPTON.
ESCAPED AS A BABY.
OR SO DER STORY GOES.
WHAT STORY?
DINK IT MEANS HOPE.
OR SUMPTIN.
I OWE HAL AN APOLOGY.
THAT IS NOT THE FIRST TIME I'VE BLOWN OFF HIS GENUINE HAND OF FRIENDSHIP.
IT'S NOT HIM. IT'S NOT HIS FAULT.
I SHOULD JUST TELL HIM THAT, INSTEAD OF FLYING AWAY.
BUT THIS IS A PERFECT EXAMPLE OF ME TAKING ADVANTAGE OF BEING SUPERMAN.
BECAUSE I'M ME--PEOPLE PUT UP WITH THAT KIND OF BEHAVIOR WAY MORE THAN THEY WOULD IF I WERE JUST CLARK KENT.
I HAVE TO REMEMBER THAT IT'S NOT AN EXCUSE TO--
BOOOOM

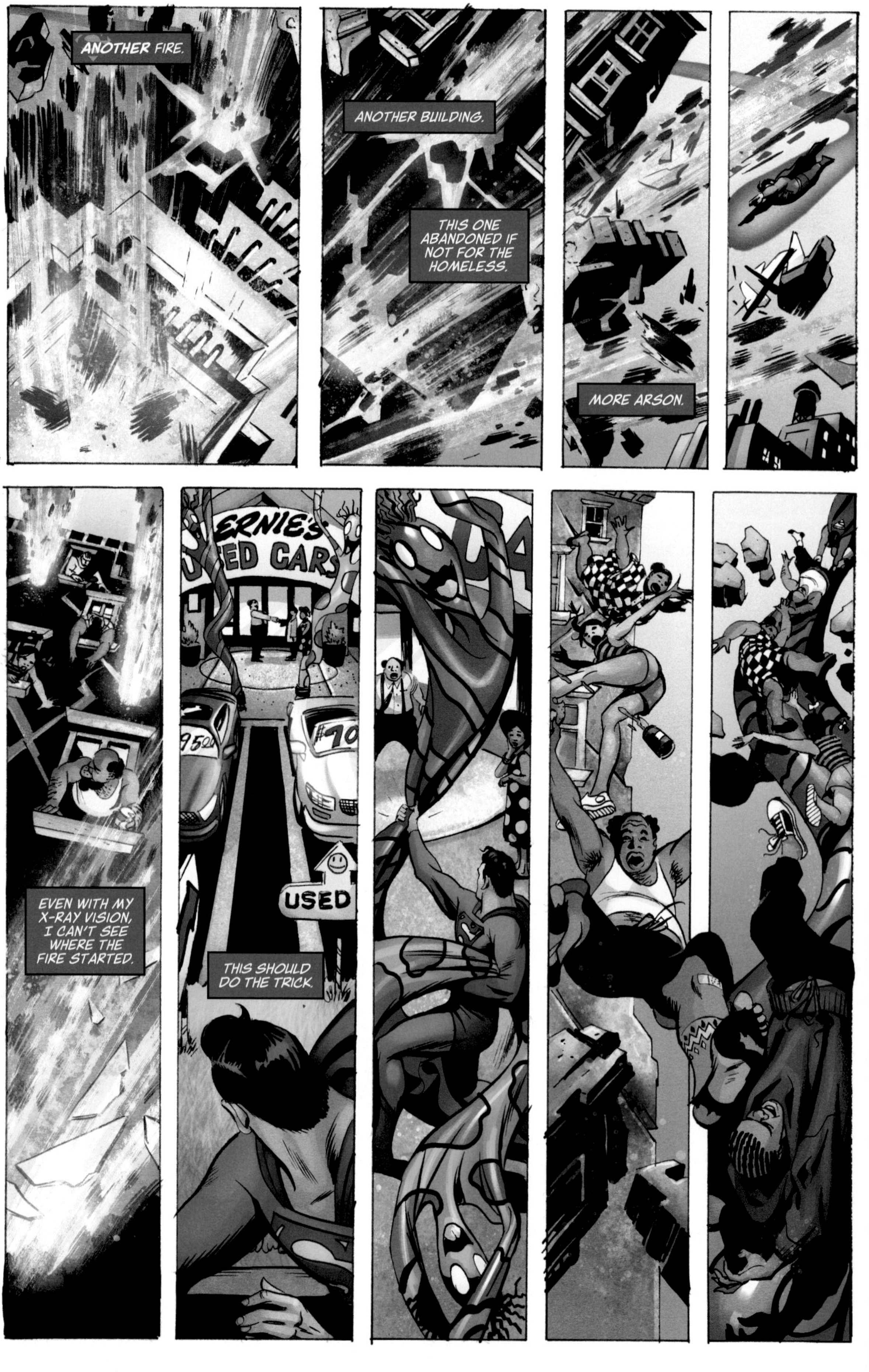
ANOTHER FIRE.
ANOTHER BUILDING.
THIS ONE ABANDONED IF NOT FOR THE HOMELESS.
MORE ARSON.
EVEN WITH MY X-RAY VISION, I CAN'T SEE WHERE THE FIRE STARTED.
ERNIE'S USED CARS
USED
THIS SHOULD DO THE TRICK.

SOMEONE IS BURNING DOWN METROPOLIS...

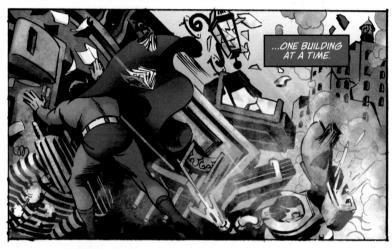

...ONE BUILDING AT A TIME.

AND THEY'RE TRYING TO DO IT RIGHT IN FRONT OF ME.

MISTER WHITE, I HAVE MORE ON THE ARSON STUFF.

OH, AND I GOT A STORY ON TOYMAN SETTING UP SHOP IN COAST CITY, BUT--

YEAH, YEAH, BIG ROBOT, SUPERMAN AND GREEN LANTERN.

YEAH, UH, HOW'D YOU KNOW?

I'M BEING SLOWLY BLED TO DEATH, KENT.

SIR?

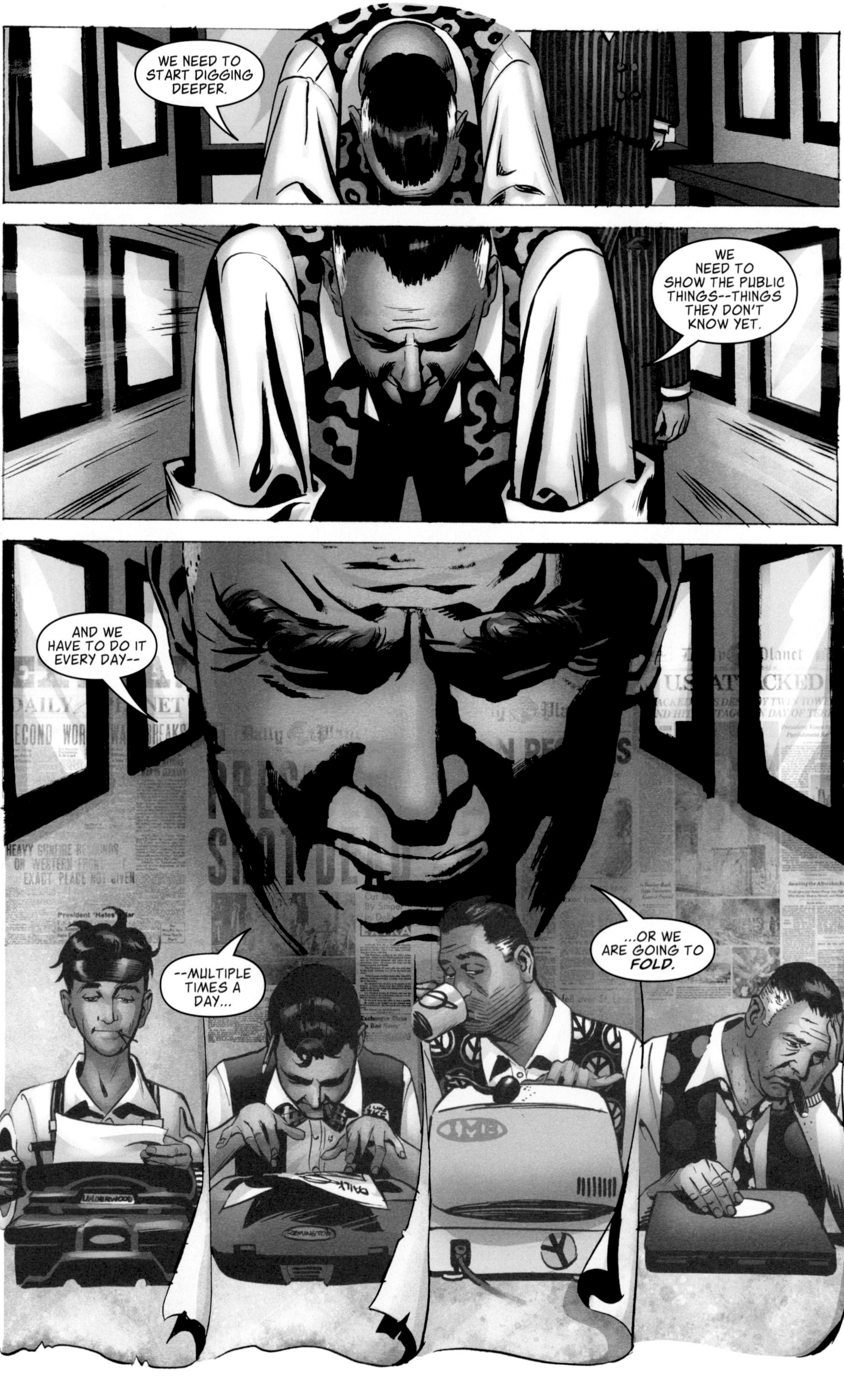
WE NEED TO START DIGGING DEEPER.
WE NEED TO SHOW THE PUBLIC THINGS--THINGS THEY DON'T KNOW YET.
AND WE HAVE TO DO IT EVERY DAY--
--MULTIPLE TIMES A DAY...
...OR WE ARE GOING TO *FOLD.*

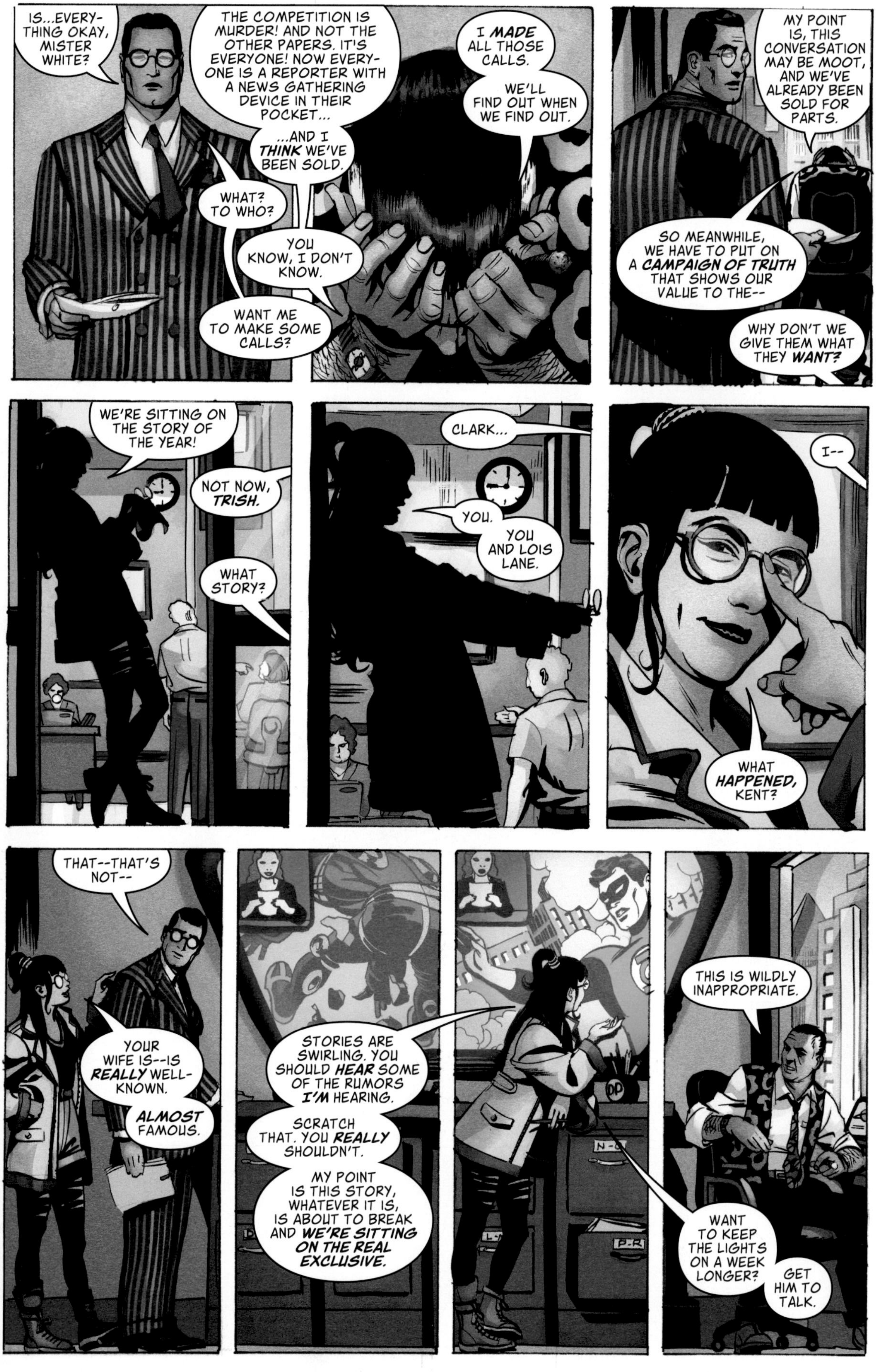

IS...EVERY-THING OKAY, MISTER WHITE?
THE COMPETITION IS MURDER! AND NOT THE OTHER PAPERS. IT'S EVERYONE! NOW EVERY-ONE IS A REPORTER WITH A NEWS GATHERING DEVICE IN THEIR POCKET...
...AND I THINK WE'VE BEEN SOLD.
WHAT? TO WHO?
YOU KNOW, I DON'T KNOW.
WANT ME TO MAKE SOME CALLS?
I MADE ALL THOSE CALLS.
WE'LL FIND OUT WHEN WE FIND OUT.
MY POINT IS, THIS CONVERSATION MAY BE MOOT, AND WE'VE ALREADY BEEN SOLD FOR PARTS.
SO MEANWHILE, WE HAVE TO PUT ON A CAMPAIGN OF TRUTH THAT SHOWS OUR VALUE TO THE--
WHY DON'T WE GIVE THEM WHAT THEY WANT?
WE'RE SITTING ON THE STORY OF THE YEAR!
NOT NOW, TRISH.
WHAT STORY?
CLARK...
YOU.
YOU AND LOIS LANE.
I--
WHAT HAPPENED, KENT?
THAT--THAT'S NOT--
YOUR WIFE IS--IS REALLY WELL-KNOWN.
ALMOST FAMOUS.
STORIES ARE SWIRLING. YOU SHOULD HEAR SOME OF THE RUMORS I'M HEARING.
SCRATCH THAT. YOU REALLY SHOULDN'T.
MY POINT IS THIS STORY, WHATEVER IT IS, IS ABOUT TO BREAK AND WE'RE SITTING ON THE REAL EXCLUSIVE.
THIS IS WILDLY INAPPROPRIATE.
WANT TO KEEP THE LIGHTS ON A WEEK LONGER?
GET HIM TO TALK.

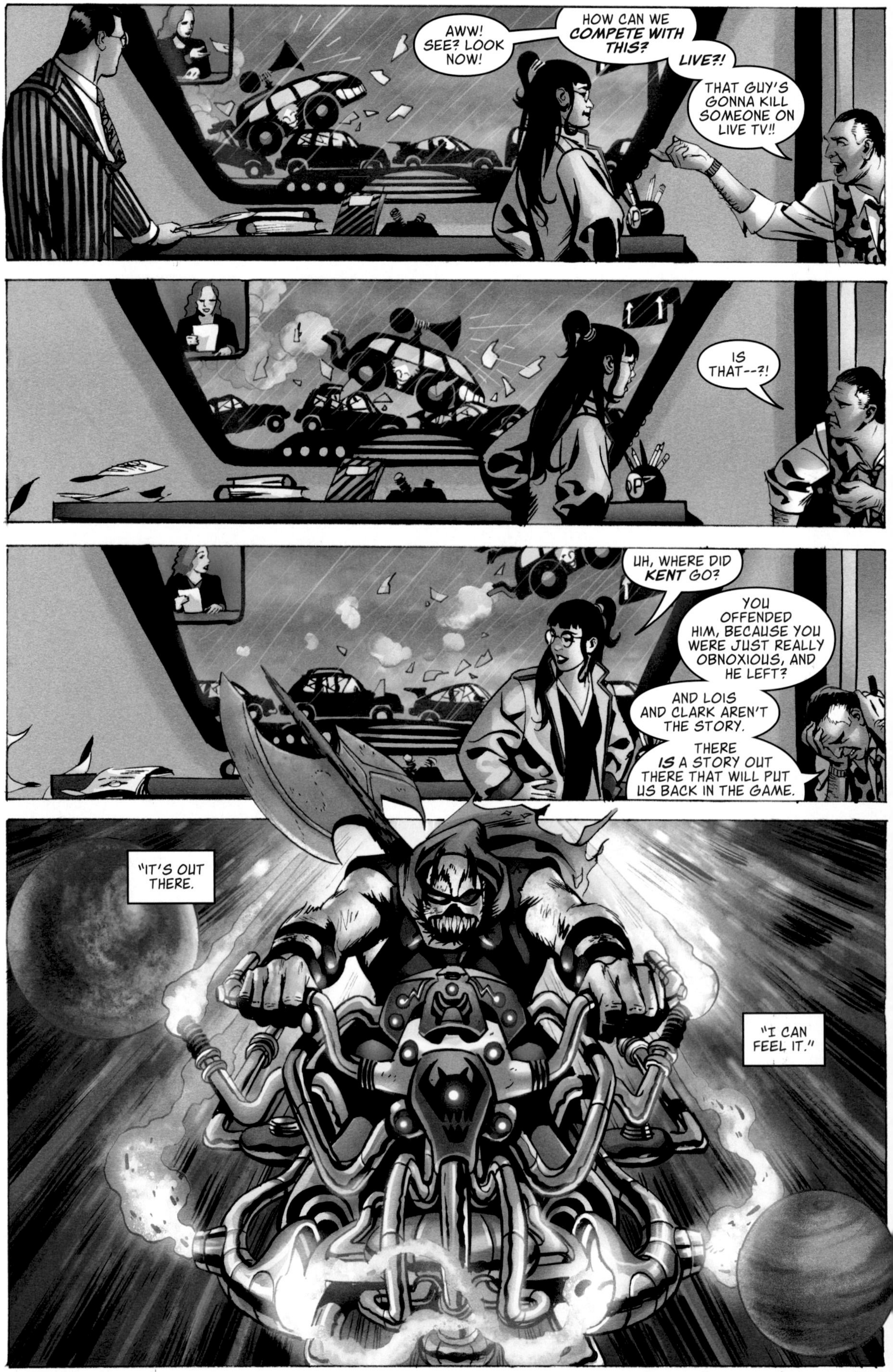
AWW! SEE? LOOK NOW!
HOW CAN WE COMPETE WITH THIS?
LIVE?!
THAT GUY'S GONNA KILL SOMEONE ON LIVE TV!!
IS THAT--?!
UH, WHERE DID KENT GO?
YOU OFFENDED HIM, BECAUSE YOU WERE JUST REALLY OBNOXIOUS, AND HE LEFT?
AND LOIS AND CLARK AREN'T THE STORY.
THERE IS A STORY OUT THERE THAT WILL PUT US BACK IN THE GAME.
"IT'S OUT THERE.
"I CAN FEEL IT."

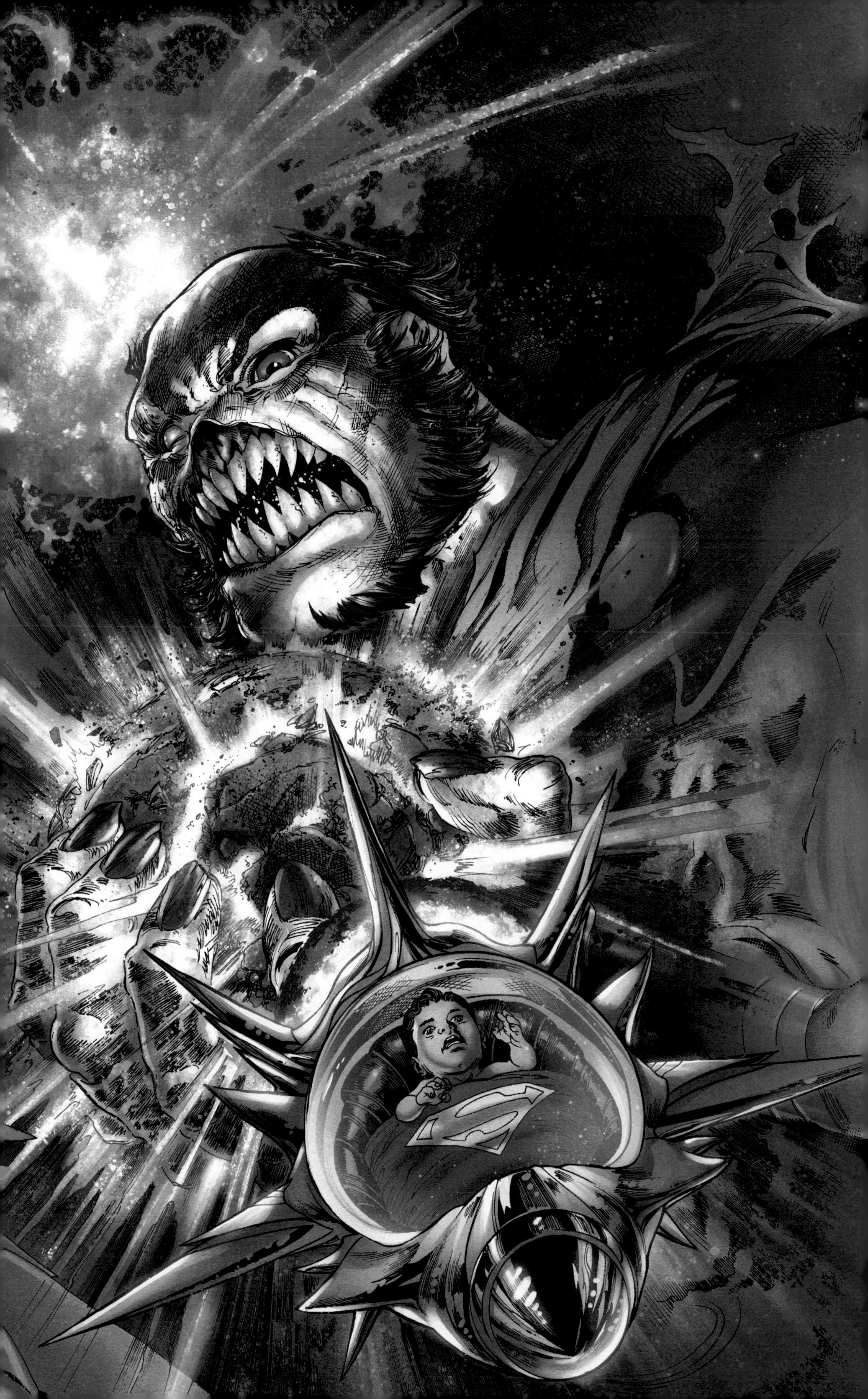

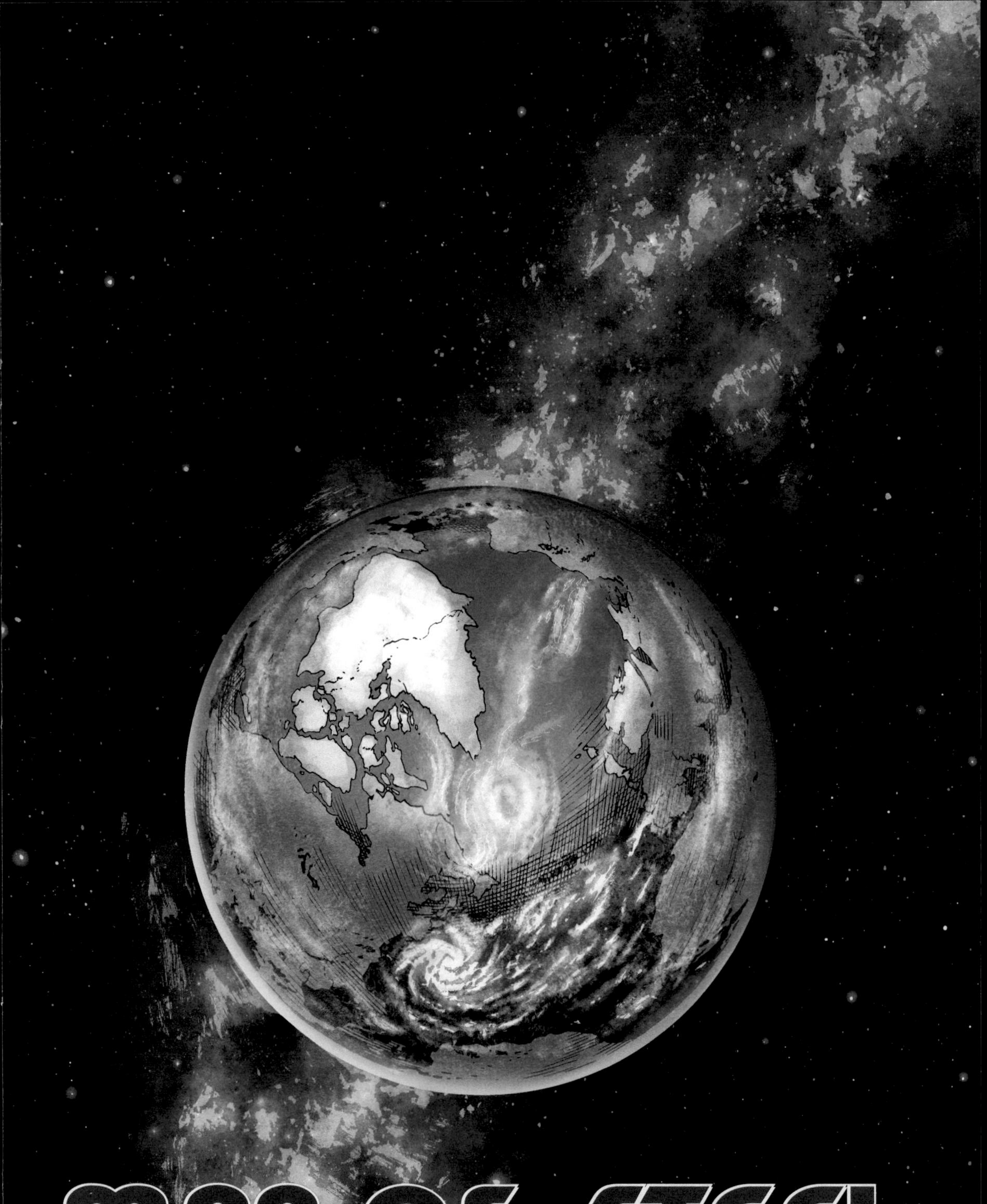

MAN OF STEEL
PART 3

BRIAN MICHAEL BENDIS WRITER
RYAN SOOK & JASON FABOK (PP16) ARTISTS WADE VON GRAWBADGER INKS (PP12-13,15)
ALEX SINCLAIR COLORS JOSH REED LETTERS IVAN REIS, JOE PRADO, SINCLAIR COVER
JESSICA CHEN ASSOCIATE EDITOR MICHAEL COTTON EDITOR BRIAN CUNNINGHAM GROUP EDITOR

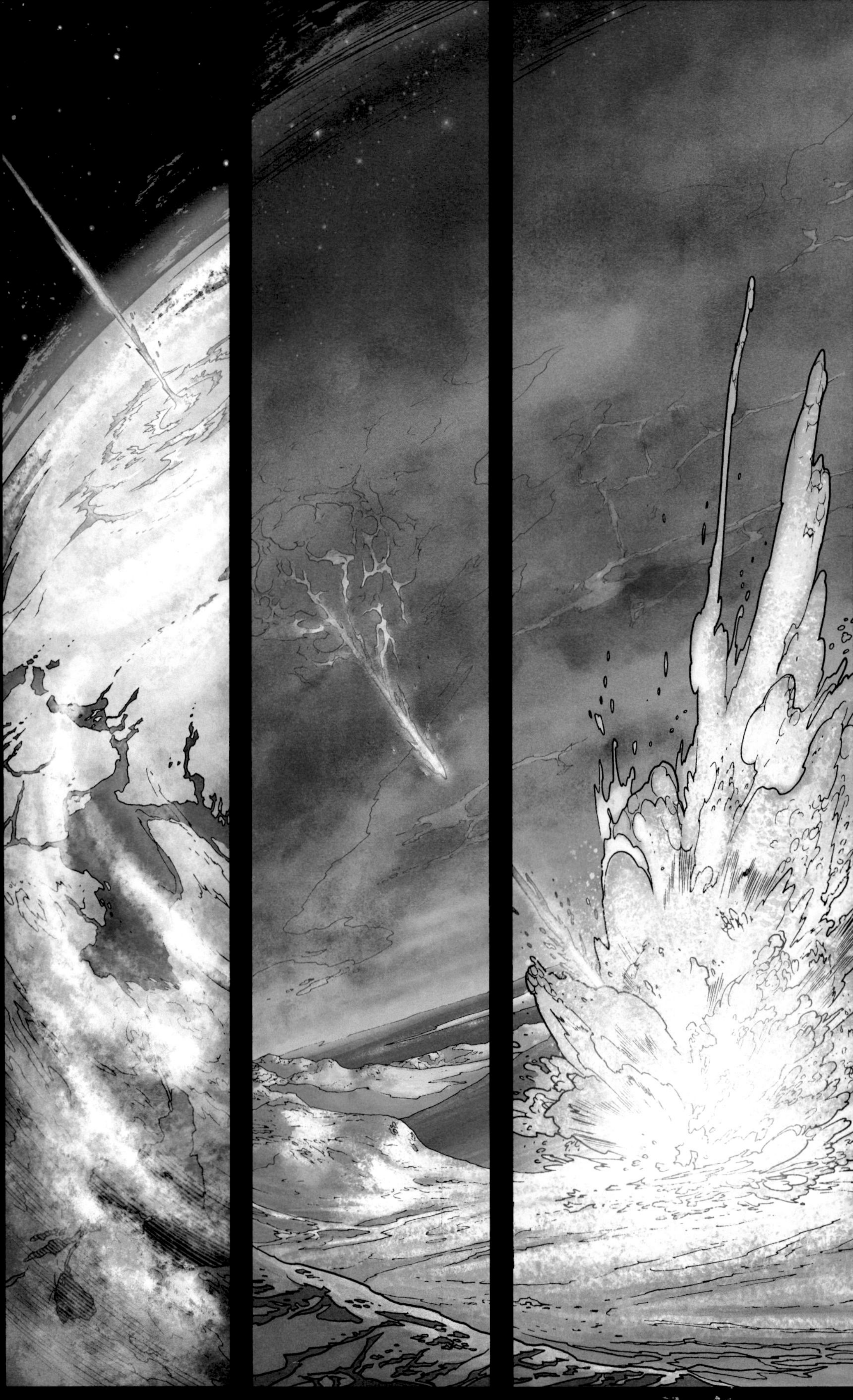

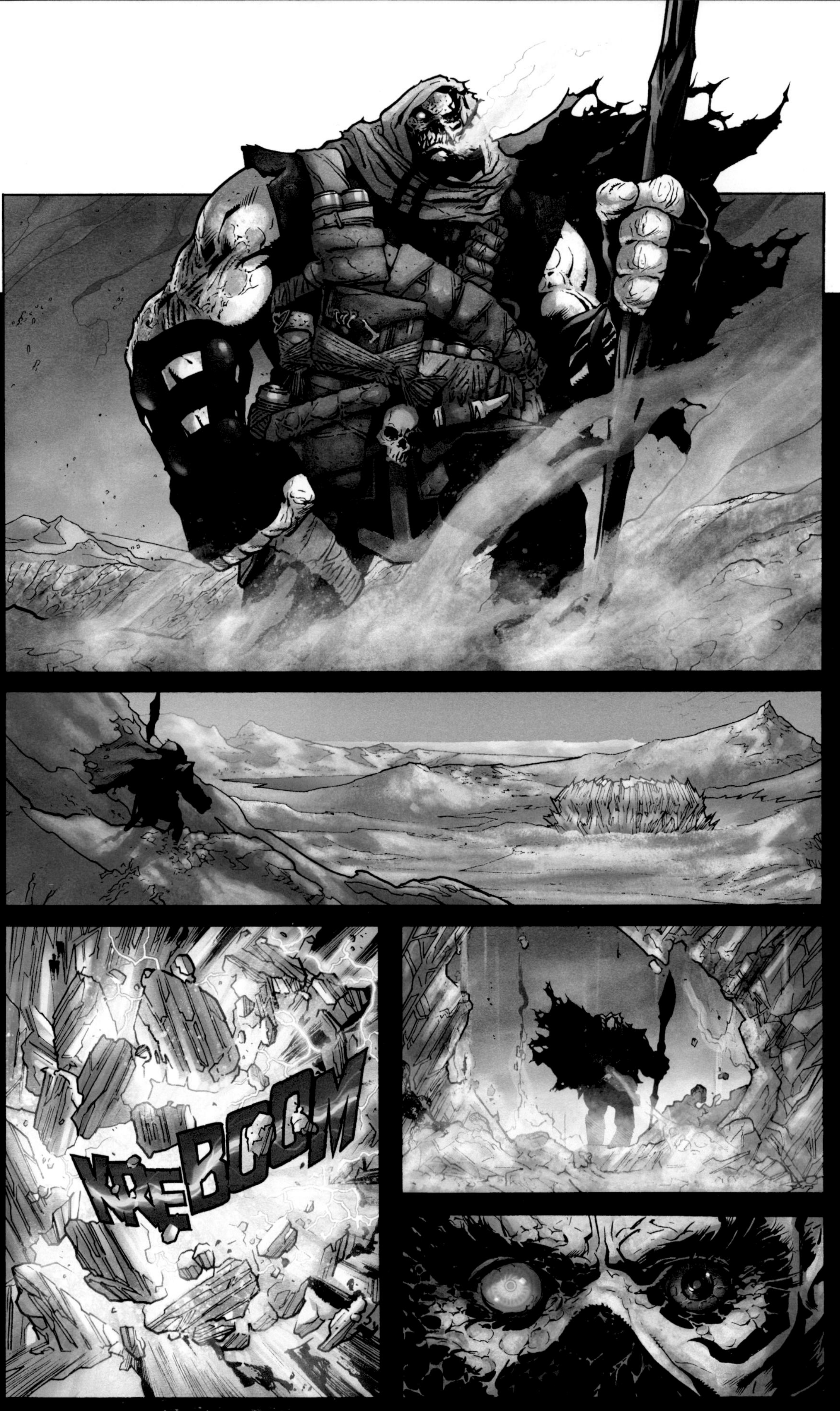
BOOM

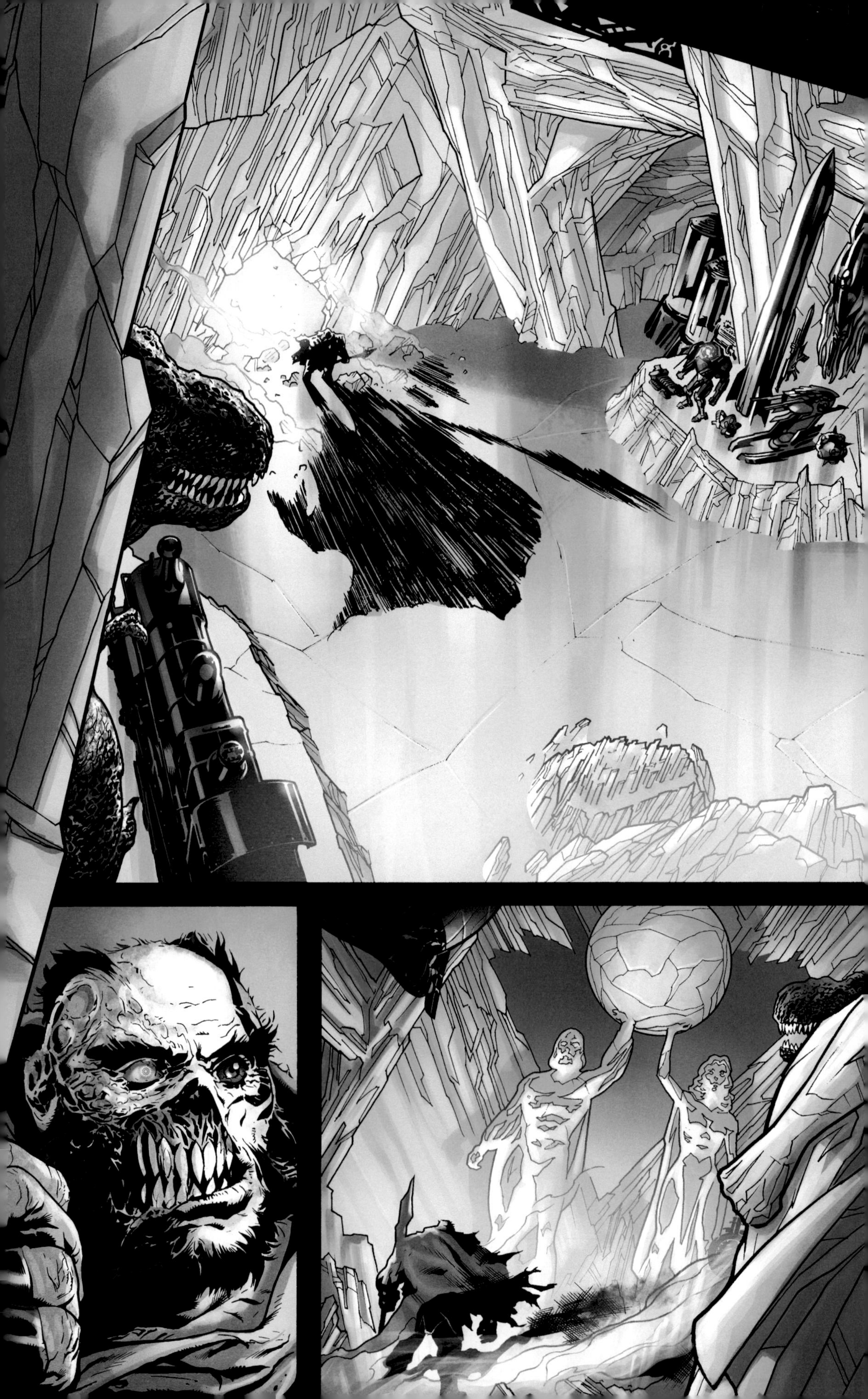

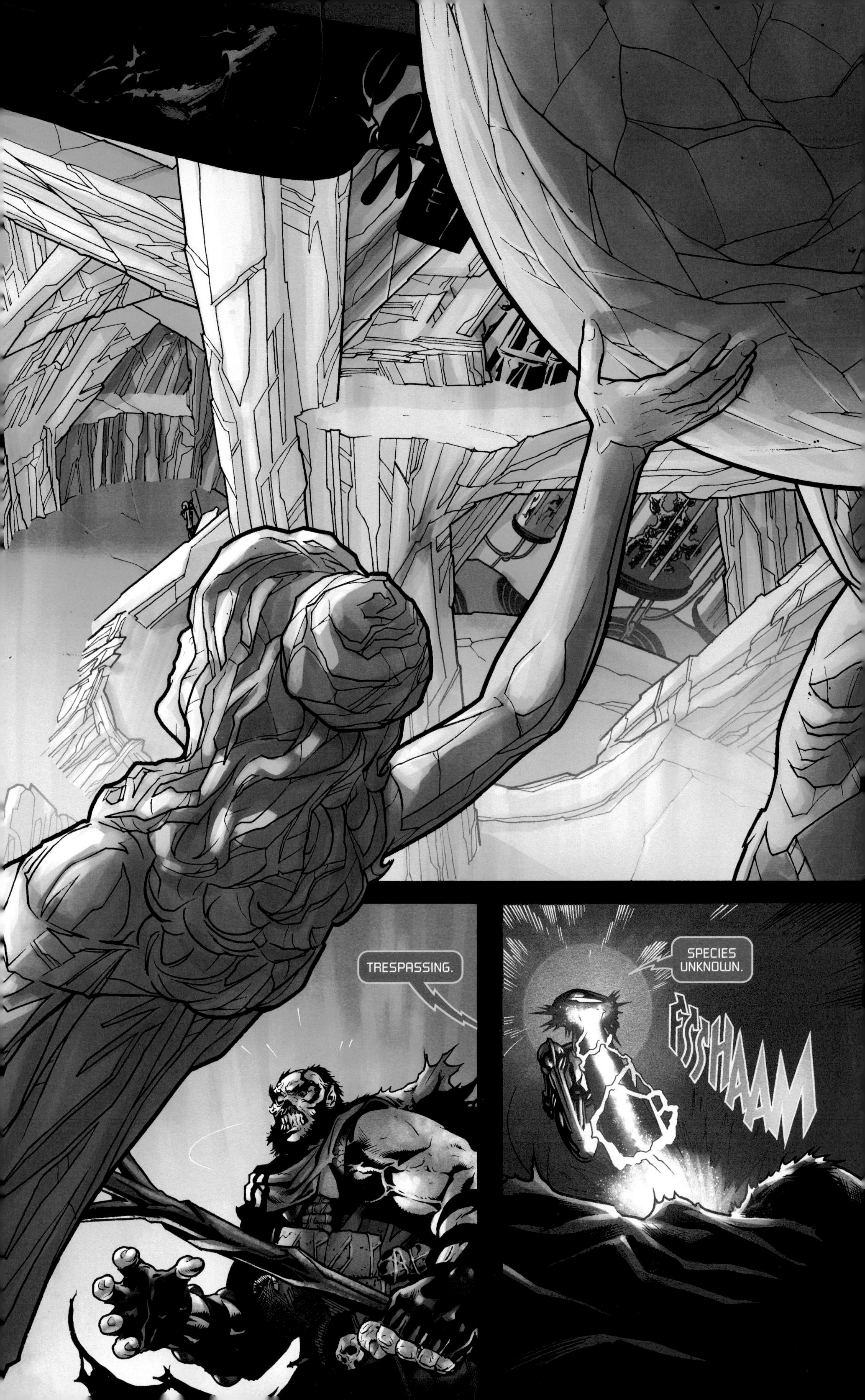
TRESPASSING.
SPECIES UNKNOWN.
FSSHAAM

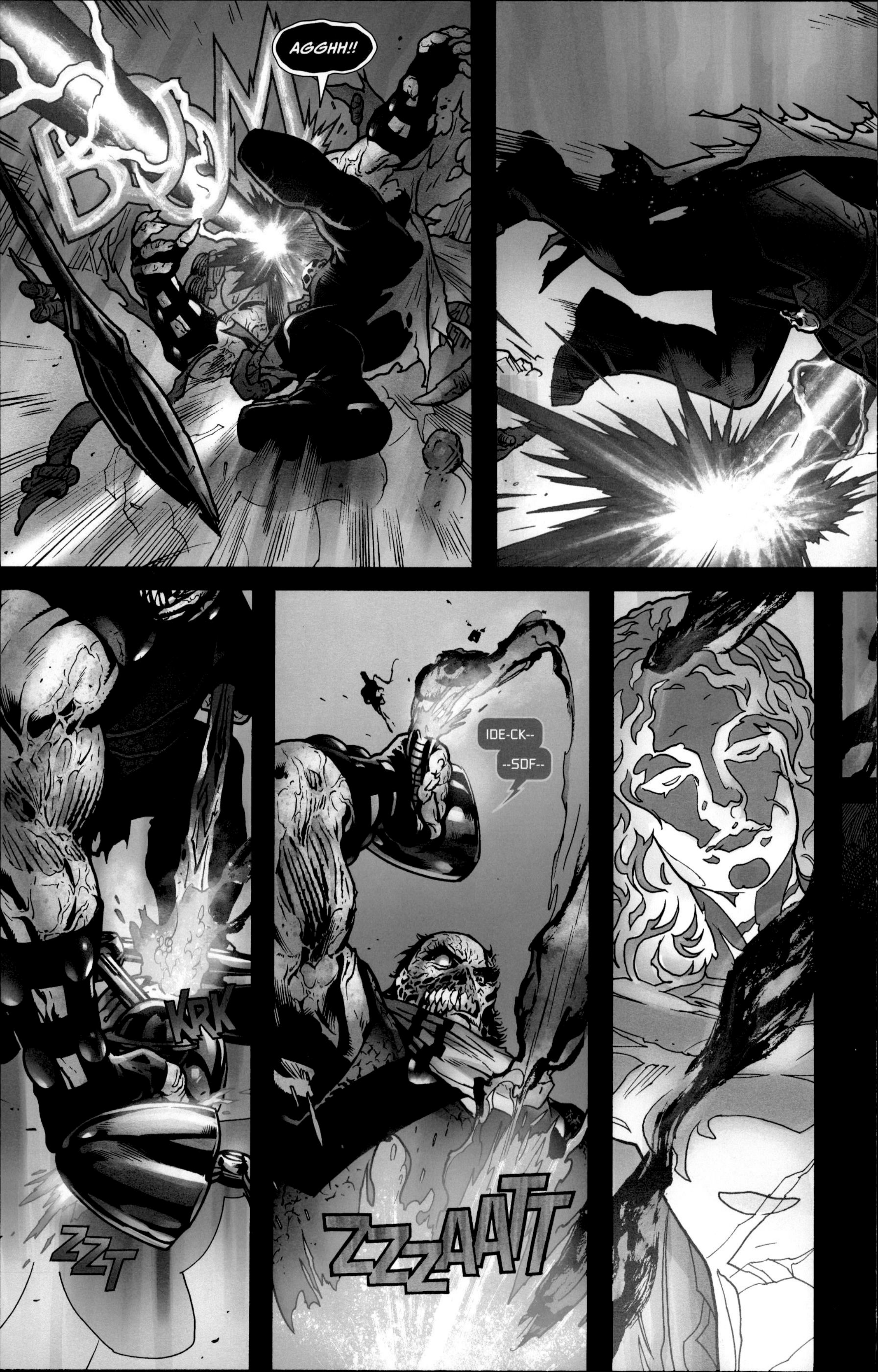
BOOM
AGGHH!!
IDE-CK--
--SDF--
KRK
ZZZT
ZZZZAATT

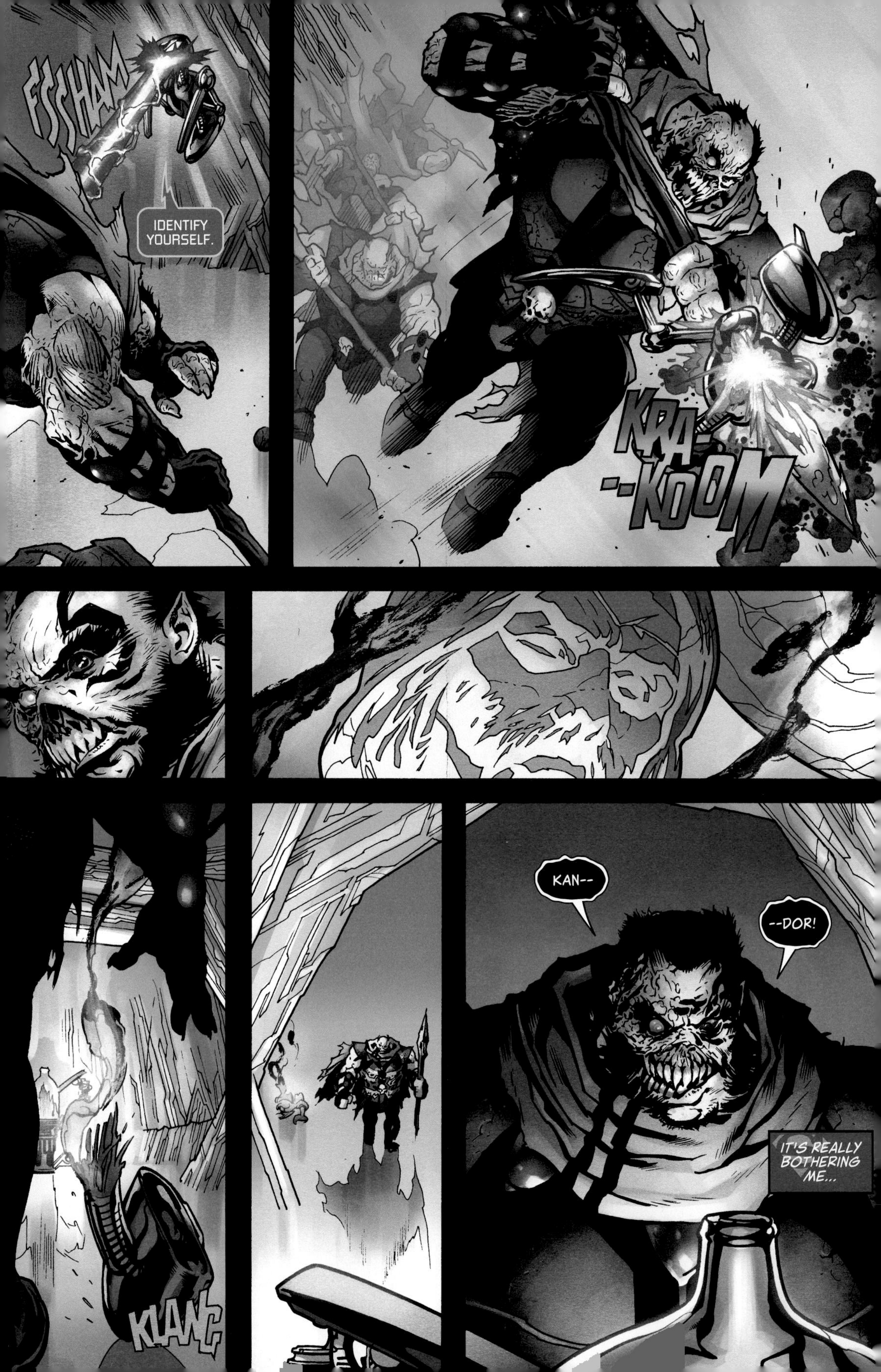
FSSHAM
IDENTIFY YOURSELF.
KRA- --KOOM
KLANG
KAN--
--DOR!
IT'S REALLY BOTHERING ME...

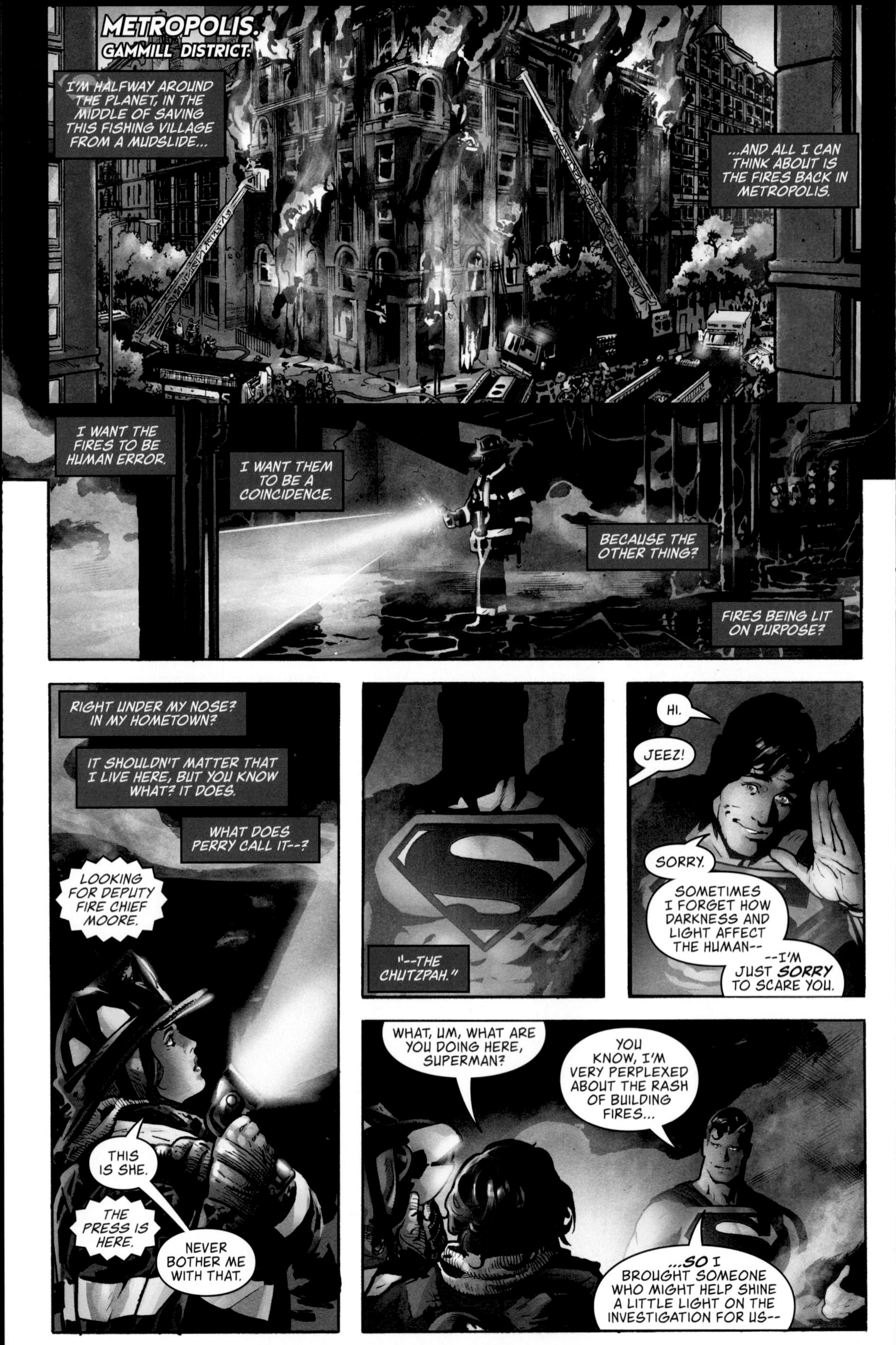
METROPOLIS.
GAMMILL DISTRICT.
I'M HALFWAY AROUND THE PLANET, IN THE MIDDLE OF SAVING THIS FISHING VILLAGE FROM A MUDSLIDE...
...AND ALL I CAN THINK ABOUT IS THE FIRES BACK IN METROPOLIS.
I WANT THE FIRES TO BE HUMAN ERROR.
I WANT THEM TO BE A COINCIDENCE.
BECAUSE THE OTHER THING?
FIRES BEING LIT ON PURPOSE?
RIGHT UNDER MY NOSE? IN MY HOMETOWN?
IT SHOULDN'T MATTER THAT I LIVE HERE, BUT YOU KNOW WHAT? IT DOES.
WHAT DOES PERRY CALL IT--?
LOOKING FOR DEPUTY FIRE CHIEF MOORE.
THIS IS SHE.
THE PRESS IS HERE.
NEVER BOTHER ME WITH THAT.
"--THE CHUTZPAH."
HI.
JEEZ!
SORRY.
SOMETIMES I FORGET HOW DARKNESS AND LIGHT AFFECT THE HUMAN--
--I'M JUST SORRY TO SCARE YOU.
WHAT, UM, WHAT ARE YOU DOING HERE, SUPERMAN?
YOU KNOW, I'M VERY PERPLEXED ABOUT THE RASH OF BUILDING FIRES...
...SO I BROUGHT SOMEONE WHO MIGHT HELP SHINE A LITTLE LIGHT ON THE INVESTIGATION FOR US--

OH !#$!@!

OKAY, I SCARED HER BY ACCIDENT.

YOU DID THAT ON PURPOSE.

I'M BATMAN.

YOU JUST COULDN'T HAVE HER NOT--

HOW MANY FIRES?

NINE.

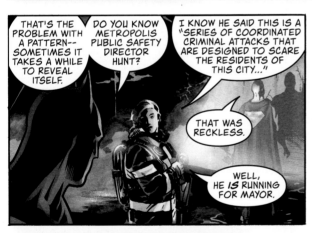

NINE? I THOUGHT IT WAS SEVEN.

I'M INCLUDING A COUPLE FROM BEFORE I JOINED METRO FIRE.

BEFORE ANYONE EVEN CONSIDERED THESE MIGHT BE A PART OF AN ACTUAL RASH OF SUSPICIOUS FIRES.

THAT'S THE PROBLEM WITH A PATTERN-- SOMETIMES IT TAKES A WHILE TO REVEAL ITSELF.

DO YOU KNOW METROPOLIS PUBLIC SAFETY DIRECTOR HUNT?

I KNOW HE SAID THIS IS A "SERIES OF COORDINATED CRIMINAL ATTACKS THAT ARE DESIGNED TO SCARE THE RESIDENTS OF THIS CITY..."

THAT WAS RECKLESS.

WELL, HE IS RUNNING FOR MAYOR.

PRACTICALLY ANYTHING THAT COULD ESTABLISH OR ARGUE HIS POINT WAS DESTROYED BY THE FIRE.

PLUS, THERE ARE SEVERAL POSSIBLE IGNITION POINTS AND SOURCES.

ANYTHING ON YOUR X-RAY OR OTHER ASSORTED SUPER-SENSES?

AN ALARM.

A SOUND ONLY SOMEONE LIKE ME CAN HEAR.

HAVE YOU MADE A LOCATION MAP OF THE FIRES? PINNED THEM?

OF COURSE.

SOMETIMES THEY MAKE A SHAPE.

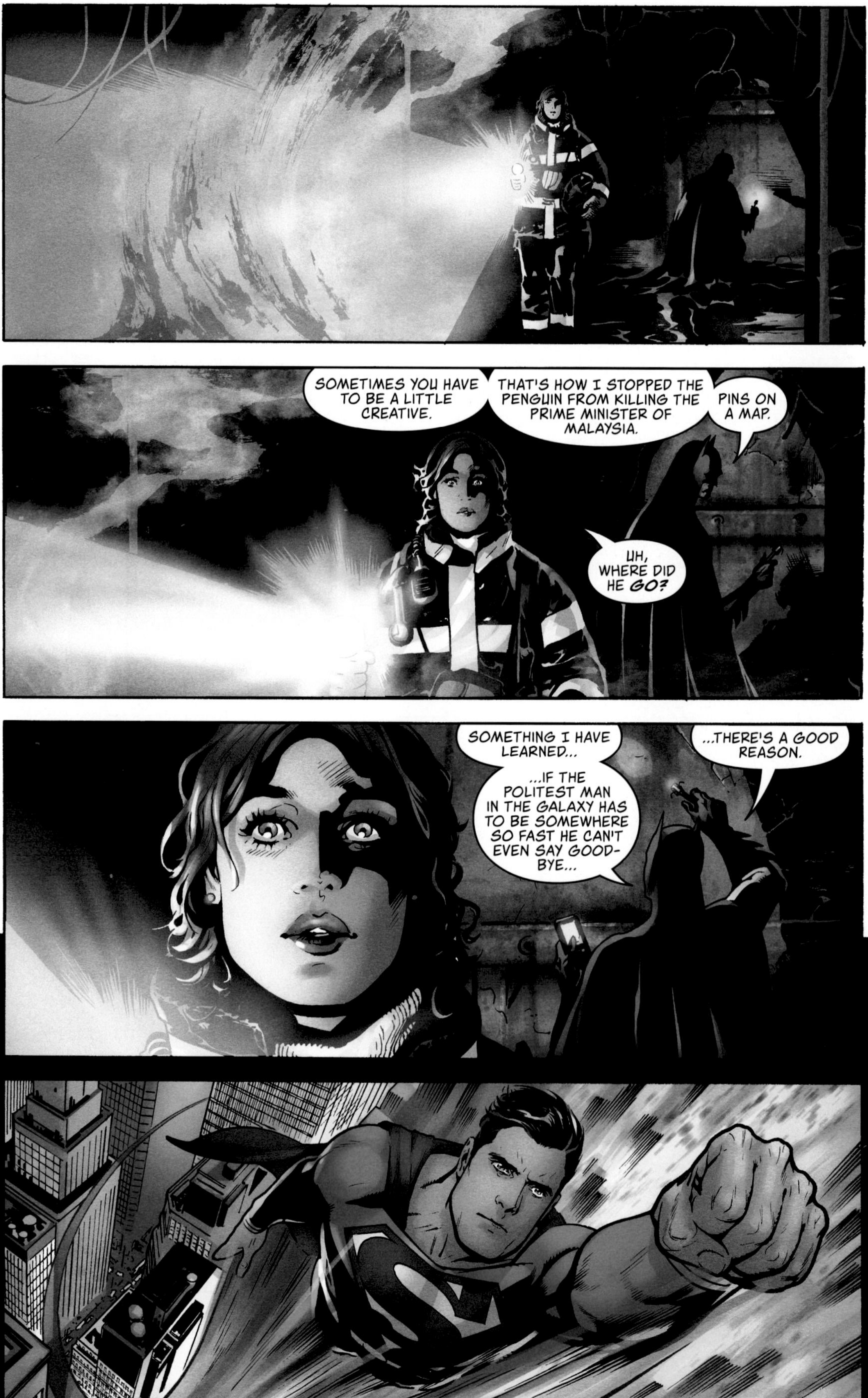
SOMETIMES YOU HAVE TO BE A LITTLE CREATIVE.
THAT'S HOW I STOPPED THE PENGUIN FROM KILLING THE PRIME MINISTER OF MALAYSIA.
PINS ON A MAP.
UH, WHERE DID HE GO?
SOMETHING I HAVE LEARNED...
...IF THE POLITEST MAN IN THE GALAXY HAS TO BE SOMEWHERE SO FAST HE CAN'T EVEN SAY GOOD-BYE...
...THERE'S A GOOD REASON.

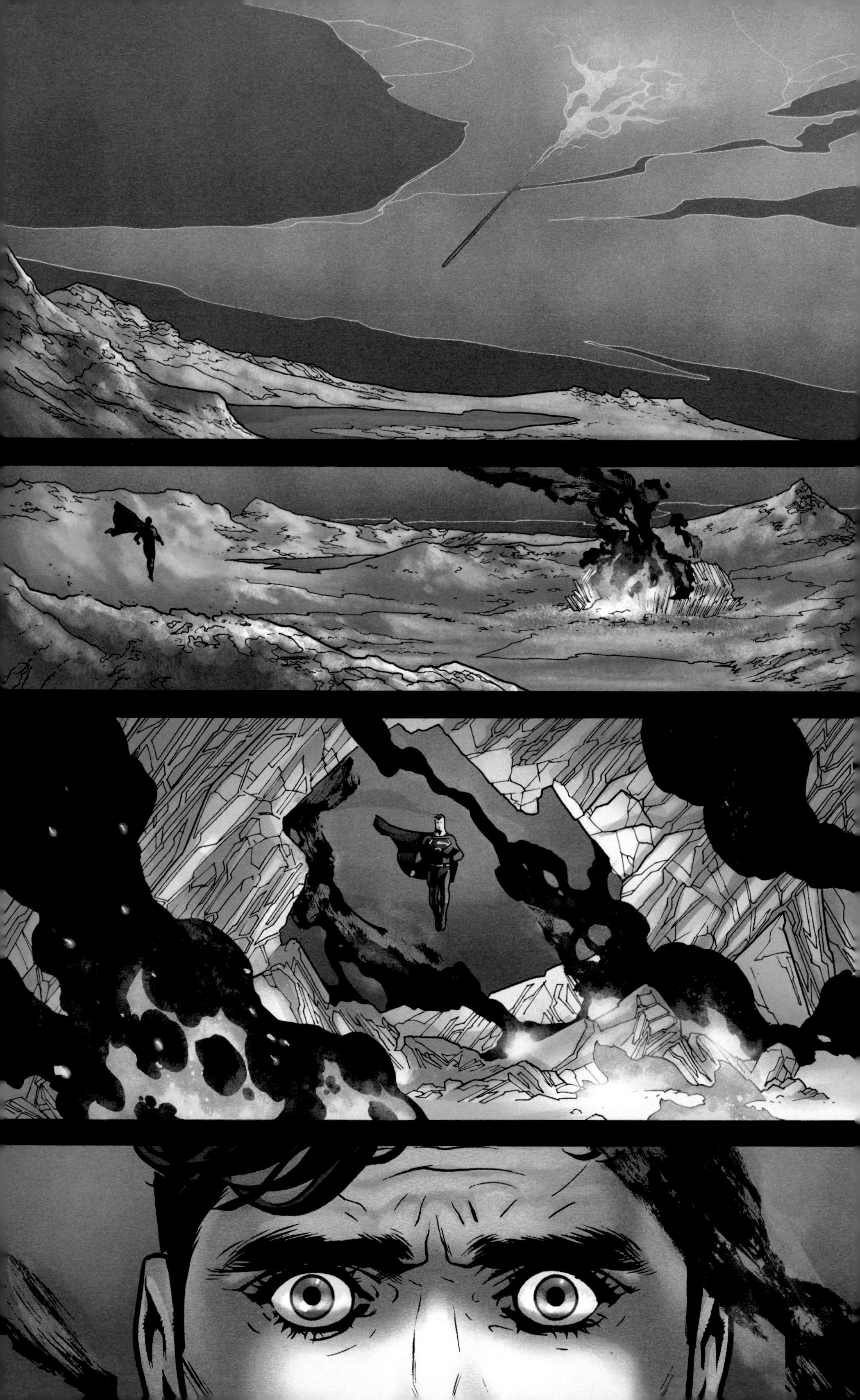

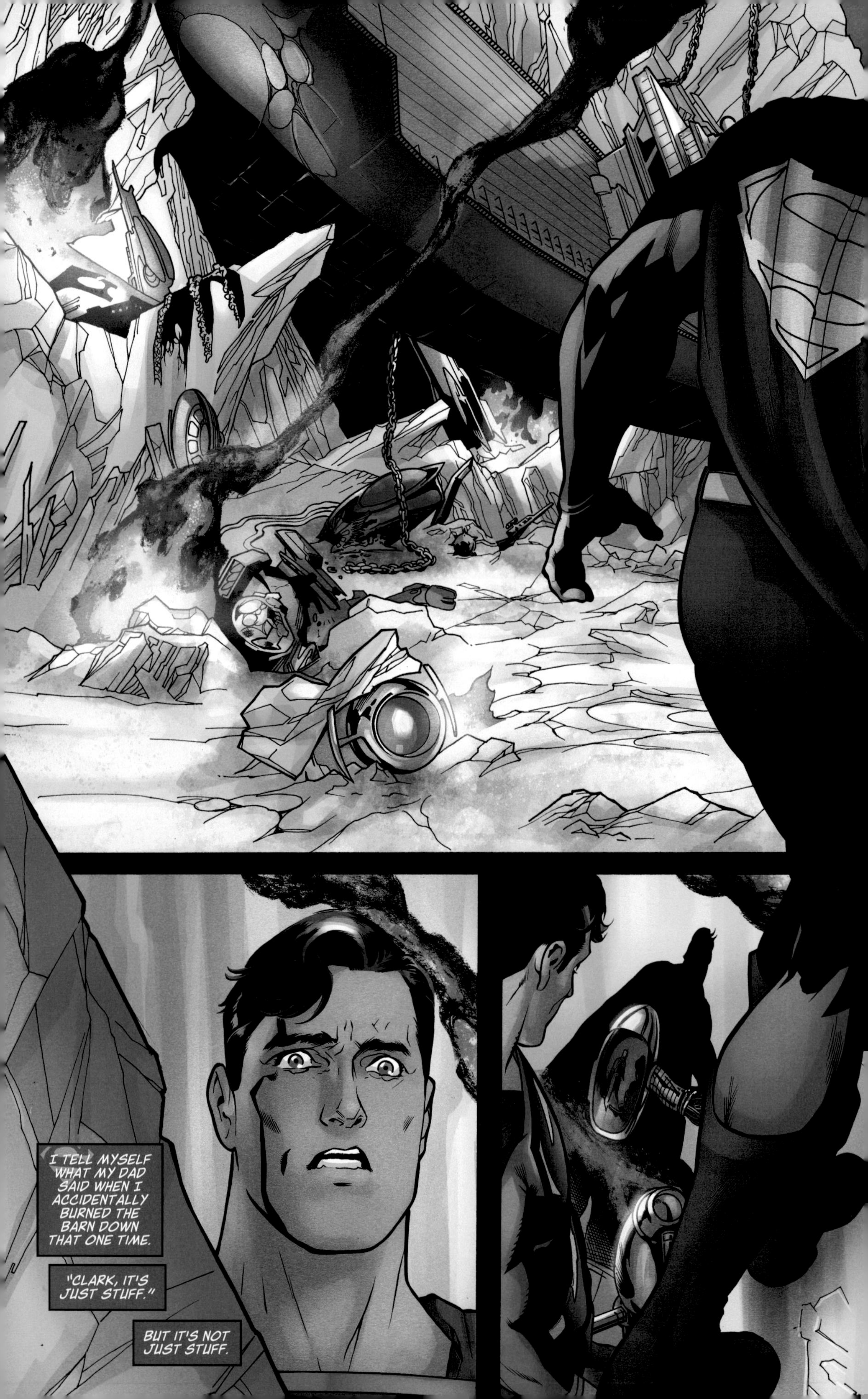
I TELL MYSELF WHAT MY DAD SAID WHEN I ACCIDENTALLY BURNED THE BARN DOWN THAT ONE TIME.
"CLARK, IT'S JUST STUFF."
BUT IT'S NOT JUST STUFF.

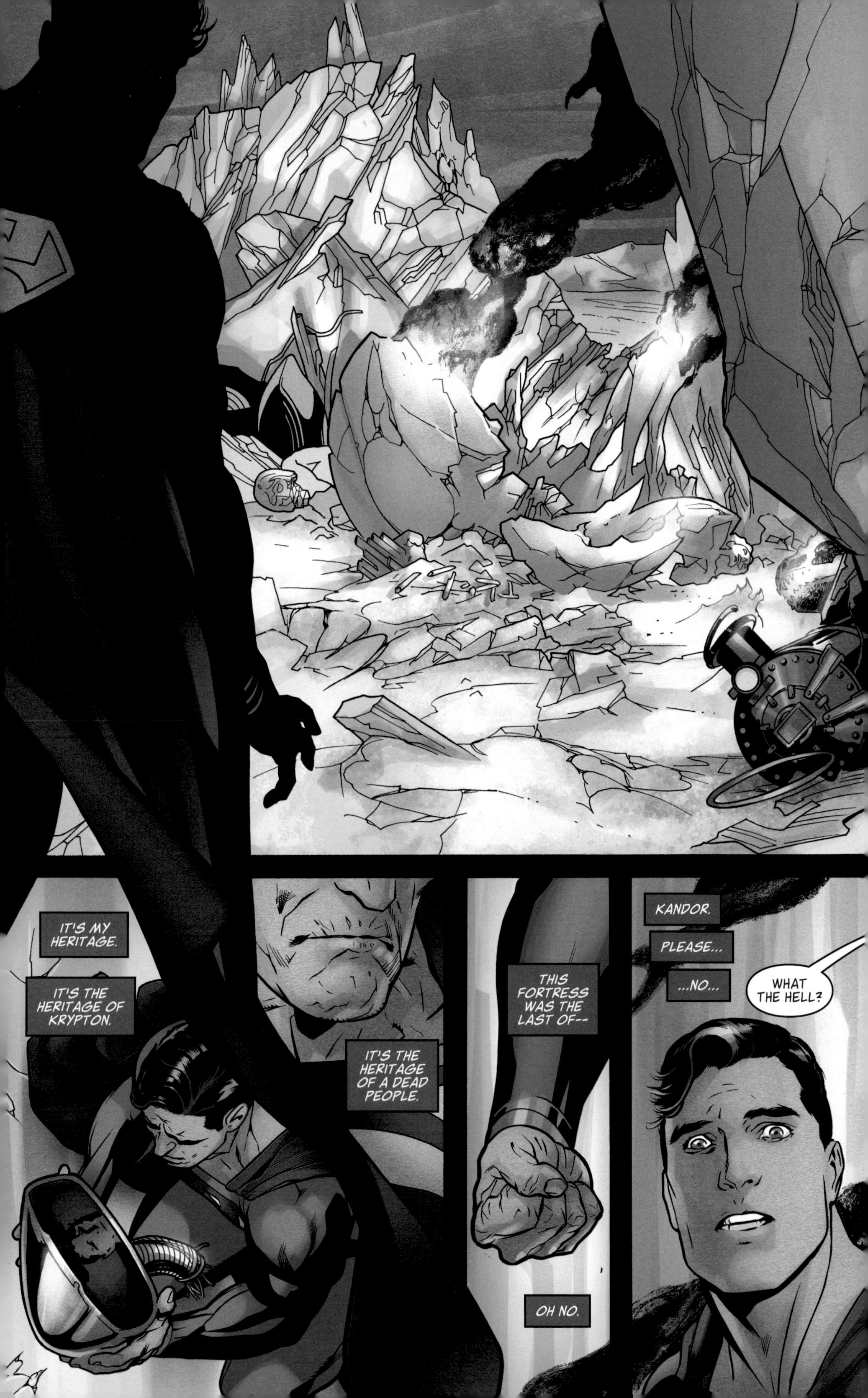
IT'S MY HERITAGE.
IT'S THE HERITAGE OF KRYPTON.
IT'S THE HERITAGE OF A DEAD PEOPLE.
THIS FORTRESS WAS THE LAST OF--
OH NO.
KANDOR.
PLEASE...
...NO...
WHAT THE HELL?

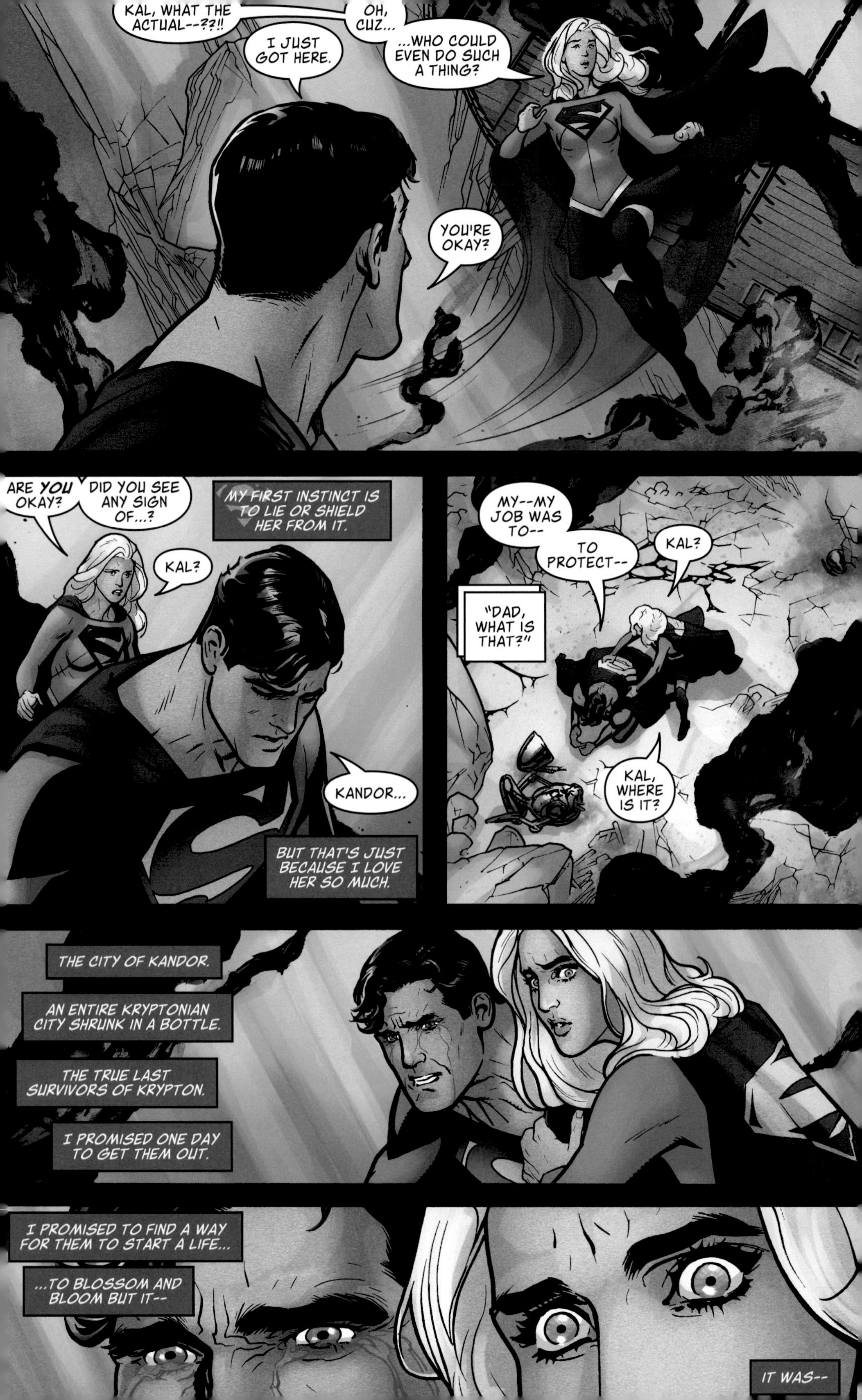
KAL, WHAT THE ACTUAL--??!!
I JUST GOT HERE.
OH, CUZ...
...WHO COULD EVEN DO SUCH A THING?
YOU'RE OKAY?
ARE YOU OKAY?
DID YOU SEE ANY SIGN OF...?
MY FIRST INSTINCT IS TO LIE OR SHIELD HER FROM IT.
KAL?
KANDOR...
BUT THAT'S JUST BECAUSE I LOVE HER SO MUCH.
MY--MY JOB WAS TO--
TO PROTECT--
KAL?
"DAD, WHAT IS THAT?"
KAL, WHERE IS IT?
THE CITY OF KANDOR.
AN ENTIRE KRYPTONIAN CITY SHRUNK IN A BOTTLE.
THE TRUE LAST SURVIVORS OF KRYPTON.
I PROMISED ONE DAY TO GET THEM OUT.
I PROMISED TO FIND A WAY FOR THEM TO START A LIFE...
...TO BLOSSOM AND BLOOM BUT IT--
IT WAS--

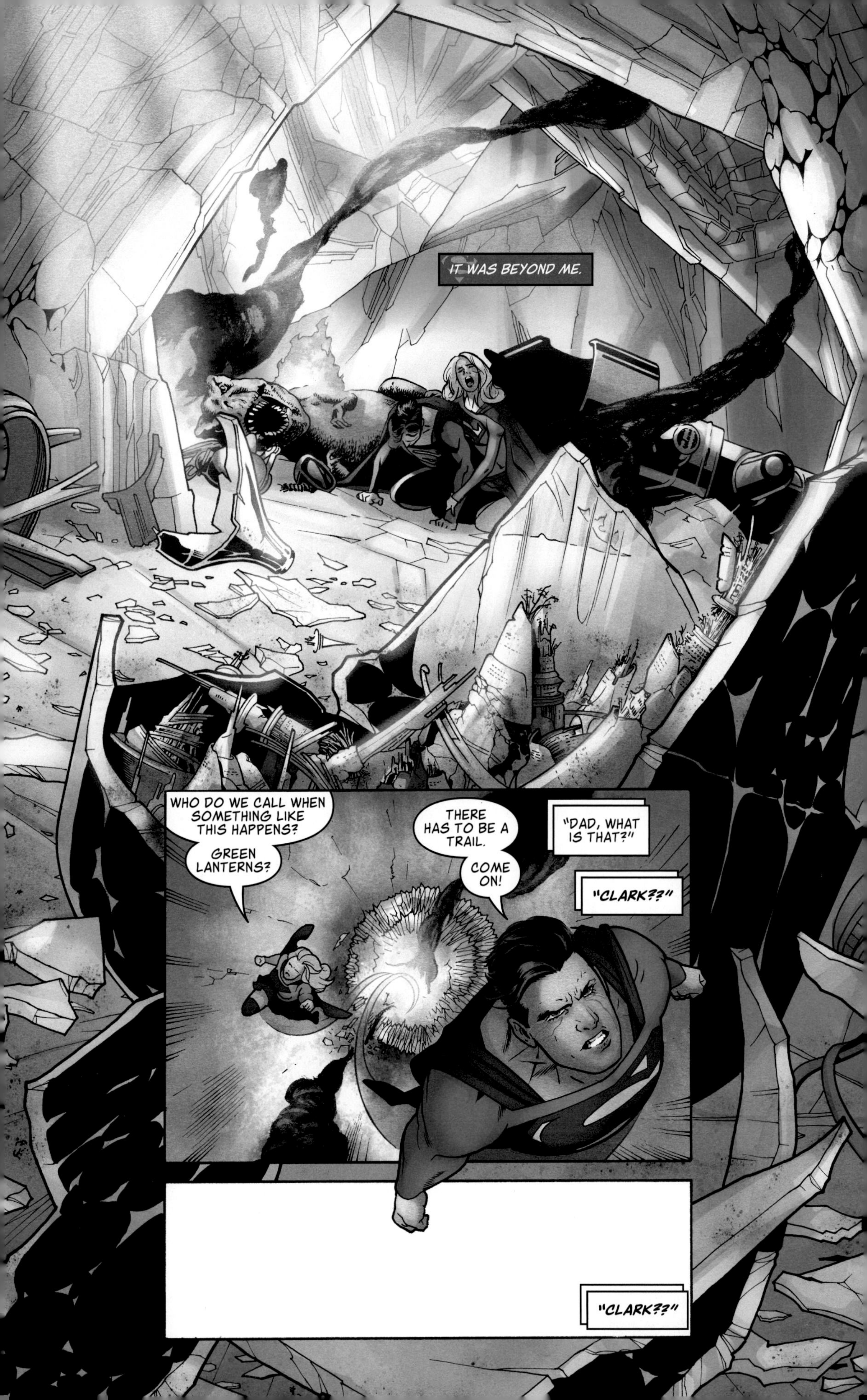

IT WAS BEYOND ME.
WHO DO WE CALL WHEN SOMETHING LIKE THIS HAPPENS?
GREEN LANTERNS?
THERE HAS TO BE A TRAIL.
COME ON!
"DAD, WHAT IS THAT?"
"CLARK??"
"CLARK??"

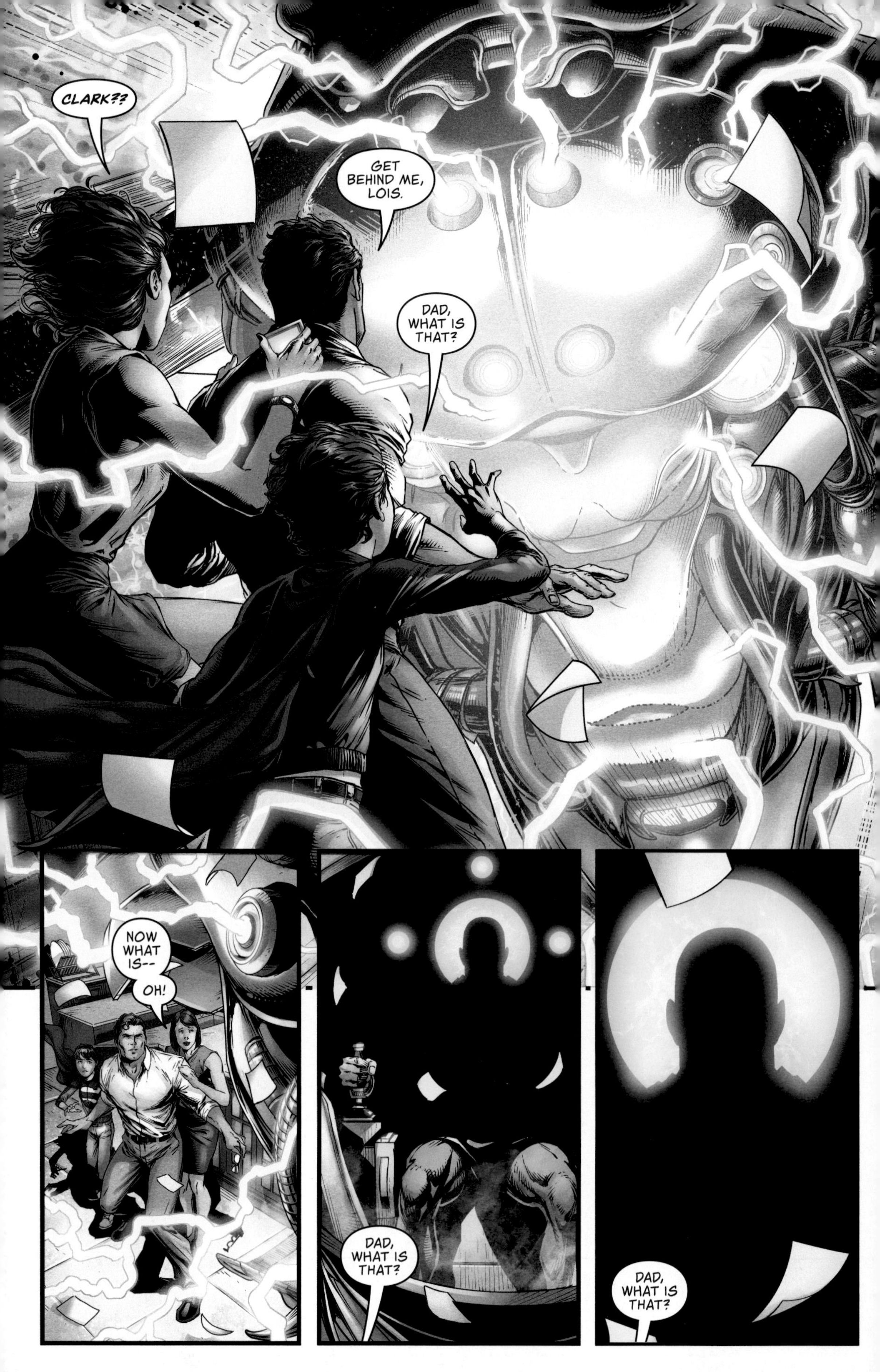
CLARK??
GET BEHIND ME, LOIS.
DAD, WHAT IS THAT?
NOW WHAT IS--
OH!
DAD, WHAT IS THAT?
DAD, WHAT IS THAT?

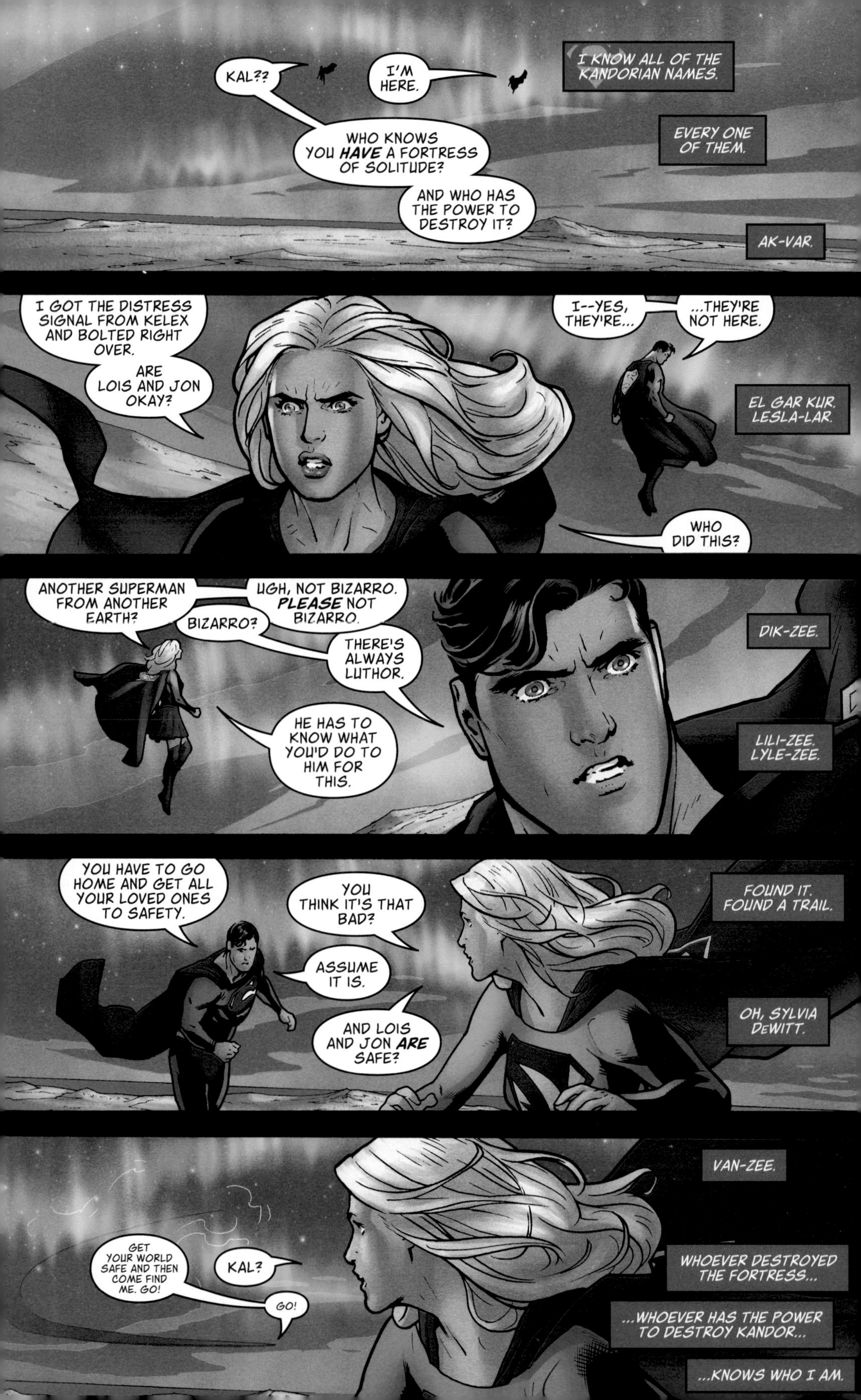
KAL??
I'M HERE.
WHO KNOWS YOU HAVE A FORTRESS OF SOLITUDE?
AND WHO HAS THE POWER TO DESTROY IT?
I KNOW ALL OF THE KANDORIAN NAMES.
EVERY ONE OF THEM.
AK-VAR.
I GOT THE DISTRESS SIGNAL FROM KELEX AND BOLTED RIGHT OVER.
ARE LOIS AND JON OKAY?
I--YES, THEY'RE...
...THEY'RE NOT HERE.
EL GAR KUR. LESLA-LAR.
WHO DID THIS?
ANOTHER SUPERMAN FROM ANOTHER EARTH?
UGH, NOT BIZARRO. PLEASE NOT BIZARRO.
BIZARRO?
THERE'S ALWAYS LUTHOR.
HE HAS TO KNOW WHAT YOU'D DO TO HIM FOR THIS.
DIK-ZEE.
LILI-ZEE. LYLE-ZEE.
YOU HAVE TO GO HOME AND GET ALL YOUR LOVED ONES TO SAFETY.
YOU THINK IT'S THAT BAD?
ASSUME IT IS.
AND LOIS AND JON ARE SAFE?
FOUND IT. FOUND A TRAIL.
OH, SYLVIA DEWITT.
VAN-ZEE.
GET YOUR WORLD SAFE AND THEN COME FIND ME. GO!
KAL?
GO!
WHOEVER DESTROYED THE FORTRESS...
...WHOEVER HAS THE POWER TO DESTROY KANDOR...
...KNOWS WHO I AM.

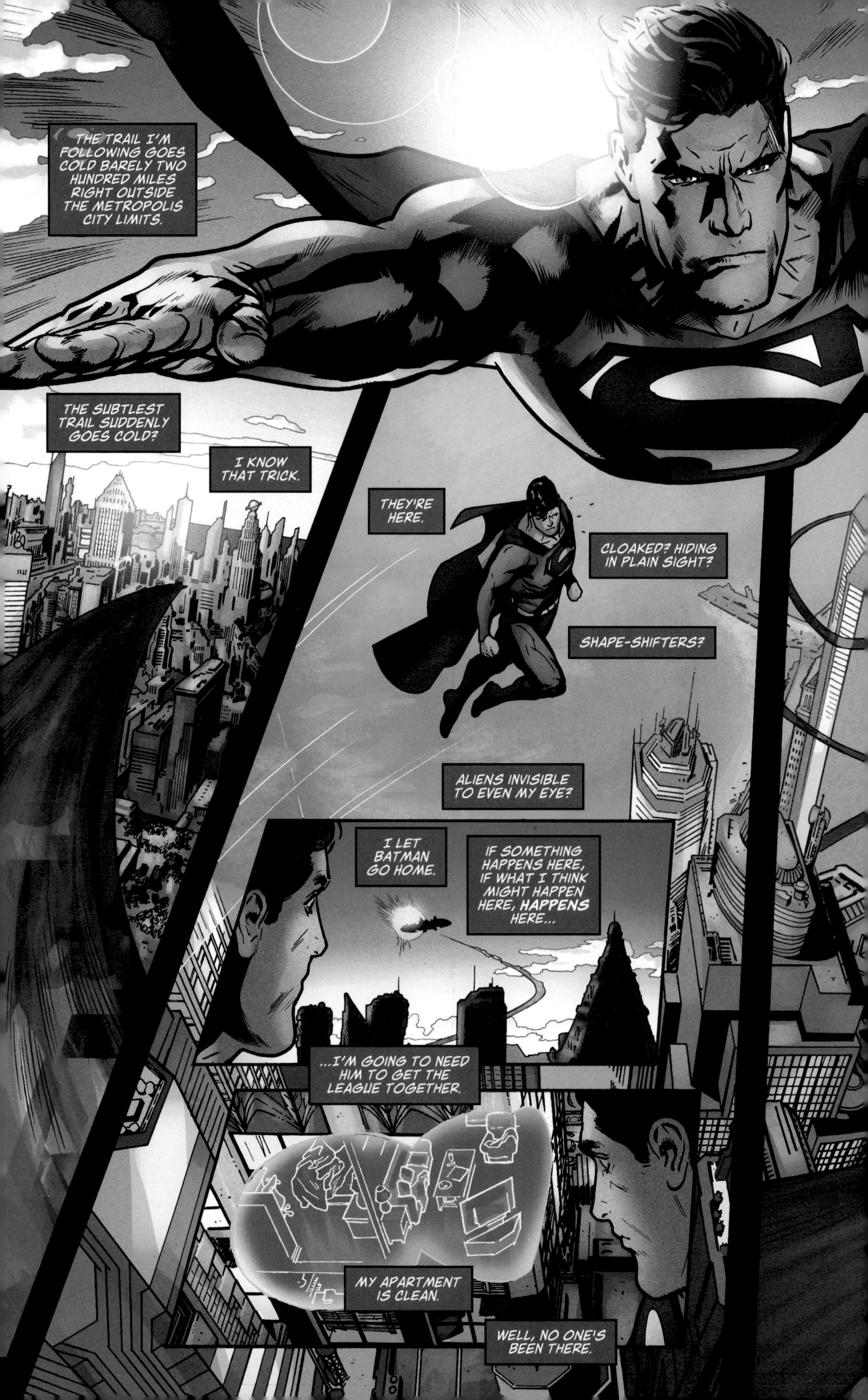
THE TRAIL I'M FOLLOWING GOES COLD BARELY TWO HUNDRED MILES RIGHT OUTSIDE THE METROPOLIS CITY LIMITS.
THE SUBTLEST TRAIL SUDDENLY GOES COLD?
I KNOW THAT TRICK.
THEY'RE HERE.
CLOAKED? HIDING IN PLAIN SIGHT?
SHAPE-SHIFTERS?
ALIENS INVISIBLE TO EVEN MY EYE?
I LET BATMAN GO HOME.
IF SOMETHING HAPPENS HERE, IF WHAT I THINK MIGHT HAPPEN HERE, **HAPPENS** HERE...
...I'M GOING TO NEED HIM TO GET THE LEAGUE TOGETHER.
MY APARTMENT IS CLEAN.
WELL, NO ONE'S BEEN THERE.

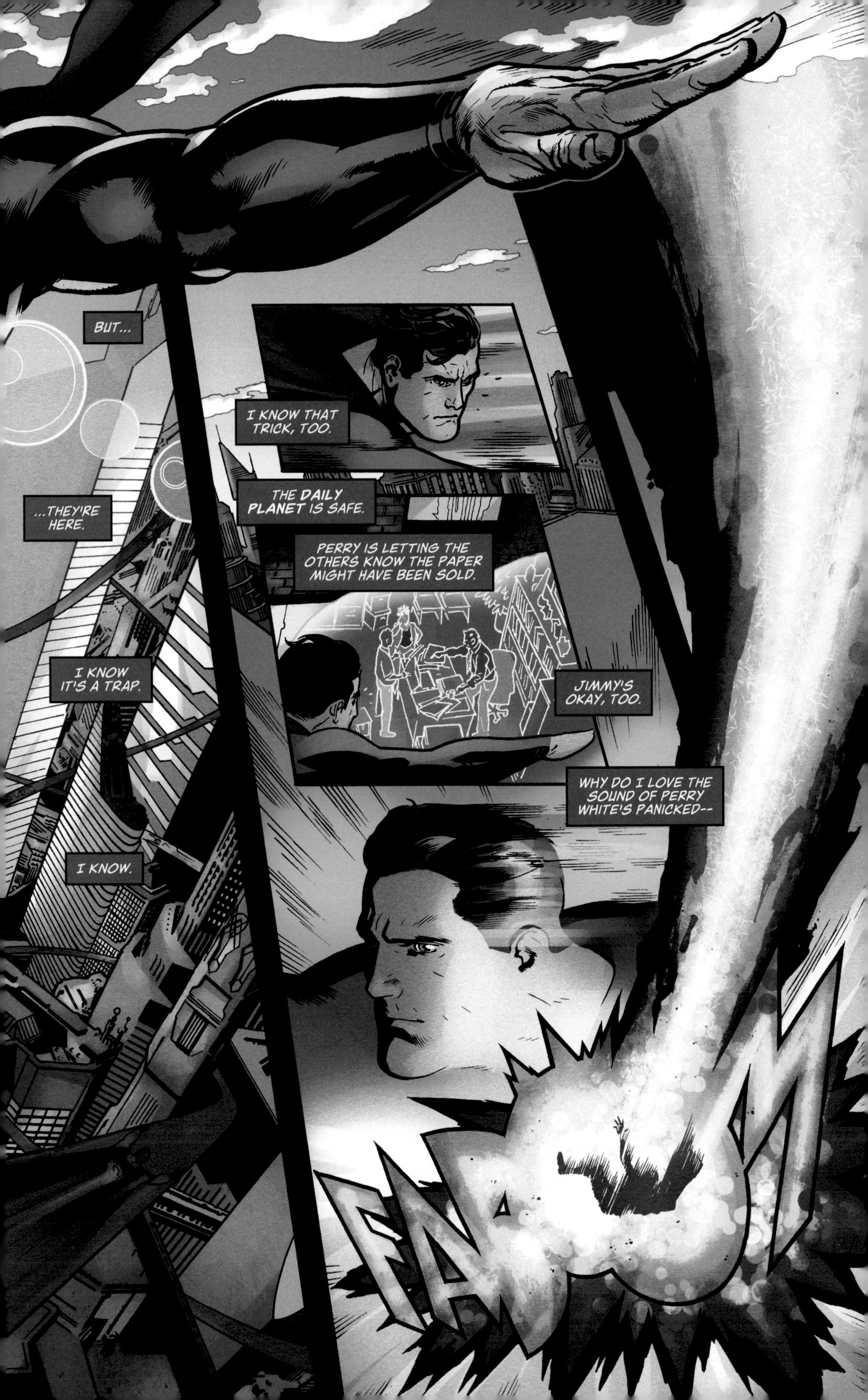
BUT...
...THEY'RE HERE.
I KNOW IT'S A TRAP.
I KNOW.
I KNOW THAT TRICK, TOO.
THE DAILY PLANET IS SAFE.
PERRY IS LETTING THE OTHERS KNOW THE PAPER MIGHT HAVE BEEN SOLD.
JIMMY'S OKAY, TOO.
WHY DO I LOVE THE SOUND OF PERRY WHITE'S PANICKED--

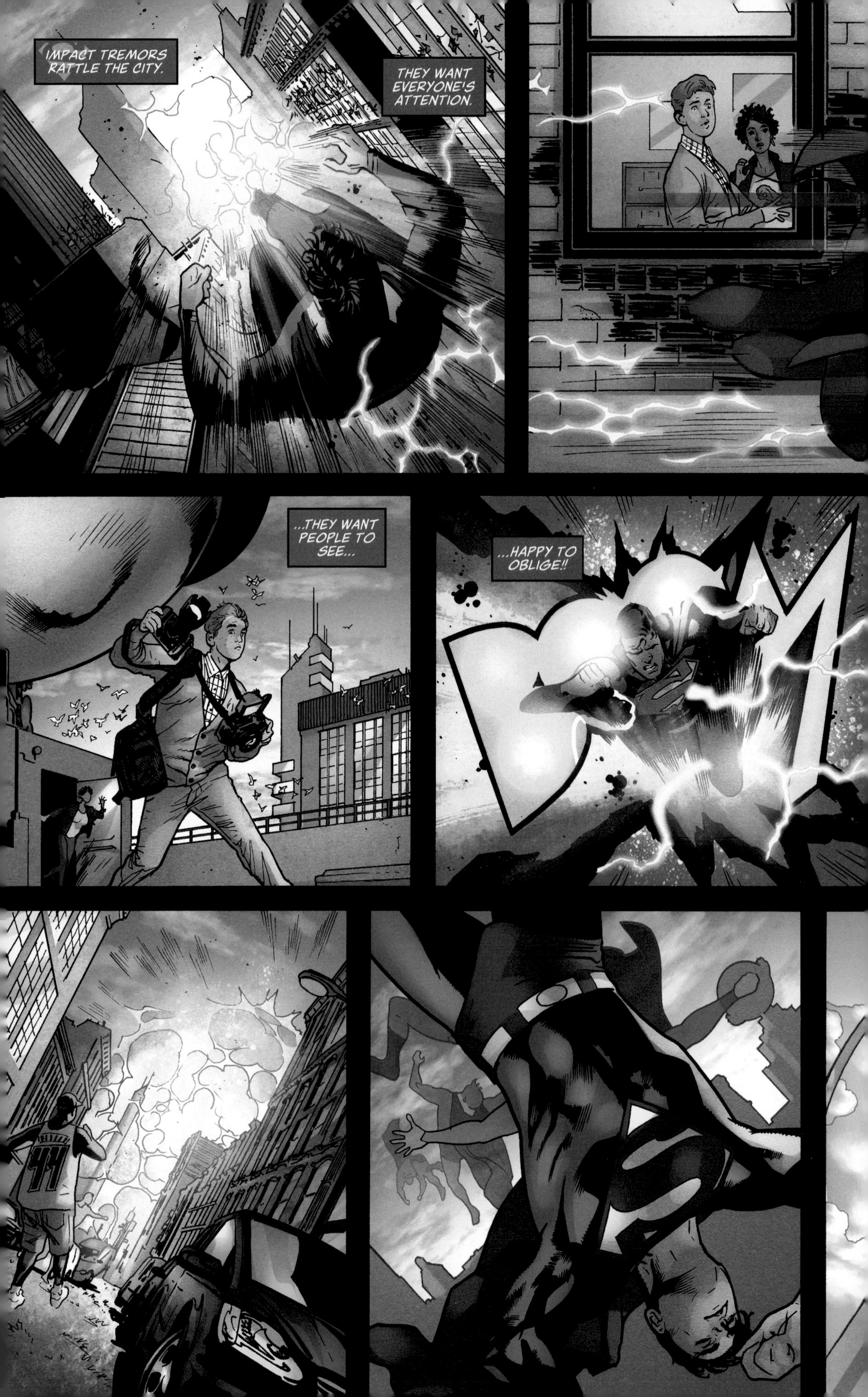
IMPACT TREMORS RATTLE THE CITY.
THEY WANT EVERYONE'S ATTENTION.
...THEY WANT PEOPLE TO SEE...
...HAPPY TO OBLIGE!!

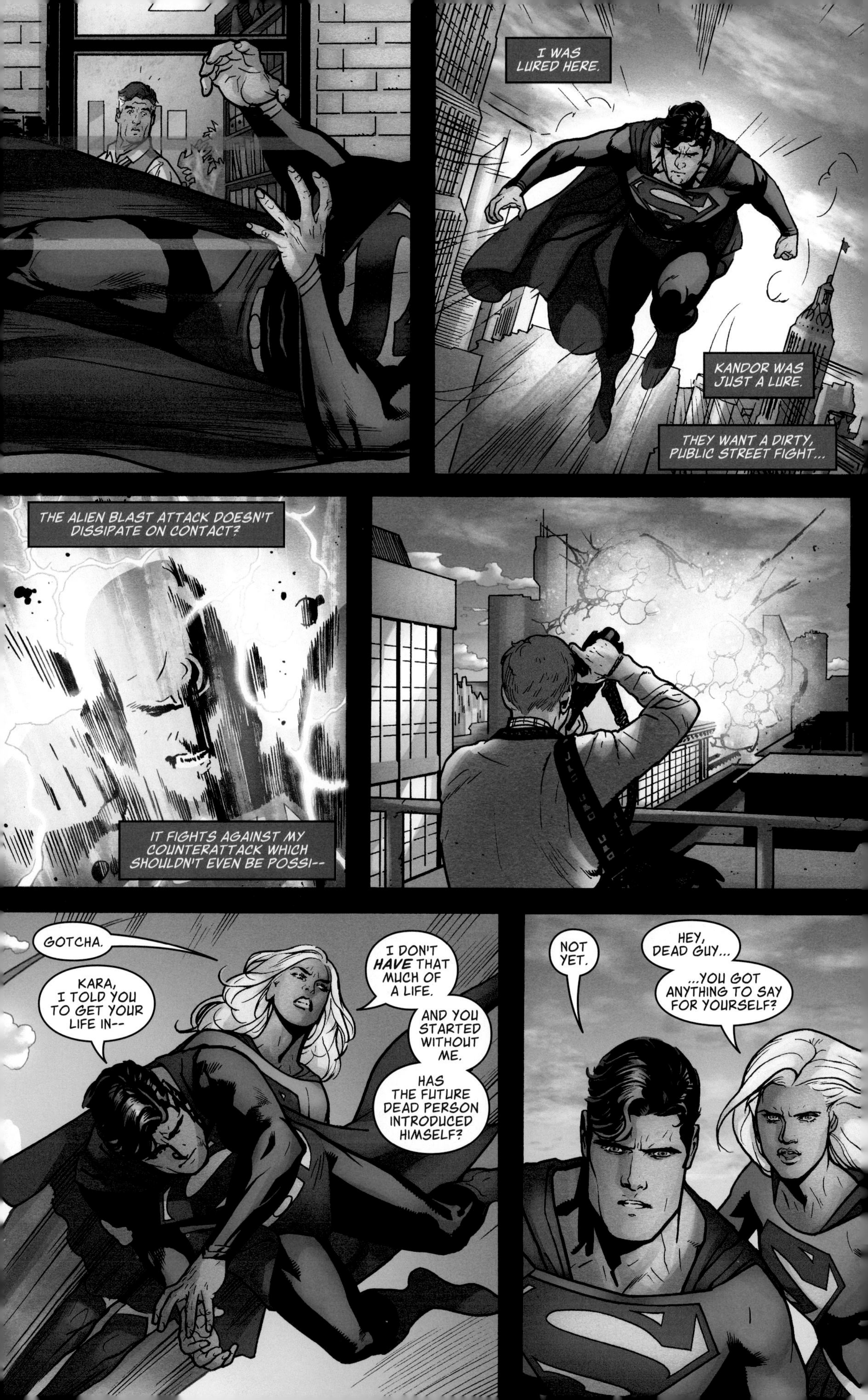
I WAS LURED HERE.
KANDOR WAS JUST A LURE.
THEY WANT A DIRTY, PUBLIC STREET FIGHT...
THE ALIEN BLAST ATTACK DOESN'T DISSIPATE ON CONTACT?
IT FIGHTS AGAINST MY COUNTERATTACK WHICH SHOULDN'T EVEN BE POSSI--
GOTCHA.
KARA, I TOLD YOU TO GET YOUR LIFE IN--
I DON'T HAVE THAT MUCH OF A LIFE.
AND YOU STARTED WITHOUT ME.
HAS THE FUTURE DEAD PERSON INTRODUCED HIMSELF?
NOT YET.
HEY, DEAD GUY...
...YOU GOT ANYTHING TO SAY FOR YOURSELF?

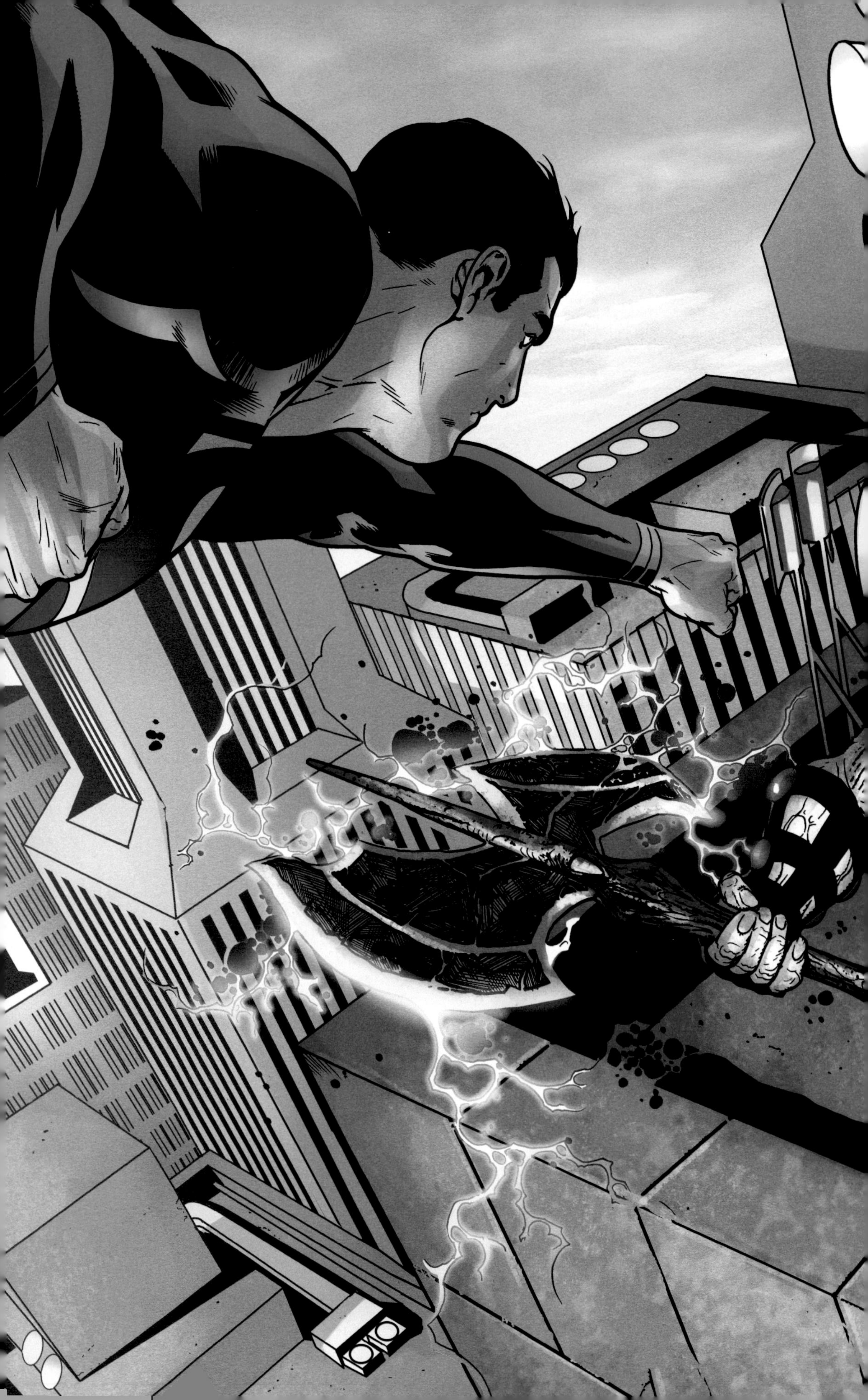

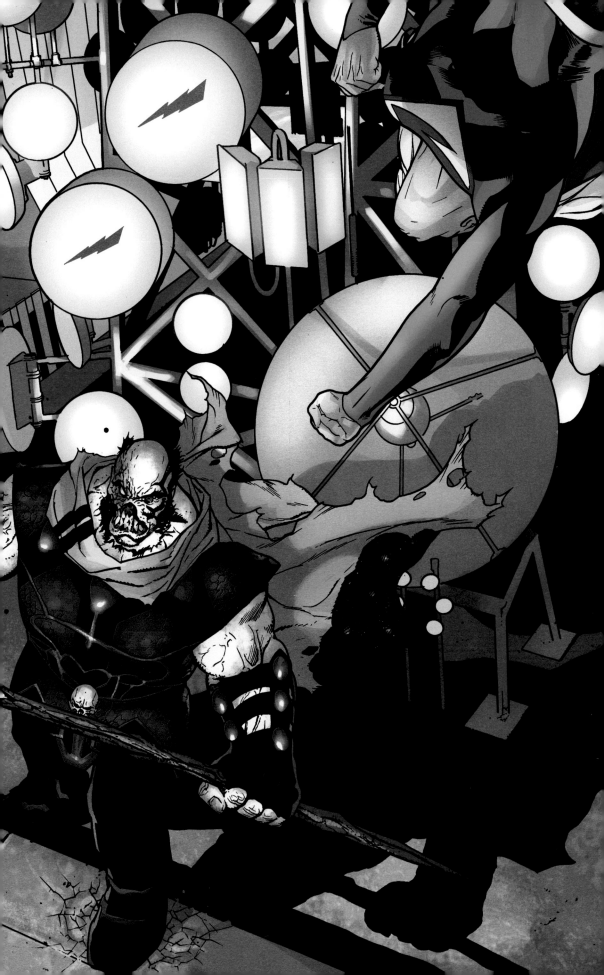

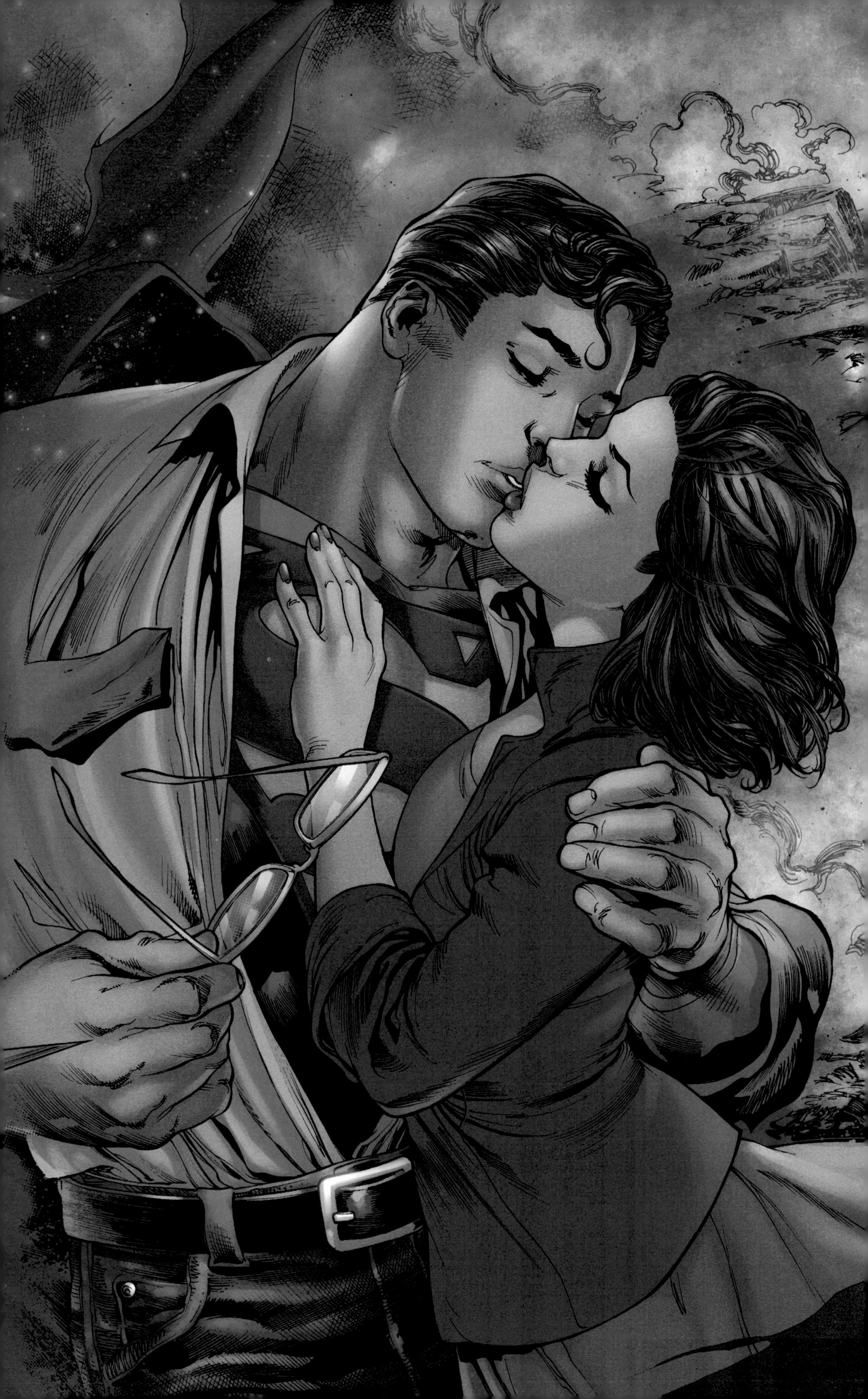

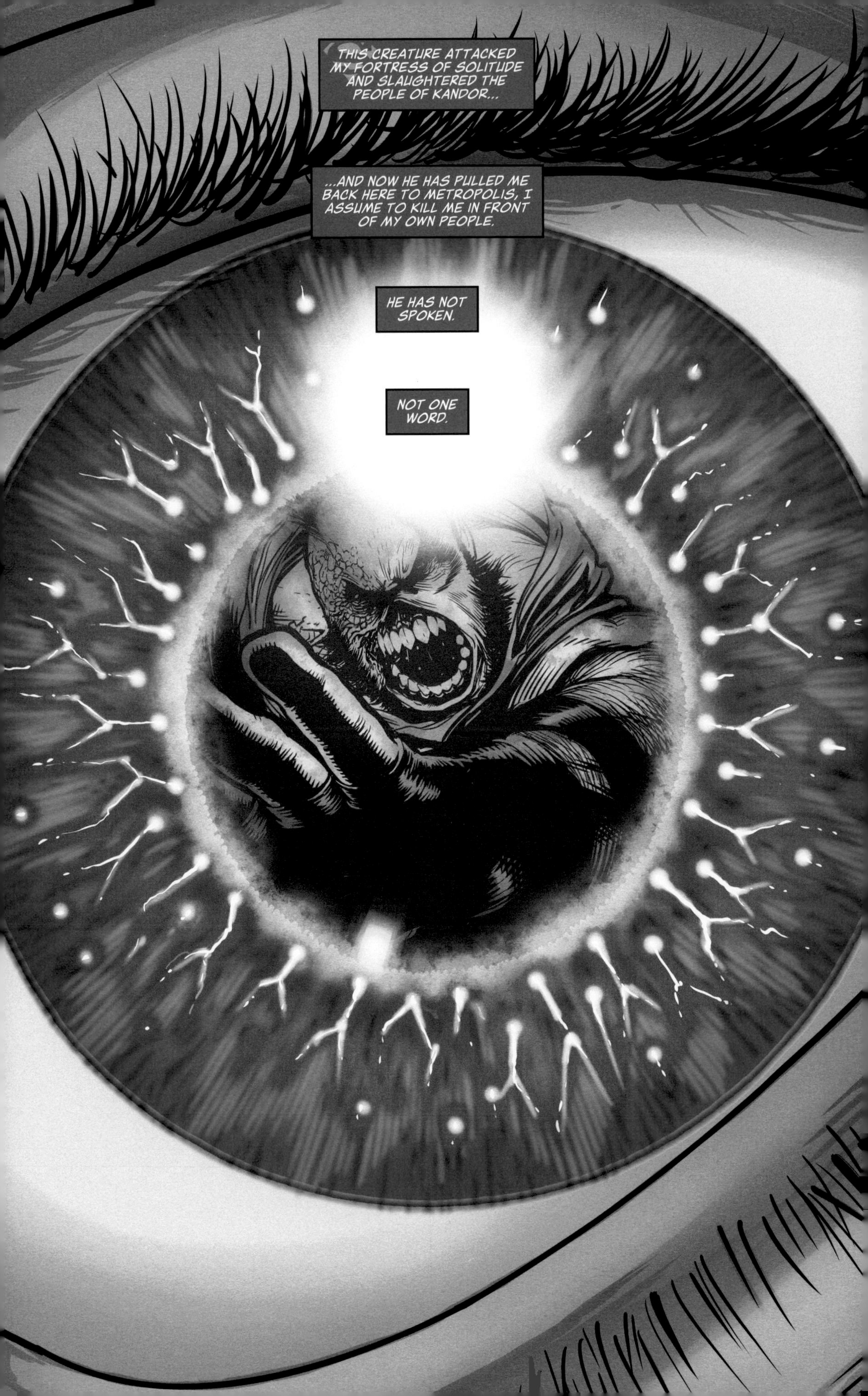
THIS CREATURE ATTACKED MY FORTRESS OF SOLITUDE AND SLAUGHTERED THE PEOPLE OF KANDOR...
...AND NOW HE HAS PULLED ME BACK HERE TO METROPOLIS, I ASSUME TO KILL ME IN FRONT OF MY OWN PEOPLE.
HE HAS NOT SPOKEN.
NOT ONE WORD.

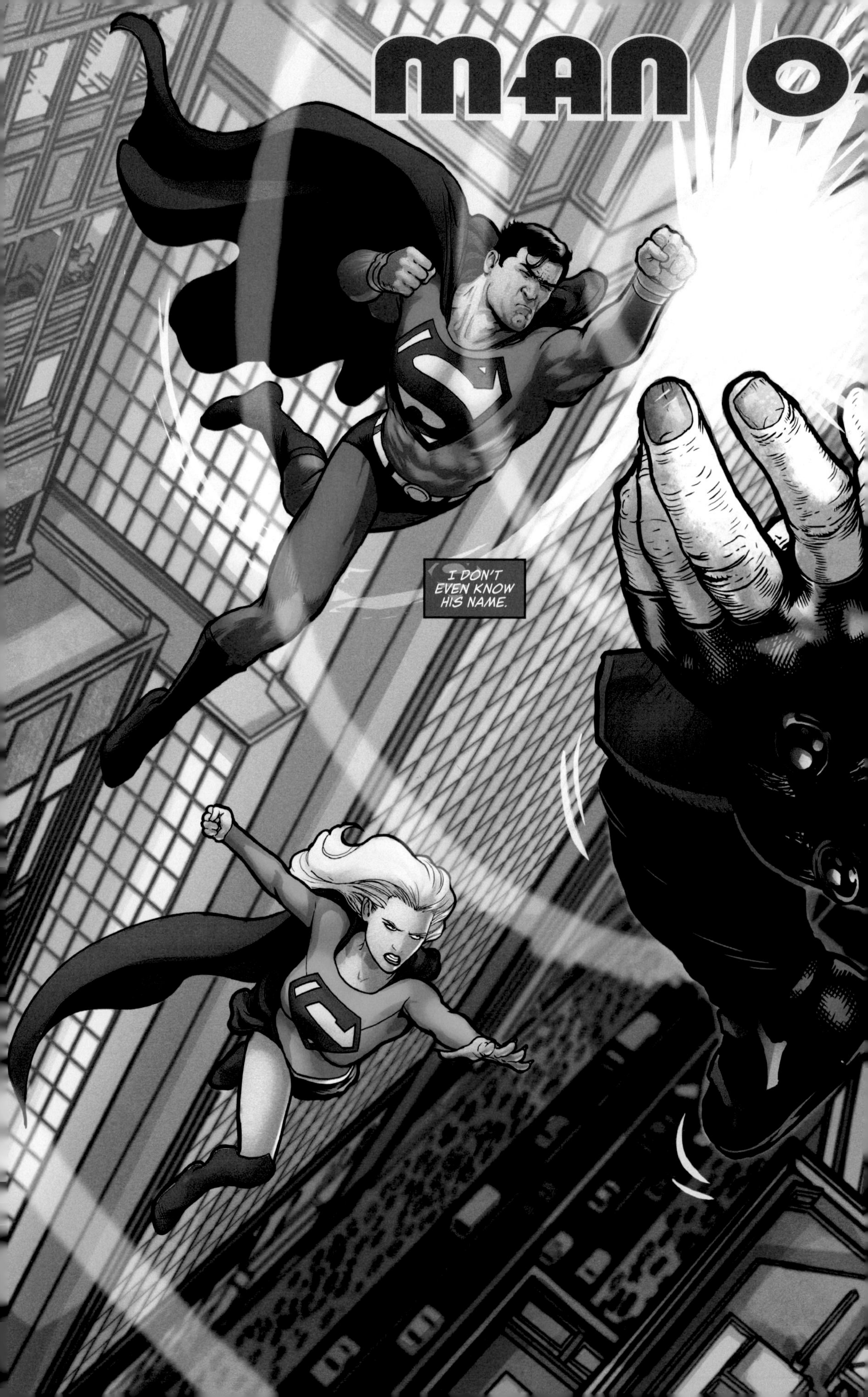
MAN O
I DON'T EVEN KNOW HIS NAME.

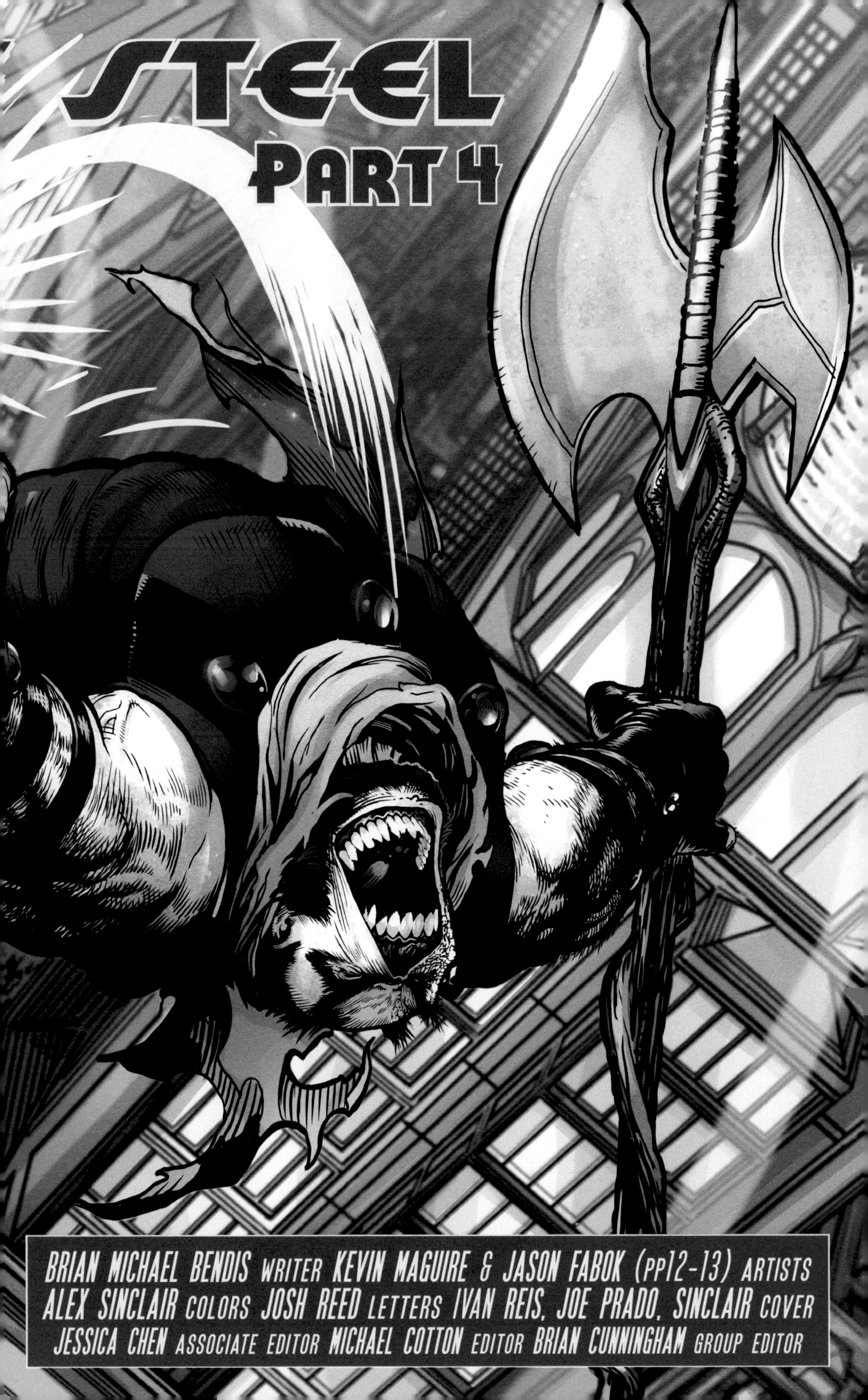
STEEL
PART 4

BRIAN MICHAEL BENDIS WRITER KEVIN MAGUIRE & JASON FABOK (PP12-13) ARTISTS
ALEX SINCLAIR COLORS JOSH REED LETTERS IVAN REIS, JOE PRADO, SINCLAIR COVER
JESSICA CHEN ASSOCIATE EDITOR MICHAEL COTTON EDITOR BRIAN CUNNINGHAM GROUP EDITOR

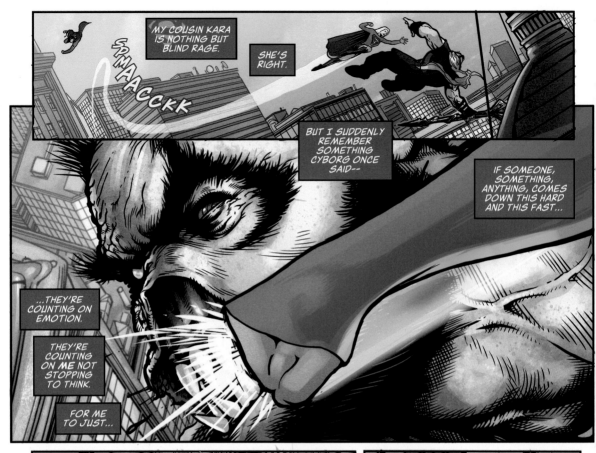

MY COUSIN KARA IS NOTHING BUT BLIND RAGE.

SHE'S RIGHT.

BUT I SUDDENLY REMEMBER SOMETHING CYBORG ONCE SAID--

IF SOMEONE, SOMETHING, ANYTHING, COMES DOWN THIS HARD AND THIS FAST...

...THEY'RE COUNTING ON EMOTION.

THEY'RE COUNTING ON ME NOT STOPPING TO THINK.

FOR ME TO JUST...

SMACK

...REACT.

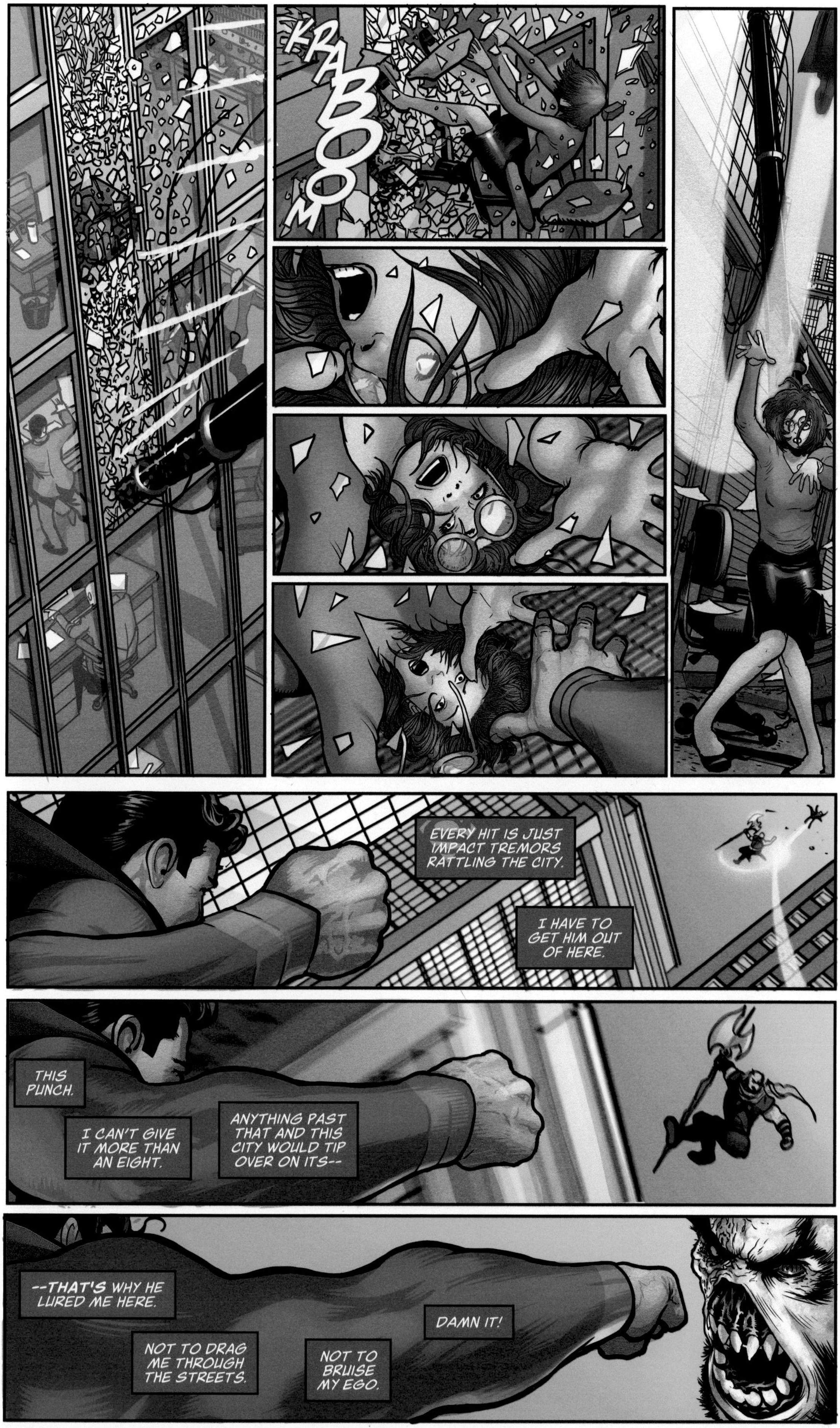
KRABOOOM
EVERY HIT IS JUST IMPACT TREMORS RATTLING THE CITY.
I HAVE TO GET HIM OUT OF HERE.
THIS PUNCH.
I CAN'T GIVE IT MORE THAN AN EIGHT.
ANYTHING PAST THAT AND THIS CITY WOULD TIP OVER ON ITS--
--THAT'S WHY HE LURED ME HERE.
NOT TO DRAG ME THROUGH THE STREETS.
NOT TO BRUISE MY EGO.
DAMN IT!

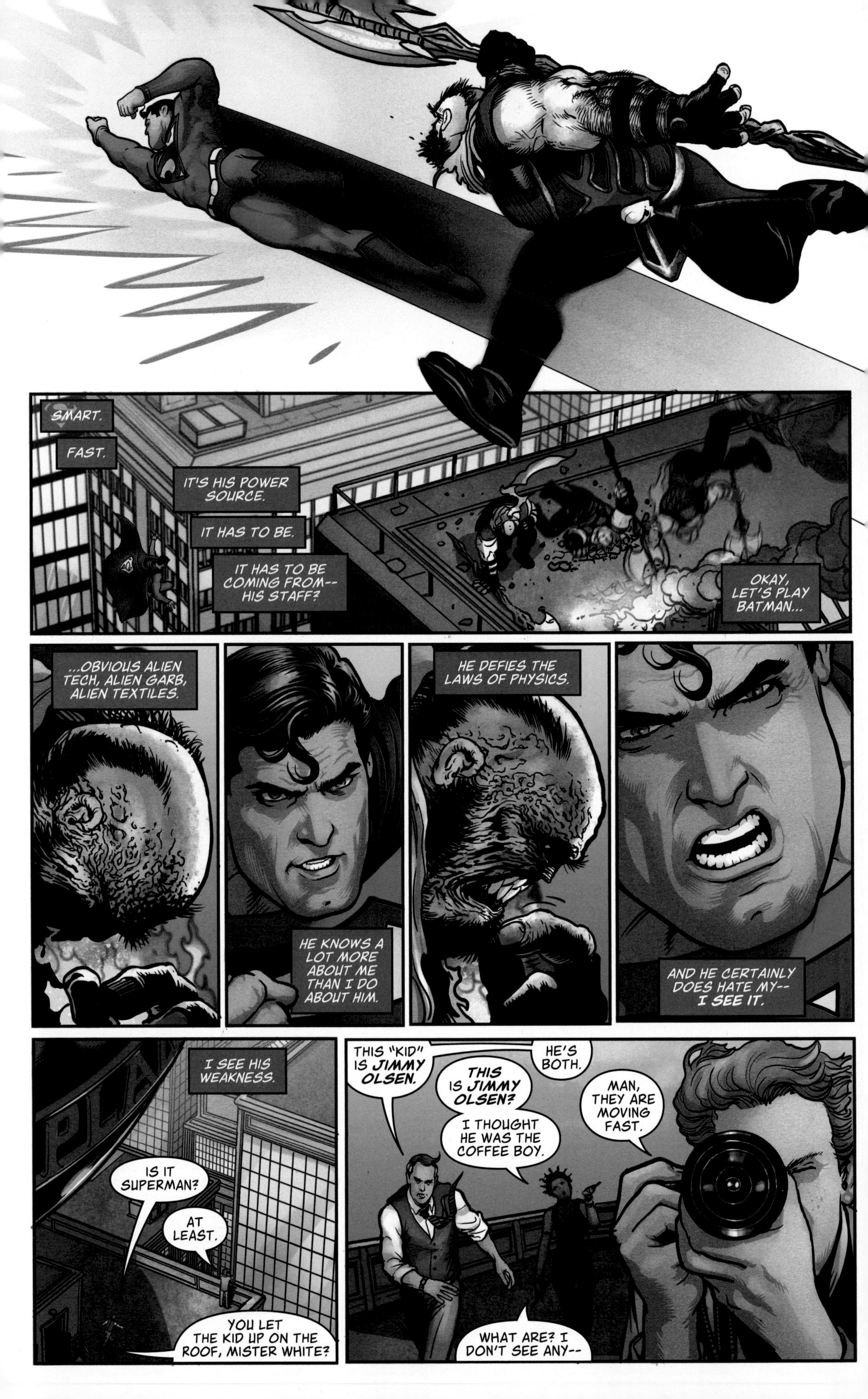
SMART.
FAST.
IT'S HIS POWER SOURCE.
IT HAS TO BE.
IT HAS TO BE COMING FROM-- HIS STAFF?
OKAY, LET'S PLAY BATMAN...
...OBVIOUS ALIEN TECH, ALIEN GARB, ALIEN TEXTILES.
HE KNOWS A LOT MORE ABOUT ME THAN I DO ABOUT HIM.
HE DEFIES THE LAWS OF PHYSICS.
AND HE CERTAINLY DOES HATE MY-- I SEE IT.
I SEE HIS WEAKNESS.
IS IT SUPERMAN?
AT LEAST.
YOU LET THE KID UP ON THE ROOF, MISTER WHITE?
THIS "KID" IS JIMMY OLSEN.
HE'S BOTH.
THIS IS JIMMY OLSEN?
I THOUGHT HE WAS THE COFFEE BOY.
MAN, THEY ARE MOVING FAST.
WHAT ARE? I DON'T SEE ANY--

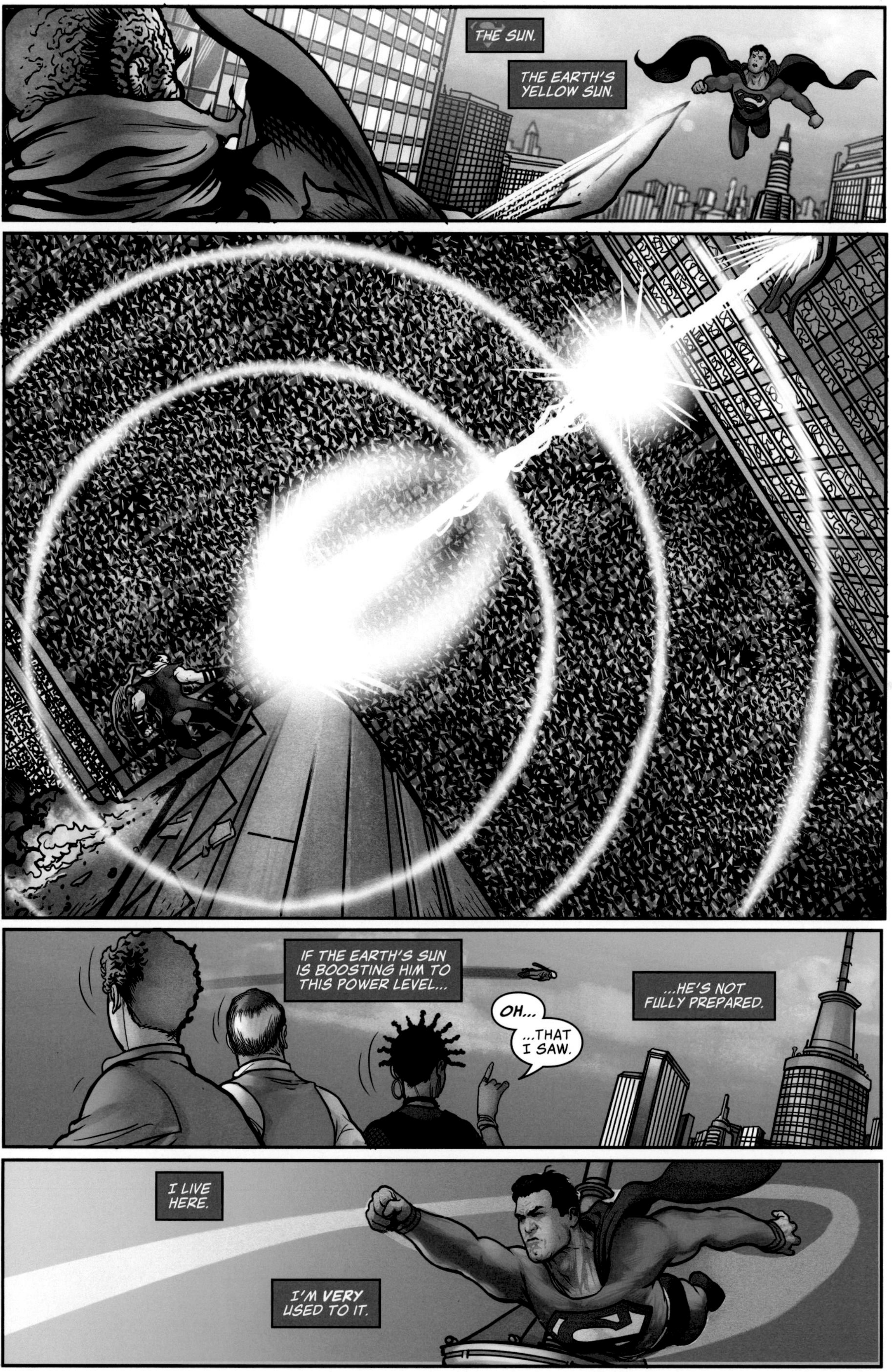
THE SUN.
THE EARTH'S YELLOW SUN.
IF THE EARTH'S SUN IS BOOSTING HIM TO THIS POWER LEVEL...
OH...
...THAT I SAW.
...HE'S NOT FULLY PREPARED.
I LIVE HERE.
I'M VERY USED TO IT.

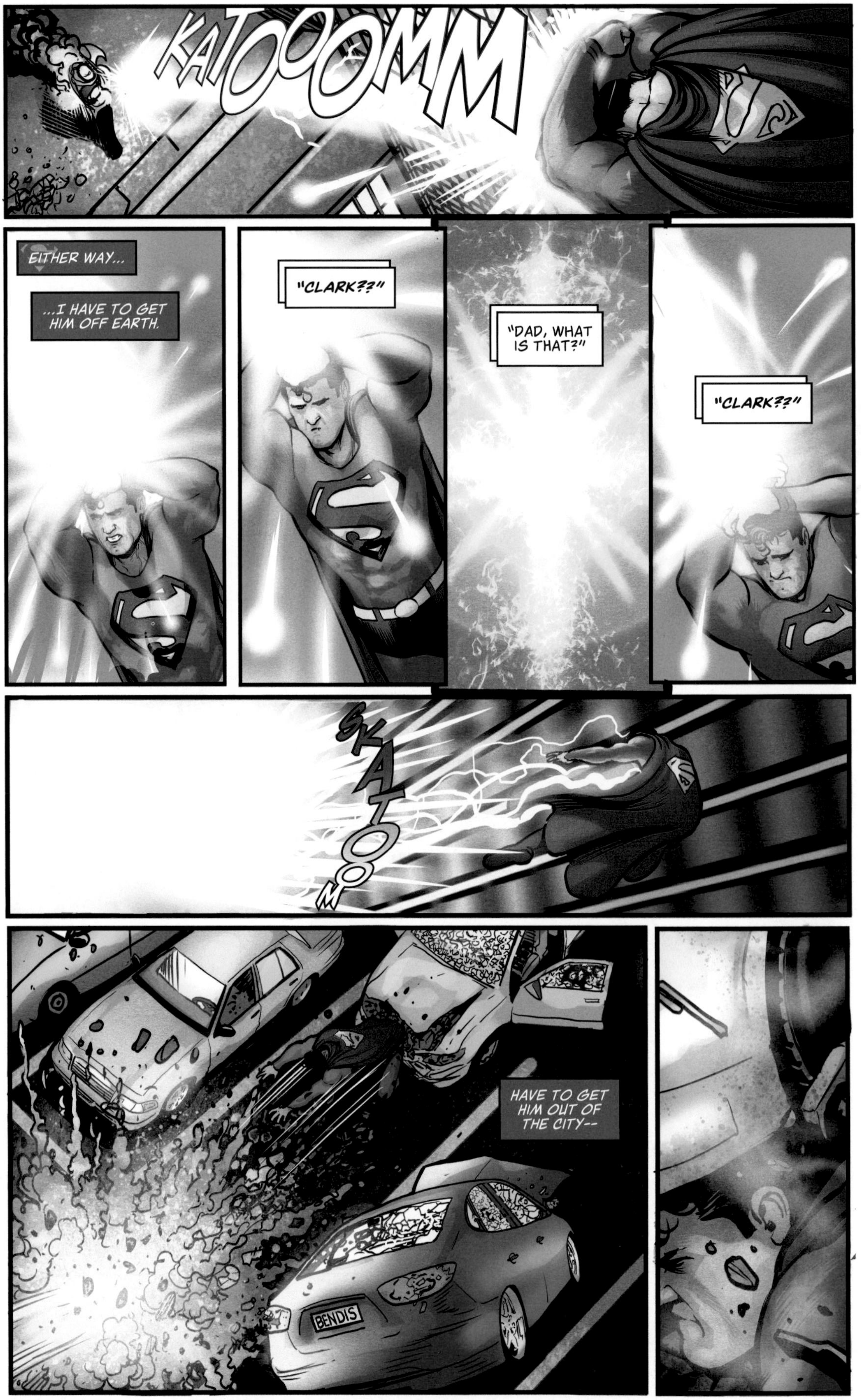
KATOOOMM
EITHER WAY...
...I HAVE TO GET HIM OFF EARTH.
"CLARK??"
"DAD, WHAT IS THAT?"
"CLARK??"
SKATOOOM
HAVE TO GET HIM OUT OF THE CITY--
BENDIS

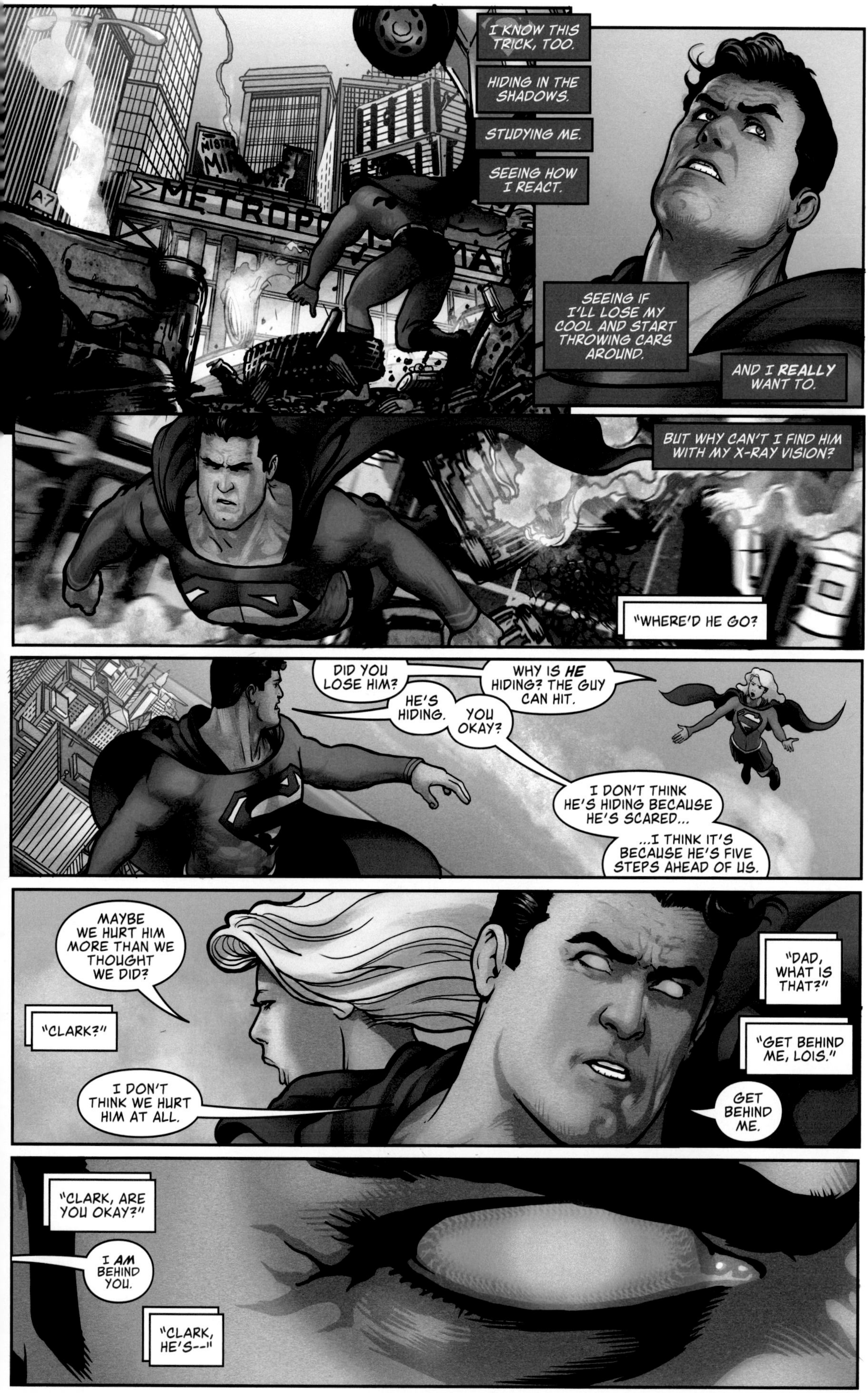
I KNOW THIS TRICK, TOO.
HIDING IN THE SHADOWS.
STUDYING ME.
SEEING HOW I REACT.
SEEING IF I'LL LOSE MY COOL AND START THROWING CARS AROUND.
AND I REALLY WANT TO.
BUT WHY CAN'T I FIND HIM WITH MY X-RAY VISION?
"WHERE'D HE GO?
DID YOU LOSE HIM?
HE'S HIDING.
WHY IS HE HIDING? THE GUY CAN HIT.
YOU OKAY?
I DON'T THINK HE'S HIDING BECAUSE HE'S SCARED...
...I THINK IT'S BECAUSE HE'S FIVE STEPS AHEAD OF US.
MAYBE WE HURT HIM MORE THAN WE THOUGHT WE DID?
"CLARK?"
I DON'T THINK WE HURT HIM AT ALL.
"DAD, WHAT IS THAT?"
"GET BEHIND ME, LOIS."
GET BEHIND ME.
"CLARK, ARE YOU OKAY?"
I AM BEHIND YOU.
"CLARK, HE'S--"

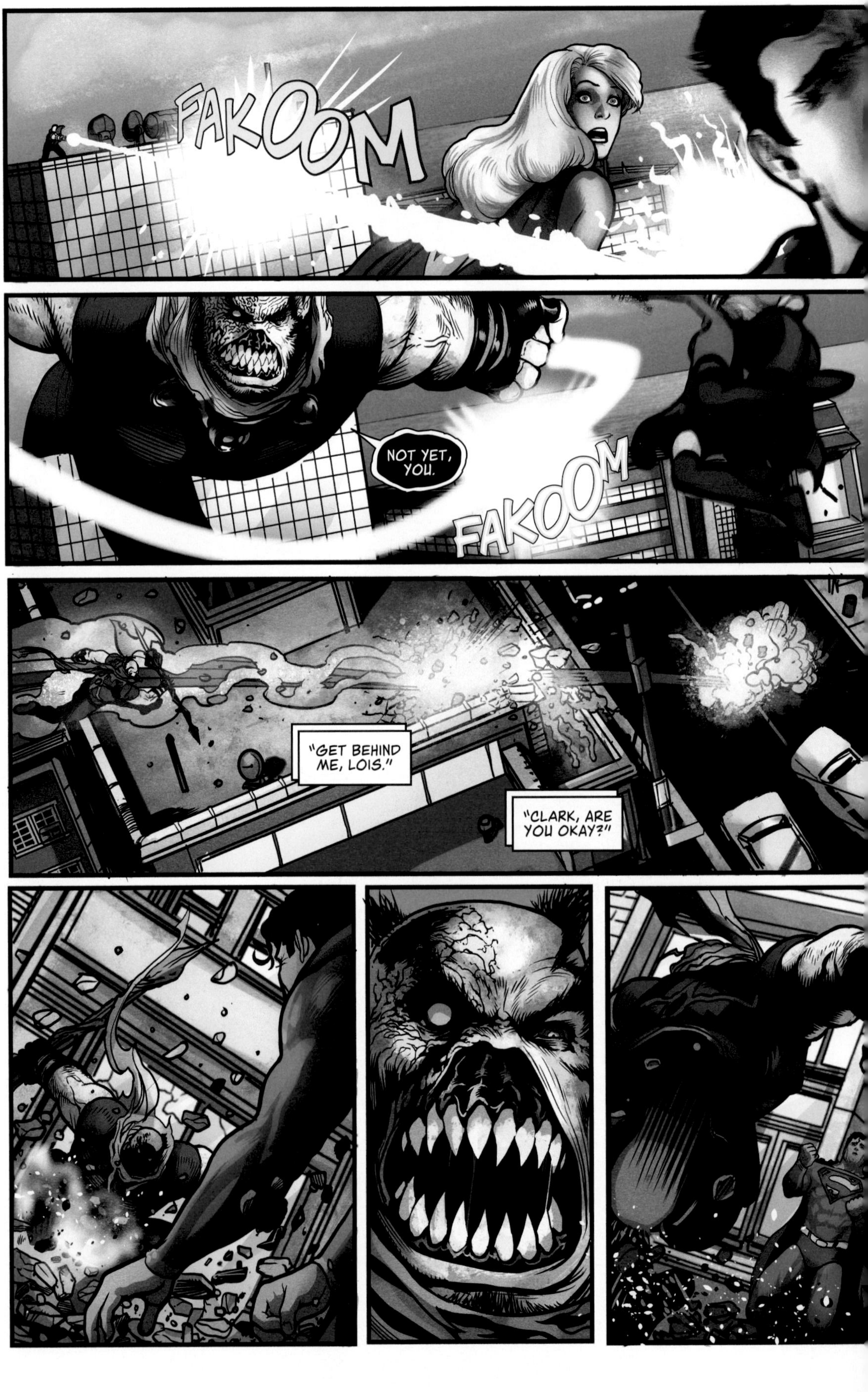
FAKOOOM
NOT YET, YOU.
FAKOOM
"GET BEHIND ME, LOIS."
"CLARK, ARE YOU OKAY?"

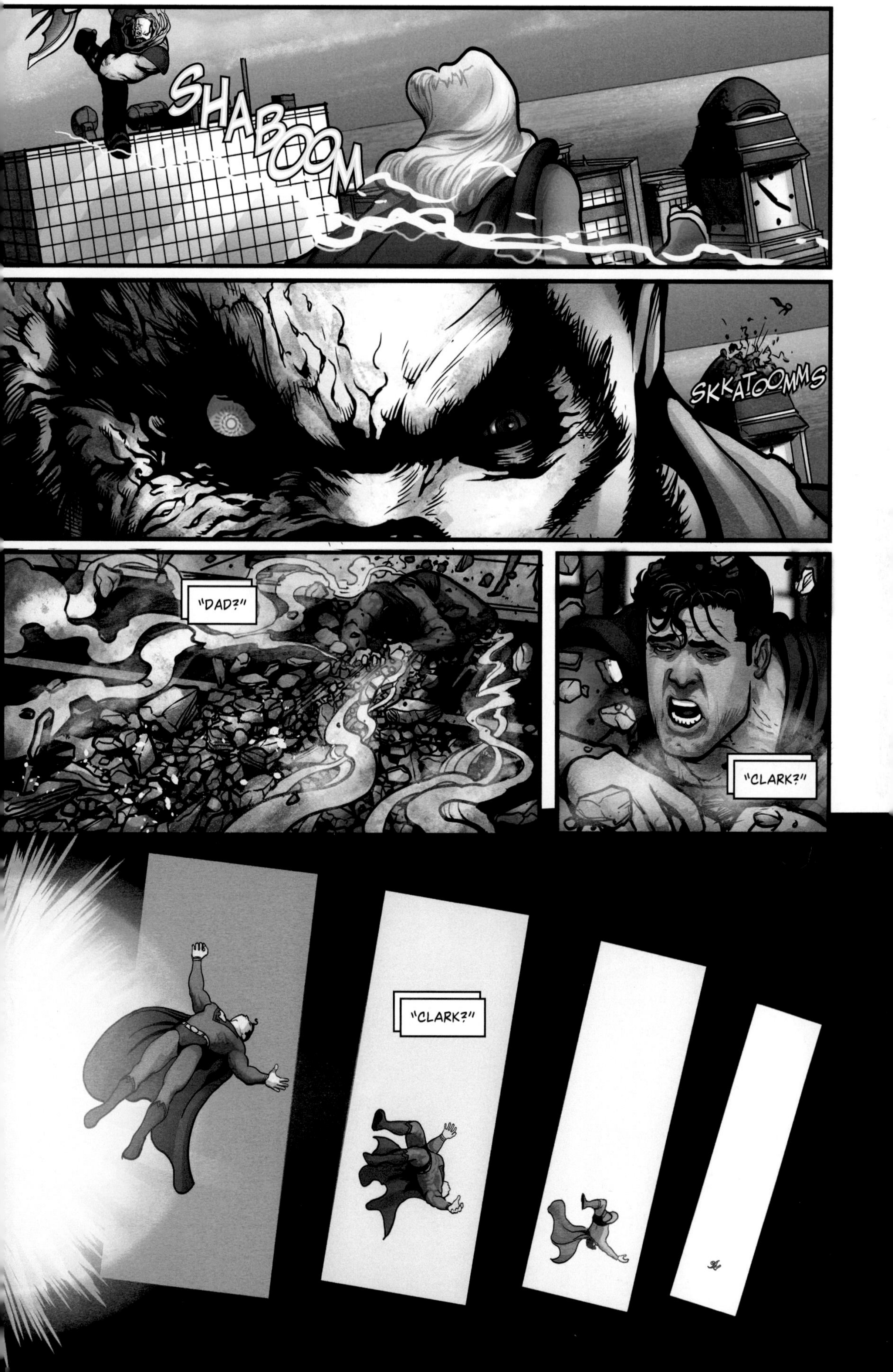
SHABOOM
SKKATOOMMS
"DAD?"
"CLARK?"
"CLARK?"

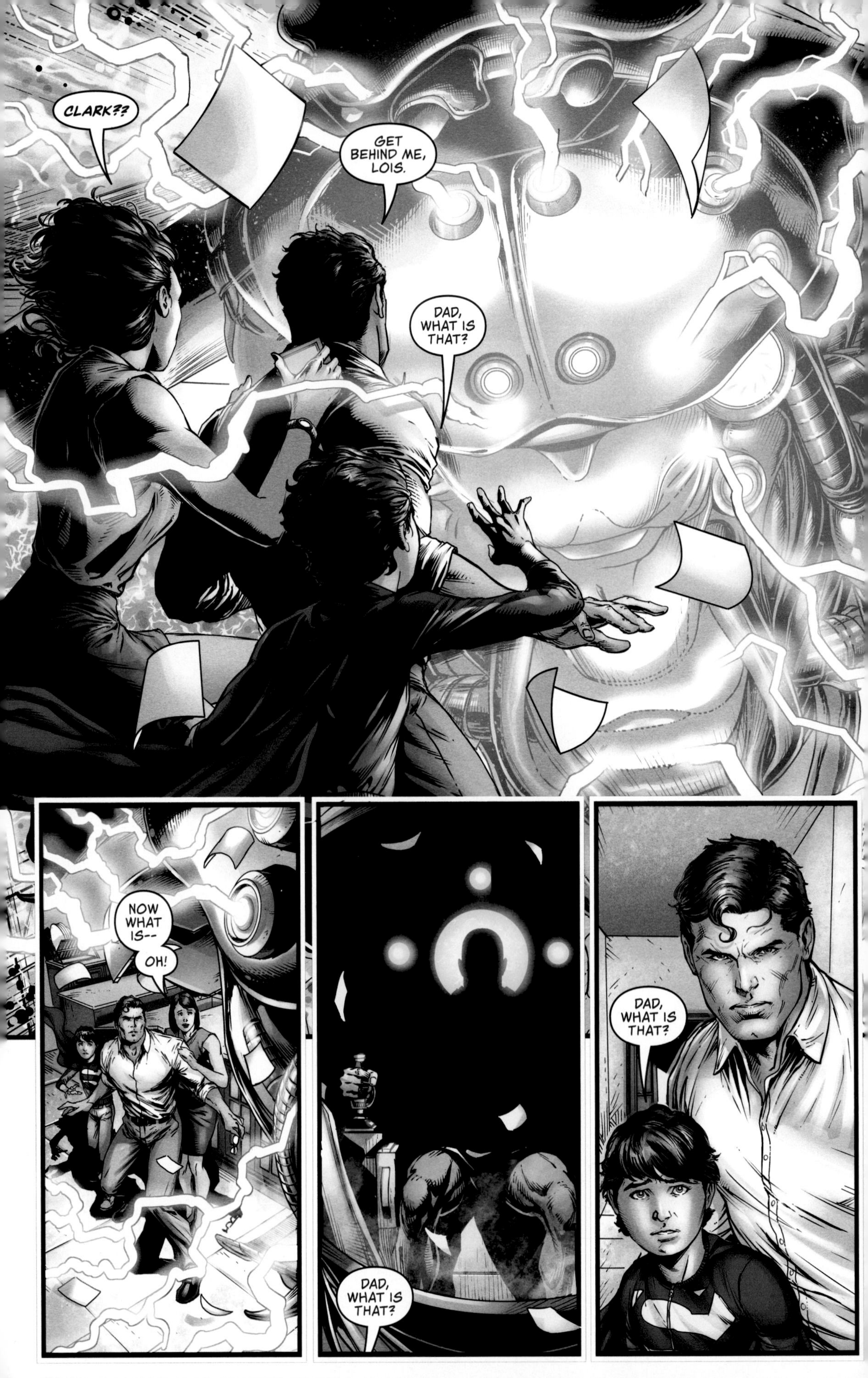
CLARK??
GET BEHIND ME, LOIS.
DAD, WHAT IS THAT?
NOW WHAT IS--
OH!
DAD, WHAT IS THAT?
DAD, WHAT IS THAT?

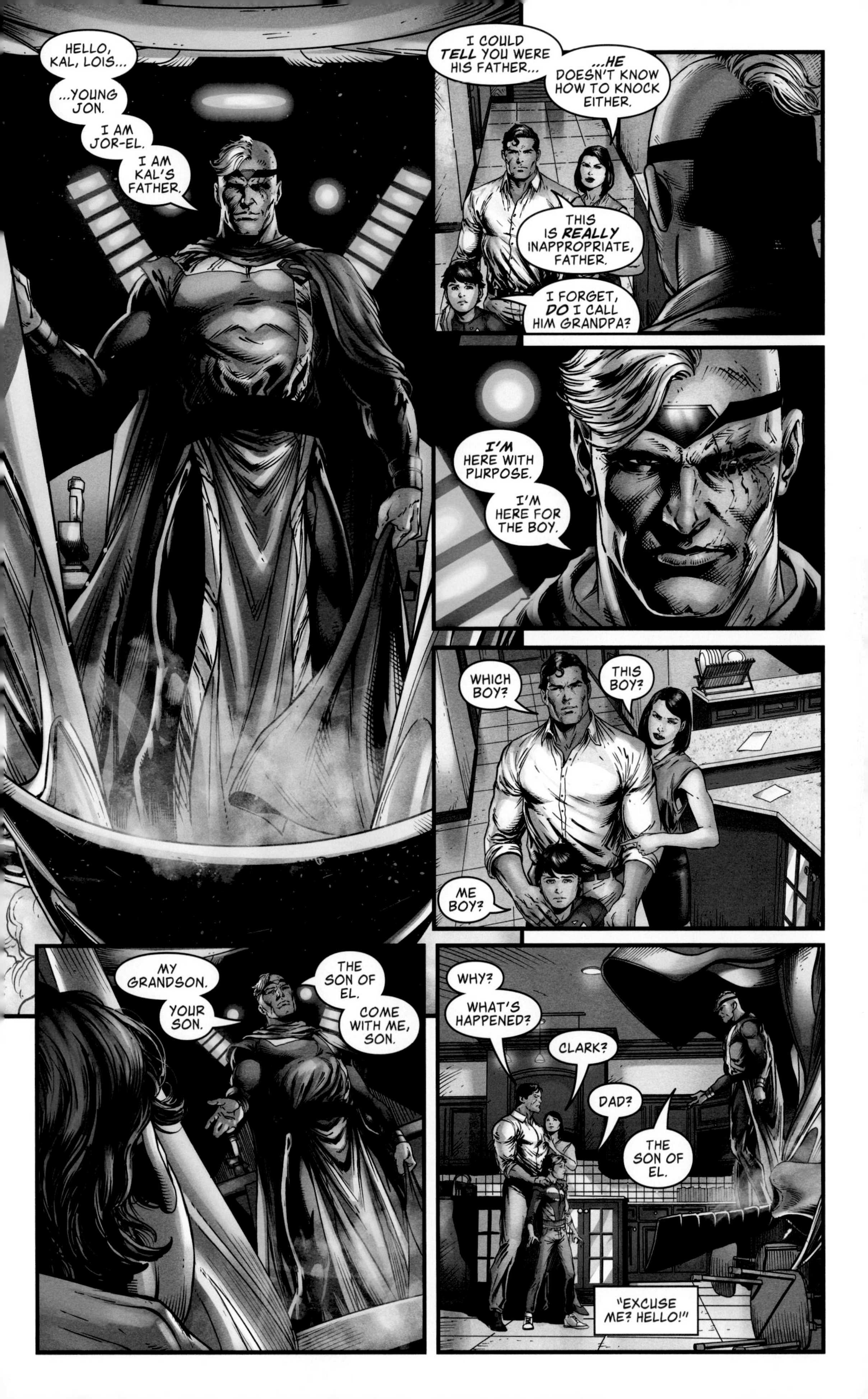
HELLO, KAL, LOIS...
...YOUNG JON.
I AM JOR-EL.
I AM KAL'S FATHER.
I COULD TELL YOU WERE HIS FATHER...
...HE DOESN'T KNOW HOW TO KNOCK EITHER.
THIS IS REALLY INAPPROPRIATE, FATHER.
I FORGET, DO I CALL HIM GRANDPA?
I'M HERE WITH PURPOSE.
I'M HERE FOR THE BOY.
WHICH BOY?
THIS BOY?
ME BOY?
MY GRANDSON.
YOUR SON.
THE SON OF EL.
COME WITH ME, SON.
WHY?
WHAT'S HAPPENED?
CLARK?
DAD?
THE SON OF EL.
"EXCUSE ME? HELLO!"

HI.
I'M THE GREEN LANTERN OF THIS SECTOR.

CAN YOU TELL ME EXACTLY WHAT YOU'VE SEEN AND HEARD?

SUPERMAN CAME CRASHING RIGHT INTO MY DELI!!

I HAVE INSURANCE. I'M NOT INSANE, BUT, STILL--

DID YOU KNOW HE WENT BACK TO WEARING THE RED SHORTS?

HEY! I'M CAPTAIN MAGGIE SAWYER, METROPOLIS SPECIAL CRIMES UNIT.

THE BIG ALIEN PERP ACCUSED SUPERMAN OF STALLING.

WHICH WAS RUDE.

AND THEN THE FIGHT HEADED DOWN PUZO PLAZA THAT WAY.

BUT I DID HEAR HIM SAY--

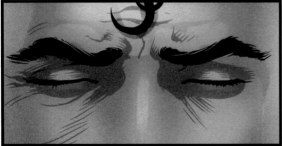

IT'S A CLEANSING

THIS IS NOT A FIGHT.

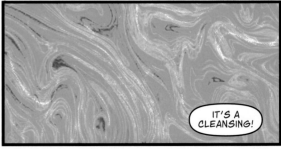

IT'S A CLEANSING!

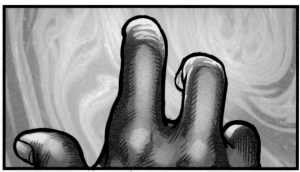

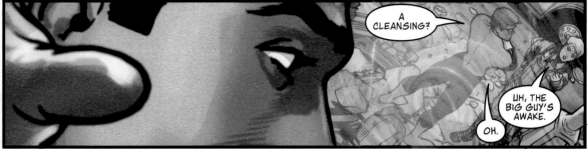

A CLEANSING?

UH, THE BIG GUY'S AWAKE.

OH.

HEY HAL... ...WHERE'S SUPERGIRL?

I JUST GOT HERE.

HEY, THANKS FOR THE ASSIST...

ARE YOU OKAY?

DID YOU SEE HIM?

NO. THE CIVILIANS SAID HE WENT THAT WAY THE SECOND BEFORE I SHOWED UP.

MAYBE HE KNEW I WAS COMING.

I WAS IN PURSUIT BUT--

HE'S OUT THERE.

I SCANNED THE AREA.

HE'S USING TECH AND TECHNIQUES I HAVEN'T FELT OR SEEN BEFORE.

HE SAID "CLEANSING"?

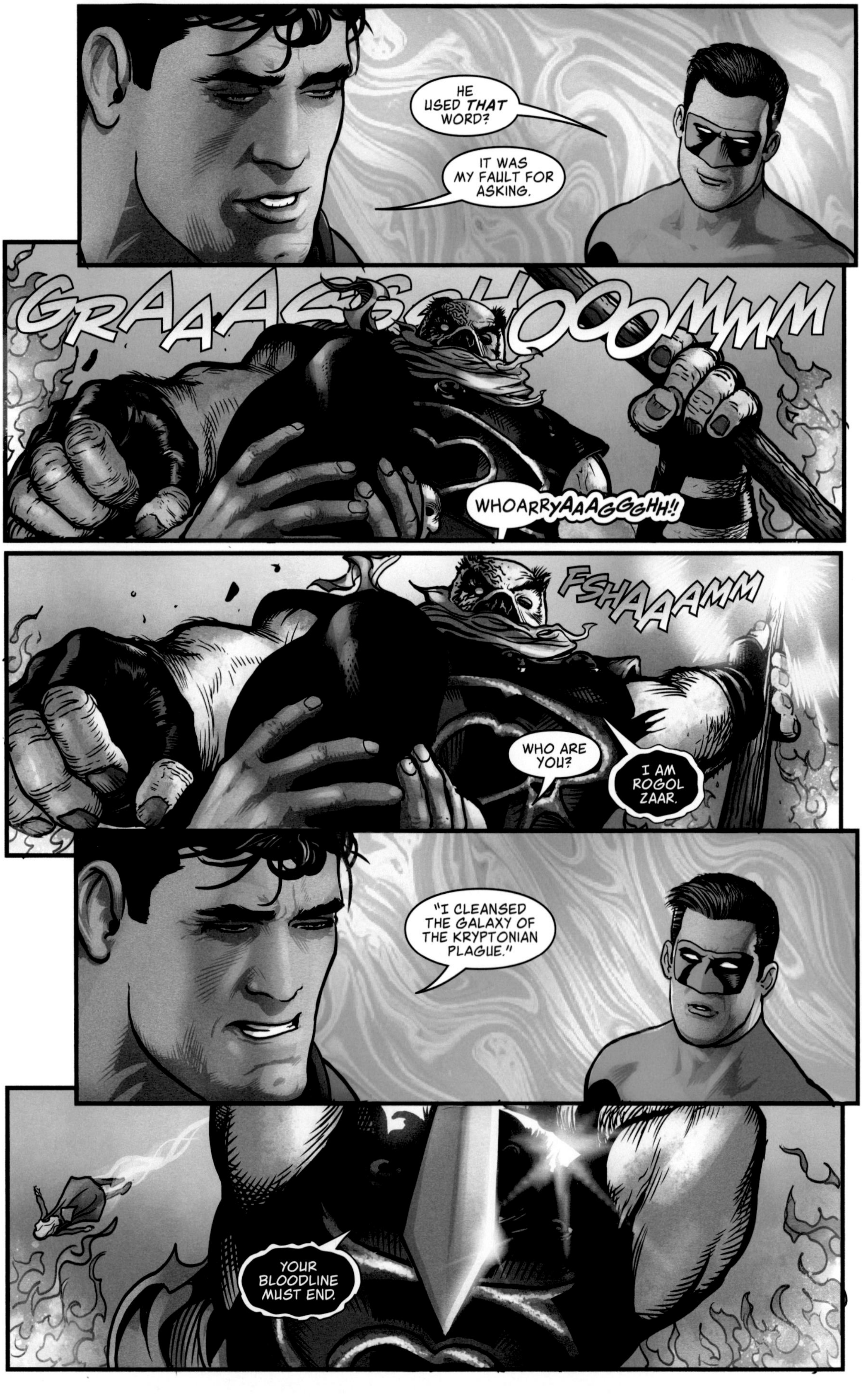
HE USED THAT WORD?
IT WAS MY FAULT FOR ASKING.
GRAAASSSHOOOMMM
WHOARRYAAAGGGHH!!
FSHAAAMM
WHO ARE YOU?
I AM ROGOL ZAAR.
"I CLEANSED THE GALAXY OF THE KRYPTONIAN PLAGUE."
YOUR BLOODLINE MUST END.

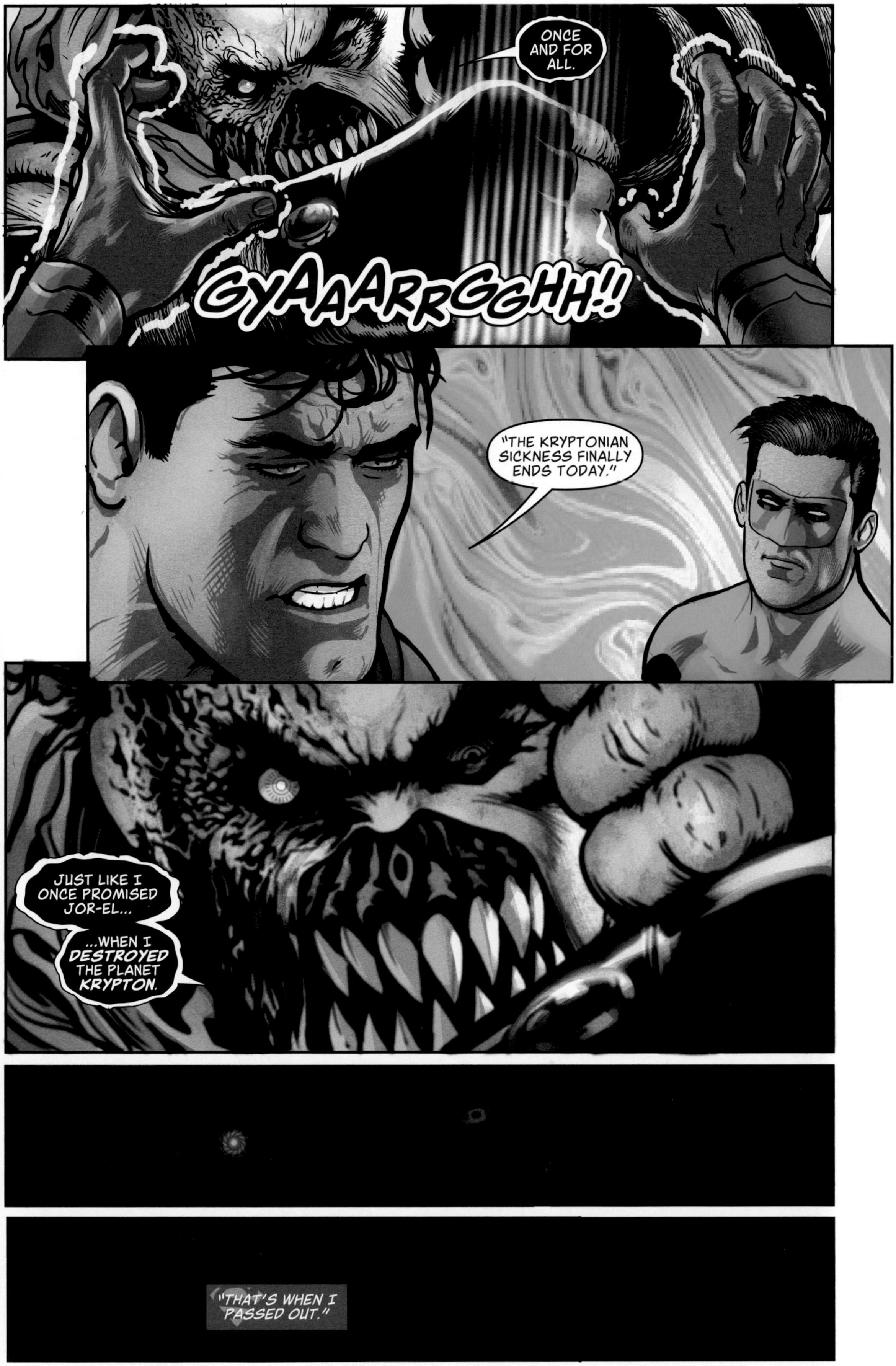
ONCE AND FOR ALL.
GYAAARRGGHH!!
"THE KRYPTONIAN SICKNESS FINALLY ENDS TODAY."
JUST LIKE I ONCE PROMISED JOR-EL...
...WHEN I *DESTROYED* THE PLANET *KRYPTON*.
"THAT'S WHEN I PASSED OUT."

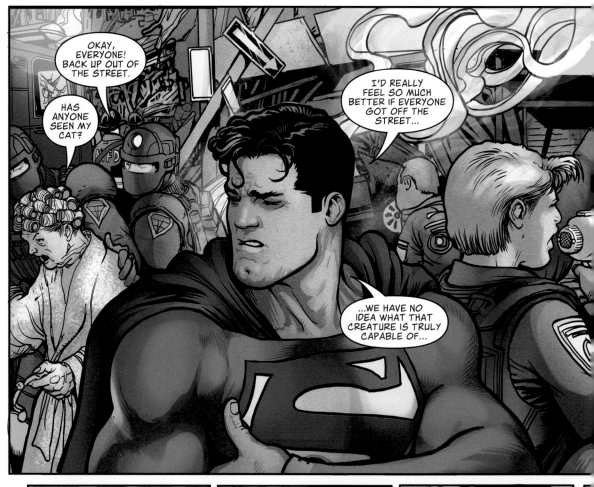

OKAY, EVERYONE! BACK UP OUT OF THE STREET.

HAS ANYONE SEEN MY CAT?

I'D REALLY FEEL SO MUCH BETTER IF EVERYONE GOT OFF THE STREET...

...WE HAVE NO IDEA WHAT THAT CREATURE IS TRULY CAPABLE OF...

NO.

DAMN IT.

WE'LL FIND HIM, KARA.

WE'LL GET THE LEAGUE TOGETHER.

KANDOR.

KANDOR.

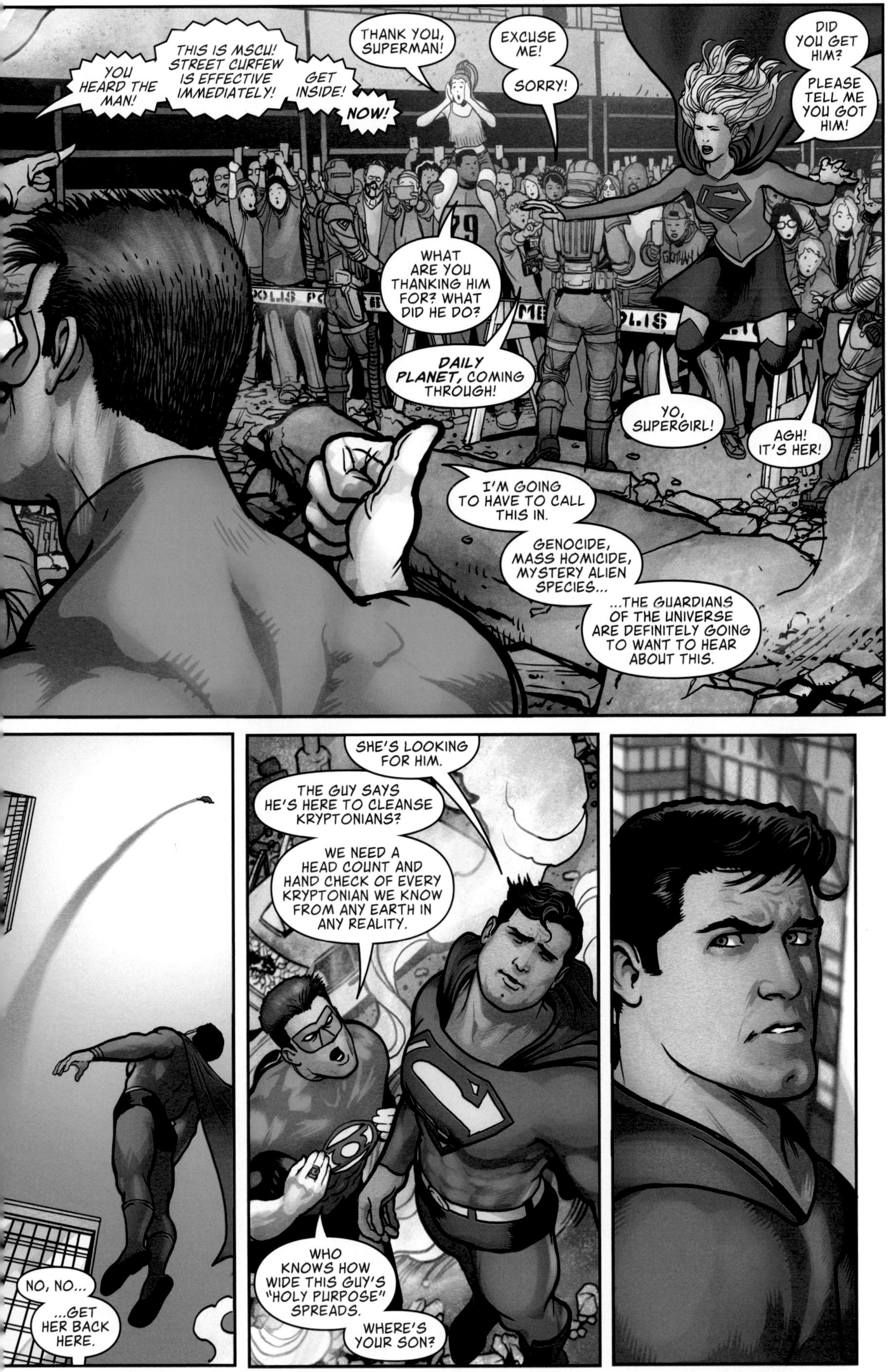
YOU HEARD THE MAN!
THIS IS MSCU! STREET CURFEW IS EFFECTIVE IMMEDIATELY!
GET INSIDE!
NOW!
THANK YOU, SUPERMAN!
EXCUSE ME!
SORRY!
DID YOU GET HIM?
PLEASE TELL ME YOU GOT HIM!
WHAT ARE YOU THANKING HIM FOR? WHAT DID HE DO?
DAILY PLANET, COMING THROUGH!
YO, SUPERGIRL!
AGH! IT'S HER!
I'M GOING TO HAVE TO CALL THIS IN.
GENOCIDE, MASS HOMICIDE, MYSTERY ALIEN SPECIES...
...THE GUARDIANS OF THE UNIVERSE ARE DEFINITELY GOING TO WANT TO HEAR ABOUT THIS.
NO, NO...
...GET HER BACK HERE.
SHE'S LOOKING FOR HIM.
THE GUY SAYS HE'S HERE TO CLEANSE KRYPTONIANS?
WE NEED A HEAD COUNT AND HAND CHECK OF EVERY KRYPTONIAN WE KNOW FROM ANY EARTH IN ANY REALITY.
WHO KNOWS HOW WIDE THIS GUY'S "HOLY PURPOSE" SPREADS.
WHERE'S YOUR SON?

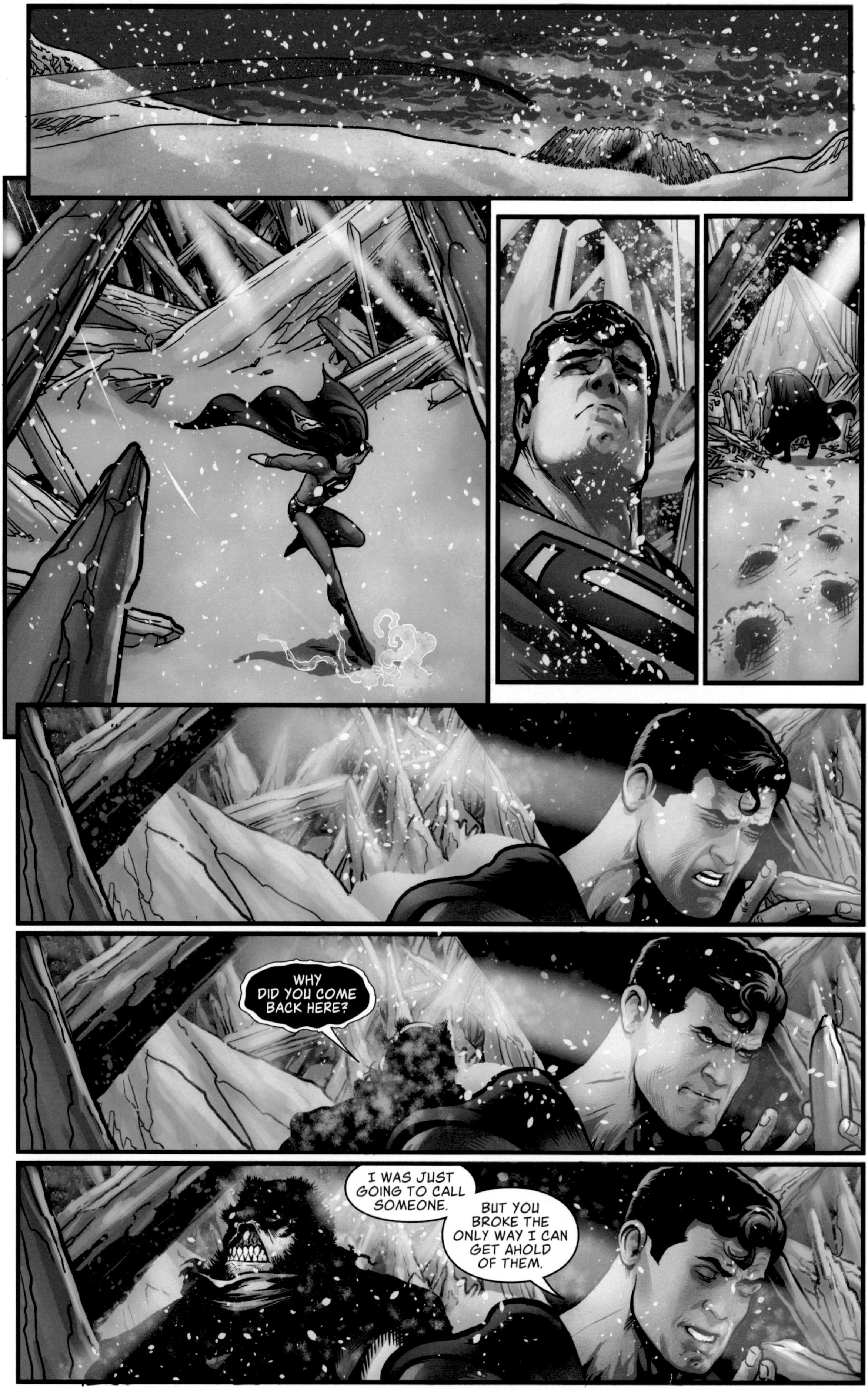
WHY DID YOU COME BACK HERE?
I WAS JUST GOING TO CALL SOMEONE.
BUT YOU BROKE THE ONLY WAY I CAN GET AHOLD OF THEM.

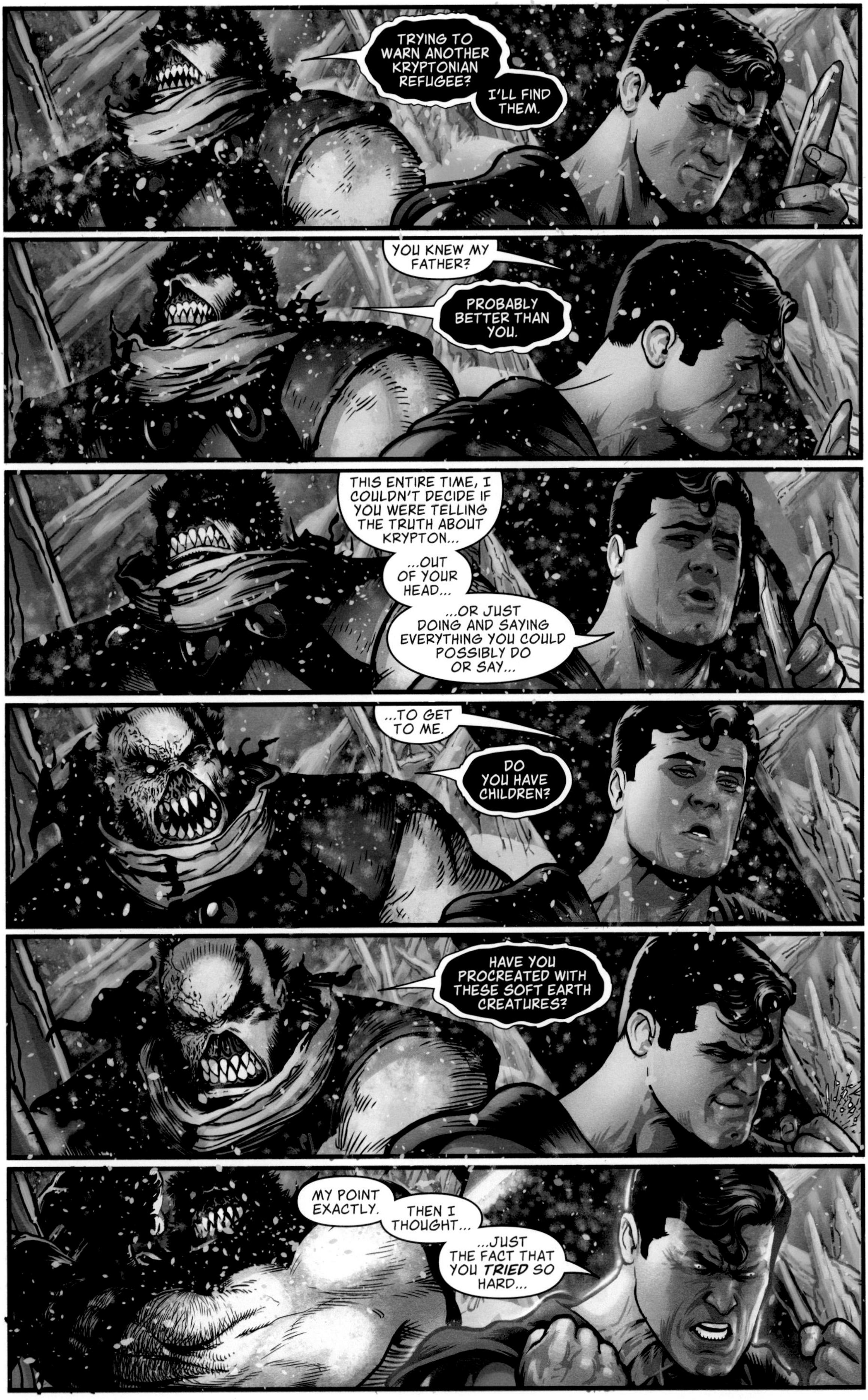
TRYING TO WARN ANOTHER KRYPTONIAN REFUGEE?
I'LL FIND THEM.
YOU KNEW MY FATHER?
PROBABLY BETTER THAN YOU.
THIS ENTIRE TIME, I COULDN'T DECIDE IF YOU WERE TELLING THE TRUTH ABOUT KRYPTON...
...OUT OF YOUR HEAD...
...OR JUST DOING AND SAYING EVERYTHING YOU COULD POSSIBLY DO OR SAY...
...TO GET TO ME.
DO YOU HAVE CHILDREN?
HAVE YOU PROCREATED WITH THESE SOFT EARTH CREATURES?
MY POINT EXACTLY.
THEN I THOUGHT...
...JUST THE FACT THAT YOU TRIED SO HARD...

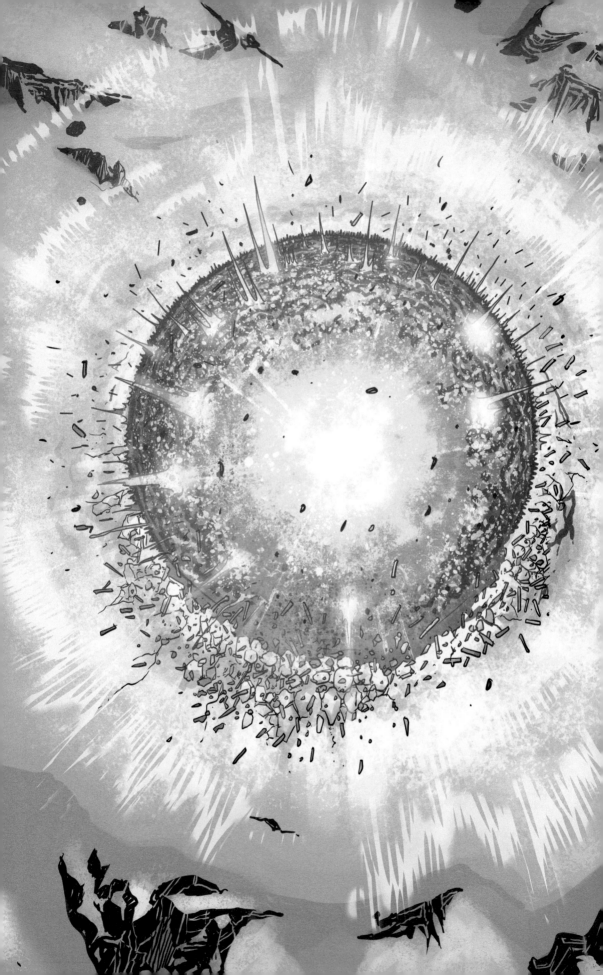

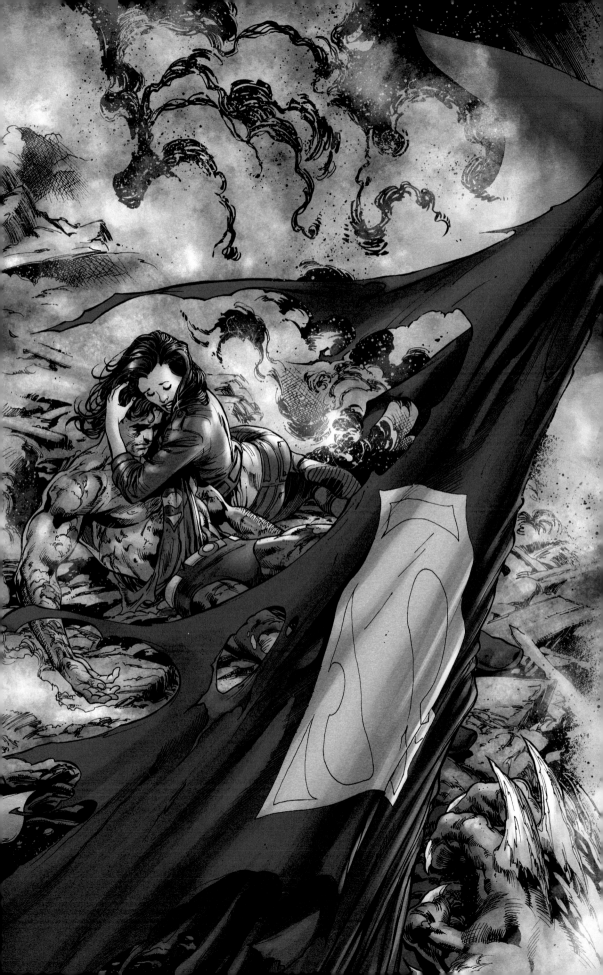

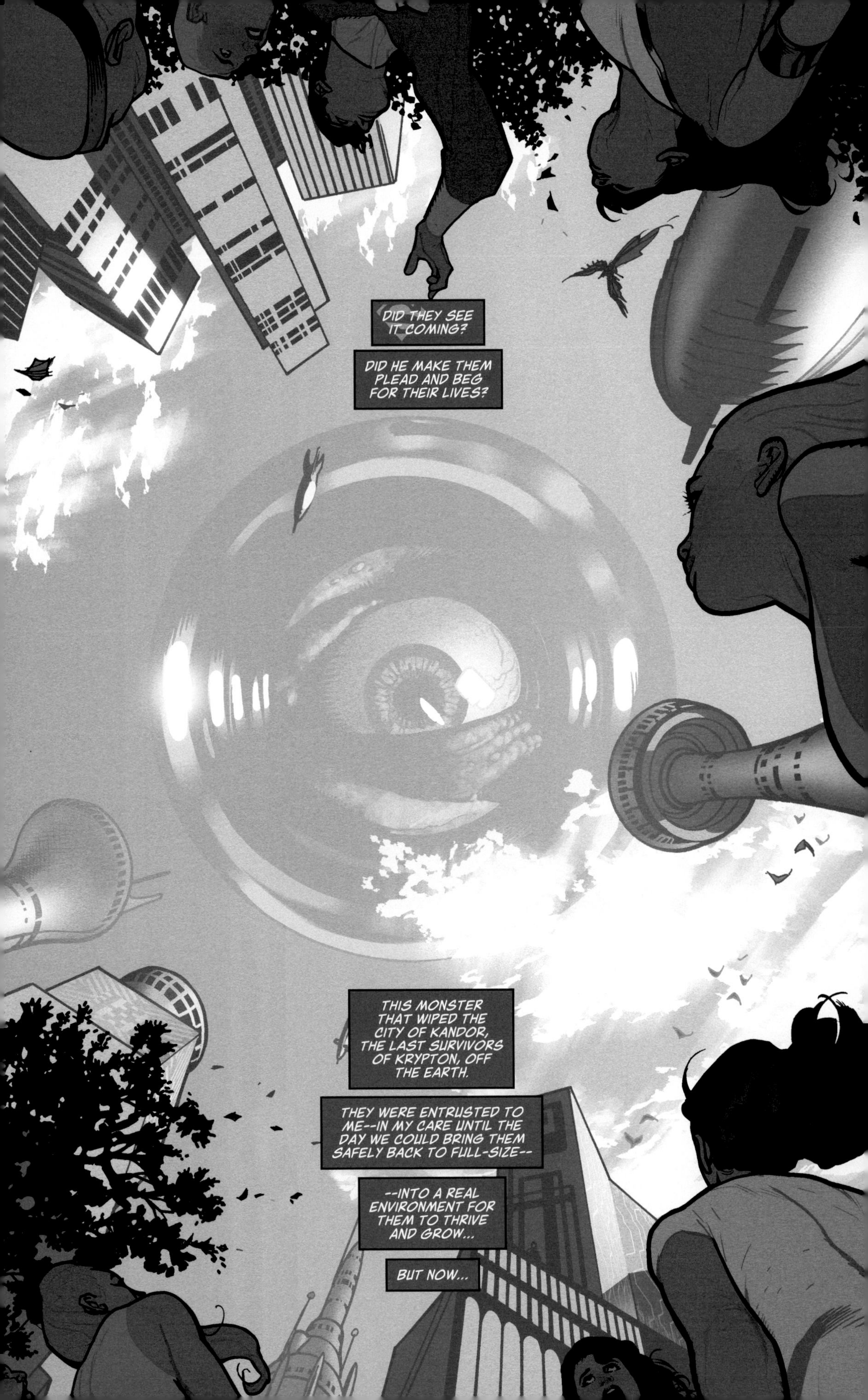
DID THEY SEE IT COMING?
DID HE MAKE THEM PLEAD AND BEG FOR THEIR LIVES?
THIS MONSTER THAT WIPED THE CITY OF KANDOR, THE LAST SURVIVORS OF KRYPTON, OFF THE EARTH.
THEY WERE ENTRUSTED TO ME--IN MY CARE UNTIL THE DAY WE COULD BRING THEM SAFELY BACK TO FULL-SIZE--
--INTO A REAL ENVIRONMENT FOR THEM TO THRIVE AND GROW...
BUT NOW...

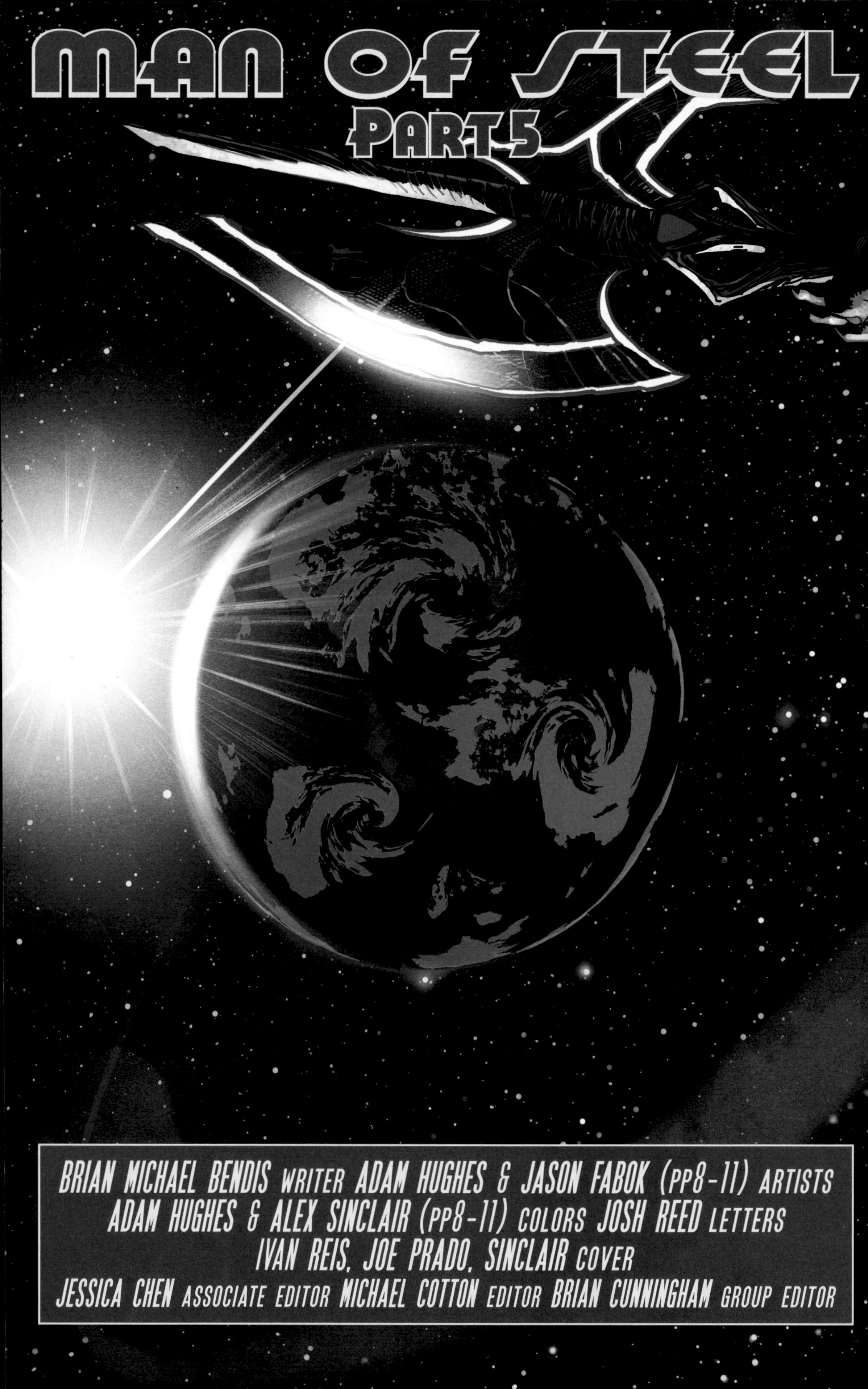
MAN OF STEEL
PART 5

BRIAN MICHAEL BENDIS WRITER ADAM HUGHES & JASON FABOK (PP8-11) ARTISTS
ADAM HUGHES & ALEX SINCLAIR (PP8-11) COLORS JOSH REED LETTERS
IVAN REIS, JOE PRADO, SINCLAIR COVER
JESSICA CHEN ASSOCIATE EDITOR MICHAEL COTTON EDITOR BRIAN CUNNINGHAM GROUP EDITOR

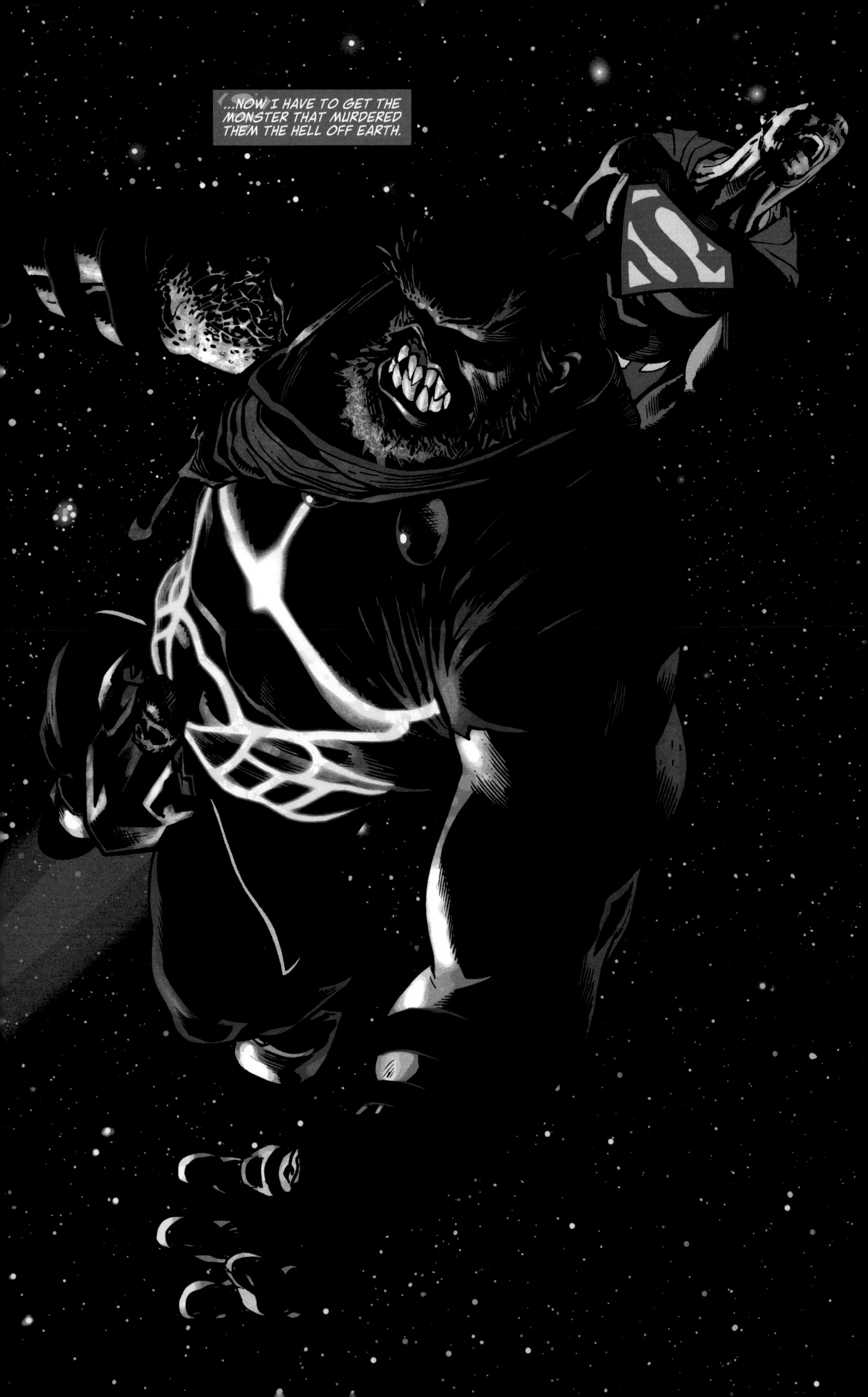
...NOW I HAVE TO GET THE MONSTER THAT MURDERED THEM THE HELL OFF EARTH.

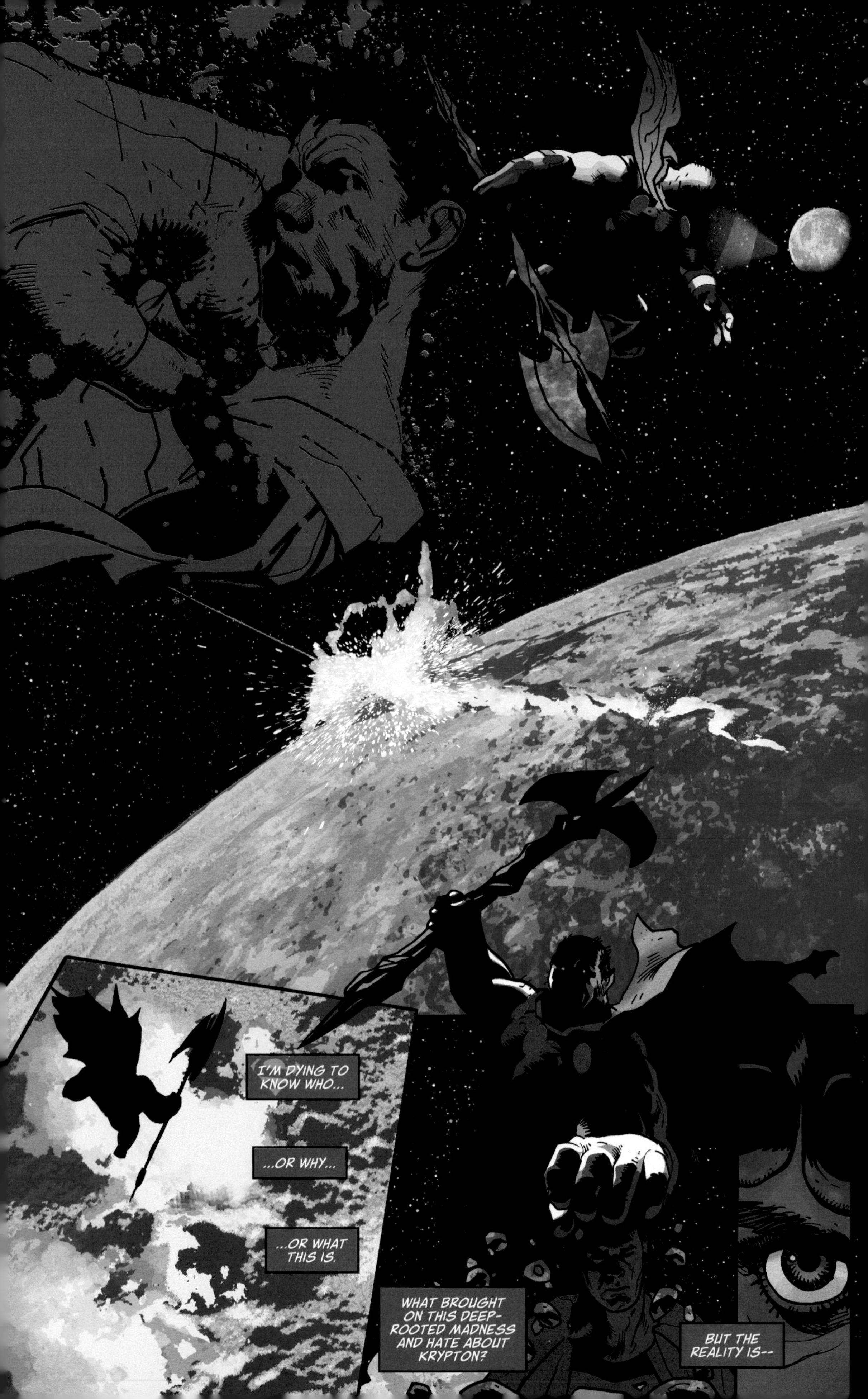
I'M DYING TO KNOW WHO...
...OR WHY...
...OR WHAT THIS IS.
WHAT BROUGHT ON THIS DEEP-ROOTED MADNESS AND HATE ABOUT KRYPTON?
BUT THE REALITY IS--

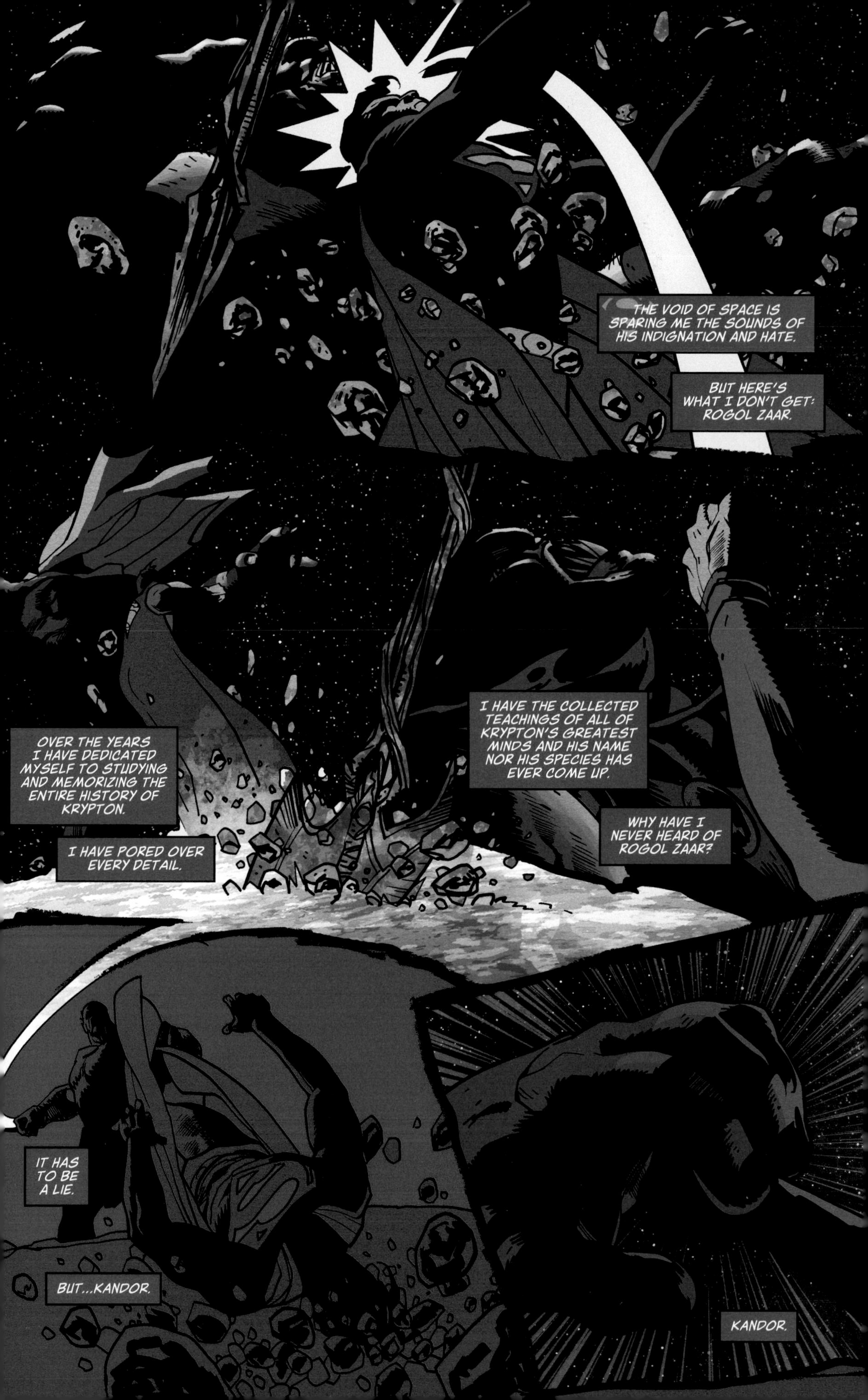
THE VOID OF SPACE IS SPARING ME THE SOUNDS OF HIS INDIGNATION AND HATE.
BUT HERE'S WHAT I DON'T GET: ROGOL ZAAR.
OVER THE YEARS I HAVE DEDICATED MYSELF TO STUDYING AND MEMORIZING THE ENTIRE HISTORY OF KRYPTON.
I HAVE PORED OVER EVERY DETAIL.
I HAVE THE COLLECTED TEACHINGS OF ALL OF KRYPTON'S GREATEST MINDS AND HIS NAME NOR HIS SPECIES HAS EVER COME UP.
WHY HAVE I NEVER HEARD OF ROGOL ZAAR?
IT HAS TO BE A LIE.
BUT...KANDOR.
KANDOR.

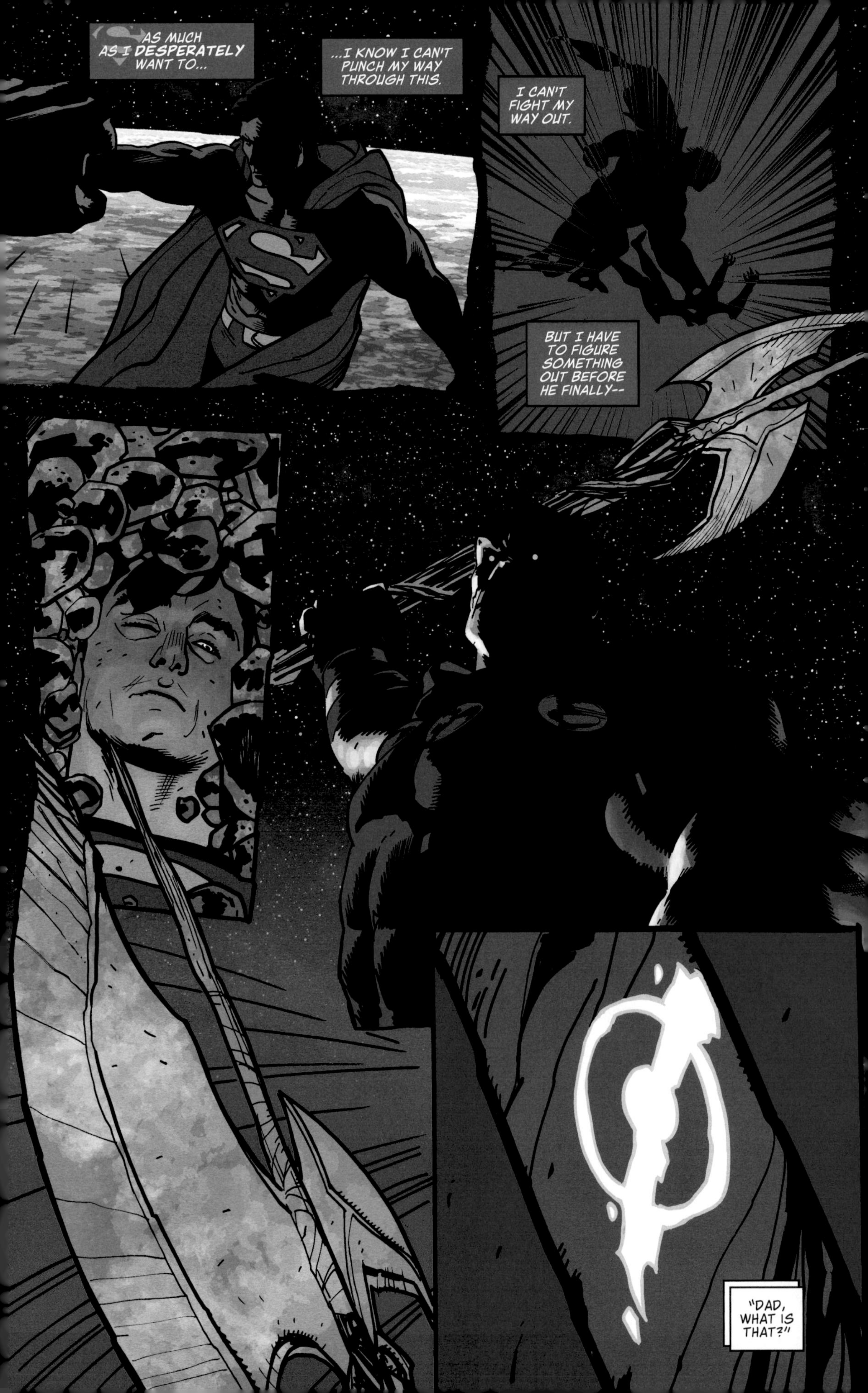
AS MUCH AS I DESPERATELY WANT TO...
...I KNOW I CAN'T PUNCH MY WAY THROUGH THIS.
I CAN'T FIGHT MY WAY OUT.
BUT I HAVE TO FIGURE SOMETHING OUT BEFORE HE FINALLY--
"DAD, WHAT IS THAT?"

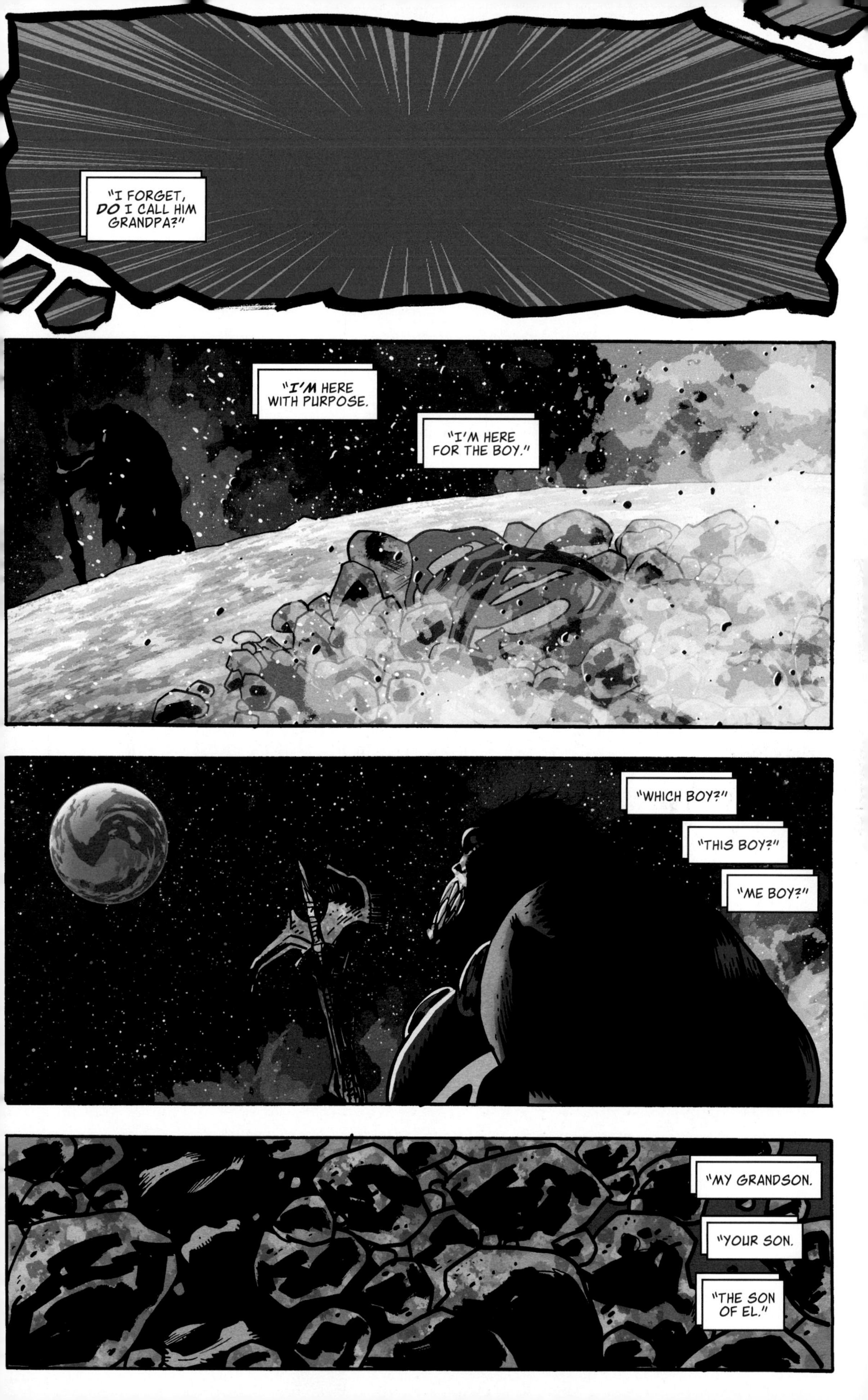
"I FORGET, DO I CALL HIM GRANDPA?"
"I'M HERE WITH PURPOSE.
"I'M HERE FOR THE BOY."
"WHICH BOY?"
"THIS BOY?"
"ME BOY?"
"MY GRANDSON.
"YOUR SON.
"THE SON OF EL."

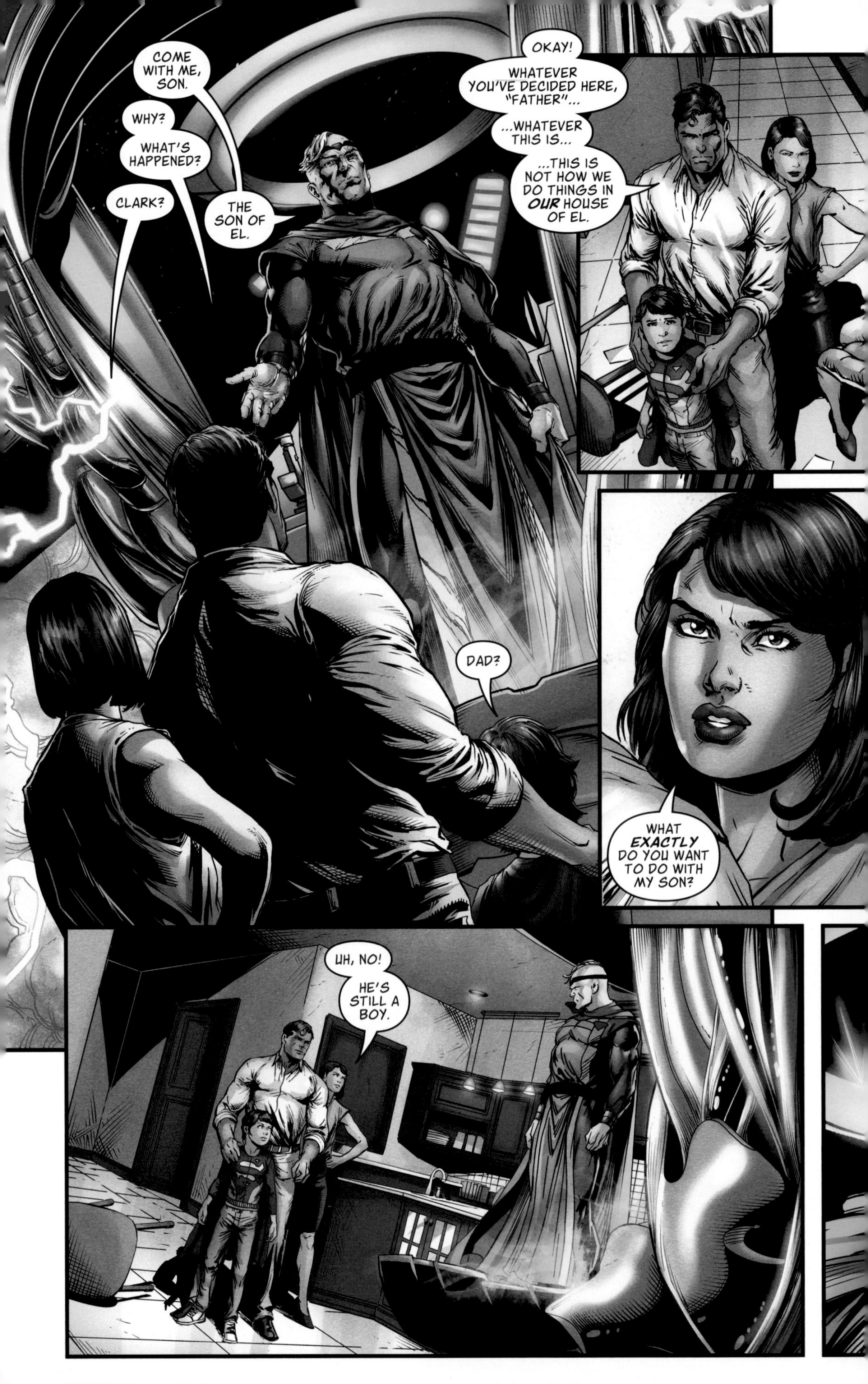
COME WITH ME, SON.
WHY?
WHAT'S HAPPENED?
CLARK?
THE SON OF EL.
OKAY!
WHATEVER YOU'VE DECIDED HERE, "FATHER"...
...WHATEVER THIS IS...
...THIS IS NOT HOW WE DO THINGS IN OUR HOUSE OF EL.
DAD?
WHAT EXACTLY DO YOU WANT TO DO WITH MY SON?
UH, NO!
HE'S STILL A BOY.

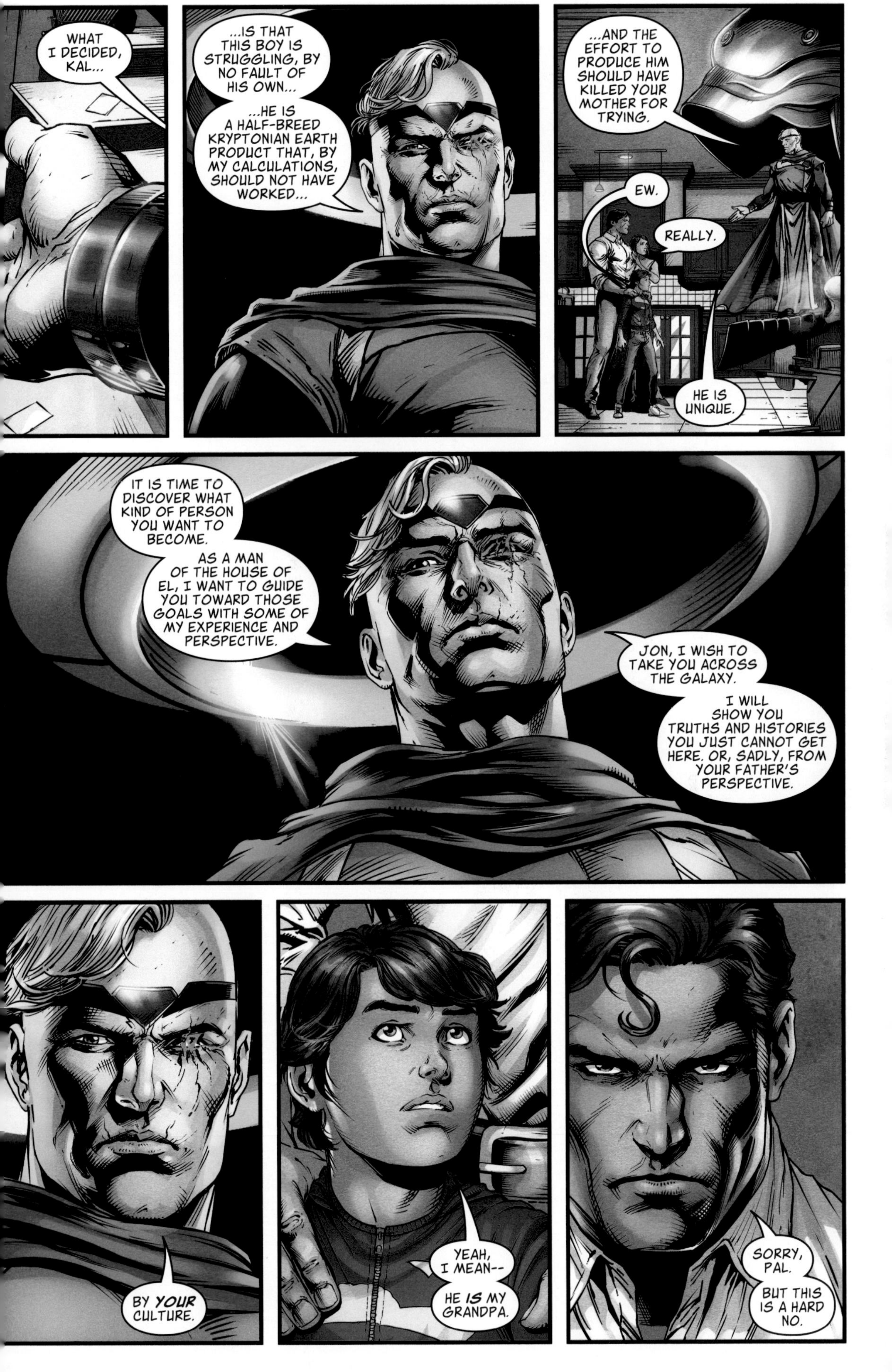
WHAT I DECIDED, KAL...
...IS THAT THIS BOY IS STRUGGLING, BY NO FAULT OF HIS OWN...
...HE IS A HALF-BREED KRYPTONIAN EARTH PRODUCT THAT, BY MY CALCULATIONS, SHOULD NOT HAVE WORKED...
...AND THE EFFORT TO PRODUCE HIM SHOULD HAVE KILLED YOUR MOTHER FOR TRYING.
EW.
REALLY.
HE IS UNIQUE.
IT IS TIME TO DISCOVER WHAT KIND OF PERSON YOU WANT TO BECOME.
AS A MAN OF THE HOUSE OF EL, I WANT TO GUIDE YOU TOWARD THOSE GOALS WITH SOME OF MY EXPERIENCE AND PERSPECTIVE.
JON, I WISH TO TAKE YOU ACROSS THE GALAXY.
I WILL SHOW YOU TRUTHS AND HISTORIES YOU JUST CANNOT GET HERE. OR, SADLY, FROM YOUR FATHER'S PERSPECTIVE.
BY *YOUR* CULTURE.
YEAH, I MEAN--
HE *IS* MY GRANDPA.
SORRY, PAL.
BUT THIS IS A HARD NO.

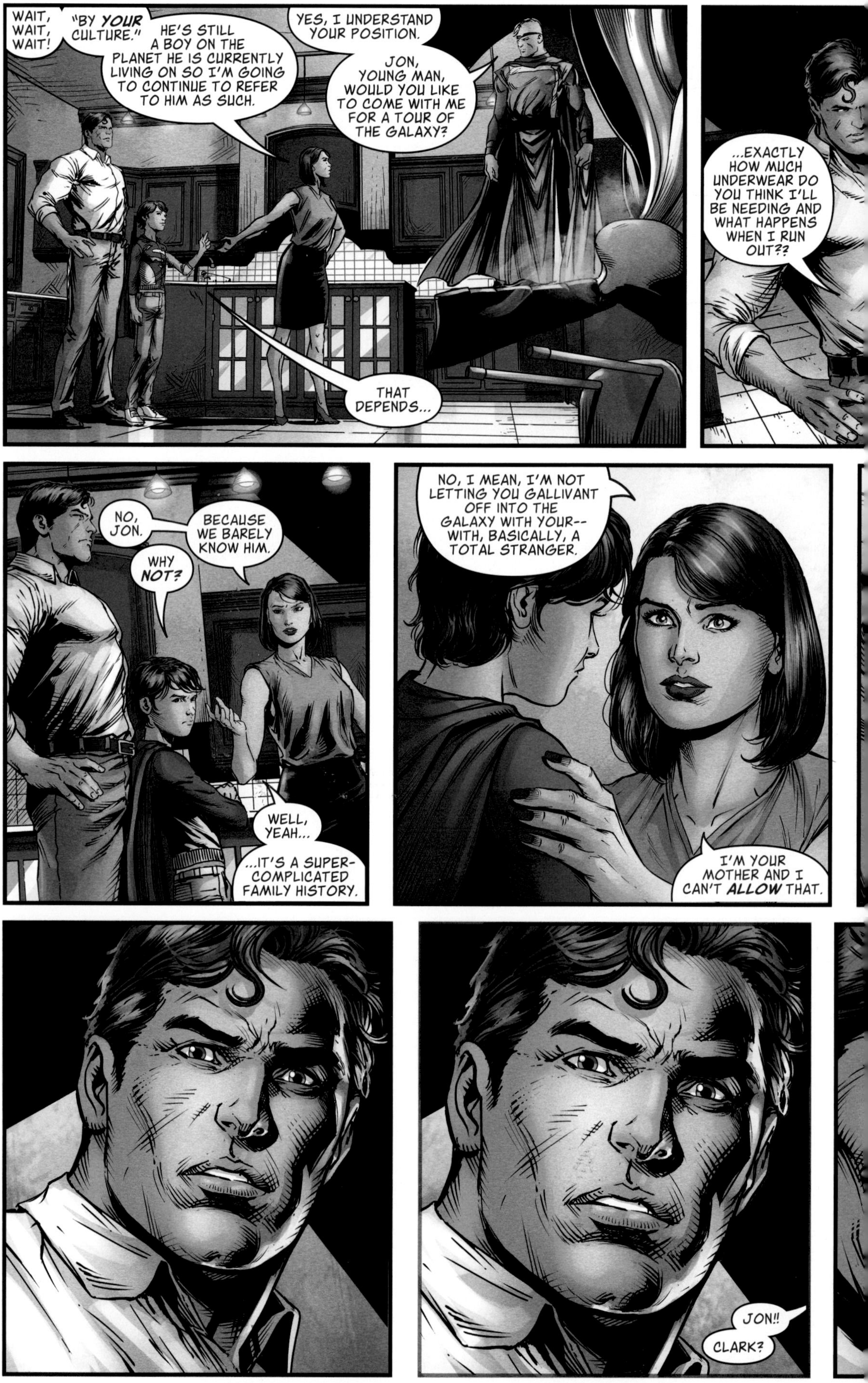
WAIT, WAIT, WAIT!
"BY YOUR CULTURE."
HE'S STILL A BOY ON THE PLANET HE IS CURRENTLY LIVING ON SO I'M GOING TO CONTINUE TO REFER TO HIM AS SUCH.
YES, I UNDERSTAND YOUR POSITION.
JON, YOUNG MAN, WOULD YOU LIKE TO COME WITH ME FOR A TOUR OF THE GALAXY?
THAT DEPENDS...
...EXACTLY HOW MUCH UNDERWEAR DO YOU THINK I'LL BE NEEDING AND WHAT HAPPENS WHEN I RUN OUT??
NO, JON.
BECAUSE WE BARELY KNOW HIM.
WHY NOT?
WELL, YEAH...
...IT'S A SUPER-COMPLICATED FAMILY HISTORY.
NO, I MEAN, I'M NOT LETTING YOU GALLIVANT OFF INTO THE GALAXY WITH YOUR-- WITH, BASICALLY, A TOTAL STRANGER.
I'M YOUR MOTHER AND I CAN'T ALLOW THAT.
JON!!
CLARK?

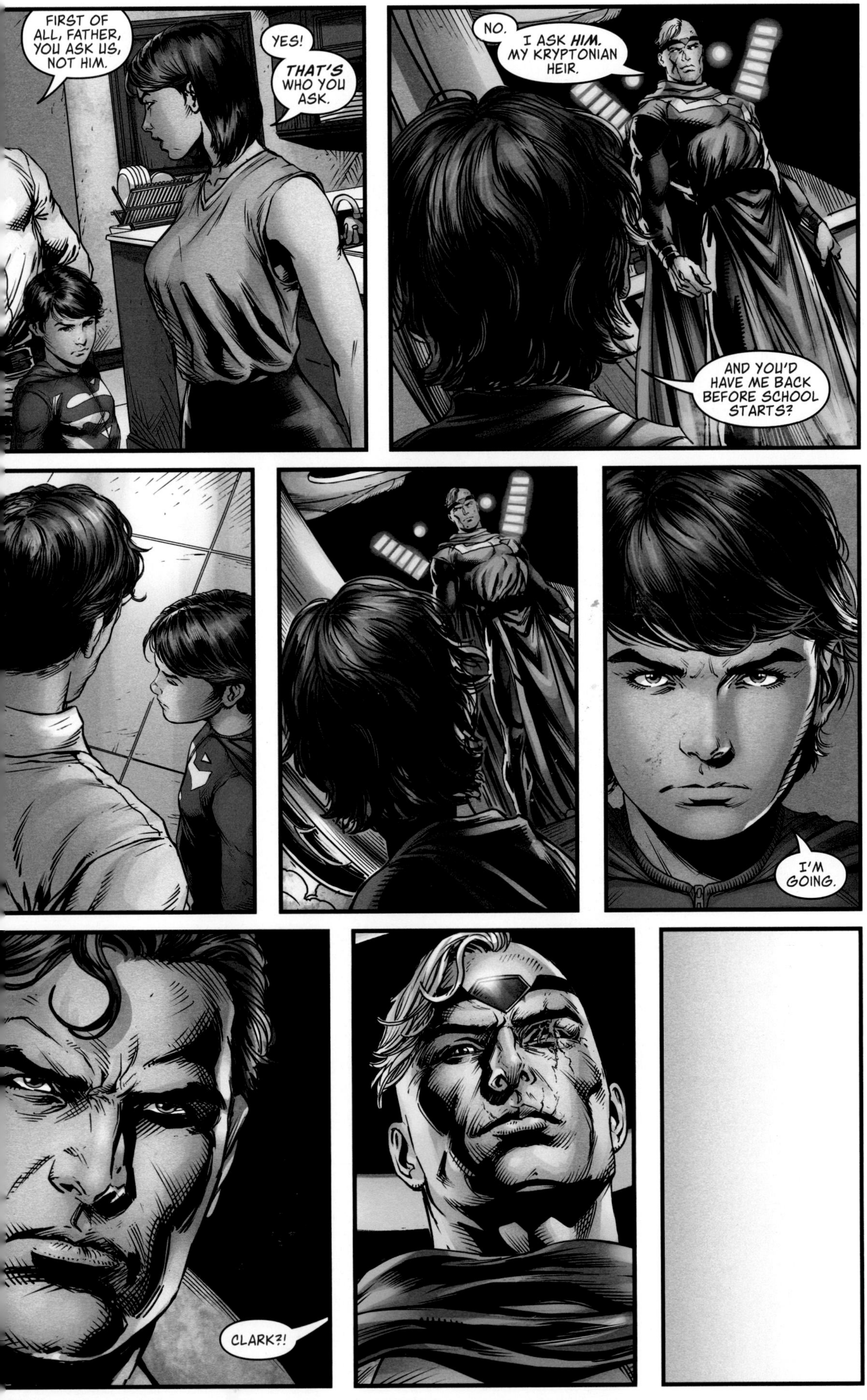
FIRST OF ALL, FATHER, YOU ASK US, NOT HIM.
YES!
THAT'S WHO YOU ASK.
NO.
I ASK HIM. MY KRYPTONIAN HEIR.
AND YOU'D HAVE ME BACK BEFORE SCHOOL STARTS?
I'M GOING.
CLARK?!

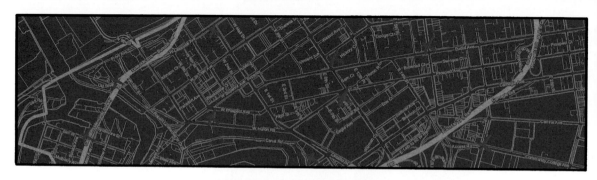

HEY GUYS, DOES THIS LOOK LIKE ANYTHING TO YOU?

IT'S METROPOLIS, CHIEF MOORE.

OH! THAT'S THE FIRES?

THAT'S MORE THAN I THOUGHT.

DUDE, THE NEW DEPUTY CHIEF IS TALKIN' ABOUT THE MAP OF THE FIRES.

I GIVE UP, CHIEF, WHAT DOES IT LOOK LIKE?

SHE'S ASKING IF WE SEE A SHAPE OR A PATTERN.

IN WHAT?

HOW THE FIRES ARE LAID OUT IN THE CITY MAP...

HE GETS IT.

LIKE A CLUE TO WHO STARTED THE FIRES?

THAT'S WHAT BATMAN SAID.

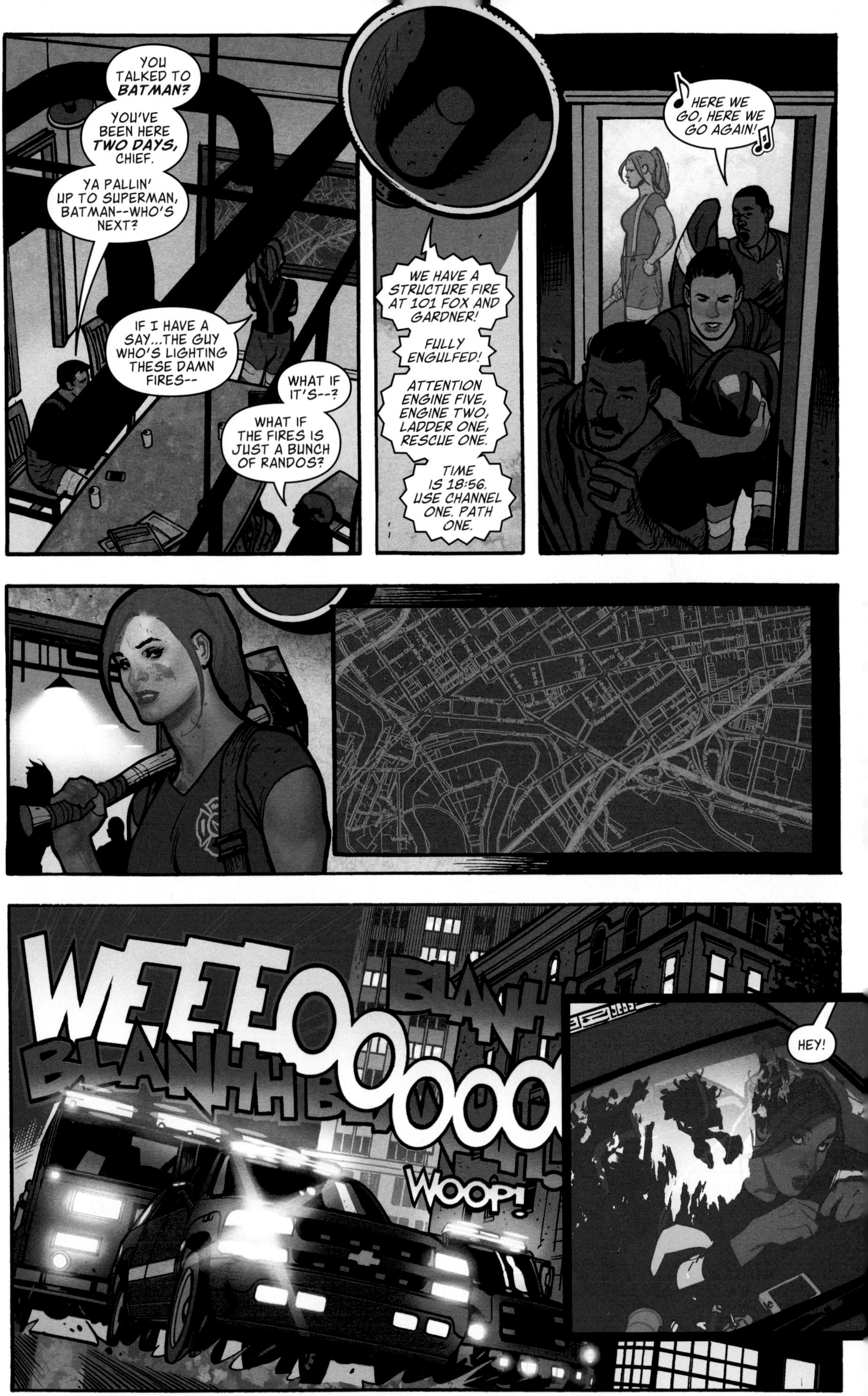
YOU TALKED TO BATMAN?
YOU'VE BEEN HERE TWO DAYS, CHIEF.
YA PALLIN' UP TO SUPERMAN, BATMAN--WHO'S NEXT?
IF I HAVE A SAY...THE GUY WHO'S LIGHTING THESE DAMN FIRES--
WHAT IF IT'S--?
WHAT IF THE FIRES IS JUST A BUNCH OF RANDOS?
WE HAVE A STRUCTURE FIRE AT 101 FOX AND GARDNER!
FULLY ENGULFED!
ATTENTION ENGINE FIVE, ENGINE TWO, LADDER ONE, RESCUE ONE.
TIME IS 18:56. USE CHANNEL ONE. PATH ONE.
HERE WE GO, HERE WE GO AGAIN!
WEEEOOOOOO
BLANHH BLANHH
WOOP!
HEY!

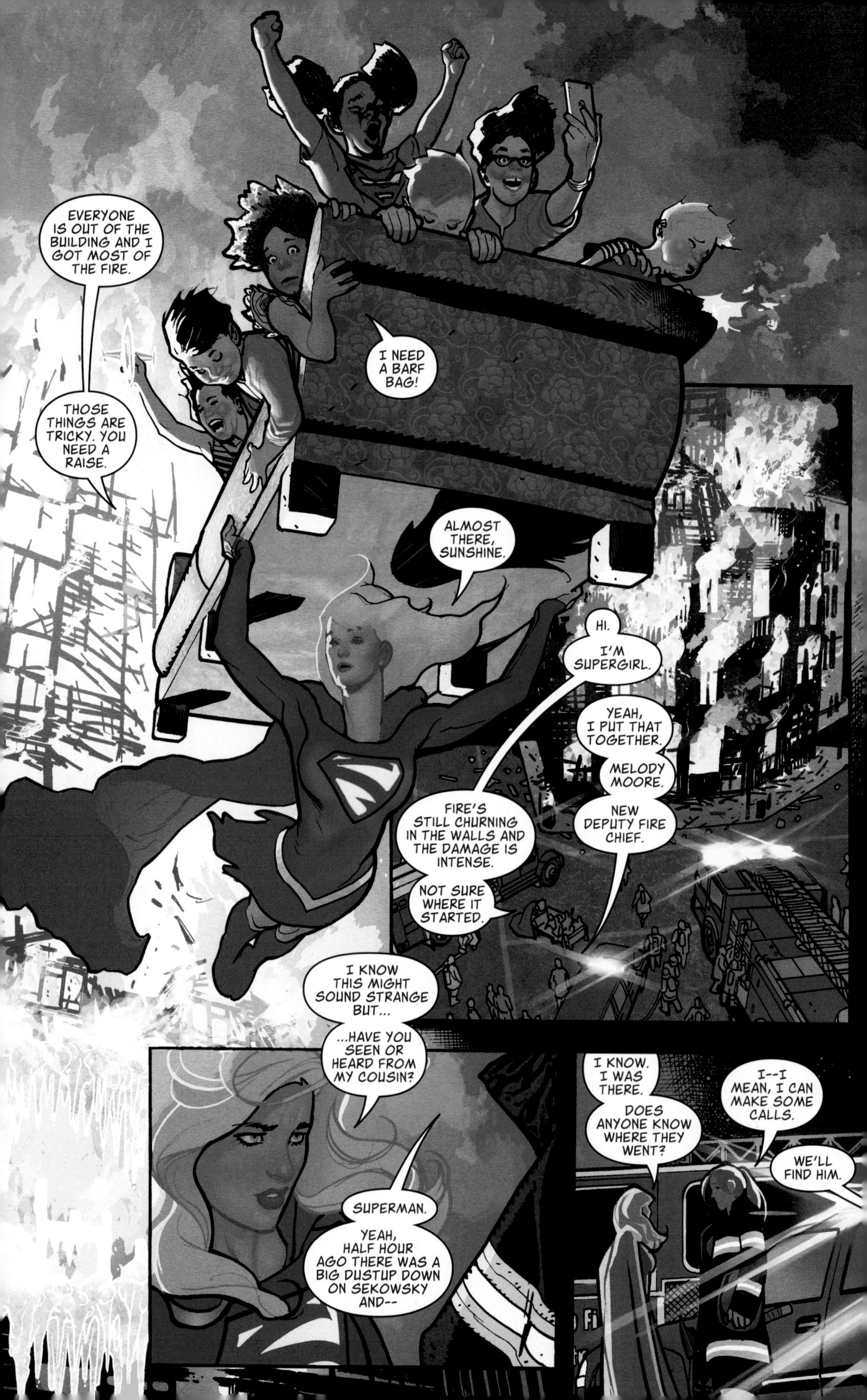
EVERYONE IS OUT OF THE BUILDING AND I GOT MOST OF THE FIRE.
THOSE THINGS ARE TRICKY. YOU NEED A RAISE.
I NEED A BARF BAG!
ALMOST THERE, SUNSHINE.
HI.
I'M SUPERGIRL.
YEAH, I PUT THAT TOGETHER.
MELODY MOORE.
NEW DEPUTY FIRE CHIEF.
FIRE'S STILL CHURNING IN THE WALLS AND THE DAMAGE IS INTENSE.
NOT SURE WHERE IT STARTED.
I KNOW THIS MIGHT SOUND STRANGE BUT...
...HAVE YOU SEEN OR HEARD FROM MY COUSIN?
SUPERMAN.
YEAH, HALF HOUR AGO THERE WAS A BIG DUSTUP DOWN ON SEKOWSKY AND--
I KNOW. I WAS THERE.
DOES ANYONE KNOW WHERE THEY WENT?
I--I MEAN, I CAN MAKE SOME CALLS.
WE'LL FIND HIM.

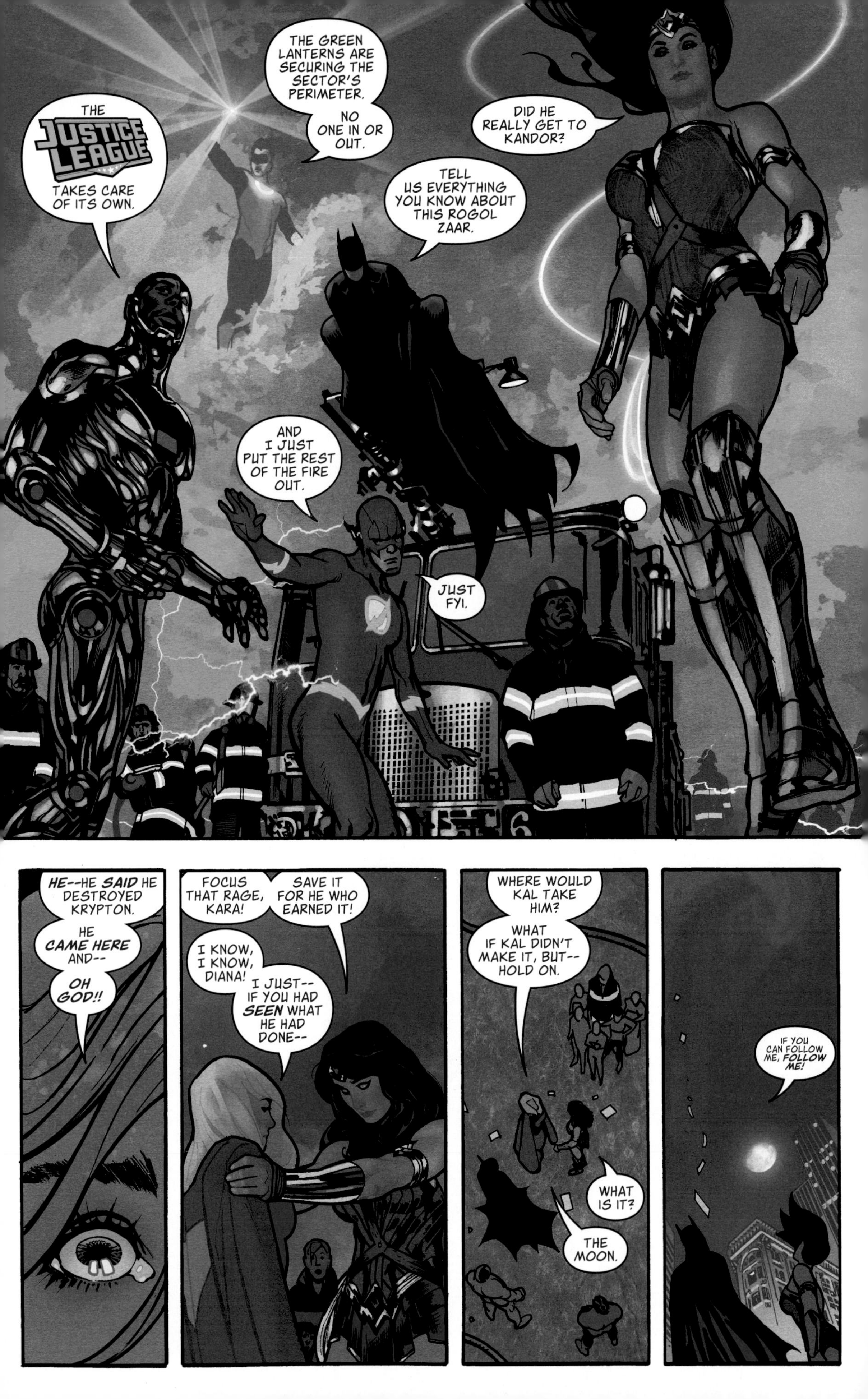

THE JUSTICE LEAGUE TAKES CARE OF ITS OWN.
THE GREEN LANTERNS ARE SECURING THE SECTOR'S PERIMETER.
NO ONE IN OR OUT.
TELL US EVERYTHING YOU KNOW ABOUT THIS ROGOL ZAAR.
DID HE REALLY GET TO KANDOR?
AND I JUST PUT THE REST OF THE FIRE OUT.
JUST FYI.
HE--HE SAID HE DESTROYED KRYPTON.
HE CAME HERE AND--
OH GOD!!
FOCUS THAT RAGE, KARA!
SAVE IT FOR HE WHO EARNED IT!
I KNOW, I KNOW, DIANA!
I JUST-- IF YOU HAD SEEN WHAT HE HAD DONE--
WHERE WOULD KAL TAKE HIM?
WHAT IF KAL DIDN'T MAKE IT, BUT-- HOLD ON.
WHAT IS IT?
THE MOON.
IF YOU CAN FOLLOW ME, FOLLOW ME!

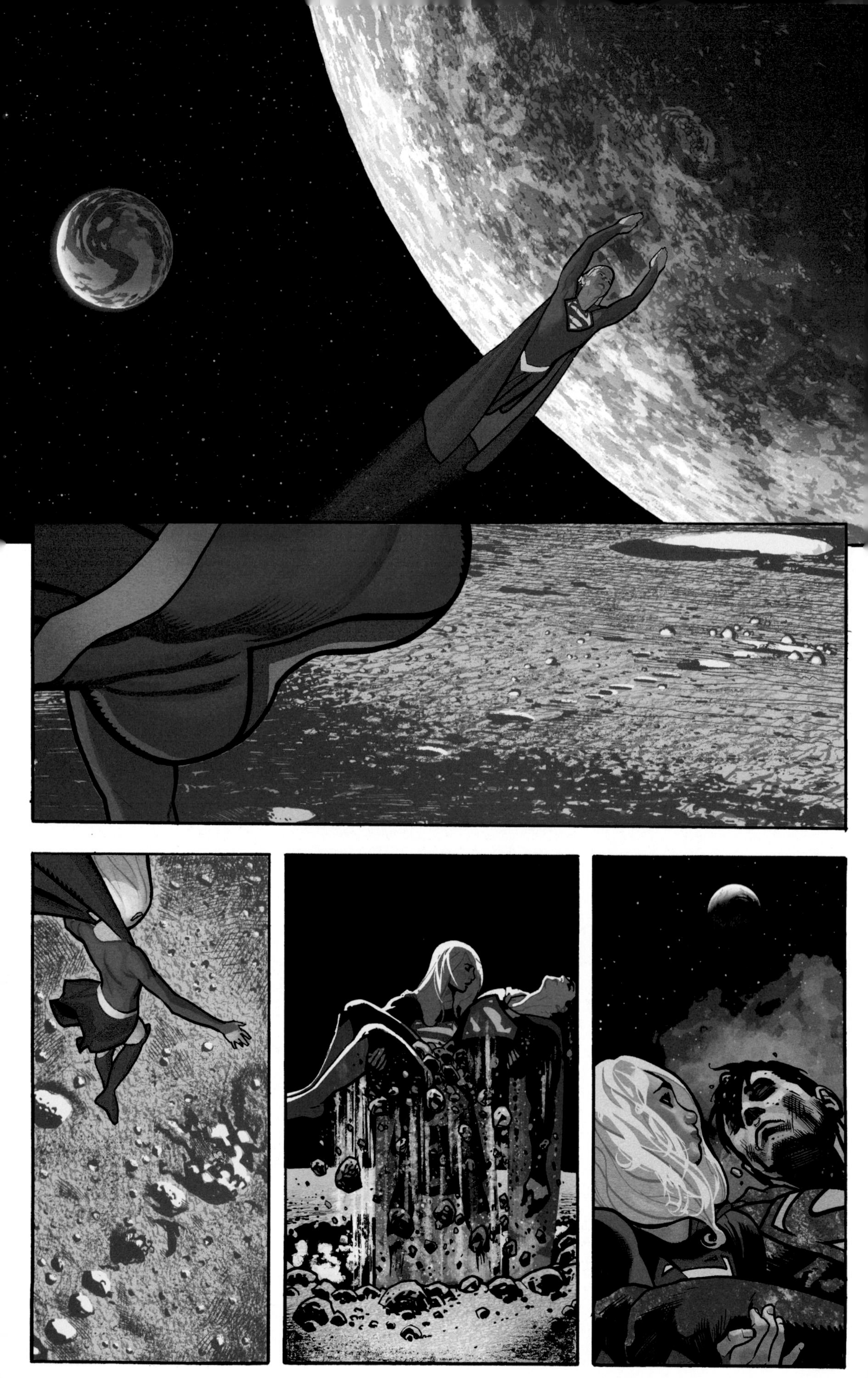

WHERE DID HE GO?

WHERE DID HE RUN OFF TO?

MAYBE HIS POWER SOURCE IS LIMITED.

MAYBE HE'S FULL OF CACA POO POO.

HE AIN'T.

HE TOOK OUT TWO OF THE SUPEREST OF SUPER-PEOPLE IN HAND-TO-HAND AND--

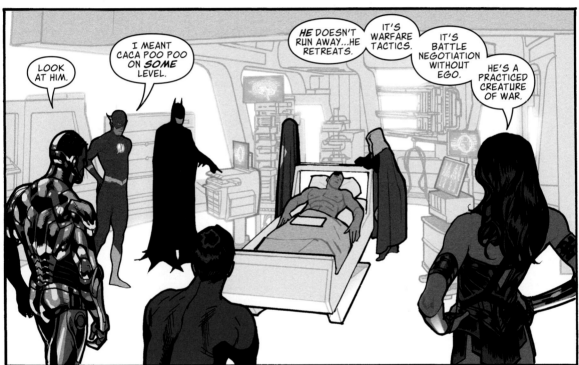

LOOK AT HIM.

I MEANT CACA POO POO ON *SOME* LEVEL.

HE DOESN'T RUN AWAY...HE RETREATS.

IT'S WARFARE TACTICS.

IT'S BATTLE NEGOTIATION WITHOUT EGO.

HE'S A PRACTICED CREATURE OF WAR.

FZZT!

TELL ME WHAT *THIS* IS.

SOME WEIRD ARTS AND CRAFTS PROJECT YOU DO TO CHILL OUT, OR--?

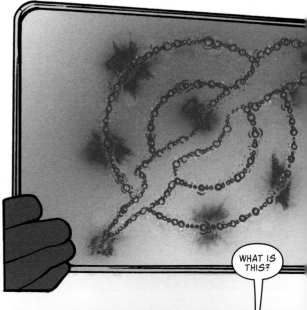

WHAT IS THIS?

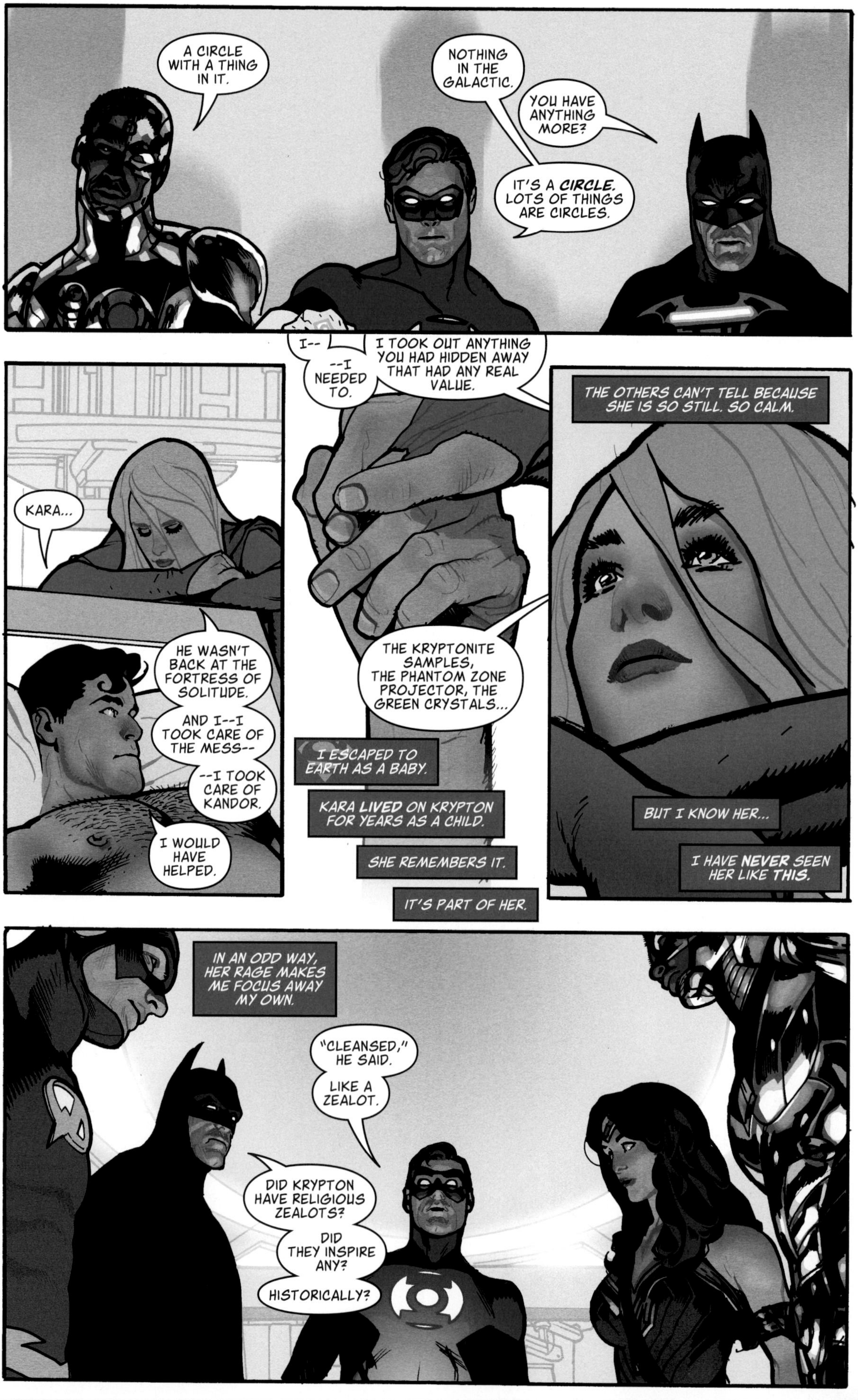
A CIRCLE WITH A THING IN IT.
NOTHING IN THE GALACTIC.
YOU HAVE ANYTHING MORE?
IT'S A CIRCLE. LOTS OF THINGS ARE CIRCLES.
KARA...
I--
--I NEEDED TO.
I TOOK OUT ANYTHING YOU HAD HIDDEN AWAY THAT HAD ANY REAL VALUE.
THE OTHERS CAN'T TELL BECAUSE SHE IS SO STILL. SO CALM.
HE WASN'T BACK AT THE FORTRESS OF SOLITUDE.
AND I--I TOOK CARE OF THE MESS--
--I TOOK CARE OF KANDOR.
I WOULD HAVE HELPED.
THE KRYPTONITE SAMPLES, THE PHANTOM ZONE PROJECTOR, THE GREEN CRYSTALS...
I ESCAPED TO EARTH AS A BABY.
KARA LIVED ON KRYPTON FOR YEARS AS A CHILD.
SHE REMEMBERS IT.
IT'S PART OF HER.
BUT I KNOW HER...
I HAVE NEVER SEEN HER LIKE THIS.
IN AN ODD WAY, HER RAGE MAKES ME FOCUS AWAY MY OWN.
"CLEANSED," HE SAID.
LIKE A ZEALOT.
DID KRYPTON HAVE RELIGIOUS ZEALOTS?
DID THEY INSPIRE ANY?
HISTORICALLY?

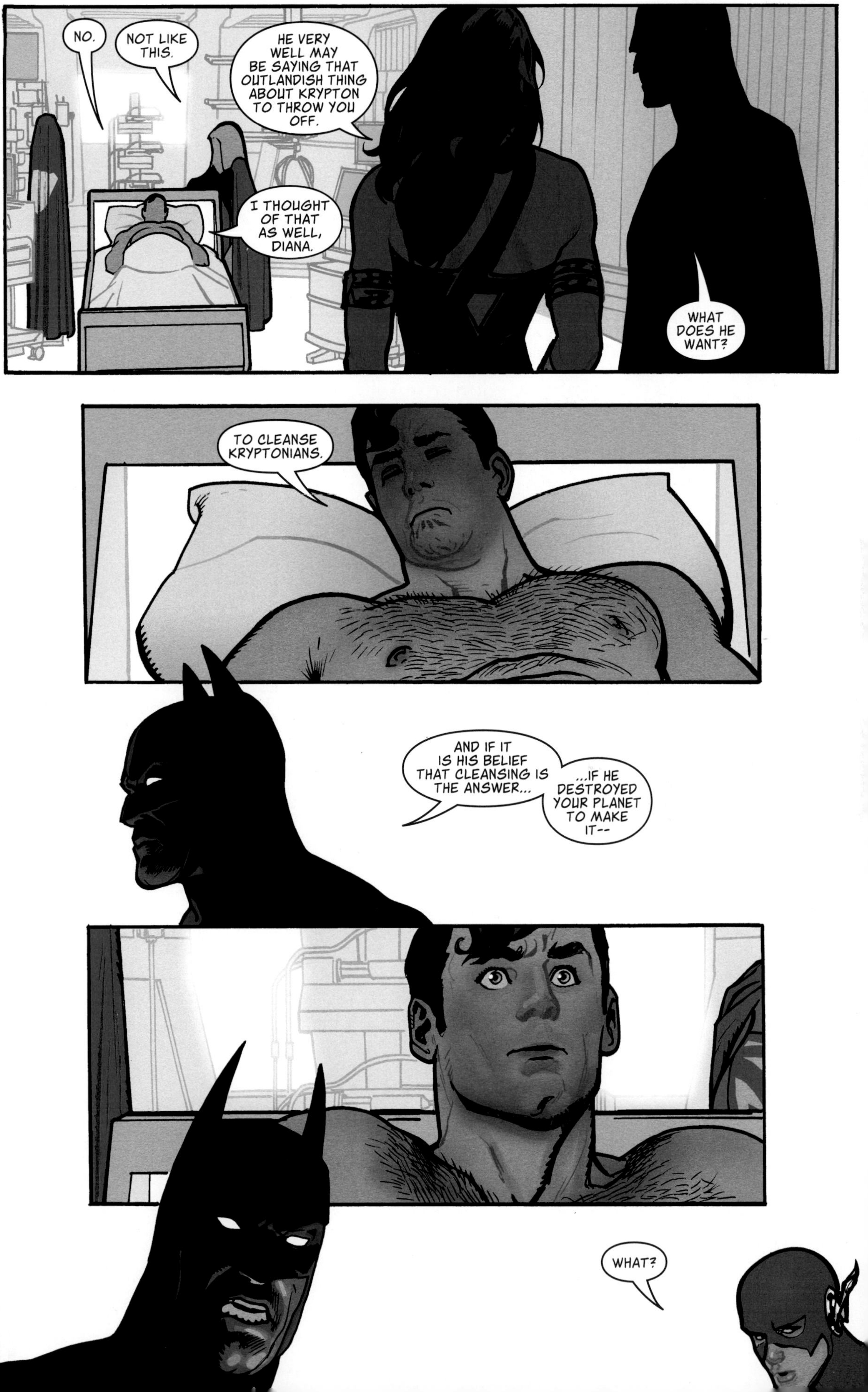
NO.
NOT LIKE THIS.
HE VERY WELL MAY BE SAYING THAT OUTLANDISH THING ABOUT KRYPTON TO THROW YOU OFF.
I THOUGHT OF THAT AS WELL, DIANA.
WHAT DOES HE WANT?
TO CLEANSE KRYPTONIANS.
AND IF IT IS HIS BELIEF THAT CLEANSING IS THE ANSWER...
...IF HE DESTROYED YOUR PLANET TO MAKE IT--
WHAT?

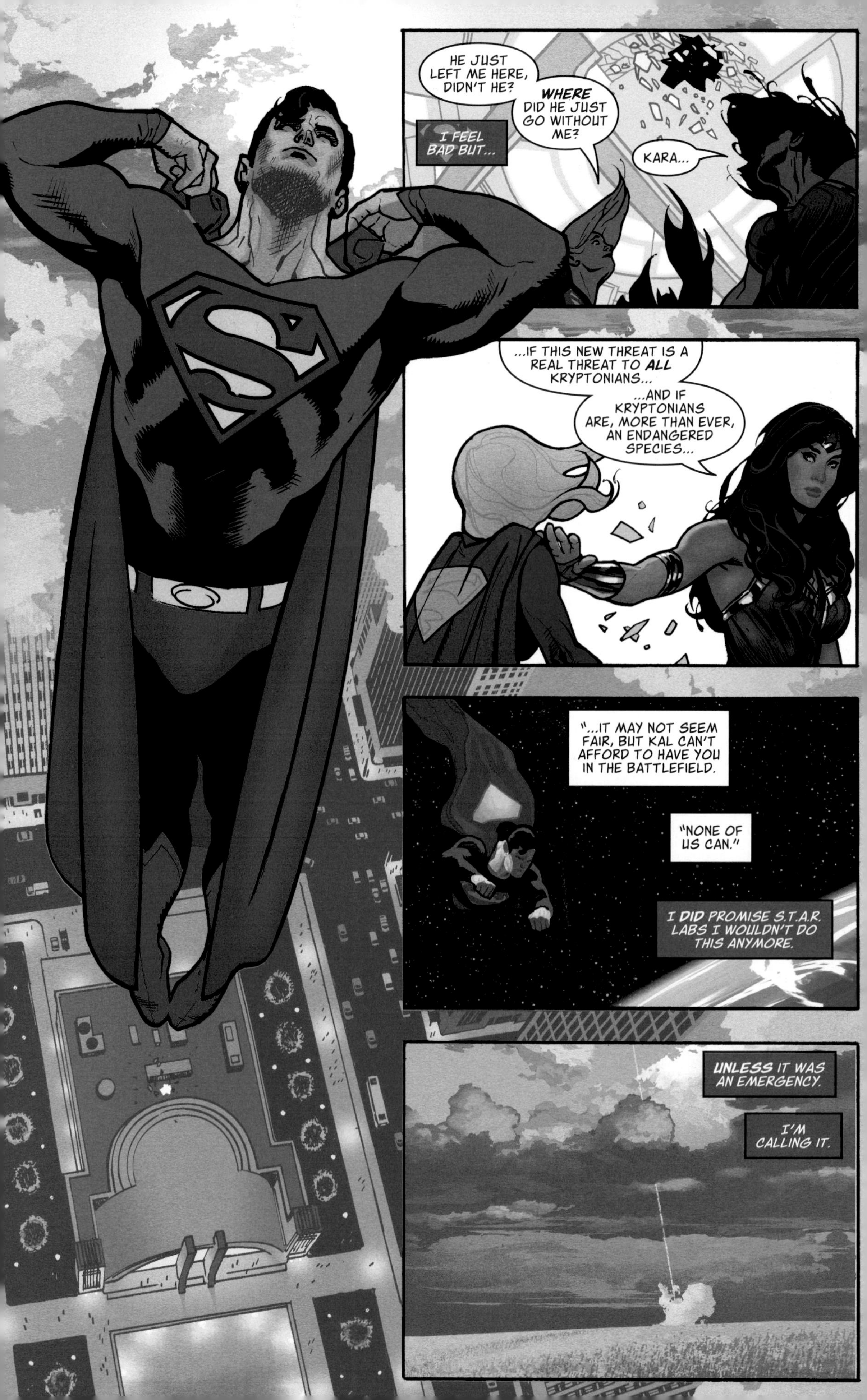
HE JUST LEFT ME HERE, DIDN'T HE?
WHERE DID HE JUST GO WITHOUT ME?
I FEEL BAD BUT...
KARA...
...IF THIS NEW THREAT IS A REAL THREAT TO ALL KRYPTONIANS...
...AND IF KRYPTONIANS ARE, MORE THAN EVER, AN ENDANGERED SPECIES...
"...IT MAY NOT SEEM FAIR, BUT KAL CAN'T AFFORD TO HAVE YOU IN THE BATTLEFIELD.
"NONE OF US CAN."
I DID PROMISE S.T.A.R. LABS I WOULDN'T DO THIS ANYMORE.
UNLESS IT WAS AN EMERGENCY.
I'M CALLING IT.

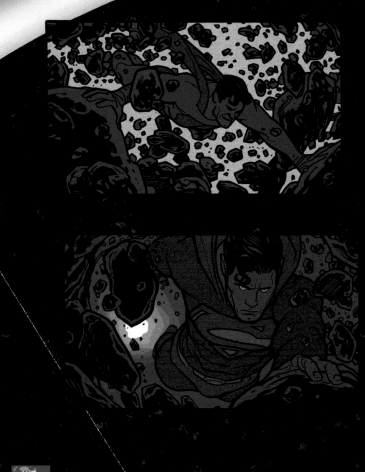

AND...

...BATMAN
WAS RIGHT...

...CLEANSING.

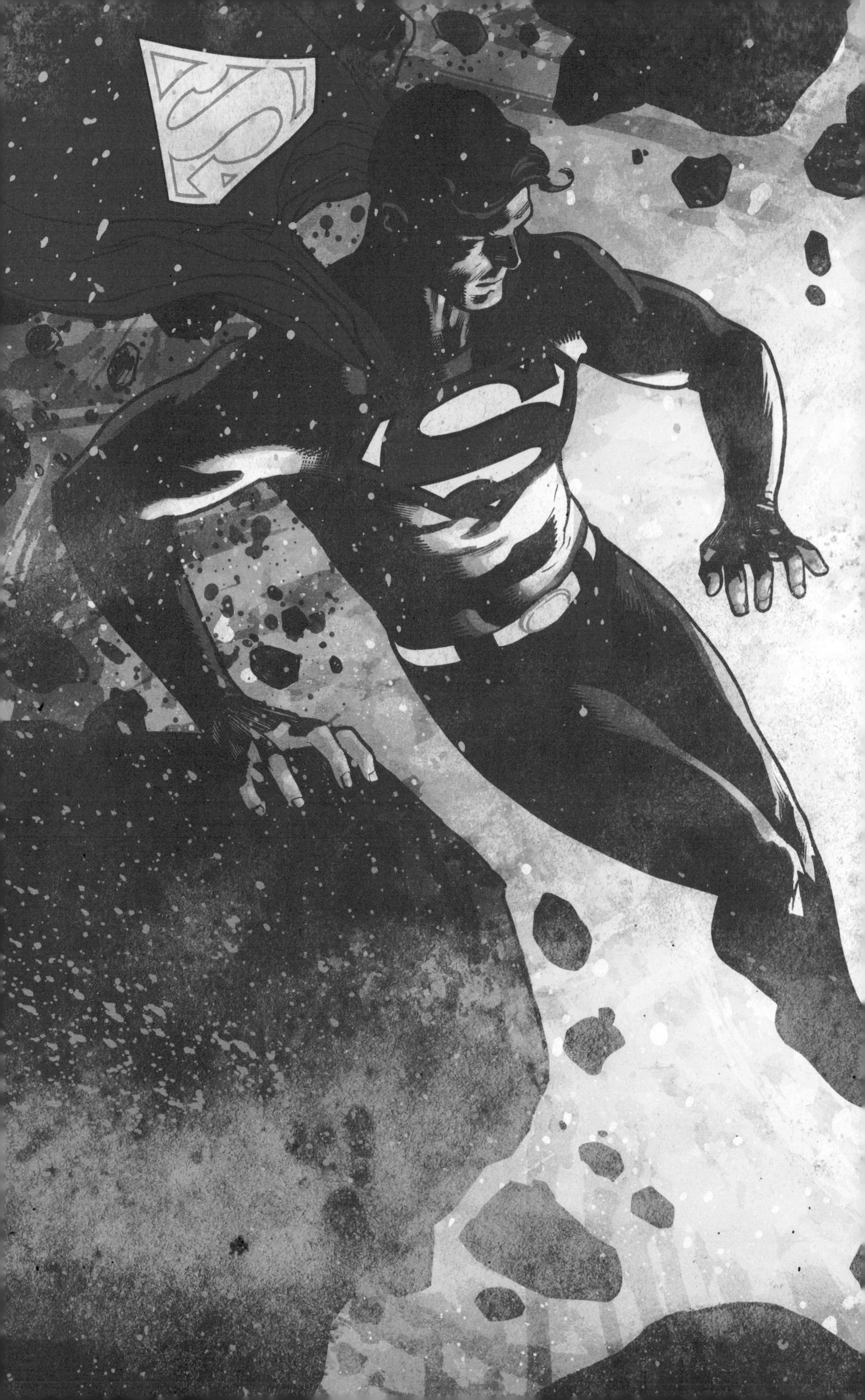

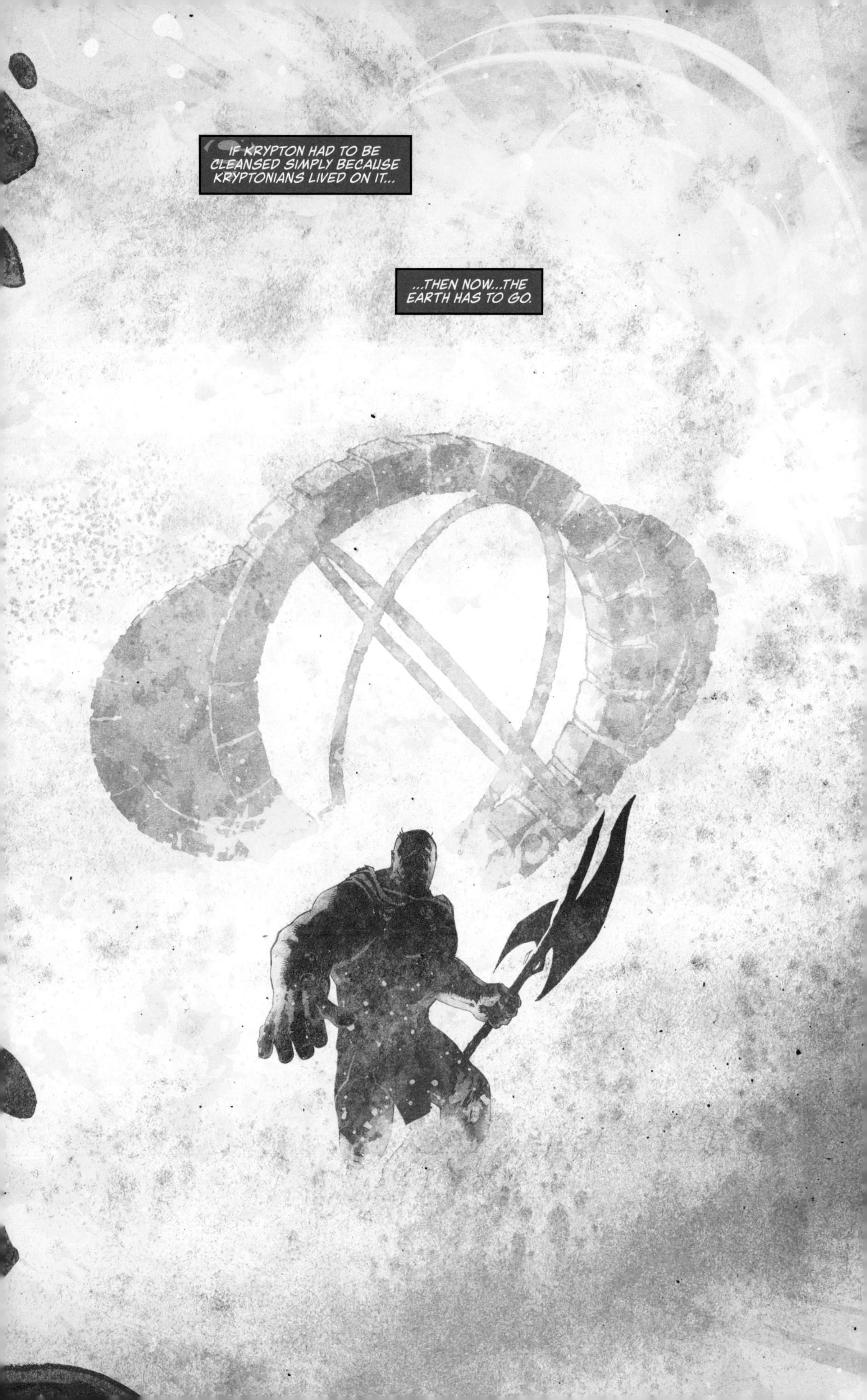
IF KRYPTON HAD TO BE CLEANSED SIMPLY BECAUSE KRYPTONIANS LIVED ON IT...
...THEN NOW...THE EARTH HAS TO GO.

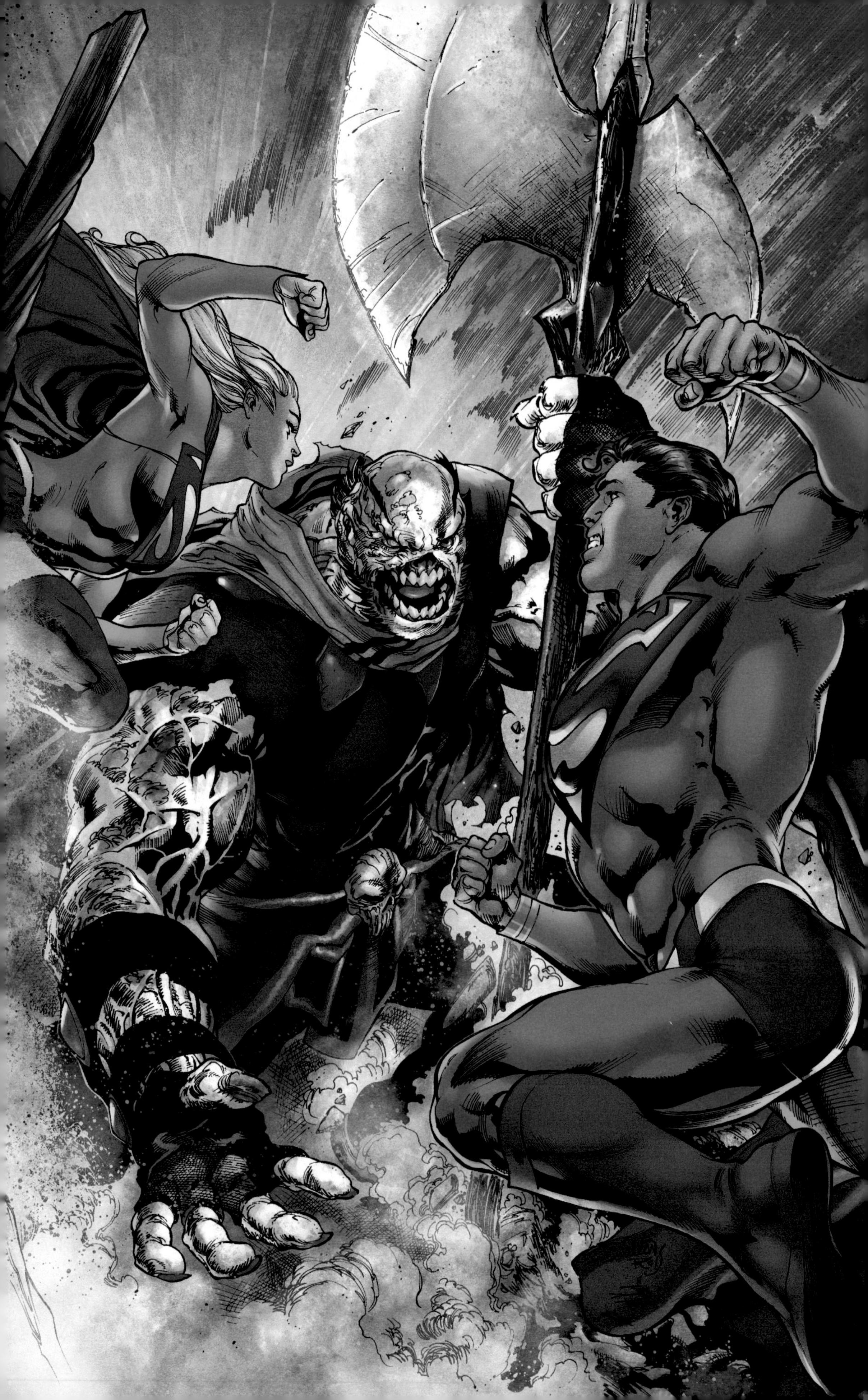

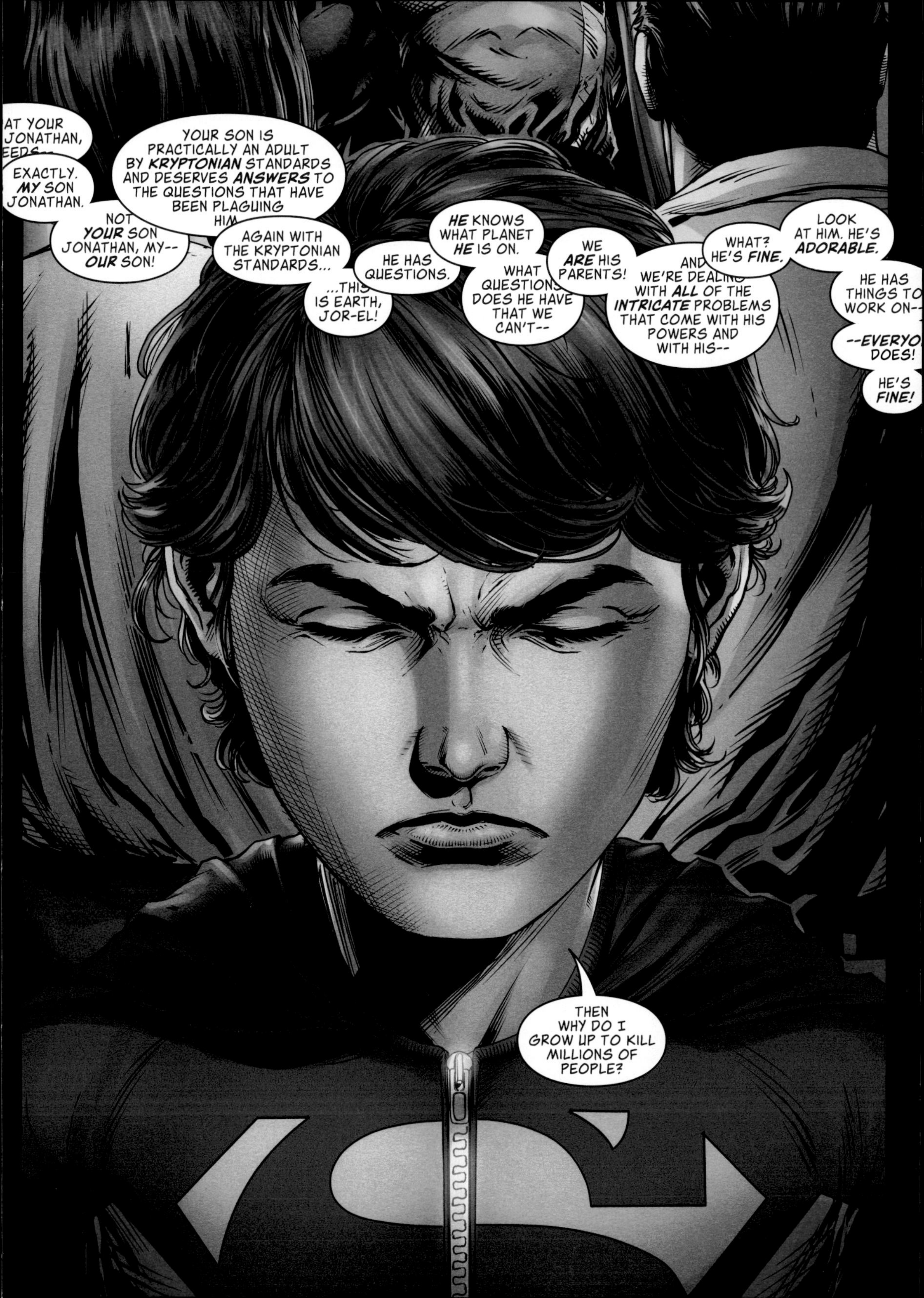
AT YOUR JONATHAN,
EXACTLY. MY SON JONATHAN.
YOUR SON IS PRACTICALLY AN ADULT BY KRYPTONIAN STANDARDS AND DESERVES ANSWERS TO THE QUESTIONS THAT HAVE BEEN PLAGUING HIM
NOT YOUR SON JONATHAN, MY-- OUR SON!
AGAIN WITH THE KRYPTONIAN STANDARDS...
...THIS IS EARTH, JOR-EL!
HE HAS QUESTIONS.
HE KNOWS WHAT PLANET HE IS ON.
WHAT QUESTIONS DOES HE HAVE THAT WE CAN'T--
WE ARE HIS PARENTS!
AND WE'RE DEALING WITH ALL OF THE INTRICATE PROBLEMS THAT COME WITH HIS POWERS AND WITH HIS--
WHAT? HE'S FINE.
LOOK AT HIM. HE'S ADORABLE.
HE HAS THINGS TO WORK ON--
DOES!
HE'S FINE!
THEN WHY DO I GROW UP TO KILL MILLIONS OF PEOPLE?

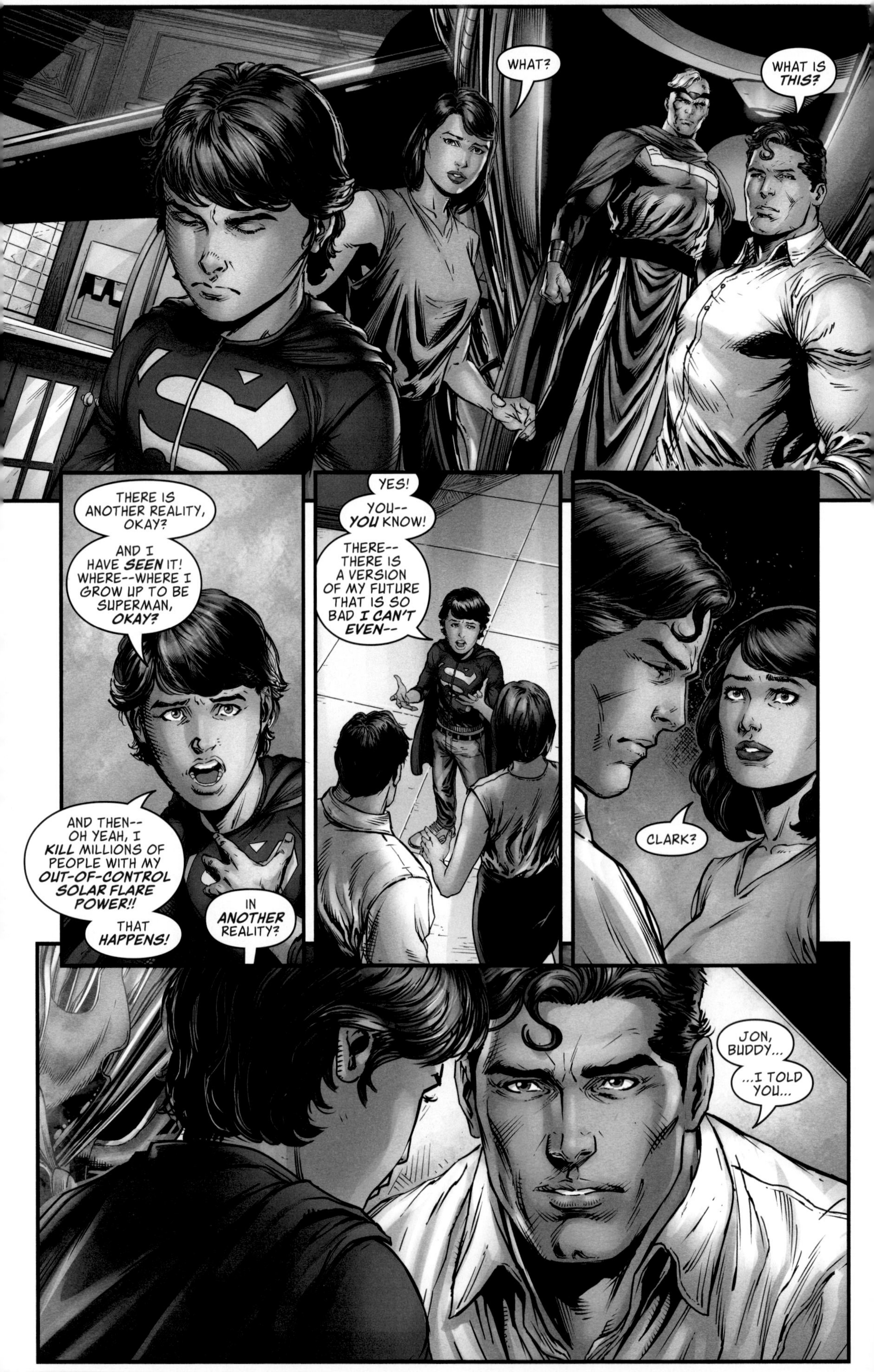
WHAT?
WHAT IS THIS?
THERE IS ANOTHER REALITY, OKAY?
AND I HAVE SEEN IT! WHERE--WHERE I GROW UP TO BE SUPERMAN, OKAY?
AND THEN--OH YEAH, I KILL MILLIONS OF PEOPLE WITH MY OUT-OF-CONTROL SOLAR FLARE POWER!!
THAT HAPPENS!
IN ANOTHER REALITY?
YES!
YOU--YOU KNOW!
THERE--THERE IS A VERSION OF MY FUTURE THAT IS SO BAD I CAN'T EVEN--
CLARK?
JON, BUDDY...
...I TOLD YOU...

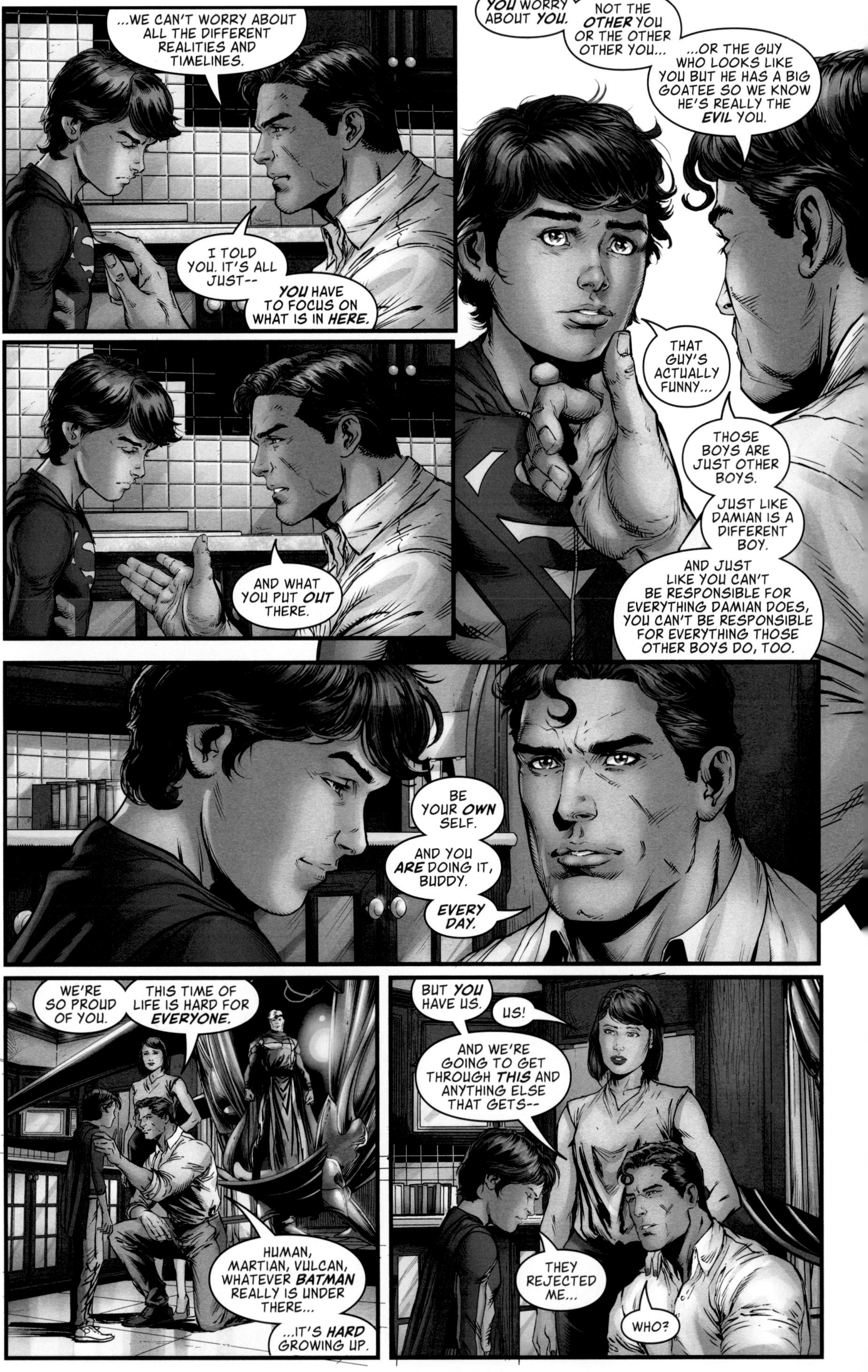
...WE CAN'T WORRY ABOUT ALL THE DIFFERENT REALITIES AND TIMELINES.
I TOLD YOU. IT'S ALL JUST--
YOU HAVE TO FOCUS ON WHAT IS IN HERE.
AND WHAT YOU PUT OUT THERE.
YOU WORRY ABOUT YOU.
NOT THE OTHER YOU OR THE OTHER OTHER YOU...
...OR THE GUY WHO LOOKS LIKE YOU BUT HE HAS A BIG GOATEE SO WE KNOW HE'S REALLY THE EVIL YOU.
THAT GUY'S ACTUALLY FUNNY...
THOSE BOYS ARE JUST OTHER BOYS.
JUST LIKE DAMIAN IS A DIFFERENT BOY.
AND JUST LIKE YOU CAN'T BE RESPONSIBLE FOR EVERYTHING DAMIAN DOES, YOU CAN'T BE RESPONSIBLE FOR EVERYTHING THOSE OTHER BOYS DO, TOO.
BE YOUR OWN SELF.
AND YOU ARE DOING IT, BUDDY.
EVERY DAY.
WE'RE SO PROUD OF YOU.
THIS TIME OF LIFE IS HARD FOR EVERYONE.
HUMAN, MARTIAN, VULCAN, WHATEVER BATMAN REALLY IS UNDER THERE...
...IT'S HARD GROWING UP.
BUT YOU HAVE US.
US!
AND WE'RE GOING TO GET THROUGH THIS AND ANYTHING ELSE THAT GETS--
THEY REJECTED ME...
WHO?

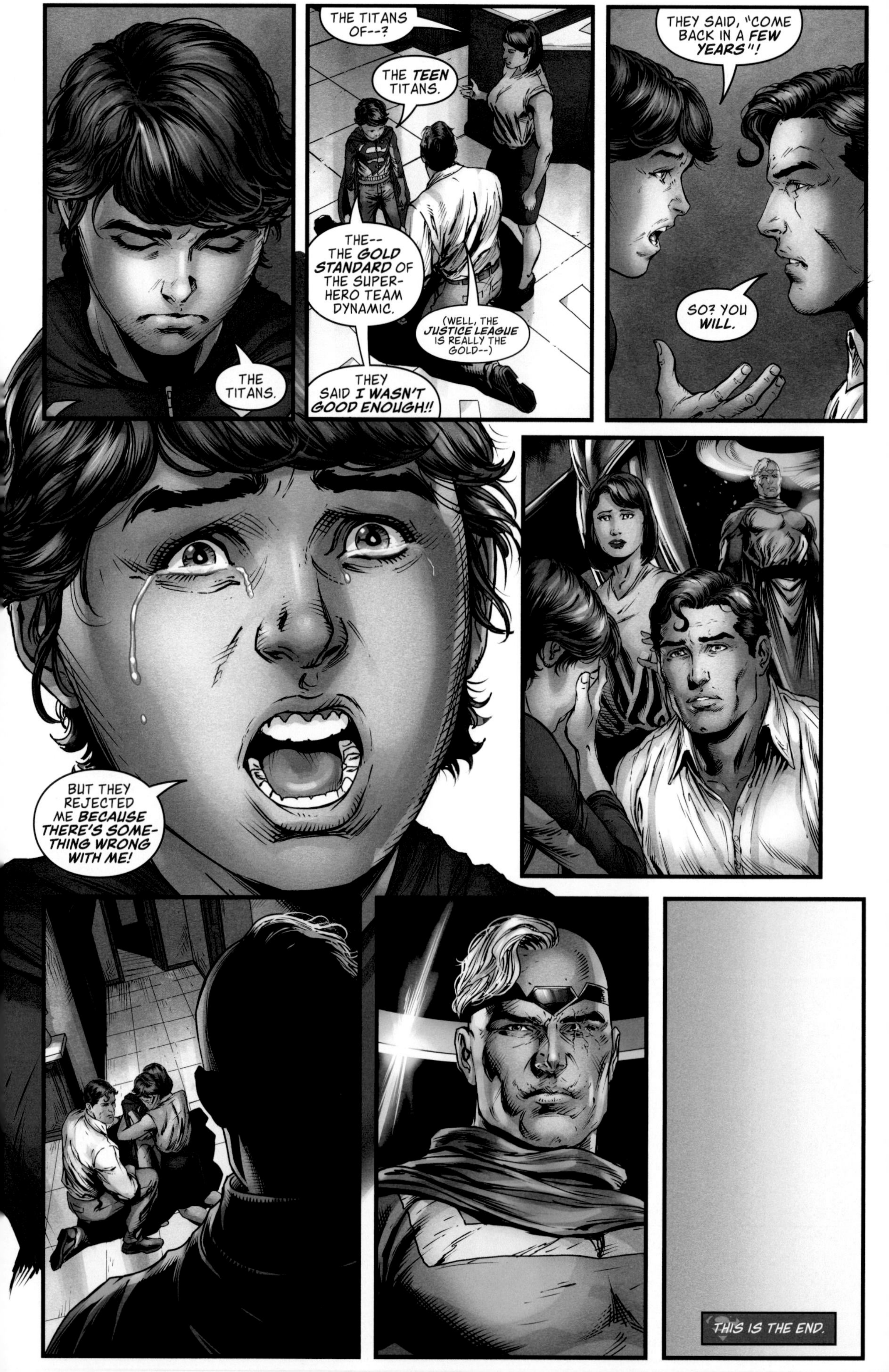
THE TITANS.
THE TITANS OF--?
THE TEEN TITANS.
THE-- THE GOLD STANDARD OF THE SUPER-HERO TEAM DYNAMIC.
(WELL, THE JUSTICE LEAGUE IS REALLY THE GOLD--)
THEY SAID I WASN'T GOOD ENOUGH!!
THEY SAID, "COME BACK IN A FEW YEARS"!
SO? YOU WILL.
BUT THEY REJECTED ME BECAUSE THERE'S SOMETHING WRONG WITH ME!
THIS IS THE END.

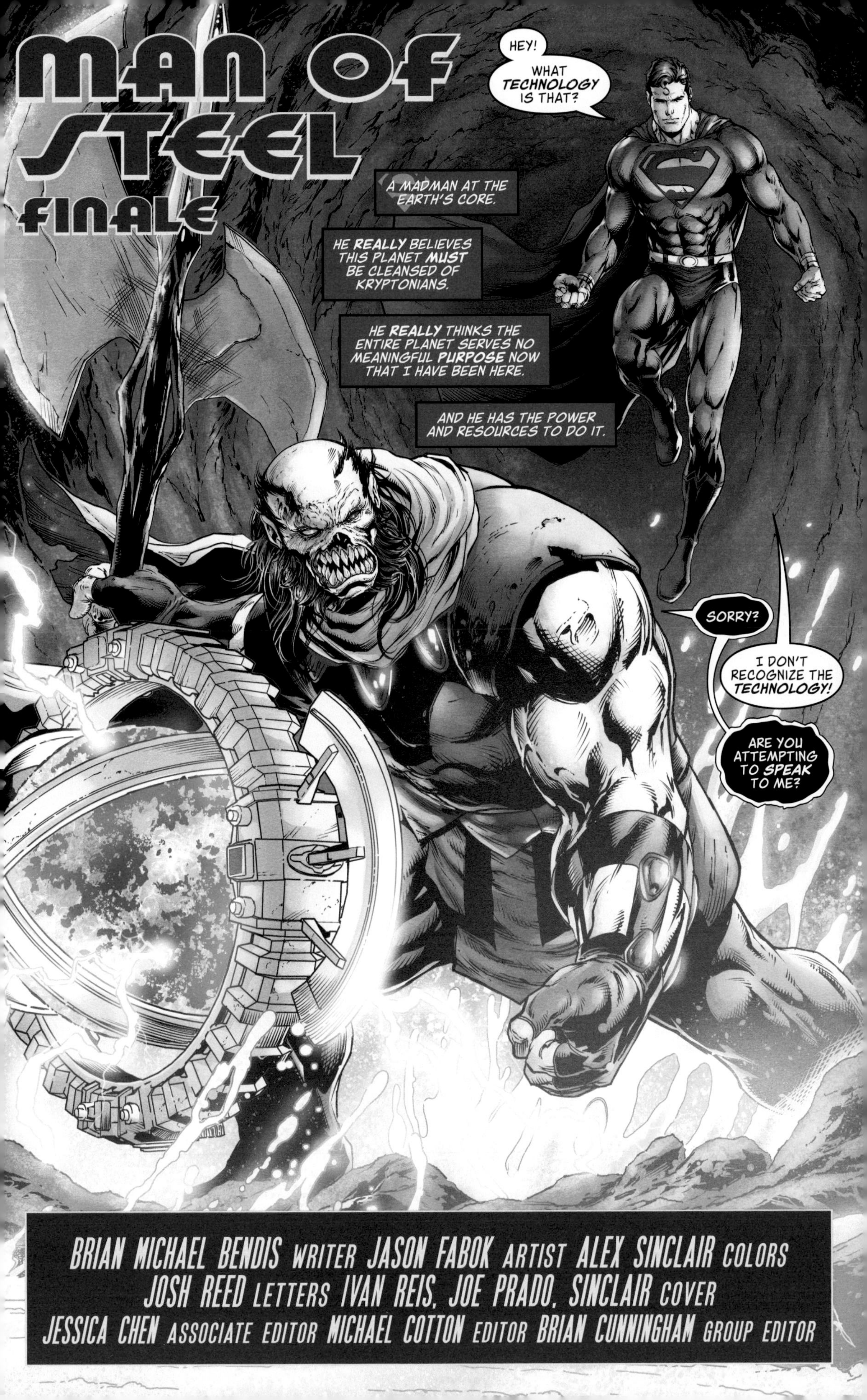
MAN OF STEEL
FINALE
HEY!
WHAT TECHNOLOGY IS THAT?
A MADMAN AT THE EARTH'S CORE.
HE REALLY BELIEVES THIS PLANET MUST BE CLEANSED OF KRYPTONIANS.
HE REALLY THINKS THE ENTIRE PLANET SERVES NO MEANINGFUL PURPOSE NOW THAT I HAVE BEEN HERE.
AND HE HAS THE POWER AND RESOURCES TO DO IT.
SORRY?
I DON'T RECOGNIZE THE TECHNOLOGY!
ARE YOU ATTEMPTING TO SPEAK TO ME?
BRIAN MICHAEL BENDIS WRITER JASON FABOK ARTIST ALEX SINCLAIR COLORS
JOSH REED LETTERS IVAN REIS, JOE PRADO, SINCLAIR COVER
JESSICA CHEN ASSOCIATE EDITOR MICHAEL COTTON EDITOR BRIAN CUNNINGHAM GROUP EDITOR

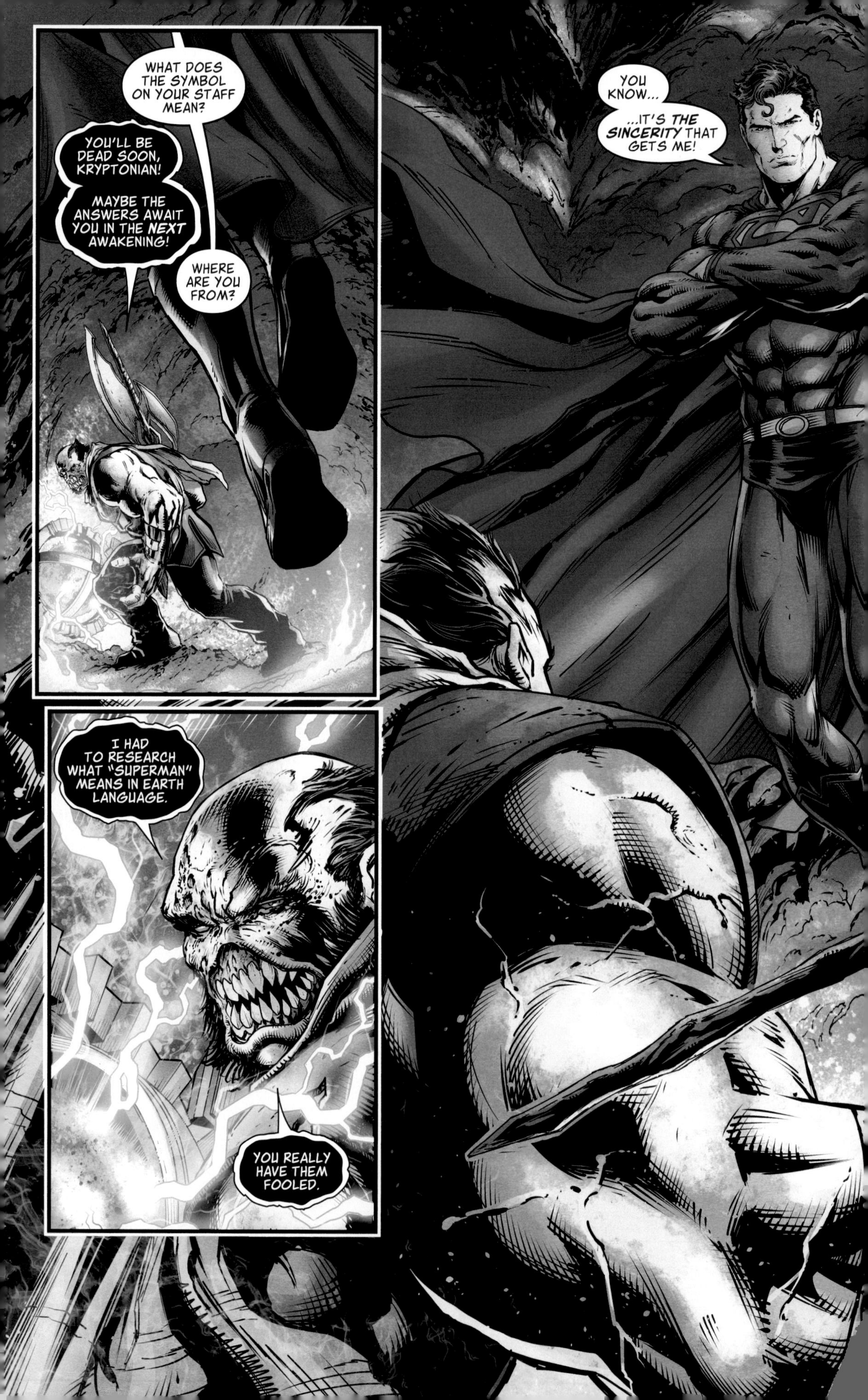
WHAT DOES THE SYMBOL ON YOUR STAFF MEAN?
YOU'LL BE DEAD SOON, KRYPTONIAN!
MAYBE THE ANSWERS AWAIT YOU IN THE NEXT AWAKENING!
WHERE ARE YOU FROM?
I HAD TO RESEARCH WHAT "SUPERMAN" MEANS IN EARTH LANGUAGE.
YOU REALLY HAVE THEM FOOLED.
YOU KNOW...
...IT'S THE SINCERITY THAT GETS ME!

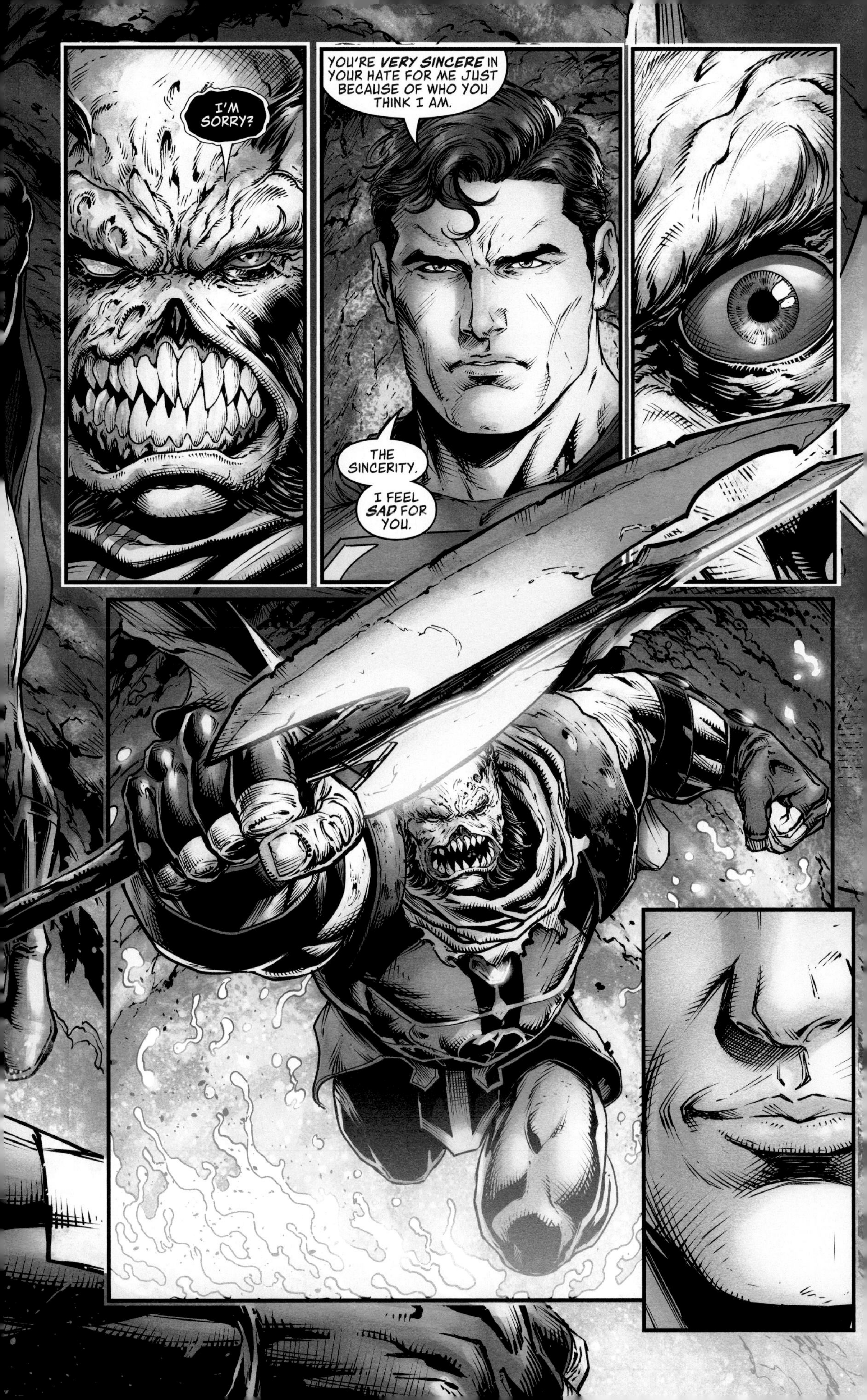
I'M SORRY?
YOU'RE VERY SINCERE IN YOUR HATE FOR ME JUST BECAUSE OF WHO YOU THINK I AM.
THE SINCERITY.
I FEEL SAD FOR YOU.

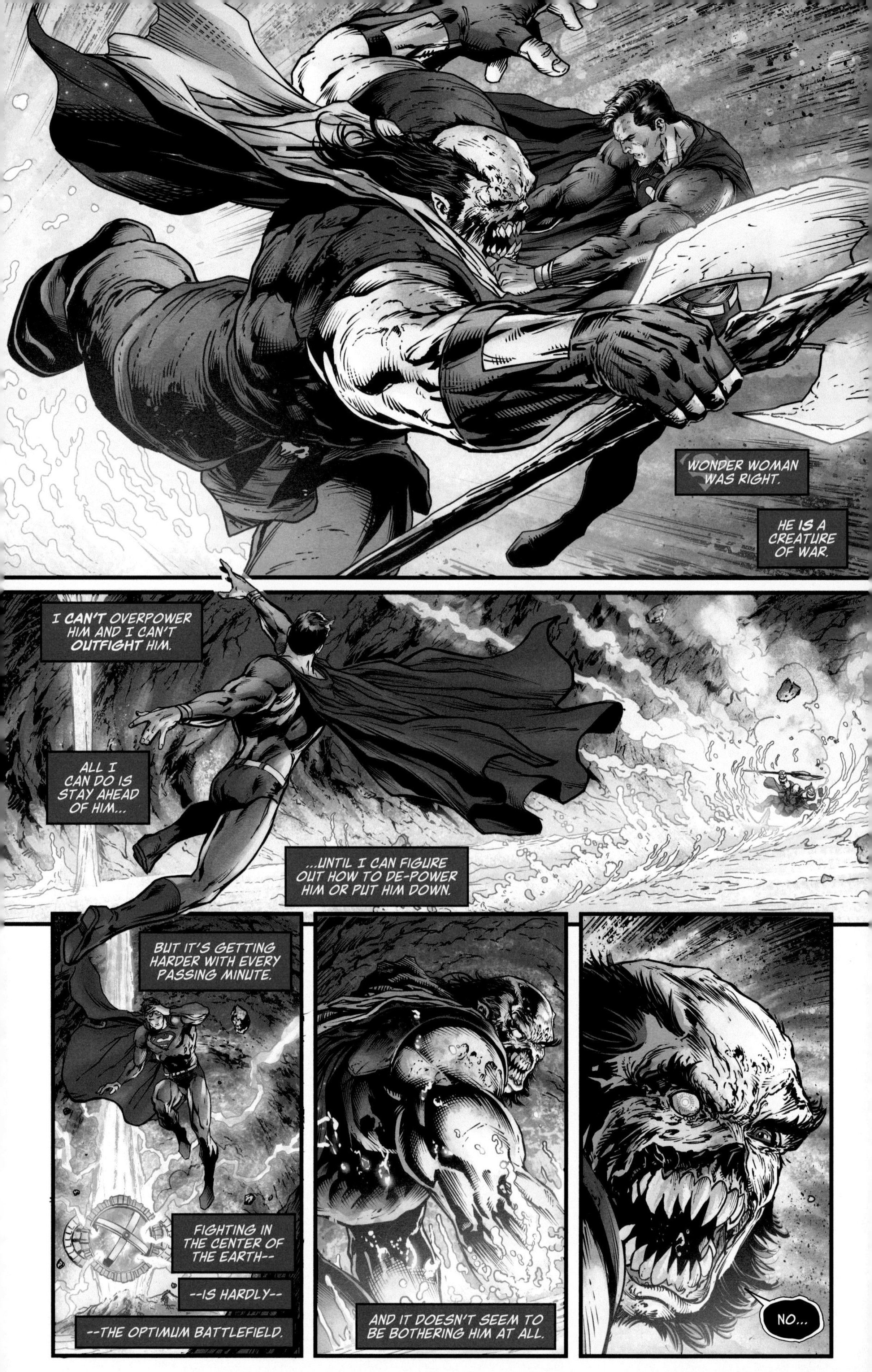
WONDER WOMAN WAS RIGHT.
HE IS A CREATURE OF WAR.
I CAN'T OVERPOWER HIM AND I CAN'T OUTFIGHT HIM.
ALL I CAN DO IS STAY AHEAD OF HIM...
...UNTIL I CAN FIGURE OUT HOW TO DE-POWER HIM OR PUT HIM DOWN.
BUT IT'S GETTING HARDER WITH EVERY PASSING MINUTE.
FIGHTING IN THE CENTER OF THE EARTH--
--IS HARDLY--
--THE OPTIMUM BATTLEFIELD.
AND IT DOESN'T SEEM TO BE BOTHERING HIM AT ALL.
NO...

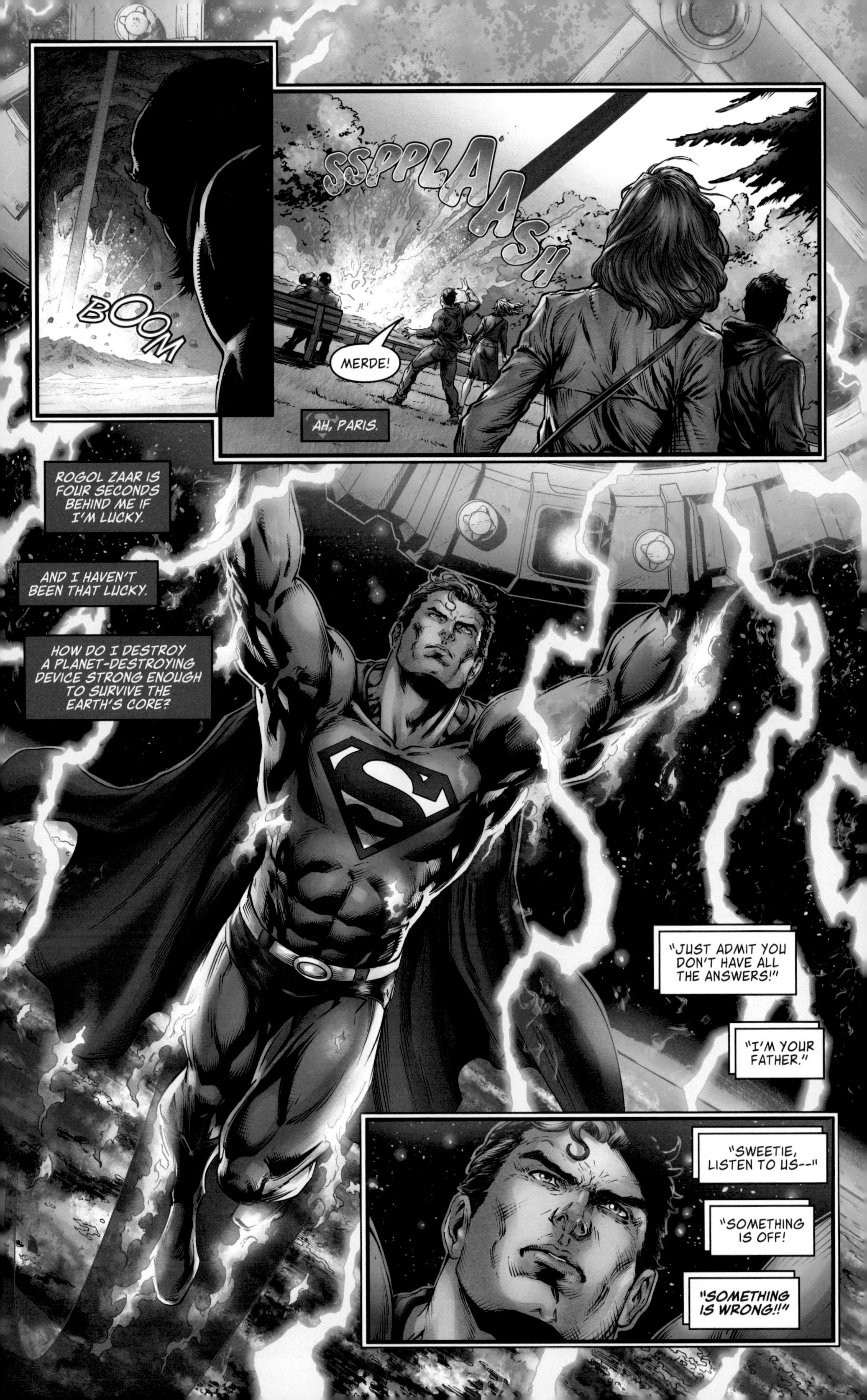
BOOM
SSPPLAAASH
MERDE!
AH, PARIS.
ROGOL ZAAR IS FOUR SECONDS BEHIND ME IF I'M LUCKY.
AND I HAVEN'T BEEN THAT LUCKY.
HOW DO I DESTROY A PLANET-DESTROYING DEVICE STRONG ENOUGH TO SURVIVE THE EARTH'S CORE?
"JUST ADMIT YOU DON'T HAVE ALL THE ANSWERS!"
"I'M YOUR FATHER."
"SWEETIE, LISTEN TO US--"
"SOMETHING IS OFF!
"SOMETHING IS WRONG!!"

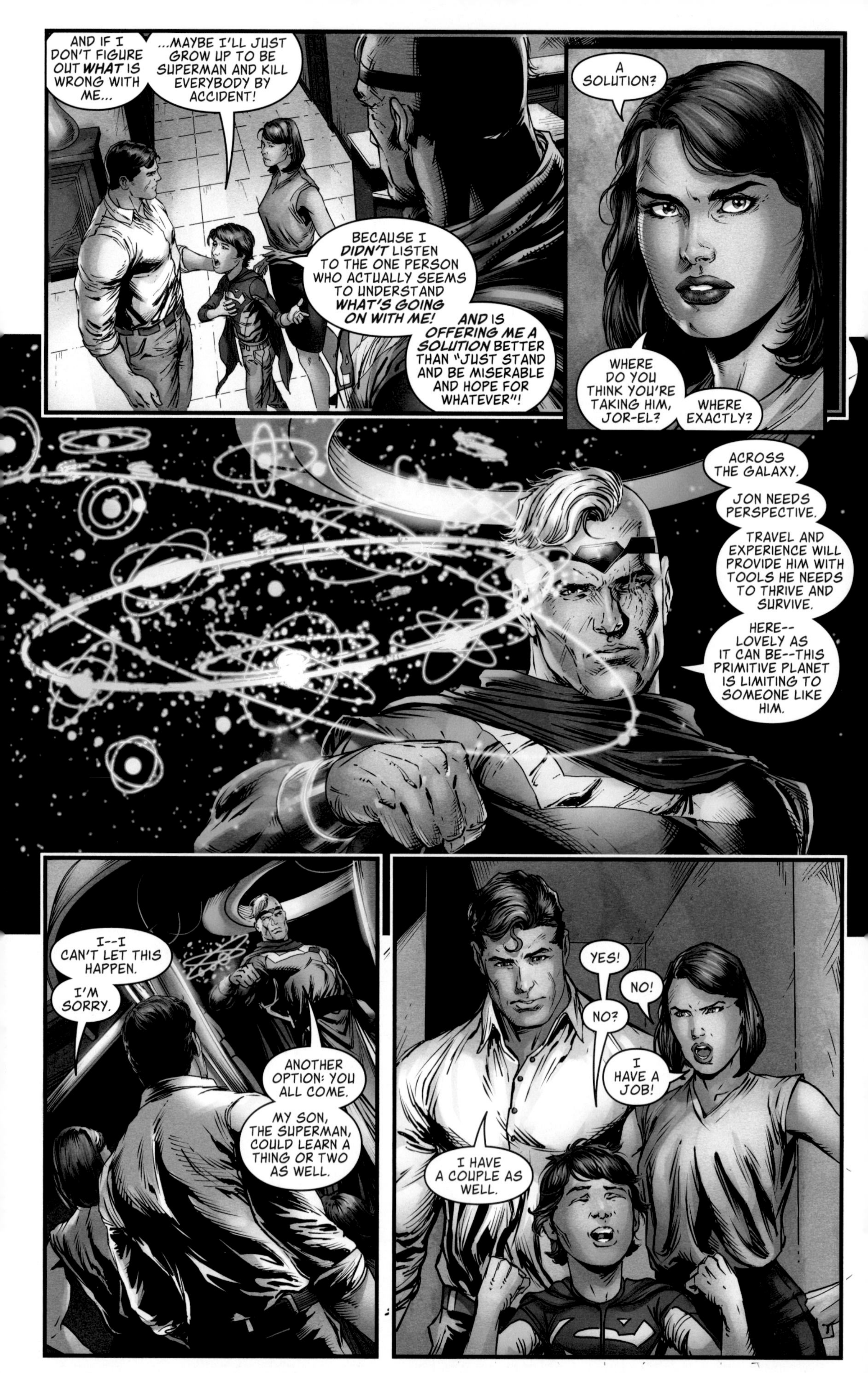
AND IF I DON'T FIGURE OUT **WHAT** IS WRONG WITH ME...
...MAYBE I'LL JUST GROW UP TO BE SUPERMAN AND KILL EVERYBODY BY ACCIDENT!
BECAUSE I **DIDN'T** LISTEN TO THE ONE PERSON WHO ACTUALLY SEEMS TO UNDERSTAND **WHAT'S GOING ON WITH ME!**
AND IS **OFFERING ME A SOLUTION** BETTER THAN "JUST STAND AND BE MISERABLE AND HOPE FOR WHATEVER"!
A SOLUTION?
WHERE DO YOU THINK YOU'RE TAKING HIM, JOR-EL?
WHERE EXACTLY?
ACROSS THE GALAXY.
JON NEEDS PERSPECTIVE.
TRAVEL AND EXPERIENCE WILL PROVIDE HIM WITH TOOLS HE NEEDS TO THRIVE AND SURVIVE.
HERE--LOVELY AS IT CAN BE--THIS PRIMITIVE PLANET IS LIMITING TO SOMEONE LIKE HIM.
I--I CAN'T LET THIS HAPPEN.
I'M SORRY.
ANOTHER OPTION: YOU ALL COME.
MY SON, THE SUPERMAN, COULD LEARN A THING OR TWO AS WELL.
YES!
NO!
NO?
I HAVE A JOB!
I HAVE A COUPLE AS WELL.

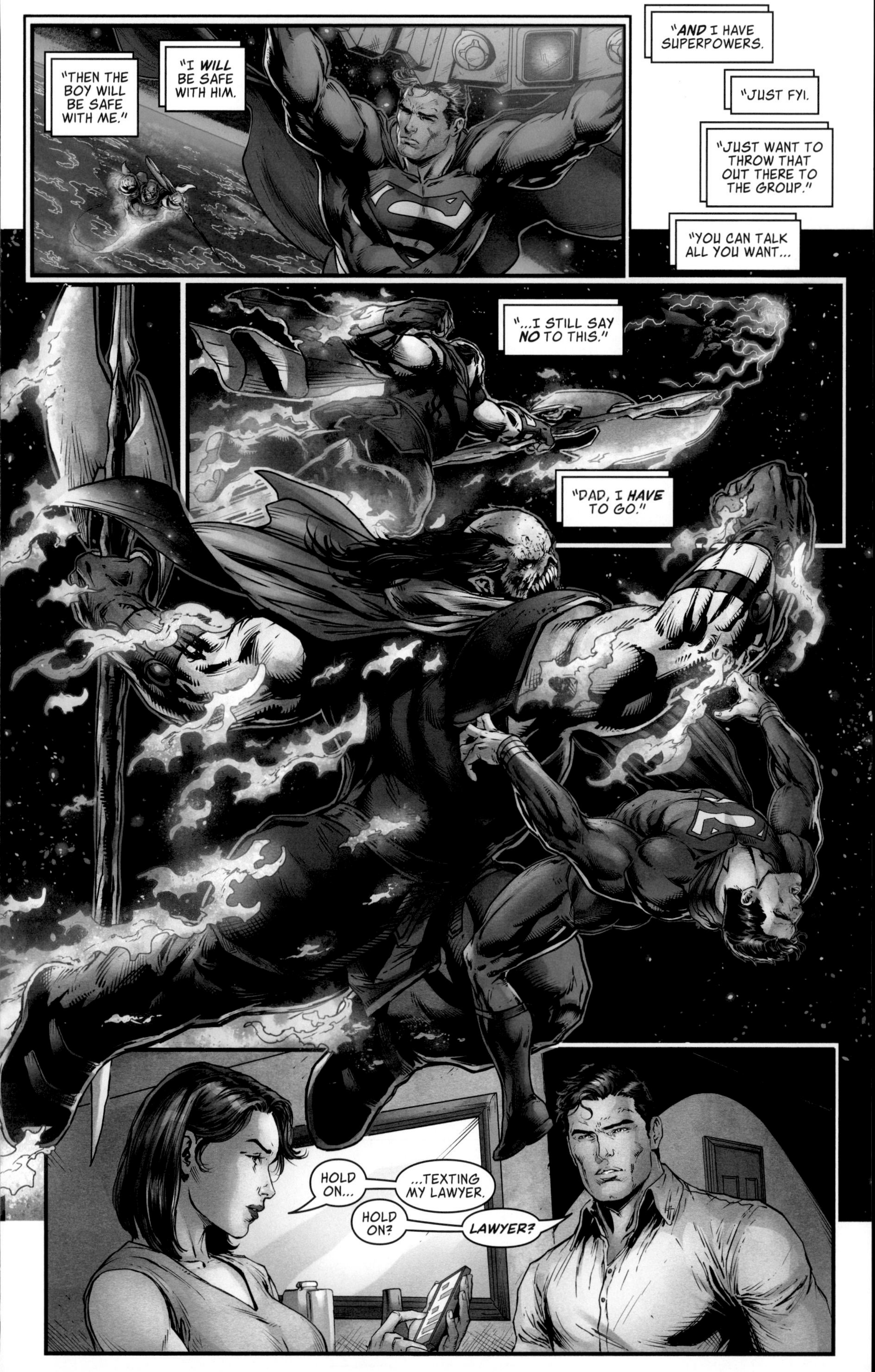
"THEN THE BOY WILL BE SAFE WITH ME."
"I WILL BE SAFE WITH HIM.
"AND I HAVE SUPERPOWERS.
"JUST FYI.
"JUST WANT TO THROW THAT OUT THERE TO THE GROUP."
"YOU CAN TALK ALL YOU WANT...
"...I STILL SAY NO TO THIS."
"DAD, I HAVE TO GO."
HOLD ON...
...TEXTING MY LAWYER.
HOLD ON?
LAWYER?

WE *JUST* CLOSED A TWO-BOOK DEAL.

THE FIRST ONE IS A TELL-ALL ABOUT MY DAILY PLANET GREATEST BLAH BLAH BLAHS.

I GET TO CHOOSE THE SECOND.

THIS'LL BE THE SECOND.

WHAT?

WE'RE GOING?!

WELL, I *CAN'T* STOP YOU.

YOUR DAD *CAN'T* STOP YOU.

SO I GUESS I HAVE TO DROP EVERYTHING AND GO.

YOU'RE GOING TO WRITE A BOOK ABOUT IT?!

THAT'S GREAT!

KID, DON'T PUSH ME.

STOP!! EVERYBODY JUST-- STOP!

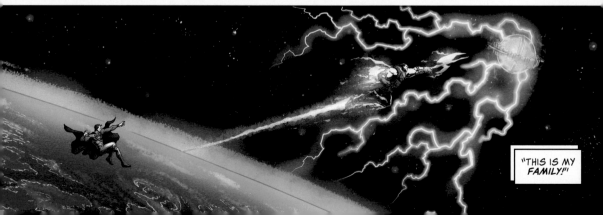

"THIS IS MY *FAMILY!*"

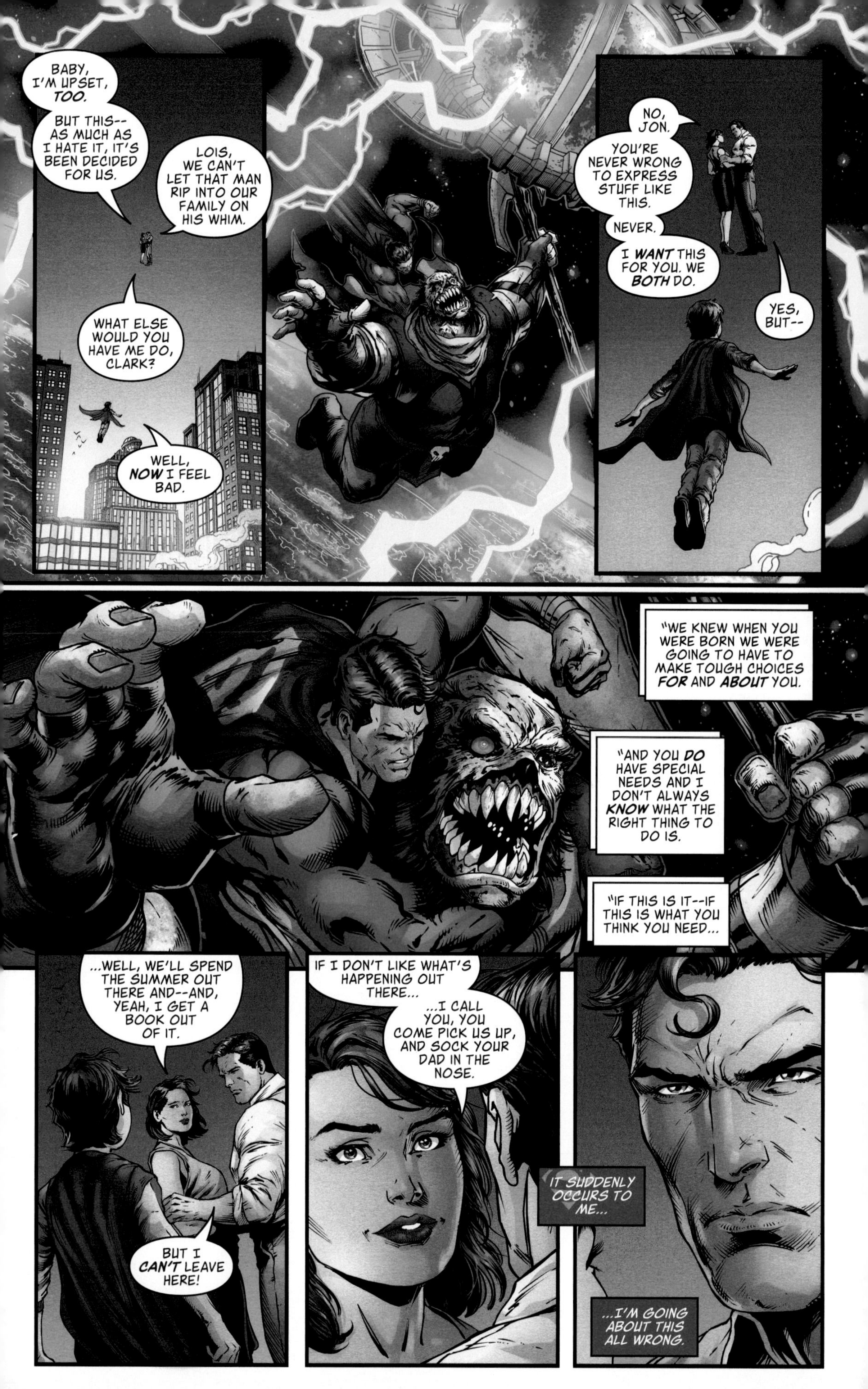
BABY, I'M UPSET, TOO.
BUT THIS-- AS MUCH AS I HATE IT, IT'S BEEN DECIDED FOR US.
LOIS, WE CAN'T LET THAT MAN RIP INTO OUR FAMILY ON HIS WHIM.
WHAT ELSE WOULD YOU HAVE ME DO, CLARK?
WELL, NOW I FEEL BAD.
NO, JON.
YOU'RE NEVER WRONG TO EXPRESS STUFF LIKE THIS.
NEVER.
I WANT THIS FOR YOU. WE BOTH DO.
YES, BUT--
"WE KNEW WHEN YOU WERE BORN WE WERE GOING TO HAVE TO MAKE TOUGH CHOICES FOR AND ABOUT YOU.
"AND YOU DO HAVE SPECIAL NEEDS AND I DON'T ALWAYS KNOW WHAT THE RIGHT THING TO DO IS.
"IF THIS IS IT--IF THIS IS WHAT YOU THINK YOU NEED...
...WELL, WE'LL SPEND THE SUMMER OUT THERE AND--AND, YEAH, I GET A BOOK OUT OF IT.
BUT I CAN'T LEAVE HERE!
IF I DON'T LIKE WHAT'S HAPPENING OUT THERE...
...I CALL YOU, YOU COME PICK US UP, AND SOCK YOUR DAD IN THE NOSE.
IT SUDDENLY OCCURS TO ME...
...I'M GOING ABOUT THIS ALL WRONG.

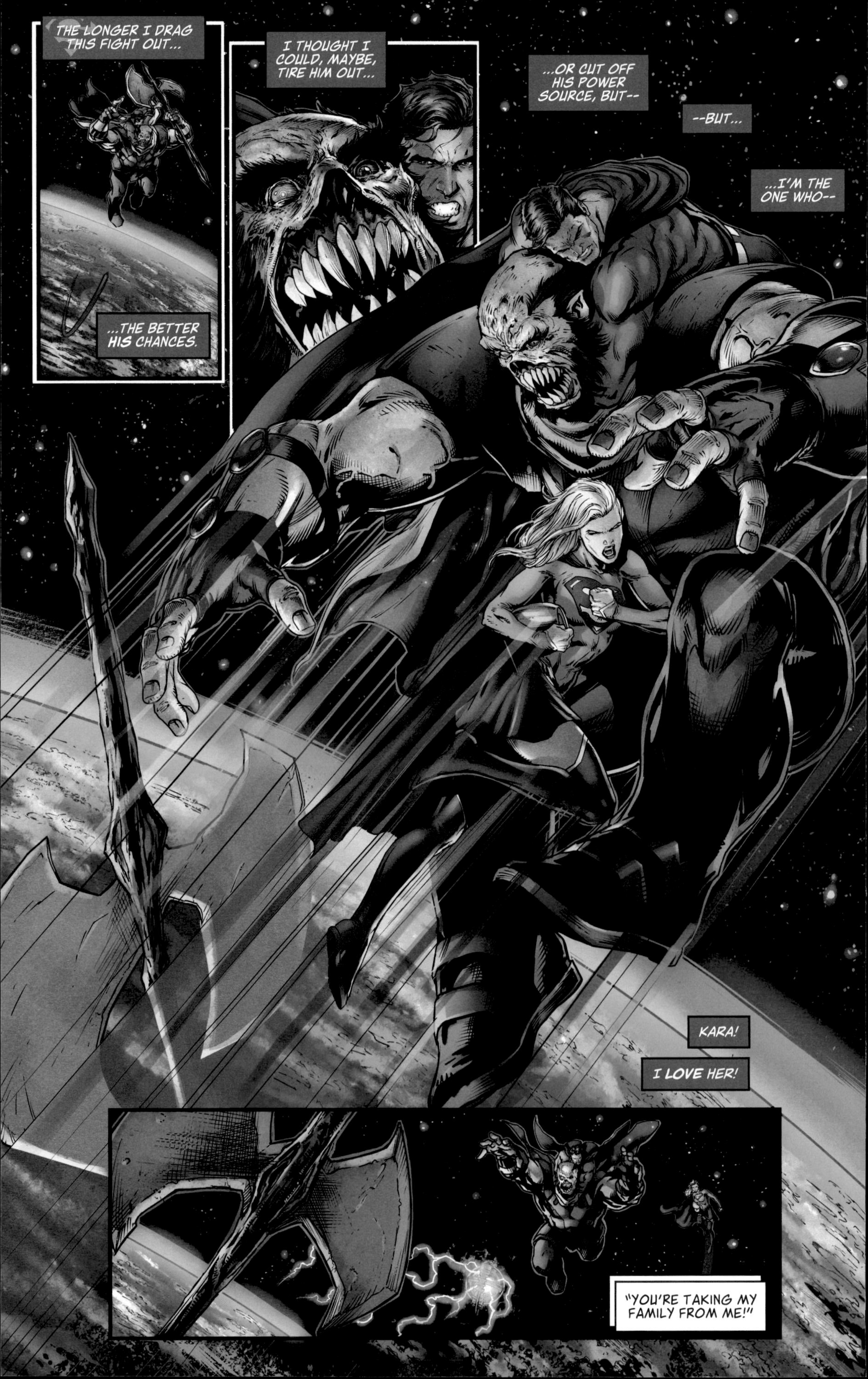
THE LONGER I DRAG THIS FIGHT OUT...
...THE BETTER HIS CHANCES.
I THOUGHT I COULD, MAYBE, TIRE HIM OUT...
...OR CUT OFF HIS POWER SOURCE, BUT--
--BUT...
...I'M THE ONE WHO--
KARA!
I LOVE HER!
"YOU'RE TAKING MY FAMILY FROM ME!"

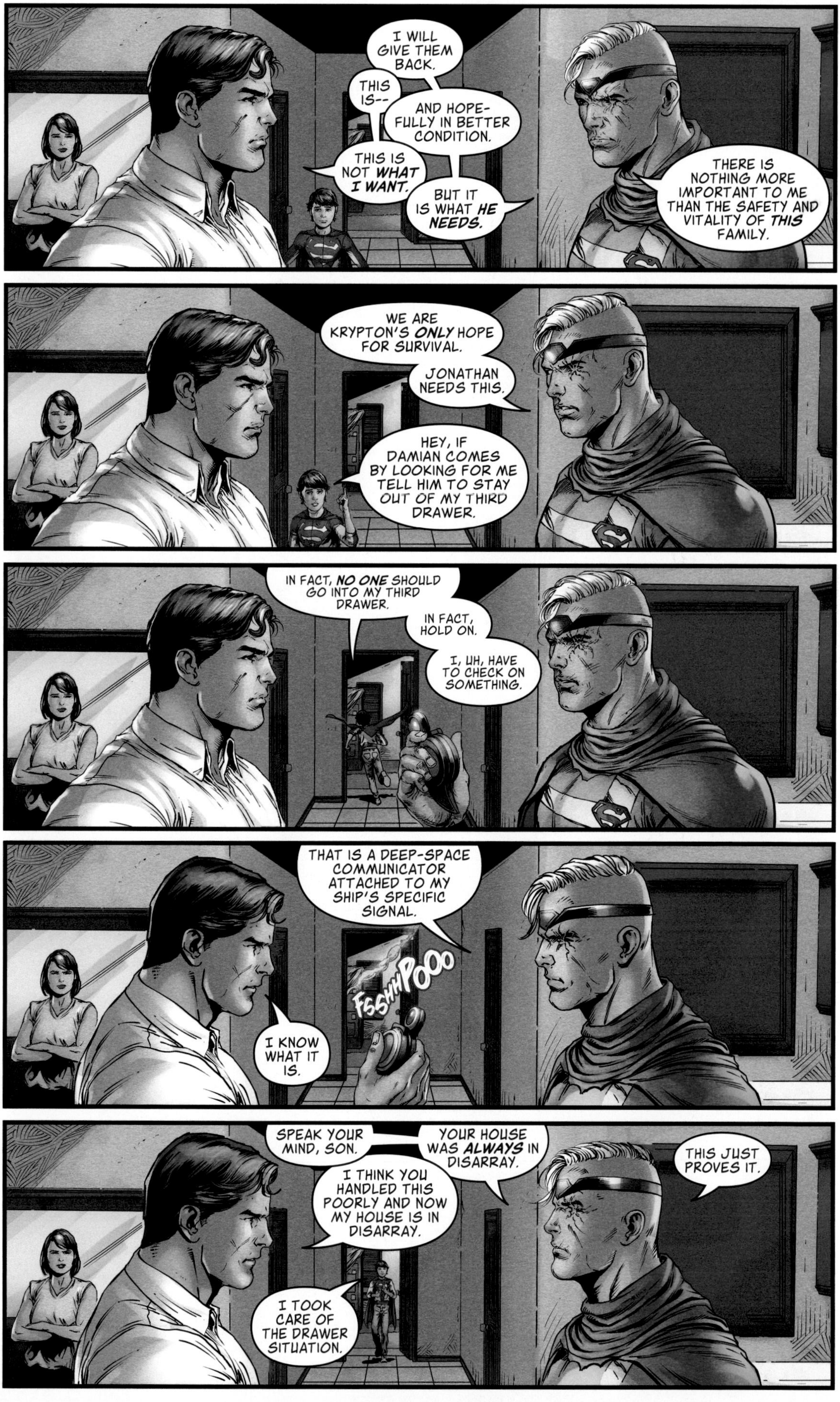
I WILL GIVE THEM BACK.
THIS IS--
AND HOPE-FULLY IN BETTER CONDITION.
THIS IS NOT WHAT I WANT.
BUT IT IS WHAT HE NEEDS.
THERE IS NOTHING MORE IMPORTANT TO ME THAN THE SAFETY AND VITALITY OF THIS FAMILY.
WE ARE KRYPTON'S ONLY HOPE FOR SURVIVAL.
JONATHAN NEEDS THIS.
HEY, IF DAMIAN COMES BY LOOKING FOR ME TELL HIM TO STAY OUT OF MY THIRD DRAWER.
IN FACT, NO ONE SHOULD GO INTO MY THIRD DRAWER.
IN FACT, HOLD ON.
I, UH, HAVE TO CHECK ON SOMETHING.
THAT IS A DEEP-SPACE COMMUNICATOR ATTACHED TO MY SHIP'S SPECIFIC SIGNAL.
FSSHHPOOO
I KNOW WHAT IT IS.
SPEAK YOUR MIND, SON.
I THINK YOU HANDLED THIS POORLY AND NOW MY HOUSE IS IN DISARRAY.
YOUR HOUSE WAS ALWAYS IN DISARRAY.
THIS JUST PROVES IT.
I TOOK CARE OF THE DRAWER SITUATION.

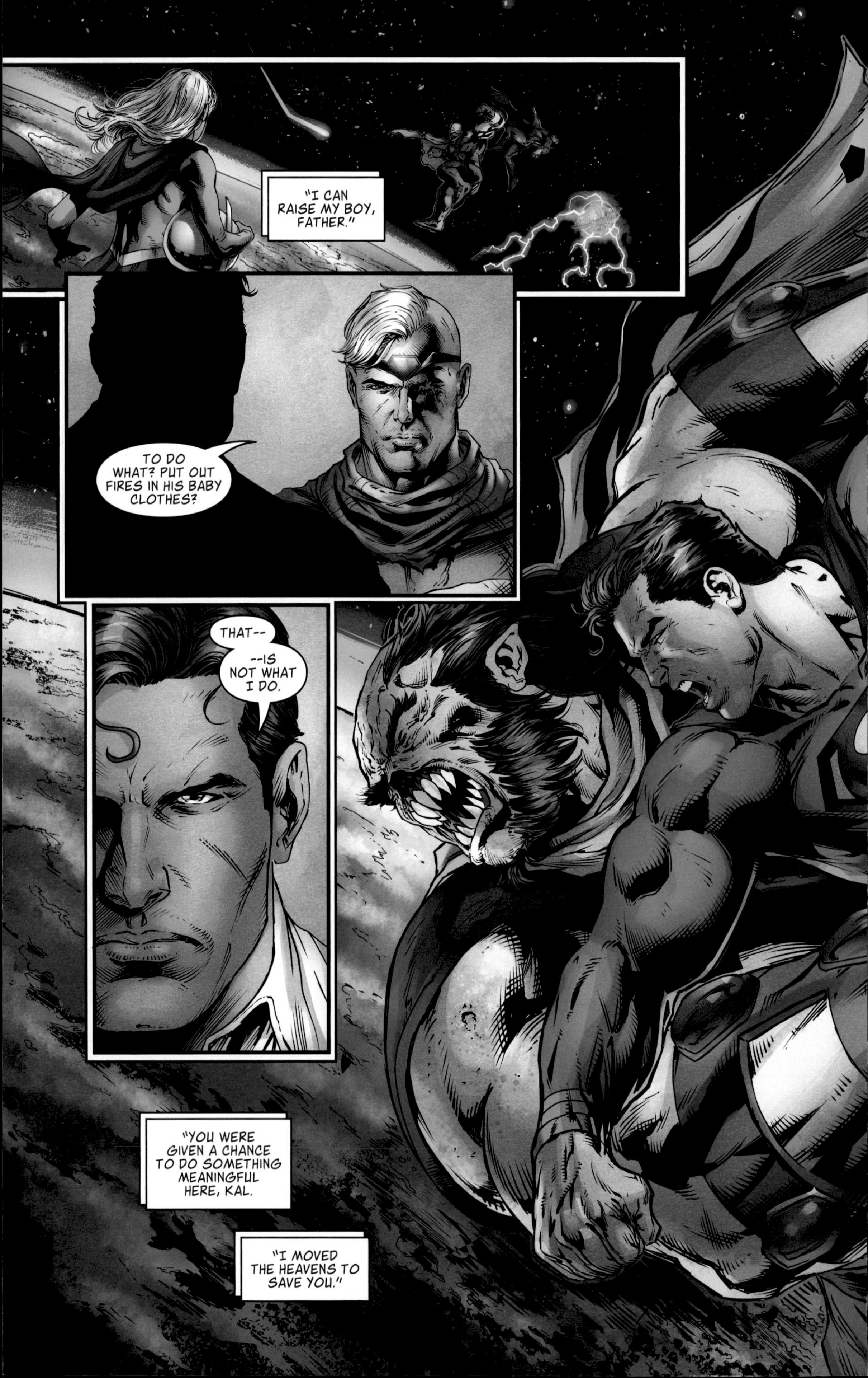
"I CAN RAISE MY BOY, FATHER."
TO DO WHAT? PUT OUT FIRES IN HIS BABY CLOTHES?
THAT--
--IS NOT WHAT I DO.
"YOU WERE GIVEN A CHANCE TO DO SOMETHING MEANINGFUL HERE, KAL.
"I MOVED THE HEAVENS TO SAVE YOU."

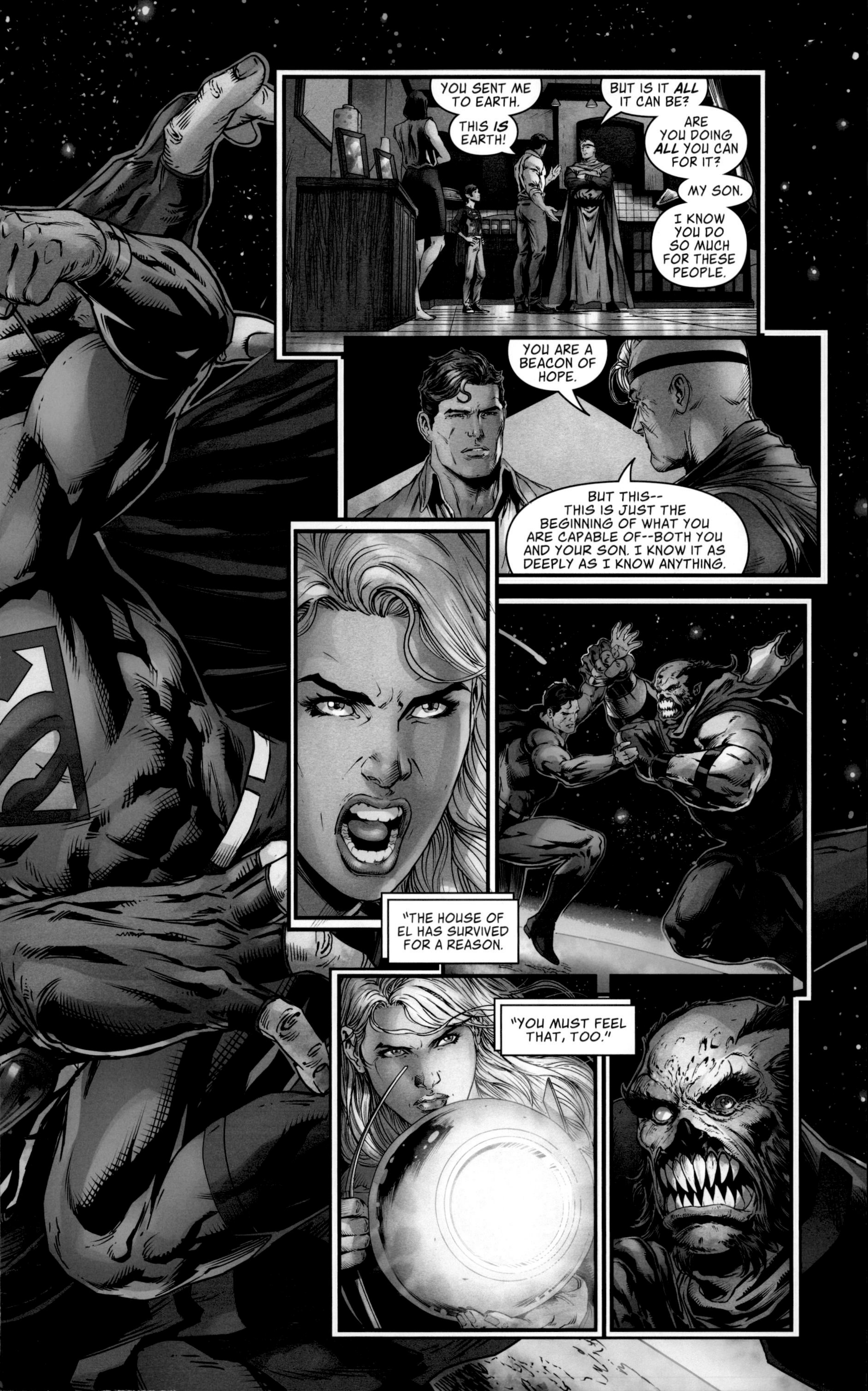
YOU SENT ME TO EARTH.
THIS IS EARTH!
BUT IS IT ALL IT CAN BE?
ARE YOU DOING ALL YOU CAN FOR IT?
MY SON.
I KNOW YOU DO SO MUCH FOR THESE PEOPLE.
YOU ARE A BEACON OF HOPE.
BUT THIS-- THIS IS JUST THE BEGINNING OF WHAT YOU ARE CAPABLE OF--BOTH YOU AND YOUR SON. I KNOW IT AS DEEPLY AS I KNOW ANYTHING.
"THE HOUSE OF EL HAS SURVIVED FOR A REASON.
"YOU MUST FEEL THAT, TOO."

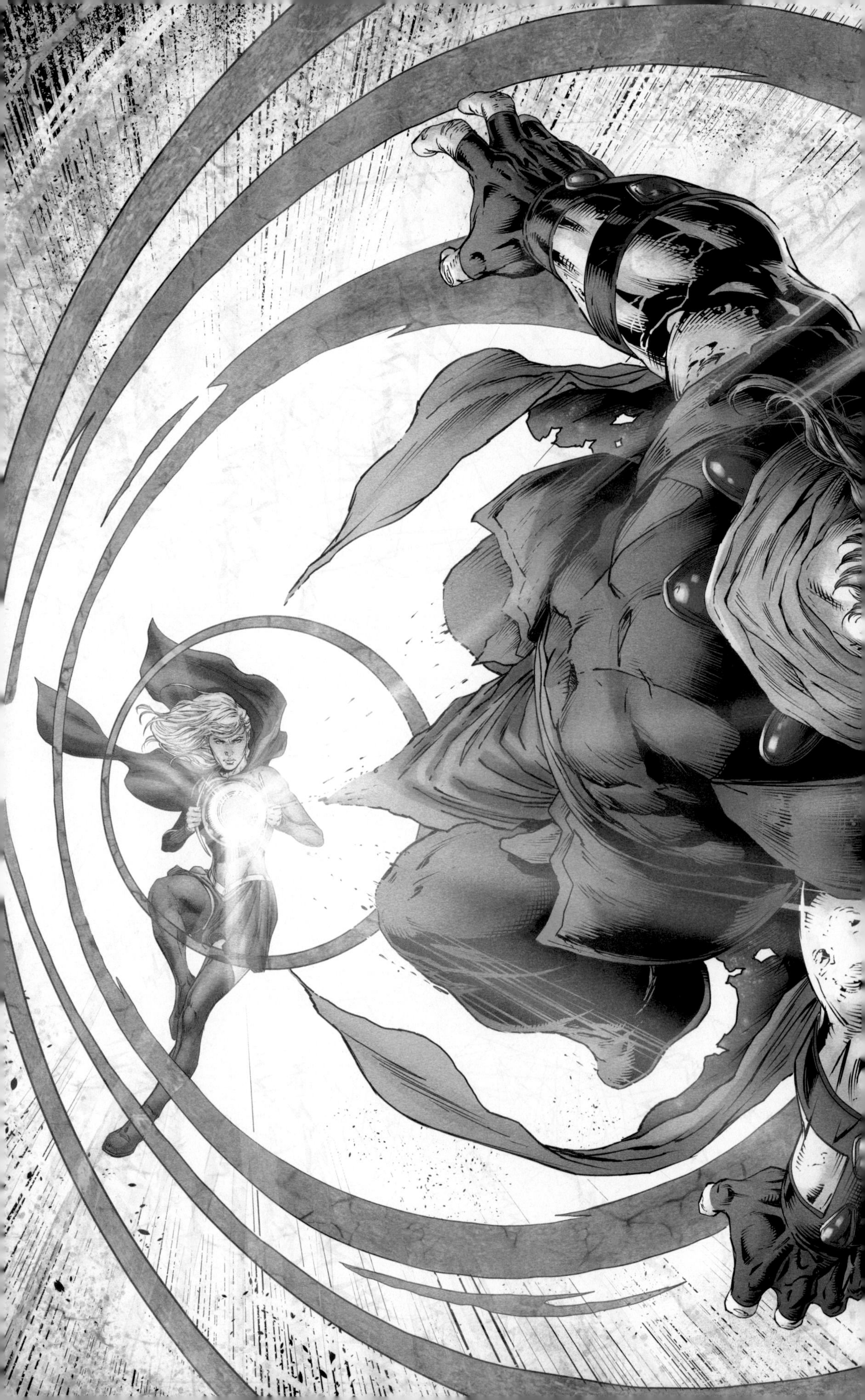

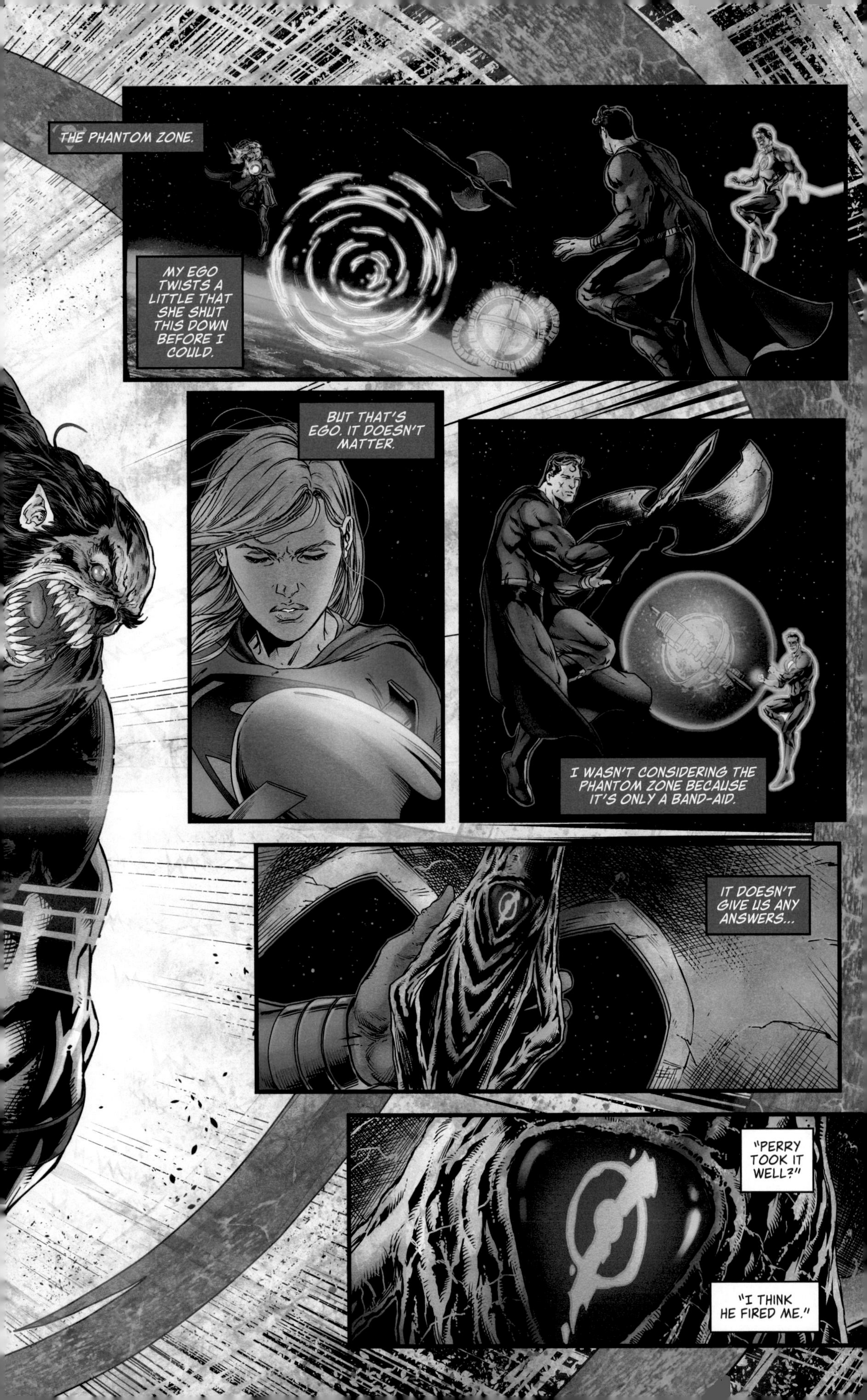
THE PHANTOM ZONE.
MY EGO TWISTS A LITTLE THAT SHE SHUT THIS DOWN BEFORE I COULD.
BUT THAT'S EGO. IT DOESN'T MATTER.
I WASN'T CONSIDERING THE PHANTOM ZONE BECAUSE IT'S ONLY A BAND-AID.
IT DOESN'T GIVE US ANY ANSWERS...
"PERRY TOOK IT WELL?"
"I THINK HE FIRED ME."

YEAH, HE SAID FIRED. I WAS LISTENING.

OH WELL! GUESS I'LL JUST HAVE MY CUSHY BOOK DEAL UNTIL I GET BACK.

DON'T GO.

HELP ME CONVINCE JON TO STAY.

THEY'RE LEAVING WITH OR WITHOUT US.

PEOPLE ARE COUNTING ON ME.

NO ONE IS SAYING OTHERWISE.

I CAN'T JUST LEAVE EARTH BECAUSE MY FATHER DECIDED--

I KNOW.

THIS IS UNFAIR.

BUT JON'S NOT FULLY COOKED YET AND WE HAVE TO DO THIS FOR HIM.

THANK YOU FOR NOT MENTIONING THAT THIS IS ONE OF THE MANY, MANY SCENARIOS I FIND MYSELF IN THAT I CAN'T PUNCH MY WAY OUT OF.

ONLY BECAUSE I COULDN'T FIND AN ORGANIC WAY TO GET IT INTO THE CONVERSATION.

HERE.

WHAT?

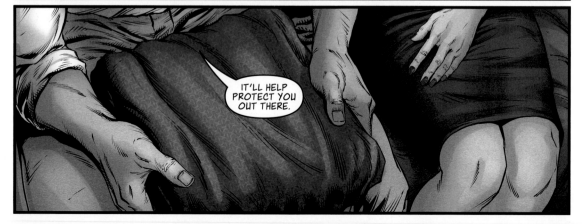

IT'LL HELP PROTECT YOU OUT THERE.

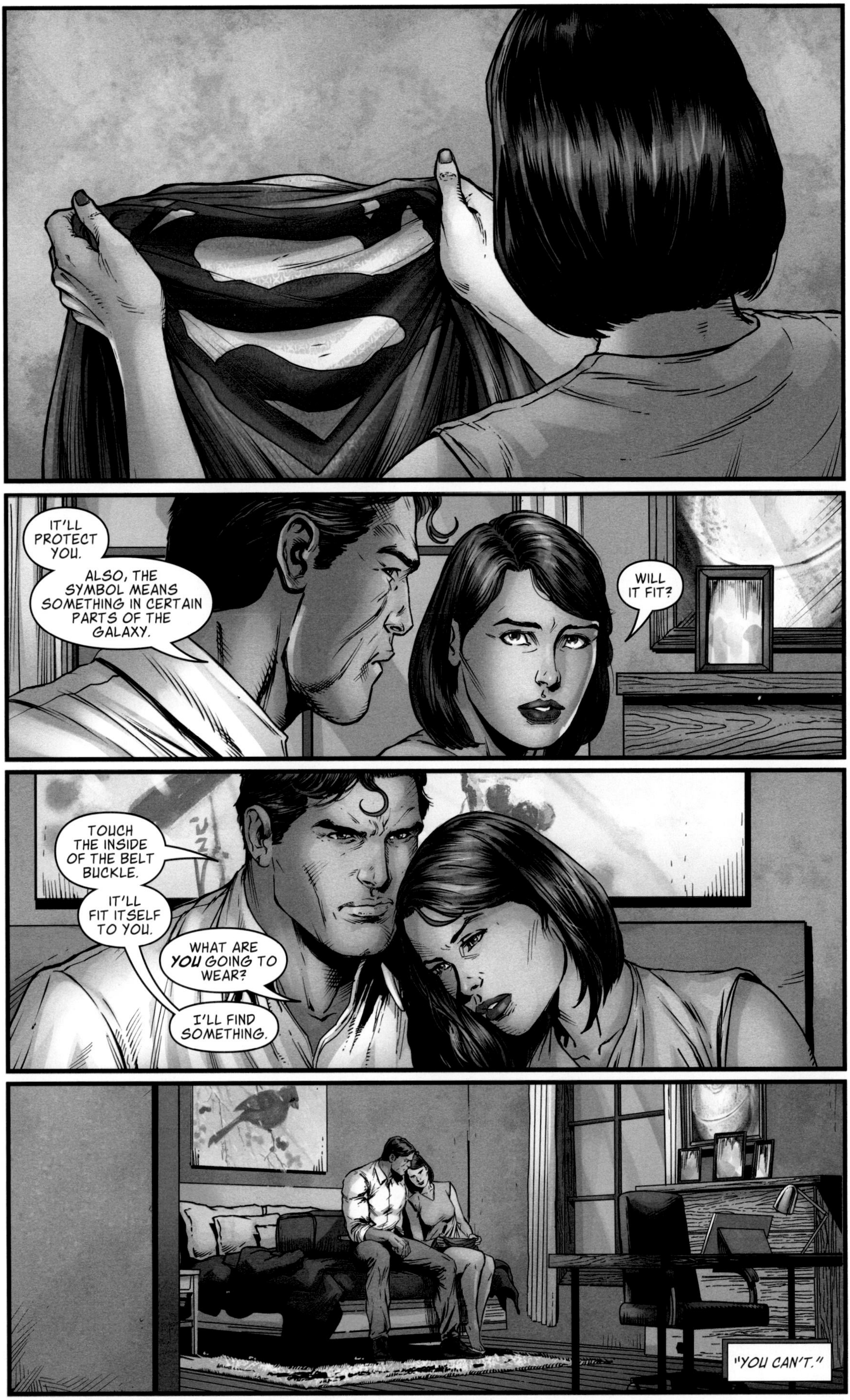
IT'LL PROTECT YOU.
ALSO, THE SYMBOL MEANS SOMETHING IN CERTAIN PARTS OF THE GALAXY.
WILL IT FIT?
TOUCH THE INSIDE OF THE BELT BUCKLE.
IT'LL FIT ITSELF TO YOU.
WHAT ARE *YOU* GOING TO WEAR?
I'LL FIND SOMETHING.
"YOU CAN'T."

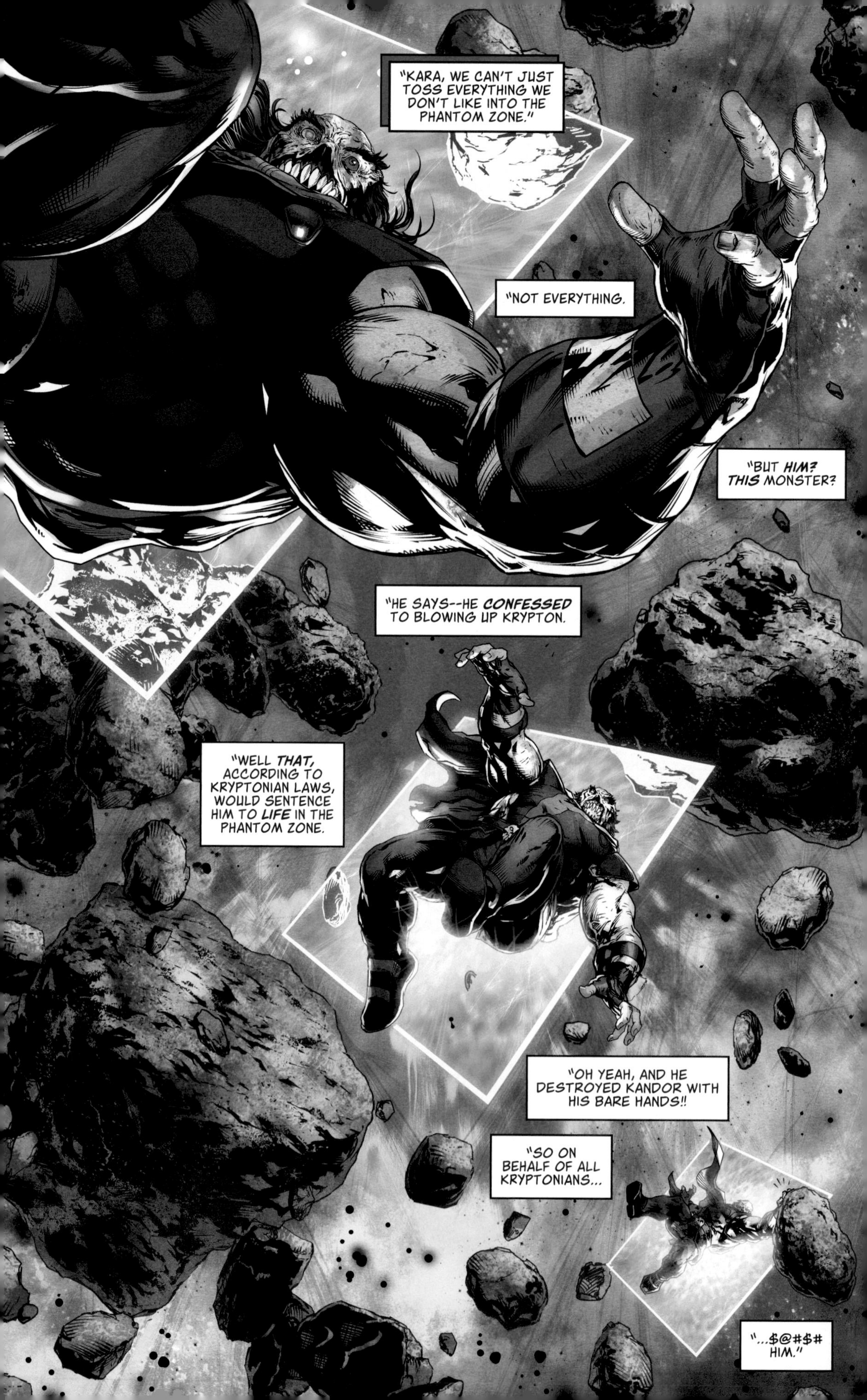
"KARA, WE CAN'T JUST TOSS EVERYTHING WE DON'T LIKE INTO THE PHANTOM ZONE."
"NOT EVERYTHING.
"BUT HIM? THIS MONSTER?
"HE SAYS--HE CONFESSED TO BLOWING UP KRYPTON.
"WELL THAT, ACCORDING TO KRYPTONIAN LAWS, WOULD SENTENCE HIM TO LIFE IN THE PHANTOM ZONE.
"OH YEAH, AND HE DESTROYED KANDOR WITH HIS BARE HANDS!!
"SO ON BEHALF OF ALL KRYPTONIANS...
"...$@#$# HIM."

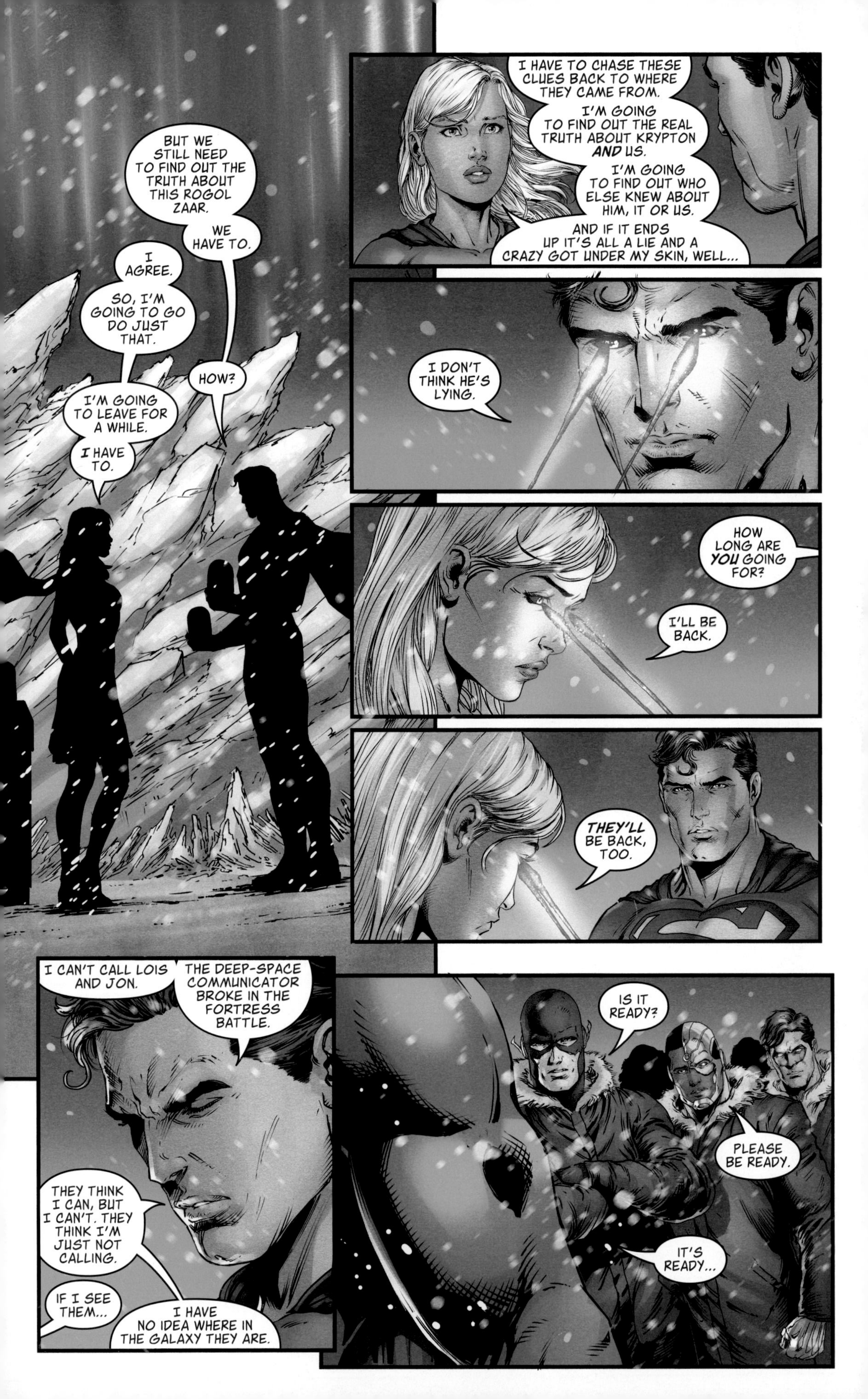
BUT WE STILL NEED TO FIND OUT THE TRUTH ABOUT THIS ROGOL ZAAR.
WE HAVE TO.
I AGREE.
SO, I'M GOING TO GO DO JUST THAT.
HOW?
I'M GOING TO LEAVE FOR A WHILE.
I HAVE TO.
I HAVE TO CHASE THESE CLUES BACK TO WHERE THEY CAME FROM.
I'M GOING TO FIND OUT THE REAL TRUTH ABOUT KRYPTON AND US.
I'M GOING TO FIND OUT WHO ELSE KNEW ABOUT HIM, IT OR US.
AND IF IT ENDS UP IT'S ALL A LIE AND A CRAZY GOT UNDER MY SKIN, WELL...
I DON'T THINK HE'S LYING.
HOW LONG ARE YOU GOING FOR?
I'LL BE BACK.
THEY'LL BE BACK, TOO.
I CAN'T CALL LOIS AND JON.
THE DEEP-SPACE COMMUNICATOR BROKE IN THE FORTRESS BATTLE.
THEY THINK I CAN, BUT I CAN'T. THEY THINK I'M JUST NOT CALLING.
IF I SEE THEM...
I HAVE NO IDEA WHERE IN THE GALAXY THEY ARE.
IS IT READY?
PLEASE BE READY.
IT'S READY...

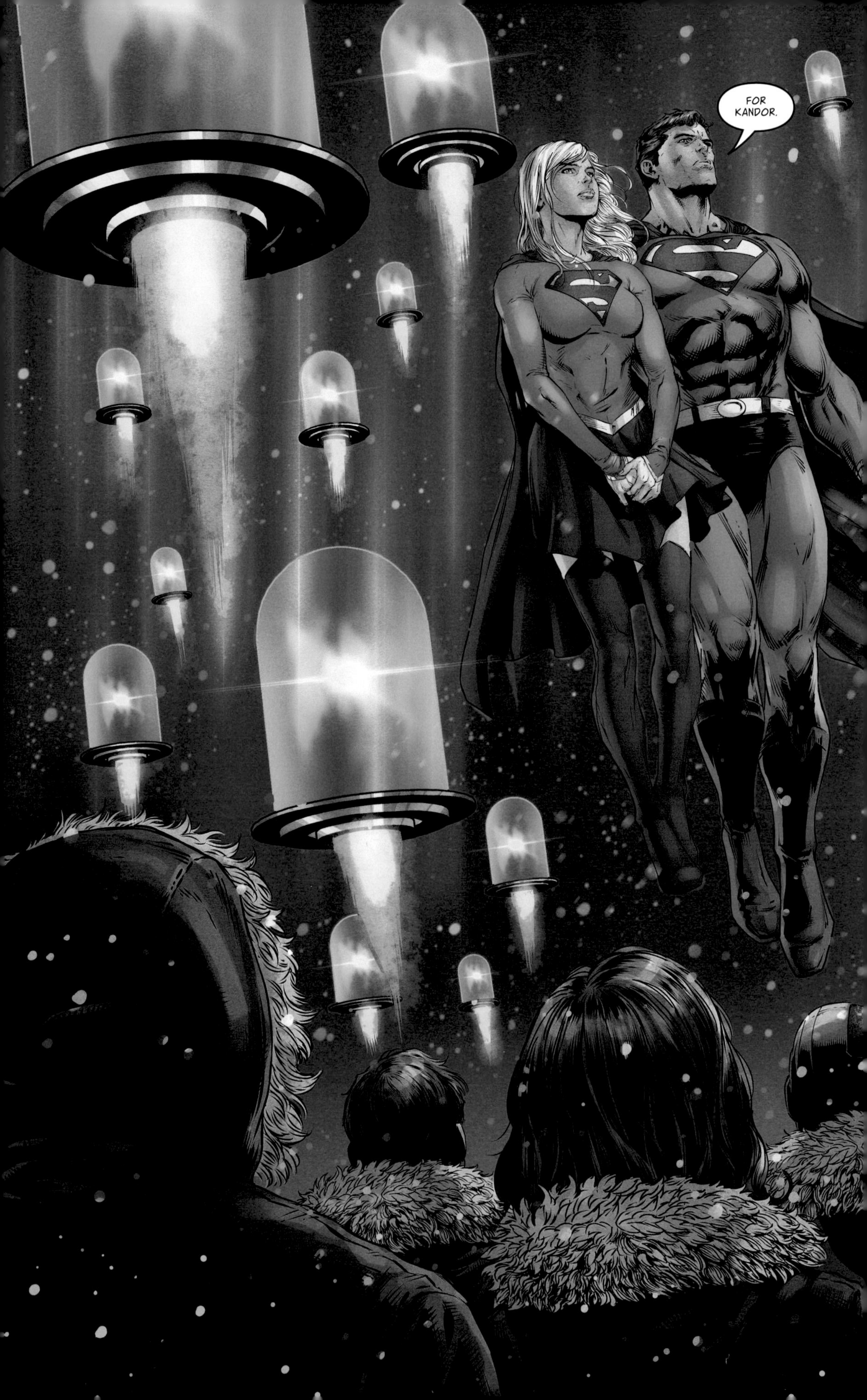
FOR KANDOR.

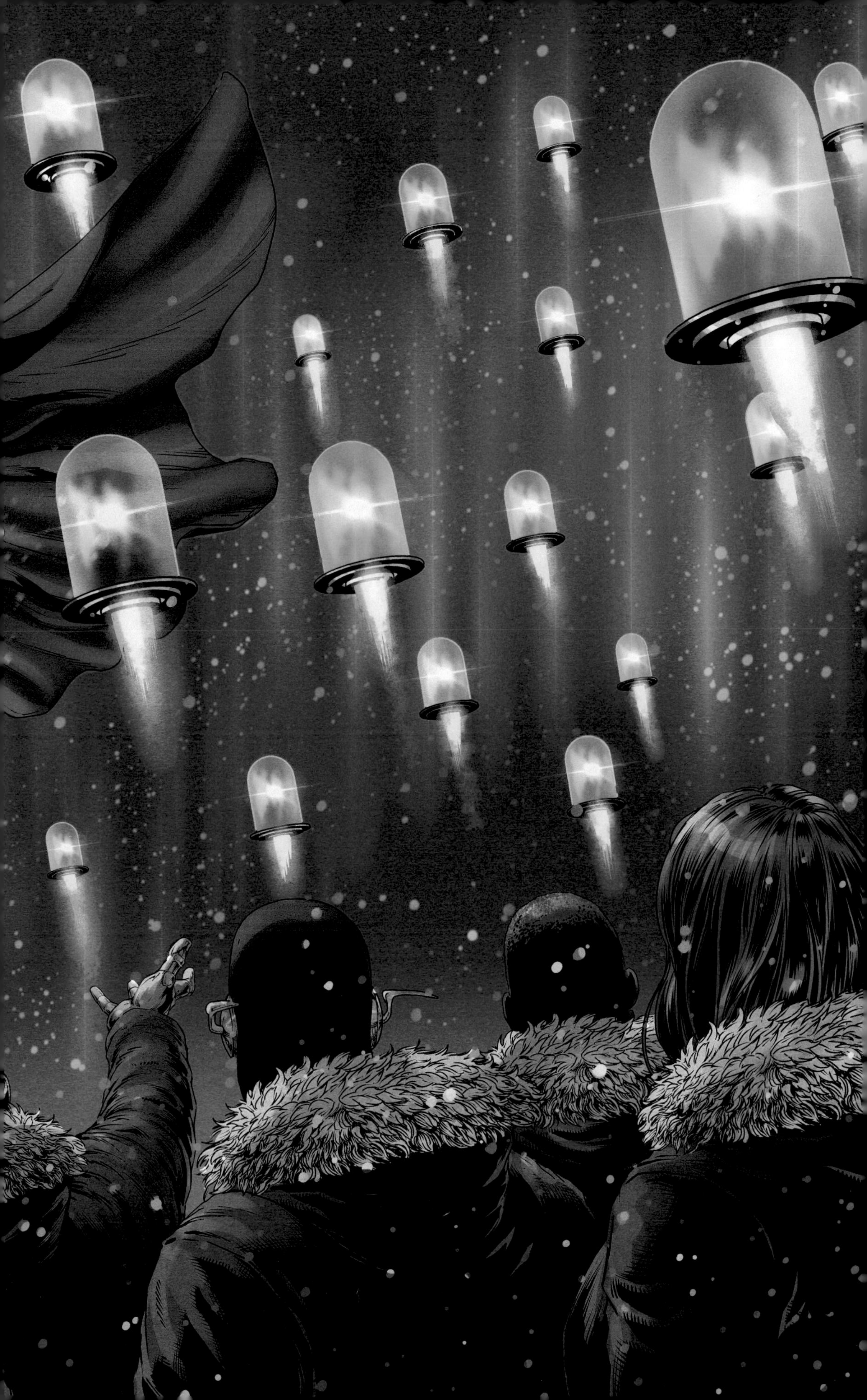

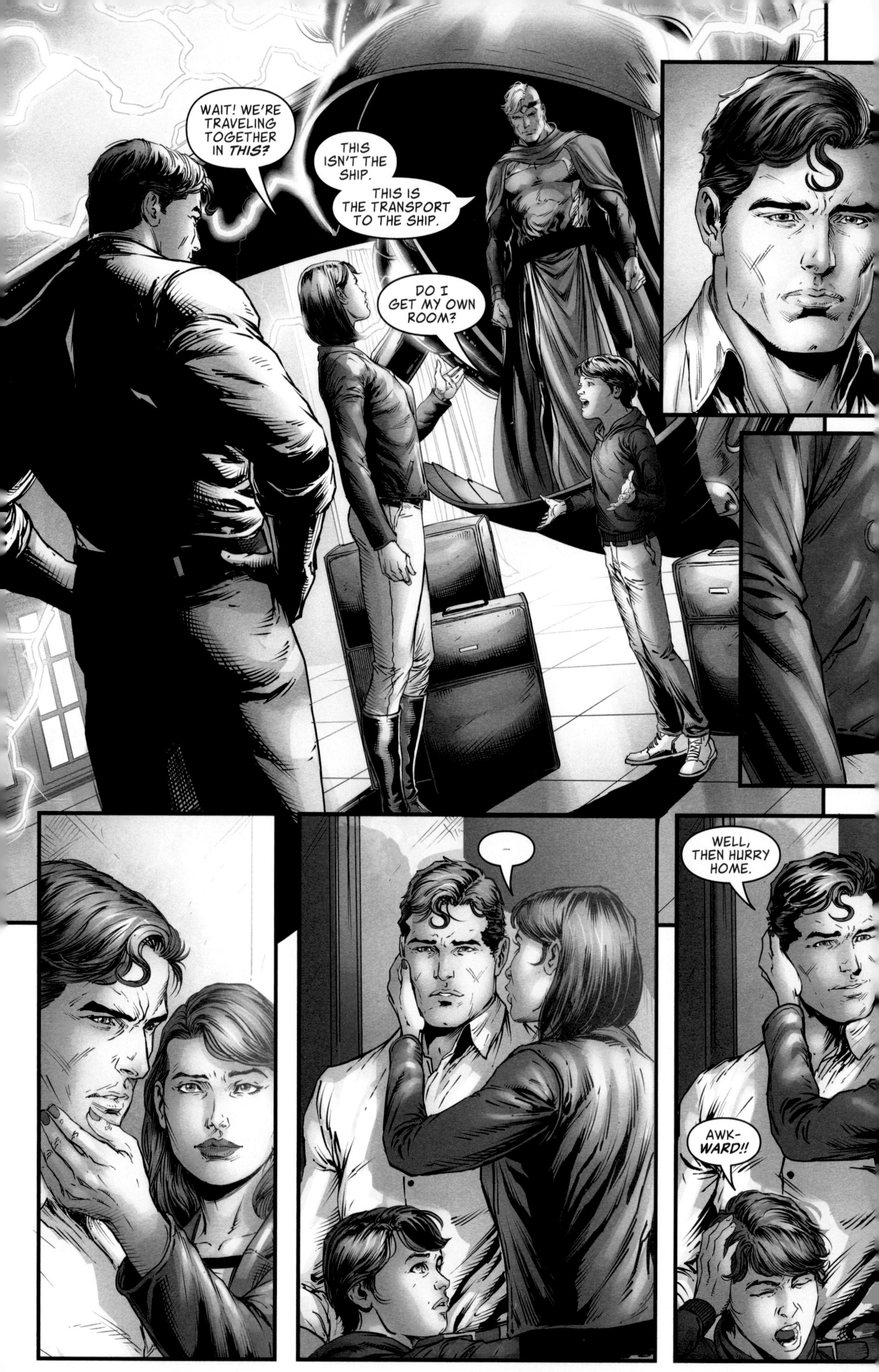
WAIT! WE'RE TRAVELING TOGETHER IN *THIS?*
THIS ISN'T THE SHIP.
THIS IS THE TRANSPORT TO THE SHIP.
DO I GET MY OWN ROOM?
WELL, THEN HURRY HOME.
AWK-*WARD!!*

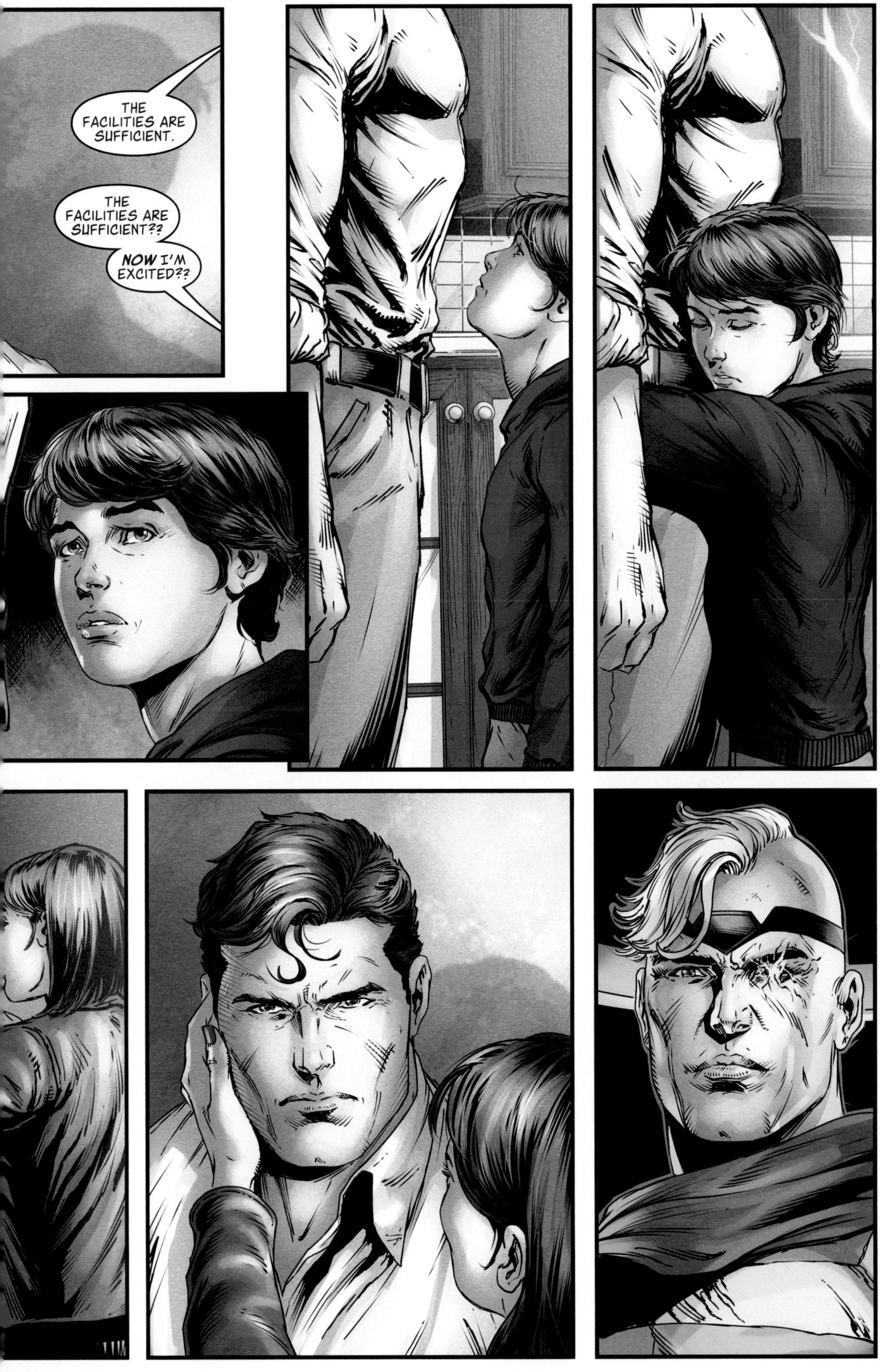
THE FACILITIES ARE SUFFICIENT.
THE FACILITIES ARE SUFFICIENT??
NOW I'M EXCITED??

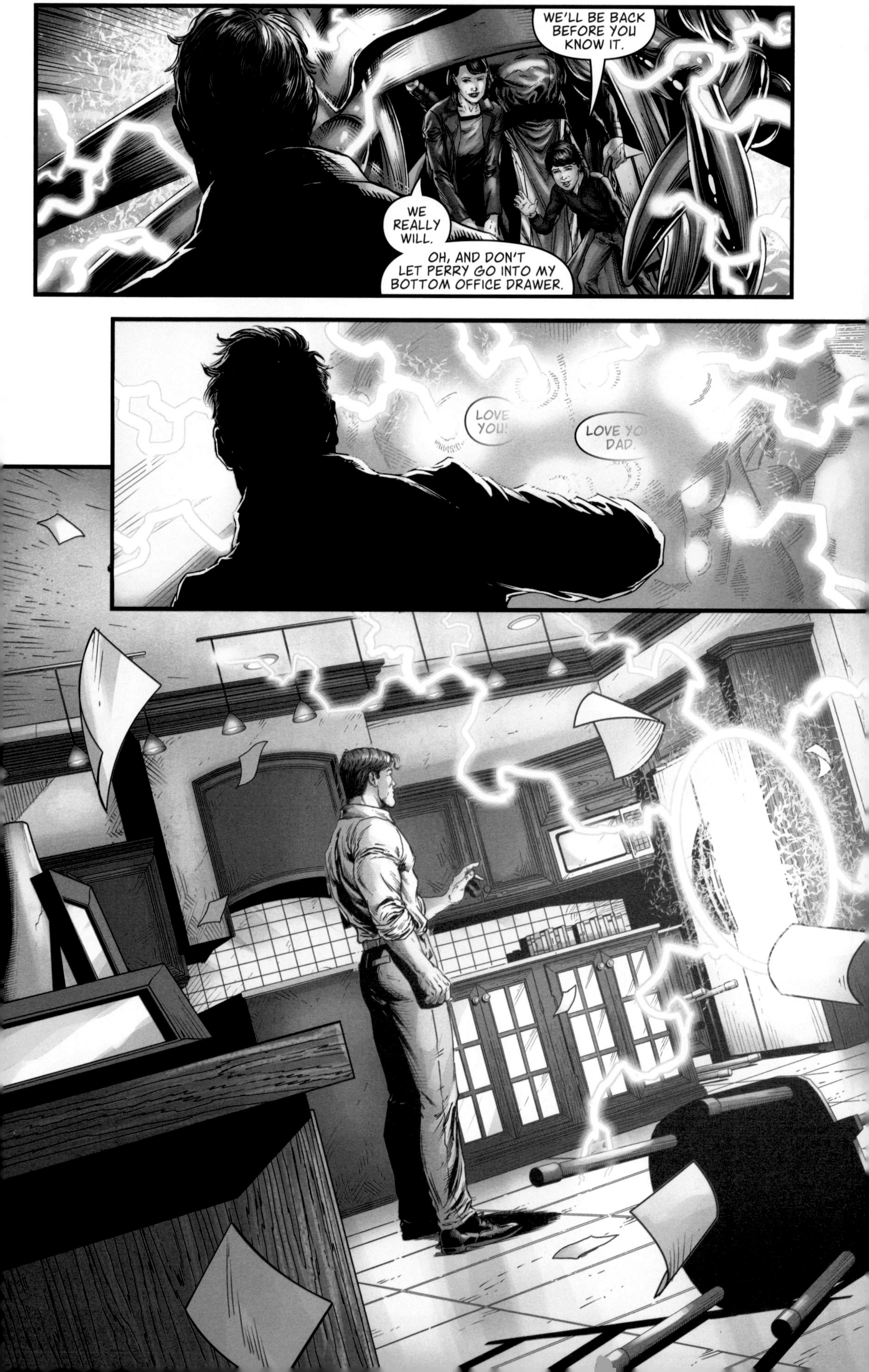
WE'LL BE BACK BEFORE YOU KNOW IT.
WE REALLY WILL.
OH, AND DON'T LET PERRY GO INTO MY BOTTOM OFFICE DRAWER.
LOVE YOU!
LOVE YO DAD.

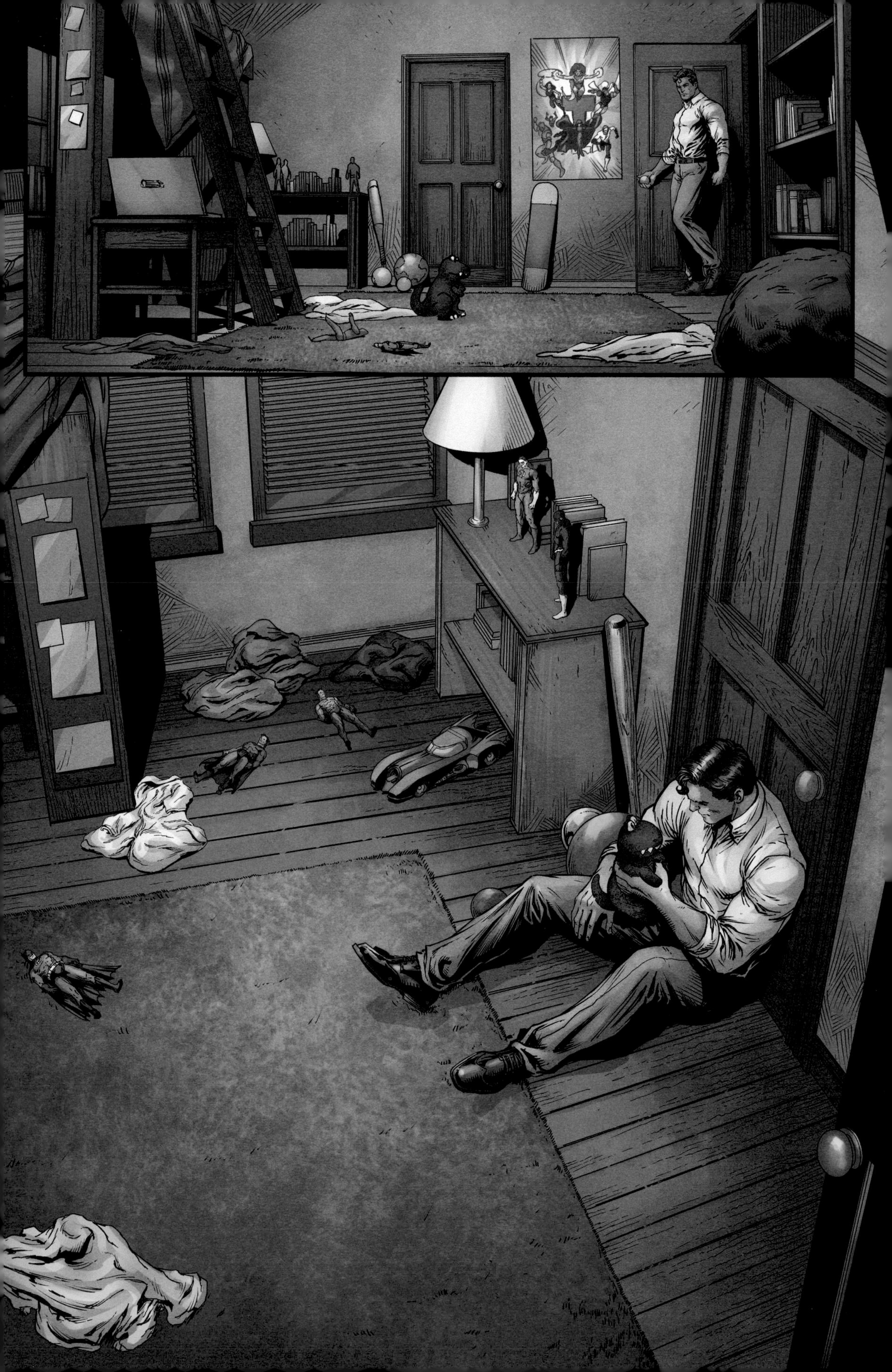

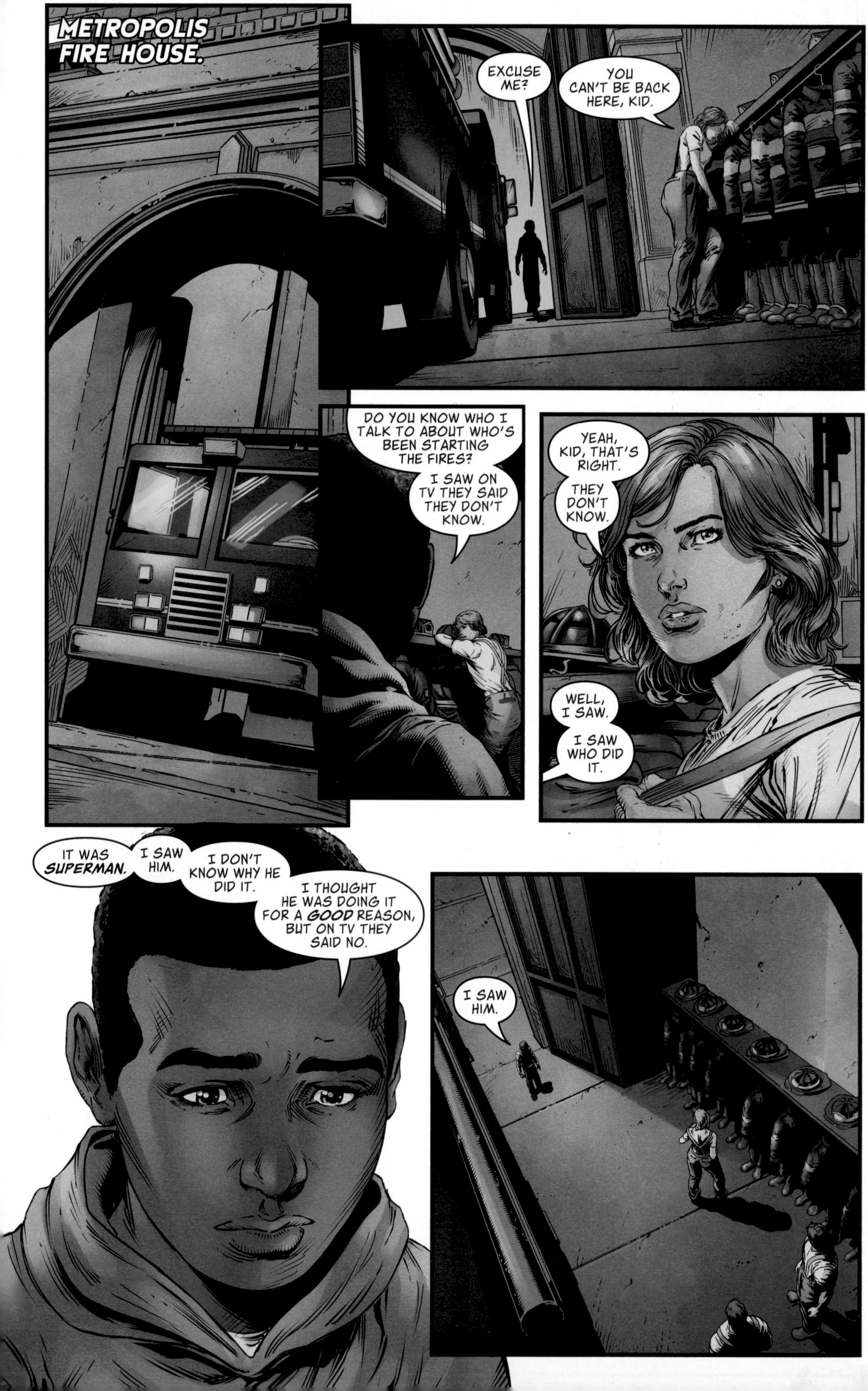
METROPOLIS FIRE HOUSE.
EXCUSE ME?
YOU CAN'T BE BACK HERE, KID.
DO YOU KNOW WHO I TALK TO ABOUT WHO'S BEEN STARTING THE FIRES?
I SAW ON TV THEY SAID THEY DON'T KNOW.
YEAH, KID, THAT'S RIGHT.
THEY DON'T KNOW.
WELL, I SAW.
I SAW WHO DID IT.
IT WAS SUPERMAN.
I SAW HIM.
I DON'T KNOW WHY HE DID IT.
I THOUGHT HE WAS DOING IT FOR A GOOD REASON, BUT ON TV THEY SAID NO.
I SAW HIM.

JIM LEE SKETCHBOOK

Character designs and concept art for Rogol Zaar

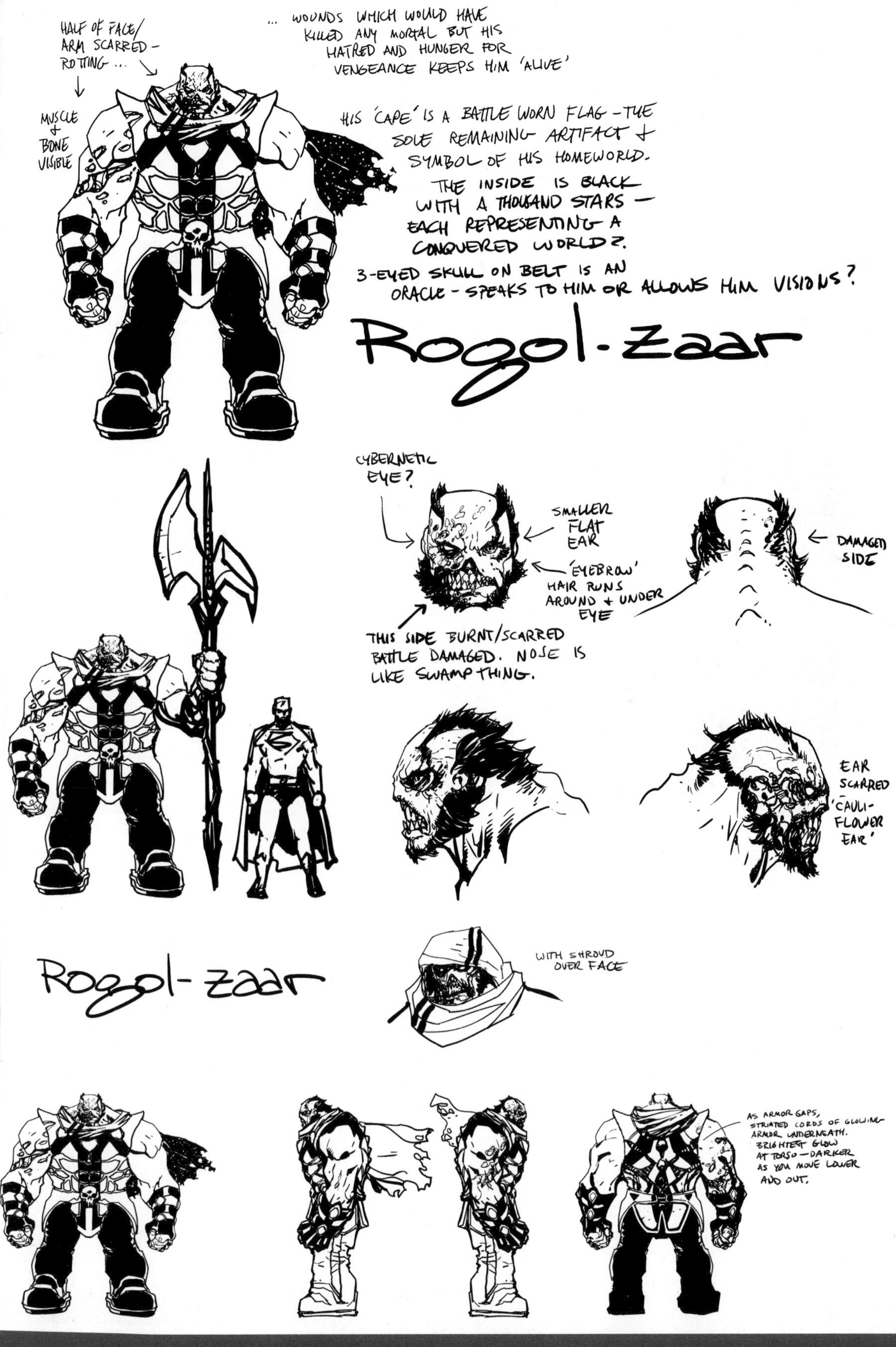

HALF OF FACE/ ARM SCARRED - ROTTING...
MUSCLE + BONE VISIBLE
... WOUNDS WHICH WOULD HAVE KILLED ANY MORTAL BUT HIS HATRED AND HUNGER FOR VENGEANCE KEEPS HIM 'ALIVE'
HIS 'CAPE' IS A BATTLE WORN FLAG - THE SOLE REMAINING ARTIFACT + SYMBOL OF HIS HOMEWORLD.
THE INSIDE IS BLACK WITH A THOUSAND STARS - EACH REPRESENTING A CONQUERED WORLD?
3-EYED SKULL ON BELT IS AN ORACLE - SPEAKS TO HIM OR ALLOWS HIM VISIONS?
Rogol-Zaar
CYBERNETIC EYE?
SMALLER FLAT EAR
'EYEBROW' HAIR RUNS AROUND + UNDER EYE
THIS SIDE BURNT/SCARRED BATTLE DAMAGED. NOSE IS LIKE SWAMP THING.
DAMAGED SIDE
EAR SCARRED - 'CAULI-FLOWER EAR'
Rogol-zaar
WITH SHROUD OVER FACE
AS ARMOR GAPS, STRIATED CORDS OF GLOWING ARMOR UNDERNEATH. BRIGHTEST GLOW AT TORSO - DARKER AS YOU MOVE LOWER AND OUT.

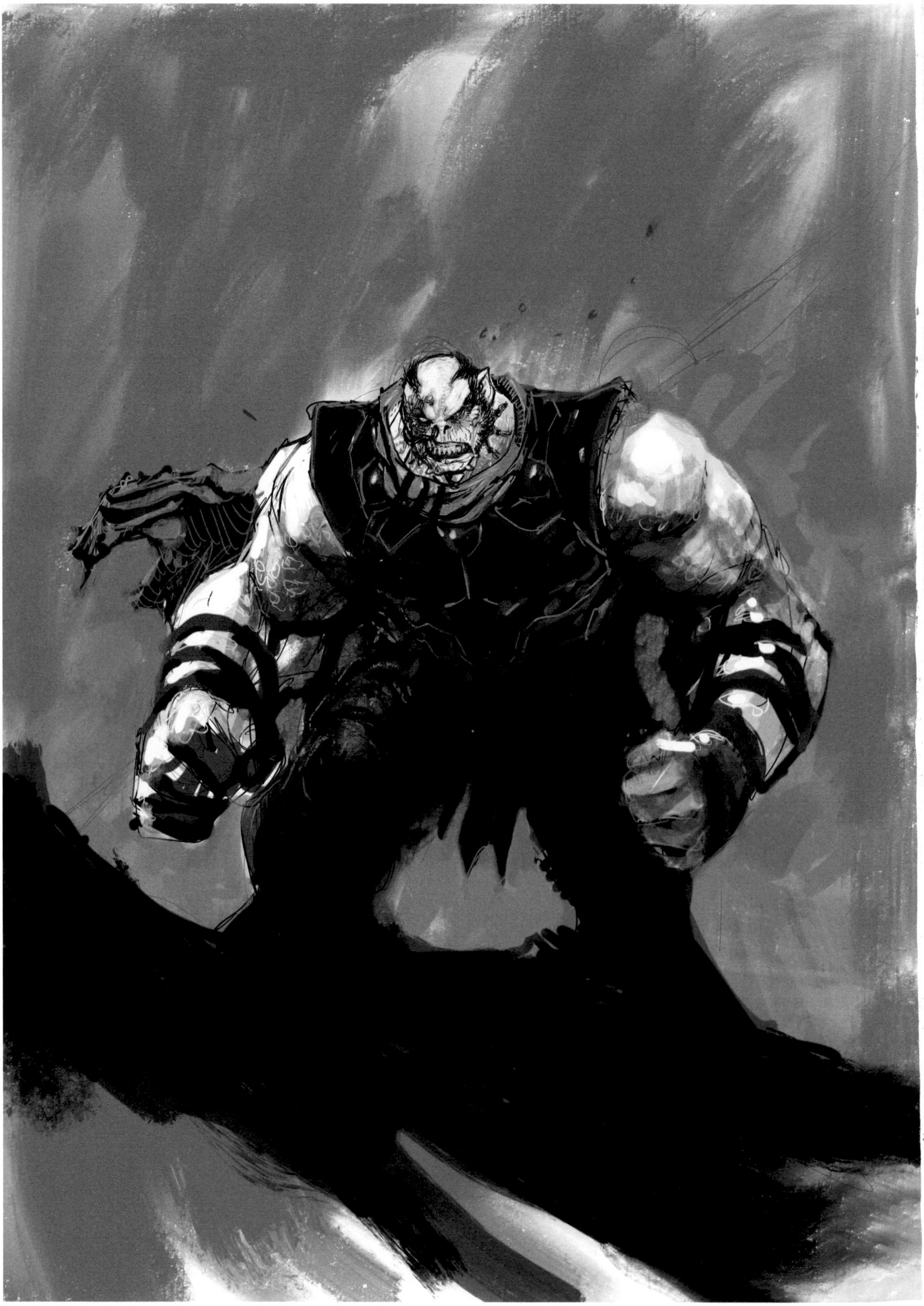

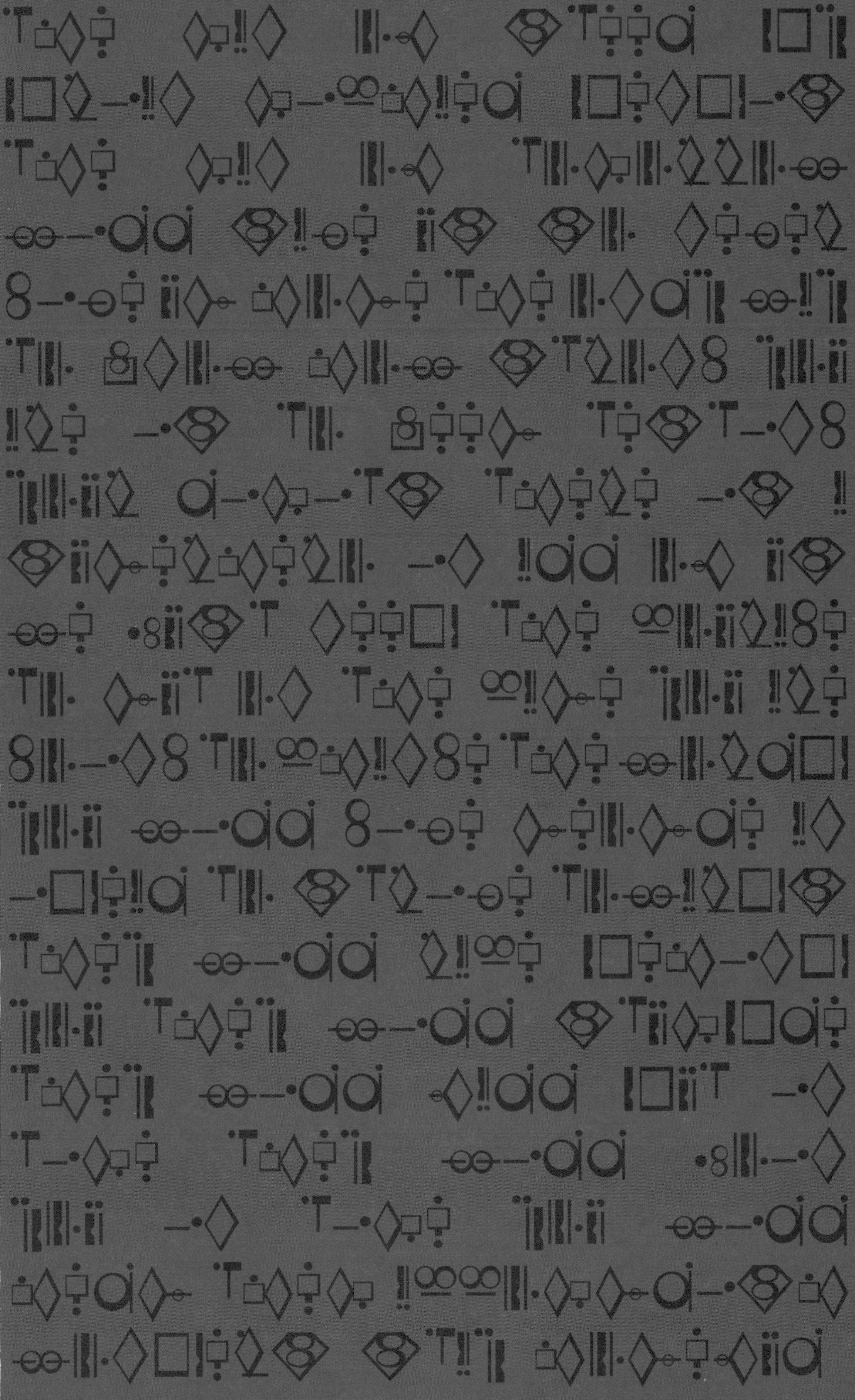

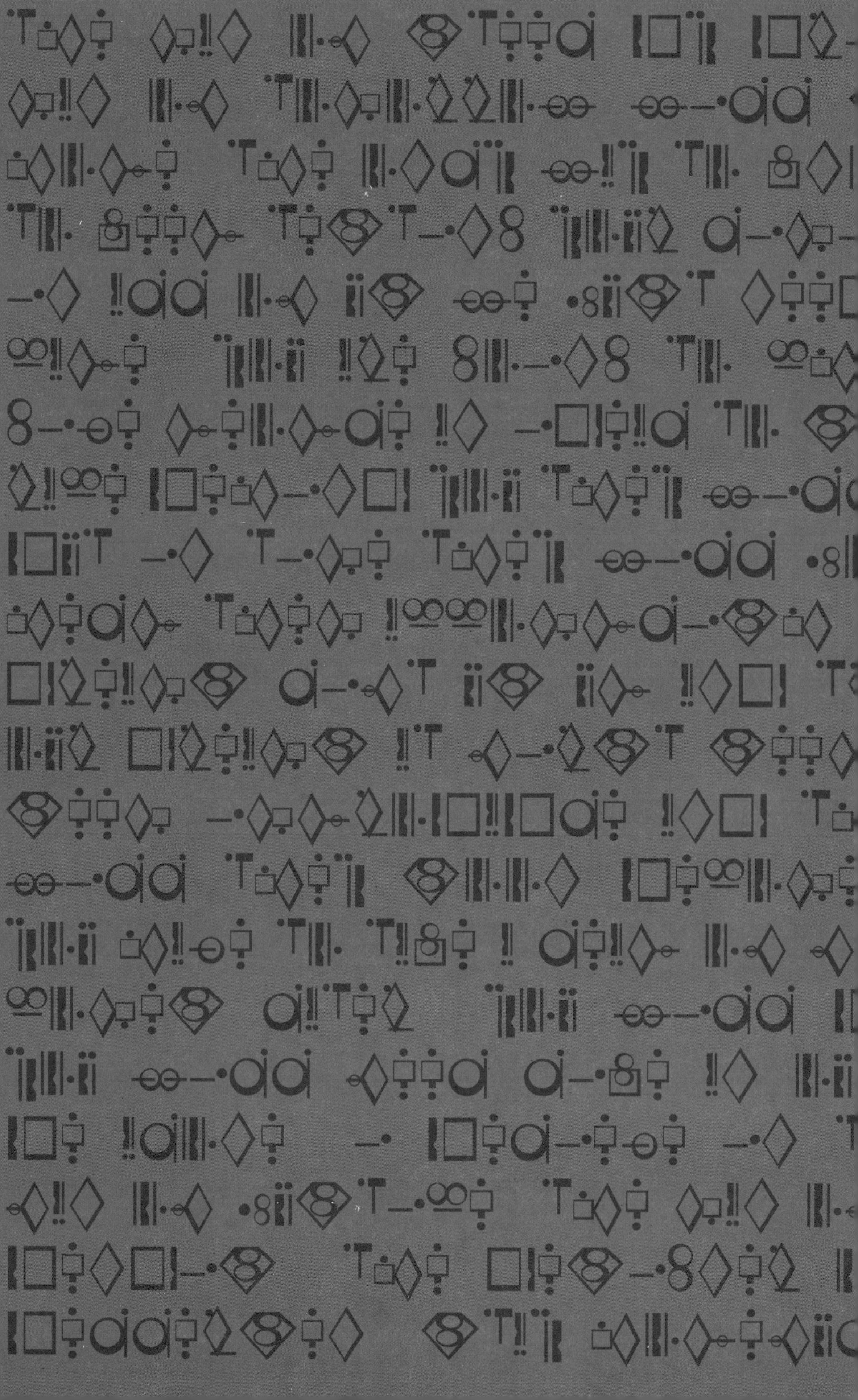